# THE MYSTERY OF
## THE YOUNG
# Rembrandt

hessische
kultur
stiftung

ERNST VON SIEMENS
KUNSTFONDS

KulturStiftung der Länder

B|BRAUN

Ministerie van
Buitenlandse Zaken

Netherlands Culture Fund (HGIS)

Ernst van de Wetering
Bernhard Schnackenburg

# THE MYSTERY OF
# THE YOUNG
# Rembrandt

## Essays

Ernst van de Wetering
Bernhard Schnackenburg
Dagmar Hirschfelder
Gerbrand Korevaar

## Catalogue

Ed de Heer
Bob van den Boogert
Bernhard Schnackenburg
Justus Lange
Ernst van de Wetering
Beate Chr. Mirsch
Marieke de Winkel
Christiaan Vogelaar

Staatliche Museen Kassel, Gemäldegalerie Alte Meister
Museum het Rembrandthuis, Amsterdam

Edition Minerva

Publication accompanying the exhibition *The Mystery of the Young Rembrandt*
Staatliche Museen Kassel, Gemäldegalerie Alte Meister, Schloss Wilhelmshöhe: from November 3, 2001 to January 27, 2002
Museum het Rembrandthuis, Amsterdam: from February 20 to May 26, 2002
The exhibition is a cooperation of the Staatliche Museen Kassel, the Museum het Rembrandthuis, Amsterdam and the Rembrandt Research Project, Amsterdam.

# Impressum

Edited by the Staatliche Museen Kassel and Museum het Rembrandthuis, Amsterdam

*Concept:* Ernst van de Wetering, Bernhard Schnackenburg

## Exhibition

*Staatliche Museen Kassel, Gemäldegalerie Alte Meister, Schloss Wilhelmshöhe*
Director: Michael Eissenhauer
Project Management: Beate Chr. Mirsch, Bernhard Schnackenburg
Curator: Beate Chr. Mirsch
Assistance: Justus Lange
Restoration: Hans Brammer, Pia Maria Hilsenbeck, Guntram Porps
Technical Organisation: Hans Brammer
Exhibition Architecture: Ernst van de Wetering, Dieter Fuchs & H. P. Tewes, Ralf Mahr
Exhibition Mounting: Helmut Jordan, Jürgen Wicke
Secretary: Ingrid Knauf, Gunda Garms
Administration: Ursula Guhr, Karl-Richard Steineck
Technical Support: Hartmut Tecklenburg
Photographs: Ute Brunzel, Baunatal; Gabriele Bößert, Arno Hensmanns, Staatliche Museen Kassel
Audiotour: Ernst van de Wetering

*Museum het Rembrandthuis, Amsterdam*
Director: Ed de Heer
Project Management: Bob van den Boogert, Ed de Heer
Scientific Support: Peter Schatborn
Curator: Bob van den Boogert
Restoration: Jan Diepraam
Technical Organisation: Jan Diepraam, Herman van der Klauw
Exhibition Architecture: Ernst van de Wetering, Peter Sas, Tessa van der Waals
Exhibition Mounting: Technischer Dienst Museum het Rembrandthuis
Secretary: Anna Brolsma
Administration: Charlotte ten Holder, Audrey Moestadja, Leonore van Sloten
Photographs: Jack Barneveld
Public Relations: Gerda van Ham, Charlotte ten Holder
Exhibition Didactics: Aernout Hagen
Audiotour: Ernst van de Wetering

*Rembrandt Research Project, Amsterdam*
Head: Ernst van de Wetering
Scientific Support: Peter Schatborn
Coordination: Margaret Oomen
Assistance: Gerbrand Korevaar, Jaap van der Veen, Marieke de Winkel

## Catalogue

*Copyeditorial*
(German): Wanda Löwe, Stefanie Heckmann
(Dutch): Bob van den Boogert, Margaret Oomen
(English): Deborah Cohen, Wanda Löwe, Stefanie Heckmann

*Translations*
from German into English: Fiona Healy
from Dutch into German: Susanne Karau, Marlene Müller-Haas, Frauke Laarmann
from Dutch into English: Lynne Richards, Murray Pearson

Catalogue Design: Gini Klose, Oberhaching
Production and Printing: Peschke Druck, Munich
© 2001 Staatliche Museen Kassel and the authors
© 2001 Museum het Rembrandthuis, Amsterdam and the authors
© 2001 Edition Minerva Hermann Farnung, Wolfratshausen

ISBN 3-932353-59-5

CIP-Data is available from the Deutsche Bibliothek.

ISBN 3-932353-59-5

# Contents

We thank the following lenders

Rijksmuseum, Amsterdam
Dr. & Mrs. Alfred Bader
Staatliche Museen zu Berlin, Preußischer Kulturbesitz,
Gemäldegalerie
Museum of Fine Arts, Boston
Maida & George Abrams, Boston
Szépművészeti Múzeum, Budapest
Fitzwilliam Museum, Cambridge
Collection Fondation Aetas Aurea
W. Baron van Dedem
Kupferstich-Kabinett, Staatliche Kunstsammlungen
Dresden
Musée de la Chartreuse, Douai
The National Gallery of Ireland, Dublin
The Provost, Fellows and Scholars of Trinity College,
Dublin
Städelsches Kunstinstitut, Frankfurt am Main
Teylers Museum, Haarlem
Royal Cabinet of Paintings Mauritshuis, The Hague
Hamburger Kunsthalle
M. P. Klaver-Hienkens
Stedelijk Museum De Lakenhal, Leiden
Prentenkabinet van de Universiteit Leiden
British Museum, Department of Prints and Drawings,
London
Spier Collection
The National Gallery, London
The J. Paul Getty Museum, Los Angeles
The State Pushkin Museum of Fine Arts, Moscow
Bayerische Staatsgemäldesammlungen, Alte Pinakothek,
Munich
Germanisches Nationalmuseum, Nuremberg
The National Gallery of Canada, Ottawa
Fondation Custodia, Institut Néerlandais, Paris
Musée du Louvre, Département des Arts Graphiques,
Paris
Nationalmuseum, Stockholm
Bridgestone Museum of Art, Ishibashi Foundation, Tokyo
Musée des Beaux-Arts de Tours
Galleria Sabauda, Turin
Museum Catharijneconvent, Utrecht
Kunsthistorisches Museum Vienna, Gemäldegalerie

and private lenders who don't wish to be mentioned.

# Foreword

Two museums, each having its own special connection with Rembrandt, joined forces for the exhibition, *The Mystery of the Young Rembrandt*. The Amsterdam Museum het Rembrandthuis needs no introduction; its function is immediately evident from its name and the building. It has been in the public eye over the past few years because of the recreation of the artist's working and living space as well as various important exhibitions which it has organised, from the first monographic exhibition on Rembrandt's teacher, Pieter Lastman (1991), to the exhibition which provided new insights into the cooperation between the young Rembrandt and his engraver, Jan van Vliet (1996). The Kassel Gemäldegalerie Alte Meister, on the other hand, possesses the oldest of all large Rembrandt collections. Its acquisitions and losses, the changing attributions during the Gallery's three-hundred-year history are themselves very much part of the history of the European museum. The 1816 inventory of paintings attributed no less that forty-three paintings to Rembrandt, nine of which are listed as having been lost during the Napoleonic period. Over the past 120 years, Rembrandt scholars have conducted a never-ending investigation into the artist's work, continually changing attributions and introducing new ones. One of positive aspects of this is the recognition afforded his best pupils, who have only in the recent past attained the position they justly deserve. A total of twelve autograph paintings are cited in the 1996 catalogue of the Gemäldegalerie, making it one of the largest and most important collections of Rembrandt's work.

Had general opinion prevailed, it would have been one work poorer. However, Dr. Bernhard Schnackenburg, the author of the catalogue and curator of the collection, was convinced of the authenticity of the *Bust of an Old Man with Golden Chain*, a painting bearing the date 1632 which had not long before been demoted. When, at a meeting in Amsterdam, he presented the concept of an exhibition focused on the painting, it became clear that his arguments in its defence were of far-reaching relevance; indeed so much so that he aroused not only the interest of the Rembrandthuis, but also that of the *Rembrandt Research Project*. It was evident that a general re-evaluation of Rembrandt's early work was necessary, and that more attention should be paid to the young Rembrandt as a painter, draughtsman and etcher from his beginnings in Leiden around 1624/25 to his early years in Amsterdam from 1631 onwards. It was thus decided to devote a special exhibition to these aspects. The obvious approach was to integrate the results of research into an exhibition that would present the public with a visual feast of exquisite works, including some usually hidden away in private collections. Another fascinating aspect of the project was that in Rembrandt's case, as indeed with other great artists, the complexities of his beginnings offer important insights into his entire artistic œuvre.

Out of the original idea for the exhibition, a three-part concept was developed. Responsibility for the first two sections, «Beginnings» and «Early Fame, Early Followers», lay with Prof. Dr. Ernst van de Wetering, while Dr. Bernhard Schnackenburg assumed control of the third, «Heads in a ‹Fine› and ‹Rough Manner›». Together with other experts on Rembrandt, they contributed essays and catalogue texts. For the latter, the contributions on Rembrandt's masterpieces by Dr. Bob van den Boogert deserve special mention.

Since the unforgettable and representative overview *Rembrandt. The Master and His Studio*, which opened in Berlin in 1991 and then travelled to Amsterdam and London, *The Mystery of the Young Rembrandt* is the first exhibition to be shown in Germany and the Netherlands that brings together a large body of autograph works, and especially of paintings. However, the point of departure and conception of the two exhibitions could not be more different. If ten years ago it was the express intention of the organisers to present the results of research that had been conducted over the previous twenty years, the present situation is much more open. New hypotheses are presented which, through confrontation     original works of art, seek to prompt discussion. So instead of starting out by presenting the fruits of a completed study of Rembrandt's early work, this exhibition hopes to reap its harvest at the end.

It was by no means certain from the onset that the exhibition concept could be realised as planned. The list of desired exhibits consisted of valuable and delicate objects, many of which were dispersed throughout the world, or indeed whose present whereabouts had first to be determined. Moreover, in many cases the presence of a particular work was essential, for it alone could clarify particular questions or illustrate certain artistic processes. It was thus immensely satisfying that, despite a few refusals, we were able to achieve our objective. An overwhelming response from some museums and private collectors provided continual encouragement for our project and its particular prerequisites. We therefore extend our sincerest thanks to all lenders.

An additional barrier for an exhibition of this calibre is the enormous cost, which was clearly beyond the financial capabilities of our institutions. Both in Kassel and Amsterdam the financial burden was met by different foundations and sponsors, to whom we here wish to express our deepest gratitude. Support for the Staatlichen Museen Kassel came from the Hessische Kulturstiftung, Wiesbaden, the Ernst von Siemens-Stiftung, Munich, the Kulturstiftung der Länder, Berlin, the firms of B. Braun Melsungen AG and Kali + Salz AG in Kassel, and for the Museum het Rembrandthuis from the HGIS (Netherlands Cultural Fund), the Stichting K.F. Hein Fonds and the Koninklijke Ahold nv.

The preparation for such a wide-ranging exhibition requires a large number of staff, without whose commitment and dedication this project could not have been realised. We would here like to express our warmest thanks for the intensive effort they invested over a long period of time in mounting the exhibition in the two venues of Kassel and Amsterdam, and in preparing the catalogue, which appears in English and German versions. Two people deserve special mention: Dr. Beate Chr. Mirsch as head of the project in Kassel, and Dr. Bob van den Boogert in Amsterdam.

Kassel and Amsterdam in September 2001

Dr. Michael Eissenhauer
Director of the Staatliche
Museen Kassel

Drs. Ed de Heer
Director of the Museum
het Rembrandthuis

Prof. Dr. Ernst van de Wetering
Head of the Rembrandt Research Project,
Amsterdam

# The Concept of the Exhibition

A museum man and a university person joined forces to realise the concept of this exhibition, supported and continually provided with new impulses by the director and the curator of the Amsterdam Museum het Rembrandthuis, Ed de Heer and Bob van den Boogert. Admittedly, this sounds very much like a division of labour, with each contributing different points of view and working methods. Is it not the responsibility of a museum to address those questions posed by the objects themselves? Is not the university the place where the larger context is established, where art history is expanded to become intellectual history? Instead of continuing this line of argument, we wish to firmly reject it. Our close co-operation was made possible only because we were motivated by similar interests, the core of which being the individual work of art in all its technical, stylistic and contextual facets. Only by studying the work of art can we hope to place it in a larger context. The exhibition is the fruit of decades of ever-increasing co-operation between the *Rembrandt Research Project* and museums and collections. As some of the research group's members have been connected with the Amsterdam University, at least periodically, the project's almost unique function as a bridge between the centres of seeing and reflection becomes apparent.

Indeed, the idea for the exhibition was not derived from the wish to undertake a more intensive and exact study of Rembrandt's beginnings and early work. Although in retrospect this has proven a worthy subject, the actual point of departure was the question of rehabilitating and reintegrating a single, apparently isolated painting. Who could have imagined that such an unpretentious, small-scale work as the *Bust of an Old Man with Golden Chain* (cat. no. 81 in the exhibition), the depiction of nothing more than a head, was the compelling force that set everything in motion? The painting, which had never before been the centre of attention, posed diverse and far-reaching questions. If,

despite its considerable divergence from the norm, the style of the painting – like that of a few comparable pictures – was considered to be autograph after all, then this would have important repercussions for our overall understanding of Rembrandt's early work. Answers were needed for questions that had rarely been asked: is there a system in the artist's early period, how is the work structured, what are Rembrandt's strategies, and the impulses for his future development? What was the dominating factor: free and independent experimentation, the search for diversity as proof of his virtuosity? Was there a difference in hierarchy between sketches and ‹finished› paintings? Did Rembrandt deliberately use different styles for different pictorial tasks? It is exactly here that the Kassel *Old Man with Golden Chain* arouses the interest of scholars, for it belongs to a category of «Study Heads» and «Heads without Meaning», for which the historical term *tronie* is becoming increasingly common. However, only a superficial glance would suggest that they form a homogenous group. The substantial differences in their depiction and the manner of painting requires explanation. This can only be found by looking beyond those areas of Rembrandt research that have already received attention and explore new territory.

Such considerations suggest that the already carefully studied field of Rembrandt's early work, which was addressed in the first two volumes of *A Corpus of Rembrandt Paintings* (1982, 1986), is destined to be subjected to renewed scrutiny. We were aware of this during our discussions. Seen from outside, this may seem an unnerving possibility, indeed provocation, designed to re-introduce turmoil into what seemed to be clarity gained only after much toil. Do we have in Rembrandt an artist who, some questions pertaining to his œuvre and person having hardly been answered, throws up new «mysteries about his beginnings»? This impression seems deceptive, for Rembrandt's many drawings, etchings and paintings from his early period make it possible to reconstruct his beginnings to a far greater extent than for many of his contemporaries. During his six years in Leiden, and to a certain extend in Amsterdam, Rembrandt produces an astonishingly large œuvre that appears to provide a step-by-step documentation of his development as a draughtsman, etcher and painter. Moreover, important documentary sources refer to the artist's early life. Nevertheless, given the number of unanswered questions about this period, the use of the term ‹mystery› in the title of the exhibition and catalogue seems appropriate.

Rembrandt is one of those artists who appears to have been born to the task, driven by so much creative energy that already in his youth he clearly did not fit into the typical historical niche of the artist who produced for the market. He clearly moved in those cultured circles that had developed an image of the artist that borders on the modern. From an art historical perspective, it is even more important that Rembrandt's understanding of his role must have been conditioned by his view of himself as a creator rather than producer; that he was not primarily the son of a Dutch miller, but above all successor to and rival of the legendary artists of antiquity and the equally famous artists of sixteenth-century Italy. It is only by way of this immense self-confidence that we can explain the extreme nature of his ambition, which continually drove him to seek out new ways. But we must also acknowledge the happy constellation of his fruitful artistic exchange with his friend and one-time child prodigy, Jan Lievens.

It is notable that Rembrandt began to take on apprentices at a very early stage in his career – and to charge the highest fees that seventeenth-century parents and guardians were prepared to pay. These pupils worked in the master's style, and their paintings must have been bought on the spot. This involvement of Rembrandt's studio and ‹school› has created enormous problems for art historical research (not to mention the art market), many of which have still not been solved, and perhaps never will be. The confrontation of paintings of disputed authorship with unquestioned originals is an essential part of any discussion on attribution. Our exhibition may in part be considered a ‹stage› for such a discussion, whereby it caters not just to the experts but is expressly intended as a ‹school of seeing› for the general public, as a challenge to both the critical and sensitive eye.

But in the absence of an historical foundation, any understanding gained through sight alone is immediately in danger of becoming a false supposition. Such a case was formulated in relation to style by Max J. Friedländer in his book *On Art and Connoisseurship*, when he wrote of the «unchangeable core of creative individuality». The third section of the exhibition will address this problem. It seeks to demonstrate that the wide spectrum of Rembrandt's style was determined not just by creative freedom and artistic curiosity, but also by art theoretical considerations. Both this exhibition and book are the result of long and intensive co-operation, whereby the different authors did not always agree and so sometimes express individual points of view. This may be taken as proof that the mysteries concerning Rembrandt's beginnings have not been solved in this publication. It is our hope that the results will stimulate viewers of the works of art and readers of the texts, be they in agreement or disagreement.

Bernhard Schnackenburg          Ernst van de Wetering

# Essays

# Leiden in Rembrandt's Time *

*Gerbrand Korevaar*

During 1573/74, in an attempt to quash the Dutch revolt against their Spanish overlords, the Duke of Alba and his troops laid siege to Rembrandt's birthplace, Leiden. The city barely survived this heavy siege, and as a result it was for some time only a shadow of the prosperous textile centre it had formerly been. Normal life gradually returned, but the threat of hunger remained for years, and several times the plague wreaked havoc, notably in 1607 and 1617. The Leiden burgomaster and city biographer, Jan Jansz. Orlers, tells that from August 1624 to October 1625, the period during which Rembrandt is believed to have stayed in Amsterdam, as many as 9,897 people died of the disease.[1]

Yet one can see the miraculous survival from this siege as a harbinger of the fruitful period that Leiden was later to enjoy. During the time that Rembrandt lived there, from 1606 to c. 1631,[2] Leiden was a flourishing and developing city in the young Republic and was gradually to become an economic and cultural centre of international significance. For a brief period it was also to be a promising centre of painting.

## The ‹New Draperies›

Economic growth was due mainly to the textile industry, which in the last decades of the sixteenth century had been given new life when innovative and decisively successful methods of production were introduced with the Flemish immigration around 1580. The so-called ‹says› industry was turning out advanced textiles, the ‹New Draperies›. The main difference between these ‹says› and the older woollen cloths they superseded was that they were thinner, more finely textured and lighter.[3] The arrival of craftsmen from the southern Netherlands at once laid the foundation for Leiden's industrial economy of the seventeenth century, an economy based on the new textile industry. A census taken in 1634 shows that an overwhelming majority – 40,000 of the

45,000 inhabitants – were «ordinary manual workers and labourers» (gemene handwerx- en arbeytsluyden), the predominant trades being tailors, bakers, say-drapers and say-workers and cobblers. Consequently there were relatively few wealthy citizens: in 1623 there were only 1600 heads of families who had to pay a tax of one 200th of all their fixed and moveable assets. Indeed, during the winter of 1633 the Leiden almoners had to distribute assistance to 20,000 people, almost half the population of the city.[4]

Thus, although the prosperity brought by the textile industry provided a higher standard of living for some, this was only a small percentage of the population. Leiden was a relatively poor city. This poverty is reflected in the drawings and etchings of beggars that Rembrandt made around 1628/29: poor men and women he would have often seen in the streets of Leiden (cf. cat. nos. 45–50). The fact that Leiden could boast so few wealthy citizens would have undoubtedly contributed to Rembrandt's decision to leave so soon for the richer trading city of Amsterdam.

## Rembrandt Hermanni Leydensis

As well as the textile industry, the presence of the university meant that Leiden's reputation extended far beyond the borders of the Republic. This university had been founded in 1575 on the initiative of the States General, with the support of William of Orange, as compensation for war damage.[5] The university grew rapidly, so that by 1630 it had some 400 students, including many foreigners and such eminent persons as Maurits and Frederik Hendrik. The lawyer Hugo de Groot and, in the mid-seventeenth century, the physicist Christiaen Huygens also studied in Leiden. On May 20, 1620, at the age of fourteen, Rembrandt was enrolled at the university, most probably after a four-year course of study at the Latin School. He appears in the university's *Album Studiosorum* under the Latinized version of his name, «Rembrandt Hermanni Leydensis», «resident still at the home of his parents».[6] It is not certain whether Rembrandt actually studied at the university,[7] but if, as is widely assumed, he began his apprenticeship with Jacob Isaacsz. van Swanenburg in 1621, he probably spent at most a year engaged in philological studies.

The presence of the university was of course an opportunity for Leiden's artists. The university collection, whose basis was laid in 1597, was gradually expanded throughout the seventeenth century, not least by portraits commissioned from local painters.[8] The graphic arts were given a similar boost by the university's presence. In 1583 the famous Antwerp printer Christofel Plantijn opened a press in Leiden; in 1595 the most important engraver of that time, Jacques de Gheyn II (1565–1629) left Amsterdam to go and work in Leiden for several years; and there were undoubtedly other artists who profited from the scientific activity in Leiden. For instance, the professor of medicine François de le Boe Sylvius possessed a substantial collection.[9]

## The ‹New City›

Immigration led to an explosive increase in the population. From c. 12,000 in 1581, the number of inhabitants had risen to 44,745 by 1622, an almost four-fold increase, making Leiden the second largest city in the Republic after Amsterdam. The inevitable consequence of this growth was a shortage of living space, and concomitantly an appreciable rise in rents. In 1611 a plan was conceived for a major expansion of the city. The city surveyor Jan Pietersz. Dou was commissioned to draw up a plan for the expansion of its northern and western areas. The year 1615 saw the first pile driven into the ground for this so-called ‹New City› which, between 1606 and 1623, was to enlarge the old city by a third, the number of houses increasing from 4886 to 6665.[10] Many Leideners saw the opportunity for financial gain, either through buying the newly developed building plots and reselling them at a profit or by renting out the houses built on them. Rembrandt's family also profited from the city's expansion. In 1614 Rembrandt's father, Harmen Gerritsz.

van Rijn, bought a plot of land on the west side of the Weddesteeg, the street where Rembrandt's family lived. The rented housing constructed on this plot would remain in the family's possession for a long time afterwards.[11]

## Religious disputes

The massive growth in population can be partly explained in terms of the fact that, for some time following the lifting of the siege, the principle of *egaliteyt* was embraced in Leiden. The city was known as a bulwark of religious tolerance, a considerable attraction to people elsewhere who were unable in their own domicile to practise their beliefs unhindered. This freedom, however, was not allowed to last long.[12] In 1604 there arose a theological discussion, first of all within the precincts of the university, but gradually spreading and becoming more public. As it was fanned by extremist preachers from their pulpits, it thus acquired a political dimension. The strict orthodox theologian working at the university, Fransiscus Gomarus (1563–1641) and his fellow professor of divinity, the more moderate clergyman Jacobus Arminius (1560–1609), clashed over the question of predestination. Gomarus, whose followers, extreme Calvinists, were known as ‹Gomarists› or ‹Counter-Remonstrants›, held that since the sin of Adam, only God's mercy could redeem mankind. Man had no free will, and by definition was incapable of earning salvation through good deeds. Arminius, with his followers, called ‹Arminians›, or ‹Remonstrants›, believed that one could elect oneself for God, and in this freedom could trust in his mercy, love and forgiveness.

The Leiden city council had of old been more sympathetic to the Remonstrant position, whilst at the same time giving the appearance of impartiality by appointing to vacant positions an Arminian or a Gomarist alternately. At first, an attempt was made to resolve the disagreement amicably and to stifle the rising dispute. But this turned out to be highly difficult and minor disturbances broke out, dividing the city even further. Despite strenuous resistance, in 1618 the Leiden city council had to concede to a Counter-Remonstrant majority in the city. This Counter-Remonstrant faction had not only gained the upper hand in Leiden, but had in the meantime also rallied a convincing majority in the States General. On October 22, 1618, Prince Maurice, who by now also supported the Counter-Remonstrant faction, came to Leiden to impose order through a change in the law. After a fierce debate, he ordered the most vehement Arminians to be replaced by equally vehement Gomarists.

In fact, the old *egaliteyt* was maintained until the Dordrecht National Synod of 1618/19, but once the Remonstrant position had been condemned officially on April 23rd, religious tolerance in Leiden was finished. All Remonstrant assemblies and preaching were forbidden, meetings disrupted, windows smashed, and people fined or banned. The city pensionary, Rombout Hoogerbeets, a leading Remonstrant, was given a life sentence and replaced by Jan van Wevelichoven. The sheriff, Loth Huygensz. Gael, who had actually been appointed for life, was banned from the city and was succeeded by the extraordinary professor of law and notorious persecutor of dissenters, Willem de Bondt. At the university, ‹suspected› Remonstrant professors had to account for their beliefs. Some endorsed the articles of Dordrecht, others were (temporarily) suspended. In this fashion, the professors Caspar Barlaeus and Gerard Vossius left for the more liberal Amsterdam, where in 1632 they would assist at the birth of the new ‹Athenaeum Illustre›, a rival to the University of Leiden.

Despite the death of Prince Maurice in 1625 and the fact that his successor, Frederik Hendrik, proved a more moderate *stadholder*, the city council of Leiden continued to persecute dissenters far into the seventeenth century.

The time when Rembrandt was active in Leiden was therefore played out against a background of religious discontent and intolerance. However, as we are not sure what religious faction he adhered to, it is difficult to say to what extent he suffered any personal consequences. Perhaps he had a Remonstrant patron in the prominent humanist Petrus Scriverius, who could have commissioned the «two rather large pieces» mentioned in his son's estate. These paintings have been connected to the *Stoning of St Stephen* (p. 23, fig. 3) and the Leiden *History Painting* (cat. no. 7) from 1626. These were possibly companion pieces that could refer to the theological differences between Remonstrants and Counter-Remonstrants.[13] But because not a single document related to the commissioning of these paintings has survived, we have no certain knowledge that Petrus Scriverius ordered these specific paintings.

We know even less about the religious convictions of Jan Lievens. Orlers records that he worked quietly through the troubles of 1618, «esteeming the love of art far more than all the commotion of the world».[14]

## Painters without guild

Closer to the daily concerns of the painter in Leiden was the unusual situation there vis-à-vis the guild system. During the first half of the seventeenth century, cities like Amsterdam, Haarlem, Rotterdam, Delft, Gouda, Utrecht and The Hague had a St Luke's Guild,[15] an association of painters and craftsmen in related fields – e.g. sculptors, glass-engravers, embroiderers, carpet-makers, etc. The survival of guilds, or the fact that they had been infused with new life around the beginning of the twelve-year truce with Spain (1609–1621),[16] points to the important role they must have played in the daily practise of the seventeenth century painter. A need apparently existed for an organisation that could provide economic and social protection. By means of special regulations, painters tried to protect themselves from unfair competition in the form of work coming from outside the city. But there were also rules concerning the master-pupil relationship, the number of pupils admitted and the duration of their apprenticeship. Internally, far-reaching social provisions were made for members. It is therefore surprising to find that in Leiden, the city where Rembrandt painted his earliest pictures, there was *no* guild of St Luke for painters throughout the first half of the seventeenth century. In 1610, at the request of the community of painters, the city council did issue a prohibition against the import and illegal sale of paintings by non-Leideners[17] which was reinforced in several subsequent years. But despite the attempt of Leiden

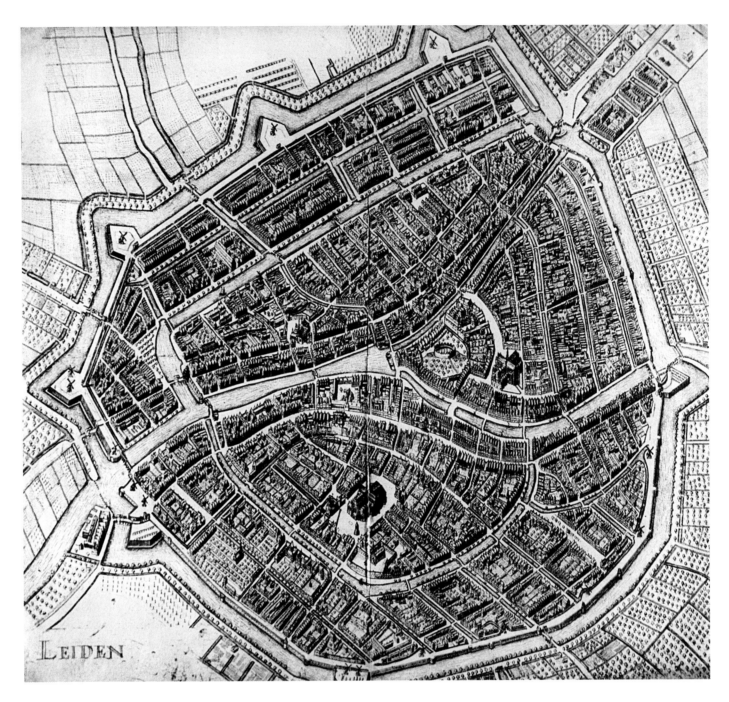

1
*Map of Leiden,* c. 1630

painters to set up a guild in 1610 and again in 1642 and 1648, it was not until 1657 that an organisation of similar legal standing to the St Luke Guilds in other cities was finally established.[18]

The question is: what were the economic consequences of this situation for Leiden painters in the period that Rembrandt was active there? The enormous growth in the production of paintings in Holland from the end of the sixteenth century went hand in hand, of course, with the growth of a potential market. With the rising economic prosperity enjoyed by the Republic in this period, the demand for luxury goods such as paintings rose concomitantly. Possessing works of art was, just as in other cities at that time, a rather normal phenomenon in Leiden. We usually encounter a few paintings in the inventories of estates, an average of probably eight to ten per household in Leiden in the seventeenth century.[19] Jan Jansz. Orlers' collection was the only one of considerable size in Leiden in the first half of the seventeenth century. In fact, as far as Leiden was

15

Isaac Claesz. van
Swanenburg,
*Spinning, Shaving of
the Chain, and
Weaving,* 1594–96
Oak panel,
137.5 x 196 cm
Stedelijk Museum
De Lakenhal, Leiden

concerned, the main period for large collections of paintings was the second half of the century.[20] Amsterdam, however, hosted far more collectors throughout the seventeenth century.[21] One could buy paintings directly from the shop of a master painter, or acquire one through an art dealer or in lotteries. However, in Leiden there were also fairs and auctions where the majority of paintings on offer were probably by non-Leideners. According to Orlers, the fairs were held in the main corridor of the city hall, «where twice a year, [they] offer many costly articles of silverware, art paintings and masses of books».[22] When in 1643 the Rotterdam painter and art dealer Leendert Hendricksz. Volmarijn wanted to open the first shop for art objects and artists' materials in Leiden, he explained that he had for years conducted a trade in various paintings at fairs in many towns, especially Leiden.[23]

As in other cities, art was in all probability also sold in Leiden outside the permitted channels, despite the presence of a guild. It is therefore remarkable that painters like Coenraet van Schilperoort (c. 1577–1636), Aernout Elsevier (c. 1580 – after 1643) and Joris van Schooten (c. 1587–1652/53), who signed the request for economic protection against the importation of art from other towns and cities, were still active in Leiden and the surrounding area in the 1620s. These Leiden painters appear no longer (or not yet) to have felt threatened by work from other cities. At least, they made no attempt to seek official protection for their own position in the market, despite the huge costs of maintaining a livelihood in the period of recession from 1622 to 1632. Rembrandt, too, who was still established in Leiden during this period, appears to have made no such move. If it is true that Rembrandt shared a studio with Lievens, both painters would certainly have benefited financially from such an arrangement.[24] Sharing rent and communal expenses for painters' materials could well have compensated both Rembrandt and Lievens for the economic disadvantages of not having a guild. Perhaps the prohibition of 1610 actually served a purpose. That there were controls on selling outside the fairs is clearly evident, as, for example, in a request submitted to the city council by Jan Lievens and three other master painters in 1630.[25] He wanted to offer paintings at a public sale but had to get special permission to do so, even as a citizen of Leiden.

Apparently the unrestricted sale of one's own paintings was not permitted.

It is evident from a detailed assessment of Leiden's art possessions in the seventeenth century that in the first half of the century, the city's bourgeoisie concentrated mainly on the Leiden market for their purchases. Of the 14 artists most in demand, eleven were actively at work in the city. In the second half of the century, the accent seems to have shifted to Haarlem painters. Of the 28 artists most in demand during the second half of the seventeenth century, only 13 were resident in Leiden, while 11 were working in Haarlem.[26] This might correlate with the high prices that Leiden fine painters were then asking for their work. During the time that there was no guild, the Leiden bourgeoisie was apparently able to satisfy its demand for fine art with the work of local painters. The fact that the rise in imports from other cities coincided with the establishment of a local guild would indicate that Leiden's guild of St Luke was not the strongest of organisations.

With the gradual growth in demand for works of art, the number of artists had risen considerably in Leiden as elsewhere. The decision to become a painter was certainly not a risky one from an economic point of view. Around 1626 there were some 46 artists at work,[27] 25 of whose birth-place is known to us: 15 were born in Leiden (60 %) and 10 became residents of the city later in life (40 %). Although these simple figures permit no general conclusions to be drawn over the geographical origins of Leiden's population of artists, it is nonetheless striking that they roughly correspond with the percentages found in Delft. Montias calculated that from 1613 to 1645, 64 % of master painters newly registered in Delft were born there, 36 % arriving from elsewhere.[28] Bearing in mind the question regarding the consequences of the absence of a guild in Leiden, the correspondence between the situations in the two cities is striking. In a city like Delft, where artists first had to become burghers and pay their entrance fee to a guild before being allowed to practise, there were virtually as many outsiders as there were in Leiden. The absence of a guild seems therefore to have had little impact on the city's attractiveness to painters.

## Leiden painters

In the generation preceding Rembrandt's Leiden period, the art life in Leiden was dominated by the painter-burgomaster Isaac Claesz. van Swanenburg (1537–1614) (fig. 2). Besides his civic duties, van Swanenburg ran a busy workshop and executed numerous commissions.[29] Indeed, van Swanenburg was the only painter of any repute in Leiden's art world around the turn of the century. By the 1620s, there were several painters working in Leiden who enjoyed a certain local reputation. In 1626 the portrait and history painter Joris van Schooten (c. 1587–1652/53) was given the most important commission of that time, to paint six large *schutters'* pieces (group portraits of the militias) (fig. 3). In fact, he and David Bailly (1584–1657) were the only Leiden painters capable of successfully executing this prestigious commission. Since Rembrandt and Lievens were still very young and had scarcely tackled the art of portraiture, it is hardly surprising that the Leiden *schutters* gave the commission to an already-established portraitist. The work of the somewhat older painters rep-

3
Joris van Schooten,
*Militias of Cornelis van Kerchem*, 1626
Oak panel, 173 x 183.5 cm
Stedelijk Museum De Lakenhal, Leiden

4
Jan van Goyen, *Summer*,
1624
Oak panel, 13.2 x 26 cm
Private Collection

5
Jan van Goyen, *Winter*,
1624
Oak panel, 13.2 x 26 cm
Private Collection

resented a rather conservative style of painting; one can well imagine that the artistic climate that Rembrandt grew up in, the context of his initial training, was relatively insignificant as a source of inspiration.

But from the year that Rembrandt returned to the city of his birth, probably in 1625, Leiden would for a short time play an important role in the field of painting. The city became a breeding ground for talented young painters who were to become well-known and popular well beyond the city walls of Leiden. Lievens returned as early as 1621, after his Amsterdam apprenticeship with Pieter Lastman. Jan van Goyen (1596–1656) had settled in Leiden around 1618, after studying with various masters, a trip to France in 1615/16 and a brief pe-

riod of study with Esaias van de Velde in Haarlem. Van Goyen was beginning to make a name for himself with the summer and winter landscapes he painted between 1620 and 1628 (fig. 4, 5). Still-life painting also experienced a revival with the Utrecht-born Jan Davidsz. de Heem (1606–1683/84), who had settled in Leiden. The latter made an important contribution to a genre that was particularly popular in Leiden, no doubt because of the presence of the university: the still-life with books (fig. 6).[30] A rather older artist who belongs to this successful group was the seascape painter Jan Porcellis (c. 1583–1632), who was resident from about 1626 in Zoeterwoude, a village close to Leiden. It was in precisely this period that he produced his most innovative work

18

(fig. 7). Around 1625 he introduced a new style of painting with a reduced palette, in tones of mainly brown and grey.[31] From about 1627 this style, known in the art historical literature as ‹monochrome›, was to influence the work of de Heem, Lievens, Rembrandt and van Goyen. We have a good picture of the work of these latter artists, but less so when it comes to the as yet little fairly unknown landscape painter Coenraet van Schilperoort (c. 1577–1636), who must have been highly popular in Leiden at the time, since we regularly come across his name in inventories.[32]

The years that Rembrandt spent in Leiden were thus a time of innovation in the art of painting, with artists striking out in new directions, both in landscape painting and in the genre of the still-life. This new generation of painters must have made Leiden an inspiring place in the 1620s; they must often have gathered at inns such as those of the painter and art dealer Aernout Elsevier or Isaeck Jouderville, whose son of the same name was one of Rembrandt's first pupils, and talked at length over the art of painting.

However, there were not so many specialists in Leiden in that area in which Rembrandt was to specialize chiefly, namely history painting. Joris van Schooten and Rembrandt's first teacher, Jacob Isaacsz. van Swanenburg, are the only two active history painters in Leiden – besides Rembrandt and Lievens, of course – of whom we are able to form any kind of picture; which, for a city of the size of Leiden, is rather few. But if one takes into account the fact that Leiden actually had very few wealthy inhabitants, on whom not only portrait painters but probably also history painters were largely dependent, the situation is more easily understood. Perhaps the absence of potential competition may have influenced Rembrandt's decision to return to Leiden. As a young, unknown but ambitious painter, he could sooner acquire a position in Leiden, whereas in Amsterdam, as a beginner, he would have had to compete with his established teacher, Pieter Lastman, and the other history painters in the city.

Opportunities to receive training in Leiden from painters who already enjoyed fame and prestige as history and portrait painters were thus not great in the 1620s. David Bailly was one possibility, but since his pupils mainly became still-life or landscape painters, his teaching was probably orientated toward these specialities.[33] Young painters or their fathers often chose as an instructor for a second or later period of study a painter whose training was oriented toward the desired speciality. Joris Schooten, who was a portraitist and history painter, was another possibility. However, we know of only one pupil of Joris van Schooten's from the period before 1630, and that was Jan Lievens who, according to Orlers, came to study with him at the age of eight and learned the basic principles of painting over two years. Van Schooten, however, despite the esteem his work enjoyed in his time, created no ‹school›. Perhaps a second period of study with this master was in fact not so obvious a choice for young ambitious painters seeking a connection with the most modern developments in the art of not only Leiden but Holland, too, in the third decade of the seventeenth century. After all, Rembrandt and Lievens had earlier had to leave for Amsterdam to pursue further training under the leading history painter of the day, Pieter Lastman. The fact that Gerard Dou (1613–1675), at the age of fourteen and after studying with two other masters, became apprenticed to the twenty-one-year-old Rembrandt is probably connected to Rembrandt's

6
Jan Davidsz. de Heem,
*Still Life with Books*, 1628
Oak panel, 36.1 x 45.5 cm
Royal Cabinet of Paintings
Mauritshuis, The Hague

7
Jan Porcellis, *River Mouth at Stormy Weather*, 1625–30
Oak panel, 58 x 80.5 cm
Museum Boijmans van Beuningen, Rotterdam

growing reputation.[34] Isack Jouderville (1612–1645/48) also entered into an apprenticeship with Rembrandt some time before November 1628.[35] Given the limited range of possibilities that existed within the Leiden community of painters, the choice of these two young painters to train under Rembrandt was not so surprising.

It was also Gerard Dou who, later in the century, would once again put Leiden on the art historical map as the founder of the so-called Leiden school of ‹fine painters›. ‹Once again› because the brief revival in painting set in motion by the new generation of painters in Leiden in the 1620s had come to an end in the '30s, mainly due to the simple fact that, either through death or departure, there were scarcely any painters of any calibre remaining in the city. Jan Lievens had left Leiden for England in 1631 – according to Orlers in order to get to know another country.[36] Jan van Goyen probably left around 1633 for The Hague. Jan Porcellis died in Zoeterwoude in 1632, Conraet van Schilperoort several years later. Jan Davidsz. De Heem disappears from the Leiden records in 1631.[37] The Leiden art world temporarily fell behind, much reduced, although those painters who had left Leiden were to pursue their careers with great success in other cities.

The usual story is that Rembrandt also cut his professional ties with Leiden and moved to Amsterdam at the end of 1631,[38] where he was to enter into a cooperative arrangement with the art dealer Hendrick Uylenburgh, whom he probably met in Leiden. The impression that this was a sudden break with his Leiden past stems primarily from the fact that from 1631 on, Rembrandt applied himself to a new field: portraiture. Indeed, between 1631 and 1635 he painted a remarkably large series of portraits, whereas, it is always assumed, he had not carried out a single portrait commission in all the six years he spent in Leiden. After 1631 the production of small history pieces – the genre in which Rembrandt had primarily specialised in Leiden – also dwindled considerably. He at once began to produce history paintings with life-sized figures.

It is, however, debatable whether the break with Leiden at the end of 1631 was quite so sudden and so drastic as this picture suggests. Dudok van Heel has suggested that Rembrandt only established himself in Amsterdam definitively in 1633, when things were going so well that he realised that his future lay in this city.[39] The distance between Leiden and Amsterdam is only fifty kilometres, and even in the seventeenth century it was no enormous problem to commute to and fro.[40] It is therefore well possible that Rembrandt initially came only sporadically to Amsterdam in order to execute his portrait commissions, making use of the facilities offered him by Uylenburgh. After all, during this time Rembrandt was also travelling to The Hague and Rotterdam to paint people's portraits.[41] Besides, Dudok van Heel points out that Rembrandt continued signing his work R(embrandt) H(armenszn) L(eijdensis) van Rijn right up till 1632.

The hypothesis that Rembrandt only left Leiden definitively in 1633 also finds strong support in the work of Hinterding.[42] Until 1635 Rembrandt worked closely with the Leiden graphic artist Jan van Vliet. When Hinterding compared the watermarks in the paper of etchings by Rembrandt and van Vliet, he discovered that the watermarks up to and including 1632 are identical. One may infer from this that prints were made in the same Leiden workshop, and that Rembrandt and van Vliet were still working together there in 1632. Only in 1633 would Rembrandt transfer his collection of copper plates to Amsterdam: from that year on, the general correspondence between the watermarks disappears. Finally, in 1634 we find the most direct evidence that Rembrandt had left Leiden for good, for in that year he purchased the *poorterschap* – citizenship – of Amsterdam and registered as a master painter with the Amsterdam St Luke Guild. Van de Wetering suggests that this late registration may correspond with the rules of the guild of St Luke that may have prevented earlier membership.[43] This would then have been the reason why Rembrandt worked for several years with Uylenburgh before being able to set up his own studio workshop. Whatever the truth of the matter, the exact date of the transition will probably never be established with any certainty. As Schnackenburg demonstrates in his essay in this catalogue, the stylistic experiments with the «rough» and the «fine manner» stand apart from the changes referred to above in Rembrandt's work.[44] As far as these are concerned, the dividing line between Leiden and Amsterdam is not an emphatic one. Indeed, Rembrandt seems in this respect to have continued on the path he had set out on in Leiden.

[*] I wish to express my gratitude to Ernst van de Wetering for his help, inspiration and repeated critical readings of earlier versions of this text. I would also like to thank Bob van den Boogert for a critical reading, Ingrid W. L. Moerman for her kindness in allowing me to see her unpublished work, and Murray Pearson, who translated this text.

[1] Orlers 1641, p. 49.

[2] With the exception of the six-month apprenticeship with the Amsterdam history painter Pieter Lastman. Schwartz dates Rembrandt's period with Lastman to 1622–23. Schwartz 1984/85/87, p. 21. Tümpel however believes this occurred around 1625. Tümpel 1992, p. 19. Broos dates the period to 1625–26. Broos 2000, p. 4.

[3] Vries 1991, pp. 78f.

[4] Taverne 1978, p. 204.

[5] «ten aensien van den grooten last ende noot van den voors. Crych by hemluyden in alder getrouwicheyt gesustineert ende gedragen». Quoted in Blok 1916, p. 64.

[6] Strauss/Meulen 1979, doc. 1620/1.

[7] Schwartz 1984/85/87, p. 21.

[8] In 1612 the Leiden painter, inn-keeper and art dealer Aernout Elsevier was paid in this way for painting several portraits *(verscheyden contrefeijtsels)*. Leiden 1976, p. 13f.

[9] Fock 1990, p. 6.

[10] Taverne 1978, p. 201.

[11] Baar/Moerman 1991, p. 27.

[12] Blok 1916, pp. 95–139.

[13] Schwartz 1984/85/87, pp. 35–38.

[14] «[...] als de liefde totte Konst meer achtende als alle tgewoel vande werelt». Orlers 1641, p. 376.

[15] On the guilds of St Luke, see Hoogewerff 1947, passim.

[16] Requests had been submitted seeking protection against imports, tightening of the rules and/or the setting up of a guild in the following cities: Amsterdam (November 1608), Rotterdam (January 1609), Gouda (May 1609), Delft (May 1611), and Utrecht (September 1611). See Obreen, vol. 3, 1881, p. 165; Hoogewerff 1947, p. 167, 162, 171 and 104.

[17] Rammelman Elsevier 1848, p. 37.

[18] Sluijter states that in the Leiden city council's service manuals, inspectors of the sale of paintings («opsienders van de vercoopinge van schilderie») were still referred to, and that the Leiden guild of St Luke was probably not officially considered a true guild. Sluijter 1988, p. 31.

[19] Fock 1990, p. 5.

[20] Fock 1990, p. 5.

[21] Gelder/Veen 1999, p. 64.

[22] «op welck tweemaels alle jaren in beyde de vrije marckten voorstaen veel kostelicke silverkrame, konstige schilderijen ende menichte van boecken». Orlers 1641, p. 165.

[23] Martin 1901, p. 86.

[24] Wetering 1991/92b, pp. 41f.

[25] Strauss/Meulen 1979, doc. 1630/3.

[26] Fock 1990, pp. 12f.

[27] Leiden 1976, pp. 111–119. This includes painters, graphic artists, engravers and glass-engravers.

[28] Montias 1982, pp. 139f.

[29] Ekkart 1998, passim.

[30] Leiden 1976, p. 80.

[31] Leiden 1976, p. 93.

[32] Egmond/Mason 1995, p. 39.

[33] In 1628 his nephew, the still-life painter Harmer Steenwijck, came to begin a five-year apprenticeship. In the same year Pieter Potter also arrived and stayed till 1631. He painted genre pieces, landscapes and still-lifes. Bailly's other nephew, Pieter Steenwijck, trained from 1632 to 1635 and became a painter of still-lifes, genre and interior pieces.

[34] Baer 2000, p. 27.

[35] Wetering 1983, pp. 59f.

[36] Orlers 1641, p. 377.

[37] Segal 1991, p. 61.

[38] See for example Gerson 1968/69, p. 42; Tümpel 1992, p. 50.

[39] Dudok van Heel 1991/92, p. 54.

[40] One could travel from Leiden to Amsterdam by boat across the Haarlemmer Meer. Prices were low because of fierce competition among the boatmen. Wetering 1986, pp. 79f. See particularly note 160.

[41] In 1632 Rembrandt painted portraits of Amalia van Solms, Maurits Huygens, Jacques de Gheyn III and Joris de Caulery in The Hague. In 1634 in Rotterdam, where he stayed throughout July of that year, he painted the brewer Dirck Pesser and his wife Haesje van Cleijburg. Strauss/Meulen 1979, doc. 1634/7.

[42] Hinterding 1996, p. 25.

[43] Wetering 1986, pp. 59f.

[44] See below, p. 92–121.

# Rembrandt's Beginnings – an Essay*

*Ernst van de Wetering*

In 1974 the Dutch art historian Henri Defoer discovered a completely unknown early Rembrandt hanging above the sideboard of an elderly lady living in Nijmegen (cat. no. 3), a discovery that was to make the front pages of the world press (fig. 1).

At the time, Defoer was the curator of the Archiepiscopal Museum in Utrecht. His original reason for visiting the old lady, as an authority on mediaeval art, was a late Gothic sculpture she had inherited as a family possession and wanted to leave as a future bequest to the museum. But in the course of the visit, his habitual curiosity led Defoer to take time out and inspect the paintings hanging on the wall. What particularly caught his attention was an old panel whose mid-joint had come loose, allowing the two boards to become misaligned. The painting brought to mind early Rembrandt and, in fact, looking in the bottom right corner he could make out a vague monogram containing a capital R and read the date 1626. Several months of his own comparative researches merely served to harden his suspicion that indeed he must be

dealing here with a very early Rembrandt and so he approached the Rembrandt experts of the time, Horst Gerson and the members of the *Rembrandt Research Project* (*RRP*) to ask their opinion.

Their initial reaction, based on the photograph that Defoer showed them, was that it could not be a Rembrandt.

In fact, Defoer's painting differed in several respects from Rembrandt's paintings then known to us from 1626. The light, which in Rembrandt's paintings almost always falls from the left, came in this painting from the right. The empty, sandy foreground with its scored paintwork and the remarkably small-seeming, rubber-like horses pulling a coach were unlike anything to be seen in any other early Rembrandt. The decorative fashion in which the trunk of the palm in the background bends together with the back of the coach was also hard to reconcile with the accepted image of the young Rembrandt. The subject, the baptism of the eunuch, was painted by the young Rembrandt in 1631 in a work since lost but whose composition is known

1
Rembrandt Harmensz. van Rijn, *The Baptism of the Eunuch*, 1626
Cat. no. 3

2
Copy after a lost painting of Rembrandt Harmensz. van Rijn, *The Baptism of the Eunuch*, 1631
Panel, 115 x 90 cm
Private Collection

to us through a surviving reproduction print by J. van Vliet as well as through a rather loosely interpreted copy (fig. 2). Rembrandt's preferred solution in that painting was entirely different from that of the newly discovered work; and above all else, the central figure in the Defoer's painting argued against the attribution. Philip, who is baptising the Moorish eunuch, looked like a wooden puppet with a head that could not have been from Rembrandt's hand. At the time, it was not evident from the photograph provided by Defoer that this head had been severely overcleaned and clumsily reconstructed by a later hand. Based only on the photograph, however, the appearance of Philip's head significantly determined the viewer's first impression of the painting. Yet there were also fine, well-preserved passages, like the young Moor holding the book, which recalled the young Rembrandt quite strongly.

As the youngest member of the *RRP*, I was at that time attached to the Amsterdam *Centraal Laboratorium voor Onderzoek van Voorwerpen van Kunst en Wetenschap* (Central Laboratory for Research on Objects from Art and Science). Josua Bruyn, chairman of the *RRP*, suggested that Defoer should have the laboratory investigate the painting, and consequently I became closely involved with Defoer's discovery. While the arguments rehearsed in cat. no. 3 began to accumulate – in short, that one really was dealing here with a Rembrandt – both Gerson and ourselves in the *RRP* came to accept that our initial rejection of the attribution had to be revised. There was a new painting to add to the Rembrandt œuvre, whose authenticity would never subsequently be in doubt.[1]

As fortuitous as Defoer's find was, it was not by chance that the new discovery concerned a very early work. It was hardly surprising that no-one among the many who must have seen the painting hanging above the sideboard over the years had seen a Rembrandt in it. Instead of the *chiaroscuro* so characteristic of later Rembrandt, one always finds in his earliest works, including of course this *Baptism of the Eunuch*, a clearly lit pictorial space containing colourful, closely crowded figures. Nor was Defoer's painting the first to go long unrecognised as a Rembrandt. Other paintings that had had to wait centuries before being rediscovered as early Rembrandts had been quite recently found, even in museum storerooms. Gerson, who initially had difficulty recognising Defoer's discovery as a work by Rembrandt, had himself several years previously discovered the earliest signed Rembrandt in the storeroom of the museum of Lyon (fig. 3).[2] One could go on telling such stories of the discovery of early Rembrandts to demonstrate how the at first sight un-Rembrandtesque part of Rembrandt's œuvre was only rather recently charted. Although our picture of the early Rembrandt has since become much more detailed, there is still much to discover and innumerable questions that await satisfactory answers. Sometimes the existing image of Rembrandt as an artist had to be radically modified, as with the discovery of the new Rembrandt recounted above. Each new discovery tends to show – and has shown – Rembrandt from another, often unexpected angle.

But the episode of Defoer's discovery also taught us that even well-established authorities on Rembrandt can sometimes have difficulty in revising their image of the painter. It demands a detached, unprejudiced gaze to see Rembrandt with new eyes and to formulate new questions. This may happen through a new discovery, as in the case of the *Baptism of the Eunuch* or of cat. no. 62 and 66, but it can also come about by bringing artworks together on one wall in an exhibition. Through such a confrontation of paintings in an exhibition, both the layman and the expert can be forced to re-think their image of the artist concerned; which in turn can lead to posing new questions.

**Rembrandt's motivation**
One question that intrigues me, particularly in

4
Jan Lievens, *Portrait of Constantijn Huygens*, c. 1628/29
Panel, 99 x 84 cm
Rijksmuseum, Amsterdam

connection with the early Rembrandt, is: What was the motivation that drove him? Did ‹it›, as we like to assume with artists, come from within? Or were there more peripheral forces and influences at play, for example the influences of what we would now call ‹market forces›? Could the enormous increase in demand for paintings in the first quarter of the seventeenth century have played a role in Rembrandt's decision to become a painter? But then how then does one account for the extraordinarily rapid development in his style? Did external influences or individuals with whom he came in contact play a role, or should one think of this primarily as a personal artistic adventure?

The few texts by contemporaries of Rembrandt that might possibly be able to throw light on the question of Rembrandt's motivation will be dealt with in their context in this essay. Two highly relevant glimpses of the young Rembrandt should be introduced here, however, since they evoke a very life-like picture of Rembrandt at work and indirectly throw light on what might have driven him. We are dealing with two fragments from a long and detailed passage devoted to the art of painting from the autobiography of one of the most exceptional figures of the seventeenth century, Constantijn Huygens (1596–1687) (fig. 4). At the time he first met Rembrandt, Huygens was secretary to the *stadholder* Frederik Hendrik (1584–1647), a civil servant and a diplomat. But in addition he was an extraordinarily versatile *homo universalis*, interested and unusually talented in many fields. Both a composer and a poet, he played the lute and drew, but at the same time was intensely interested in the development of science.[3] Huygens' versatility was the intentional product of his education. We know a good deal about this education from his autobiography, written in Latin at the age of 33 not published until 1891, when the handwritten manuscript was discovered.[4] It is important for us to know that, beyond the detailed account of the education and upbringing that he and his brother Maurits received, a large part of this text is devoted to the painters Constantijn knew.

Huygens, who presumably visited Rembrandt in 1628, gives in his autobiography one of the most intelligent analyses of his work to be found in all

5
Rembrandt Harmensz.
van Rijn, *Self-portrait*,
c. 1628/29
Pen in brown, grey wash,
127 x 95 mm
Benesch 53
British Museum,
London

6
Rembrandt Harmensz.
van Rijn, *Jan Lievens in
His Studio*, c. 1630
Pen in brown,
205 x 70 mm
Benesch 390
The J. Paul Getty
Museum, Los Angeles

seventeenth-century writings on the artist (see Appendix).[5] It, as well as other surviving texts, will be quoted frequently in this essay. These texts are invaluable windows onto the past. Having lain dormant for centuries in dusty piles of paper in some file or other, it is a wonder that it was possible for them to be fished from the stream of time by some fortunate hand. In some of these texts we hear the words of individuals who knew and had spoken with Rembrandt, who lived in the same world of ideas and who had sometimes watched him at work. The remarkable thing about historical texts is that, time and again, depending on the context in which they are studied, they provide new insights. This is partly because these texts – like all texts, those of our time, as well – were written under the influence of certain conventions of which the author was probably not consciously aware, but which make it essential that the present-day reader should not simply take them at face value. If this proviso is borne in mind, the historical sources can often offer a rich and detailed picture of the past.

In a long passage in his autobiography, Huygens bracketed Rembrandt (fig. 5) with his younger Leiden colleague, Jan Lievens (fig. 6). As a result, it is mostly impossible to lift the passages on Rembrandt from the text without also referring to Jan Lievens.

To return to the question of what motivated Rembrandt, Huygens has nothing to say explicitly about this, but his text does contain implicit indicators that can help us. The passage in Huygens' text where he regrets that Rembrandt and Lievens are so self-assured «that up till now they have found it unnecessary to spend a few months on a study tour of Italy» has often been quoted and analysed; less well known, however, is the following passage in which several reasons are given for the painters having declined the Italian study trip. One of these was that

> «they are now at the height of their youthful powers and must first and foremost make the best use of them; they have no time to waste on distant travel.»[6]

A few lines later, Huygens takes up this remark:

> «I have to say that I have never witnessed a comparable dedication and tenacity in any group of people, in any occupation or at any age. For truly, they make the most of their time. That is the only thing that matters to them. It is most remarkable that they dismiss even the innocent pleasures of youth as a waste of time. It concerns them so little, one might think one was dealing with old men, full of years, who have long since put such trivialities behind them. This indefatigable industry should soon lead to great results, yet I have often wished that these

outstanding young men would temper their exertions and also take into account their constitution which, because of their sedentary way of life, is neither so robust nor healthy.»[7]

This last remark is undoubtedly coloured by the belief in Huygens' circles that a young man should exercise the body as well as the mind.

One does not get the impression from the text quoted above that this «dedication and tenacity» of Rembrandt and Lievens had primarily to do with outside pressures in the form of a stream of commissions. Nowhere in Huygens' text is there any mention of a commission. On the contrary, one of the paintings dealt with most prominently in his text was not, according to Huygens' own account, a commission but was painted by Lievens on his own initiative: Huygens' portrait (see fig. 4; see Appendix). The document cited by Korevaar in his essay, in which Lievens asks the city council of permission to sell two paintings at a sale (see p. 16), indicates that these too had been painted on his own initiative. The diligence shown by Rembrandt and Lievens is primarily seen by Huygens as a path that «would quickly lead to great results.» Should one then conclude that both painters were consciously working on their own development as artists, that in their early works they were practising and experimenting, mainly preoccupied with finding their artistic direction rather than with producing for the market?

There is another passage from Huygens suggesting that it was not primarily commissions that determined <u>what</u> or <u>how</u> they painted but the young painters themselves:

> «So off-hand I would venture to suggest that in precision and vividness, Rembrandt is the superior of Lievens. Conversely the latter wins through a grandeur in conception and in the daring of subjects and forms. Everything this young spirit strives for must be majestic and exalted. Rather than conforming to the true size of what he depicts, he gives his painting a larger stature. Rembrandt, on the other hand, would rather concentrate totally on a small painting and achieves a result on a small scale that one looks for in vain in the largest paintings of others.»[8]

Referring back to the question of Rembrandt's motivation, the passages quoted above are important because they suggest that the two young artists were apparently in certain respects following their own bent. But we cannot help wondering whether such an interpretation is coloured by our nineteenth and twentieth-century ideas of *art pour l'art*, taking it for granted that artists are driven by their own motivation (and if an interested party shows up, they can buy a work if they so wish).

In the current art historical literature on the sixteenth and seventeenth centuries, the question of the artist and his patrons is a normal and proper matter for discussion: the painter as a rule produced for churches, castles, city halls, ancestral galleries, etc. From this perspective, painters seem first and foremost like either craftsmen or suppliers, on the one hand, running small independent businesses, or else courtiers in the service of kings and princes, who produced paintings for various functions. And then there is the fact that people like to refer to the ‹art market›. Particularly in seventeenth-century Holland, the role of this art market in the art of painting warrants emphasis. As Gerbrand Korevaar makes clear in his essay in this volume, many of the millions of paintings produced along with other luxury goods in the seventeenth century were indeed sold as ‹skilful paintings› at annual markets to decorate house interiors. The existence of public sales and art dealers in the seventeenth century is also of course well known.[9]

The image created, however, is to a considerable extent misleading when it comes to an artist like Rembrandt. As suggested above and as will be more closely developed later on in this essay, his early work is characterised by an astonishingly rapid development that can scarcely be explained unless one accepts that Rembrandt was <u>not</u> primarily producing for sale but was rather possessed of a questing and exploratory approach to the art of painting. In this respect he seems to be the type of artist considered exemplary in the late nineteenth and twentieth centuries. But did he quest and explore solely for the purpose of solving artistic problems of various kinds for himself? It will turn out that, just as in our own day, there was at that time a public, a select company, which followed certain artists' developments closely, and in the case of the young Rembrandt we know this for certain. The writings of Constantijn Huygens already quoted are enough to demonstrate this.

We have become used to thinking that art criticism and art history only arose as disciplines in the nineteenth century, and that the museum, which functioned as an institution where art could be publicly shown, commented on, or raised for discussion, was a parallel development. This does not mean, however, that art was not seriously regarded or studied earlier. Indeed, even before Rembrandt was born, art and artists were already being written and talked about from historical and theoretical perspectives. It is general knowledge, of course, that Giorgio Vasari's *Le vite de'più eccelenti Pittori, Scultori e Architettori* (Lives of the Greatest Artists, Sculptors and Architects) appeared in the sixteenth century, inspiring Karel van Mander's *Schilderboeck*, published in the Netherlands in the early seventeenth century.[10] These and other similar books that appeared in various European countries in the course of the seventeenth century did not restrict themselves to details of the lives of painters and their works. They also provided a good deal of technical and art historical information. This is true, for example, of Karel van Mander's *leerdicht* or didactic poem, *Grondt der Edel vrij Schilder-const* (The Essence of the Noble Art of Painting), that forms part of his *Schilderboeck*. At first thought, one assumes that such books were written by artists for artists; but when one analyses the often highly verbose titles, forewords and dedicatory verses of such publications it is evident that they were also, and perhaps even predominantly, written for art lovers.

## Art lovers and connoisseurs: a stimulating ‹art scene›

Before the invention of photography, of course, innumerable representations of diverse sorts were needed and there was great demand for well-trained people who could create such images. But just as today, there was then too a privileged set of artists surrounded by an informed public seriously interested in the developments in the art of their own time, a public that was al-

so educated in the history of art – not least thanks to the above-mentioned books of Vasari, van Mander and others.

In a text of 1657, Rembrandt's pupil Samuel van Hoogstraten discusses the knowledge that a cultivated citizen in Rembrandt's time would be required to have where painting was concerned. The book was aimed at the «Honourable Young Man» (Den Eerlyken Jongeling) and deals with all that a young man from a good background might need. As far as the art of painting was concerned, the passage runs:

> «Therefore my advice is that one should in general learn to understand the basic principles [of painting] familiarise oneself with the great masters and learn to distinguish between their styles. One also should know in what countries, cities and palaces the best works are to be seen.»[11]

Van Hoogstraten goes on to add that the books of Karel van Mander, Albrecht Dürer and Junius are very useful for acquiring this knowledge.[12]

The travel journals of well-bred young men who were required to use their general knowledge on the ‹Grand Tour› tend to suggest that their knowledge of art usually fell far short of Hoogstraten's standard.[13] But unquestionably, van Hoogstraten's advice gives a fair idea of the knowledge art-lovers aspired to.

It would seem from seventeenth-century travel reports that only painters betray the kind of curiosity and knowledge that Hoogstraten advised the «honorable young man» to acquire.[14] It is as well to realise that Rembrandt too must have possessed such knowledge. The collection he built up and the art historical erudition evident in his own works are witness to this.[15] Undoubtedly, mixing with the older connoisseurs who, as will be seen below, surrounded him from an early stage must have contributed to the development of that erudition.

In exploring the ‹art scene› surrounding the young Rembrandt, it is worth knowing that these connoisseurs and art-lovers maintained active contacts with living artists and with each other, cultivating the judgement that would enable them to judge the quality of art works and to discuss the art of painting competently.

Constantijn Huygens' autobiography sheds further light on the background context of this

field of painting (with which one is currently everywhere confronted) it is impossible
to arrive at even a partially founded judgement unless one has actively tried to practise the basic principles of this art oneself.
He had remarked that important persons
who were renowned for their wide learning
had nevertheless brought upon themselves
the ridicule of professional practitioners
when they vented their own opinions on the
art of painting. This had led him to an un-
shakeable decision to ensure – since we
could simply not be experts in all branches
of the art – that we [Constantijn and his
brother Maurits] should never cut a ridicu-
lous figure with our judgement, at least in
the most prominent arts.»[17]

Here a remarkable and, for our view of art history, extremely important symbiosis is revealed
between the practise of a profession – that of the
painters – and a public, also including «the great
of the earth,» in which one did one's best to be
well-informed on the art of painting so as not, as
Alexander the Great did of front of Apelles'
pupils, make a fool of oneself when art was discussed.[18] No wonder that Rembrandt and more
especially Jan Lievens were, according to Huygens, «rather self-assured» since, in a certain
sense, the «great of the earth» solicited their
favours. It was precisely in connection with
painters that Huygens let slip the remark: «I am
always keen on friendship with celebrities.»[19]

Beside Huygens, another typical representative
of the sixteenth and seventeenth-century art
*scene* was Aernout van Buchell (1565–1641), also known as Arnoldus Buchelius (fig. 7). We
shall meet him as an early witness regarding the
growing reputation of the still-young Rembrandt. Van Buchell was a lawyer in Utrecht
who kept a record of the many things that occupied him. From a part of these innumerable
notes, many of which have been preserved, it
turns out that he was a great connoisseur of
painting and print-making. He browsed the
premises of art dealers, bought prints and visited
artists in their studios; he met other connoisseurs of painting and discussed art with them,
and on his many journeys he visited collections
and other places where paintings and prints
were to be seen. He also read van Mander's

need for the cultivated Dutchman to be initiated
into the art world. The most important motive
for this derives from texts of classical antiquity,
which report that in Greece and subsequently in
Rome, particular importance was attributed to
the arts of drawing and painting. These arts were
not only important for artists; the practical pursuit of draughtsmanship was also important and
played a major role among non-artists. In this
connection, Constantijn Huygens quotes the
Roman writer Pliny the Elder (23–79 AD) who
reports that drawing in Greece «was accorded
the first place in the educational curriculum.»
Huygens continues with his own contention:

> «On whether the art of painting enjoys the
> same prestige in our own time I will not
> comment, but her esteem is sufficiently evi-
> dent from the love that the great of the
> earth have for her: those who practise her
> are noble or her practitioners become eno-
> bled if they are successful.[16] Her rewards
> (understood in the material sense) have al-
> ways been very great. Yet these were not
> the motives for which my father let himself
> be guided. [Huygens writes this in the pas-
> sage where he is dealing with the educa-
> tional ideas of his father.] He had seen the
> result that the Greeks had also undoubtedly
> had in mind. As a complete layman, as he
> said himself, he had observed that in the

*Schilder-boeck* attentively and excerpted passages from it. Many of his loose notes on art and artists were assembled in a file under the heading *Res pictoriae* (concerning painting).[20]

It is not known whether Arnoldus Buchelius ever met Rembrandt but by 1628 he had certainly heard him discussed. Rembrandt was then 22 years old and had only been active a few years as an independent painter. That Rembrandt should have been spoken about so early by art connoisseurs in Buchelius' circle of acquaintances says a great deal about those connoisseurs, but as we shall see it says even more about Rembrandt.

The brief note Buchelius wrote on Rembrandt may at first glance scarcely seem worth attention, but on closer consideration one realises how revealing it actually is:

> «Also, the son of a miller in Leiden is esteemed highly, though prematurely.»[21]

The «prematurity» of the praise remarked by Buchelius implies that he has been talking with others who admired Rembrandt, art-lovers who it seems were *au fait* with the latest news from the ‹art scene› and that Rembrandt apparently was such news.

These connoisseurs reappear in a brief biographical account of the young Rembrandt written by the Leiden burgomaster Jan Jansz. Orlers (1570–1646). In the second expanded edition of his *Descriptions of the City of Leiden*, which appeared in 1641 (following the first edition in 1614), Orlers added a series of brief biographies of famous Leideners, including one on Rembrandt.[22] Orlers tells us here that Rembrandt spent three years under his first master, Jacob Isaacsz. van Swanenburg, ending this passage with the words:

> «during which time, his progress was so great, that the art lovers [underlining E.v.d.W.] were amazed, for it was clearly evident that he would one day become an exceptional painter.»[23]

These «art-lovers» who might also have been Buchelius' interlocutors thus apparently followed closely the progress of even young, apprenticed painters. Constantijn Huygens too refers to anonymous connoisseurs and to the high expectations they had for the duo of Rembrandt and Lievens.

«Were I to say that they are the only ones who can hold their own against the absolute geniuses among the [in the same text] aforesaid masters, I would even then not be doing these two justice. And were I to say that they will soon surpass those geniuses, I would merely be expressing what their astonishing beginning has led connoisseurs [underlining E.v.d.W.] to expect.»[24]

The question that immediately arises is who these anonymous art-lovers and connoisseurs – referred to by Buchelius implicitly and by Orlers and Huygens explicitly – could have been. Our picture of these observers of the young painters in their whirlwind development, who must have followed Rembrandt and Lievens over some time, is considerably enriched by the identification of four of them. One was the learned schoolmaster Theodorus Schrevelius (1572– 1649), who taught in Haarlem until 1625 and subsequently became rector of the Latin school in Leiden, the same school that Rembrandt attended between 1615 and 1619 (fig. 8). Buchelius, on one of his trips from Utrecht, visited Schrevelius in Leiden in 1628. From one of his subsequent notes it is clear that the two had extensively talked about painting, during which conversation also the «son of a miller in Leiden» was discussed. Apparently, when he came to write his notes, Buchelius had forgotten Rembrandt's name – a name which then too was unusual.[25]

Then there is Pieter Schrijver, or Petrus Scriverius (1576–1660) who had left Haarlem and established himself in Leiden at the end of the sixteenth century (fig. 9). On the basis of various documents on Scriverius, Gary Schwartz has shown that he must have had an exceptional love of the art of painting.[26] For instance, in 1604 he wrote the first eulogy in Karel van Mander's *Schilder-boeck*. Three years after his death, paintings from his collection were auctioned off, including «two rather large pieces by Rembrandt.»[27] Scriverius may well have been one of those ‹art-lovers› who, according to Orlers, avidly followed Rembrandt's progress during the period of his apprenticeship with Jacob Isaacsz. van Swanenburg.

Besides Scriverius, the other purchasers of works by the young Rembrandt who are known to us were also devotees of the art of painting

rather than some burgher merely buying paintings for wall decoration. From a letter written by a French art dealer in 1641, it is evident that Rembrandt's *Balaam and the Ass,* from 1626 (cf. fig. 24), was bought directly from the young Rembrandt by the French art-lover and collector Alfonse Lopez (1582–1649)[28], originally a goldsmith, who was in the Netherlands between 1624 and 1630 under orders from Richelieu to make purchases for the French army and navy.[29] Lopez had many contacts with the *stadholder's* court in The Hague (including, no doubt, with Constantijn Huygens) and, as his correspondence reveals, he often travelled up and down between Amsterdam and The Hague – and therefore via Leiden. The suggestion can hardly be avoided that Lopez too had heard of «the astonishing beginning» of the young Rembrandt and that, as early as 1626 or during the years immediately following, he had visited him in his studio and that it was here that he bought the *Balaam* from him.

One of the most intriguing art-lovers and purchasers of Rembrandt's early work was Jacques de Gheyn III (1596–1641), son of the brilliant, multi-faceted artist of the same name, Jacques de Gheyn II (1565–1629) (see p. 70, fig. 20), who was highly regarded at the *stadholder's* court. Constantijn Huygens called Jacques

Gheyn II «the most outstanding of my friends» but he was also greatly concerned about him. It is worth quoting Huygens' severe criticism of him. His disgust that such a gifted painter as De Gheyn had sunk into indolence may well explain the creation of one of the young Rembrandt's earliest remarkable paintings. Huygens wrote:

«If I think back on De Gheyn's promising beginning, it incenses me that someone could have so carelessly treated such promise, that someone who was so evidently born in the Netherlands to be for ever a pearl in the crown of his fatherland, can bury his talent in this way and can slumber in barren and ignoble indolence. I would almost say that this is the result of too many material comforts.»[30]

These comforts, combined with his understanding of art, put Jacques Jr. in a position to buy one of Rembrandt's most ambitious and revolutionary early paintings (see fig. 18), *Peter and Paul Disputing.* (This painting, now in the National Gallery of Victoria in Melbourne, is in such a fragile state that unfortunately it could not be included in this exhibition).

The other early work by Rembrandt owned by Jacques Jr. is described in the testament as

«A man sitting near a fire, asleep with his hand on his breast.» (cat. no. 31)[31]

It would have been immediately clear to a seventeenth-century viewer that this painting represented the vice of sloth (Acedia). It is tempting to speculate whether it was commissioned by Jacques' friend Constantijn Huygens as a «Wraeke des Penseels» (the revenge of the brush) as it was called in the seventeenth century, a reflection of Huygens' irritation at his friend's «barren and ignoble indolence».[32]

It is evident from this discussion of those with whom the young master had dealings in the early stages of his career that he was surrounded by experts on art who, with the possible initial exception of Buchelius, must have been full of admiration for his work. Such admiration must surely have had a stimulating effect on Rembrandt himself.

That this interest of art-lovers and connoisseurs in his work has hitherto scarcely been recognised in a broader context in the Rembrandt literature is perhaps due to the fact that in the art historical literature on Rembrandt's period, art-lovers are implicitly treated as exceptional individuals who, through their own bent, had an unusually developed interest in art. However, since Castiglione in his *Libro del Cortegiano* (The Courtier) of 1528 makes it clear that the well-informed discussion of art, and particularly of the art of painting, was one of the recommended topics of conversation for a courtier, there must have developed a certain social pressure on this point.[33] The concern felt by Constantijn Huygens' father that his sons should not make fools of themselves when they discussed the art of painting in particular (in the passage quoted earlier) is a telling witness to this social pressure. Besides, there was the usual evolution of what had first gained currency as courtly conversation and deportment under the influence of Castiglione, subsequently penetrating the lower levels of society, first in Antwerp and later throughout Europe, particularly in the northern Netherlands. In the 1624 diary of David Beck, a schoolmaster from The Hague (1594–1634) we find his record of reading van Mander's *Schilderboeck* and exchanging ideas on art with a cabinet-maker during a journey of many hours in the tow-barge from The Hague to Dordrecht.[34]

Van Hoogstraten's book, in which the recommended curriculum, cited above, covering the art of painting appeared, bore the telling title *Den Eerlyken Jongeling, of de edele Kunst, Van zich by Groote en Kleyne te doen Eeren en Beminnen* (The Honourable Young Man, or the Noble Art of Being Honoured and Loved by Great and Small). The book, published in 1657 for the seventeenth-century Dutch citizen, was clearly based on Castigliano's *Libro del Cortegiano* of 1528. Its existence demonstrates the process of the spread of aristocratic culture into the world of the bourgeoisie. As far as the art of painting is concerned, Hoogstraten was explicit on this point: his passage on the art of painting begins with the declaration that the latter «is loved in all Courts of the world ...» In the context of this essay, it is significant that he continues this sentence as follows:

> «... and to be able to discourse well on her will often compel Monarchs and Princes to hear us ...»[35]

These latter words indicate that the painter was the most important source of knowledge for the art-lover and for the monarch who, *ex officio*, had to be an art-lover.

Studio visits indeed were an inherent part of the symbiotic relation between art-lovers and painters. A manual for connoisseurs of painting, written at this same time in Paris, that has survived in manuscript form, includes this advice:

> «... to know how to discourse on this noble profession [painting on a flat surface, one of the most noble arts of the world, as set out earlier by the author] you must have frequented the studios and disputed with the masters, have seen the magic effects of the pencil and the unerring judgement with which the details are worked out.»[36]

The illustrations accompanying this quotation seem to be supplied by a number of seventeenth-century Dutch paintings in which visitors to a studio are represented closely inspecting paintings in the presence of the artist (fig. 10), or in intense conversation with the artist (fig. 11). The word ‹illustration› is of course ill-chosen. Such paintings presumably constitute only one category of a whole genre, the studio representation, which could be described as ‹a visit to a painting studio›, in which perhaps not the entire ‹essence› of the art of painting was dealt with but one or several relevant aspects. In the

Pieter Codde, *Visitors in the Studio*, c. 1635
Panel, 38.3 x 49.3 cm
Staatsgalerie, Stuttgart

Boston *Studio* (cat. no. 61) for instance, the creative moment of invention in the mind is depicted in the context of the plain, but in several of its technical aspects, precisely and informatively represented studio. In a studio representation by one of Rembrandt's pupils the young Rembrandt is portrayed with his tufts of hair and the Rembrandt beret, standing by his easel, the still-life in the foreground apparently as a demonstration of «the magic effects of the brush and the unerring judgement with which the details are worked out» (fig. 12). In the background an expensively dressed young man is entering the studio, the «honourable young man,» perhaps, or the aspiring art connoisseur? Or should he be seen as the attribute standing for the symbiosis between the art-lover and the artist, a symbiosis that was undoubtedly of great importance to the young Rembrandt's development as an artist.

## Rembrandt's gift and the underrated importance of his apprenticeship with Jacob Isaacsz. van Swanenburg

History is witness to countless examples of certain children's overwhelming urge to draw and their conviction that there is no possible future for them other than as painters. Many of us, from our own acquaintance, know of such instances of juvenile obsession. This early need to draw and paint is one of the *topoi* of the genre of the biography of artists, but these are nonetheless stories that seem to be mostly based on fact. When Orlers writes in his one-page biography of Rembrandt that the latter «had absolutely no desire nor inclination» to follow a university education, «whereas his natural bent was directed solely to the art of painting and drawing» we can assume that this was indeed the case, all the more so since Rembrandt's entire career betrayed the same obsessive single-mindedness.[37] Apart from those interested art-lovers who were so astonished by his progress during his time of apprenticeship, there were three individuals who played a major role in his early years as a

11
Pieter Codde, *Conversation about Art*, c. 1630
Panel, 43 x 56.5 cm
Fondation Custodia
(Collection F. Lugt),
Paris

painter: his first master, Jacob Isaacsz. van Swanenburg (1571–1638), with whom Orlers tells us he stayed three years; his second master Pieter Lastman (1583–1633) in Amsterdam, where according to the same source he stayed for six months; and the child prodigy Jan Lievens, one year his junior, who was to play such a complex if still only partially understood role in Rembrandt's development as an artist. Huygens' remarks about Rembrandt's and Lievens' masters (the latter was with Joris Schooten from 1615 to 1617 and with Pieter Lastman from 1617 to 1619) are at first sight surprising, but from a particular point of view they may be very relevant:

> «When I ask about the masters that they had in their childhood, I am confronted by individuals who are scarcely known beyond the lower social strata. Because of their parents' slender means, these lads were sent to masters whose fees were not so high. Were one to confront these masters with their pupils now, they would feel embarrassed in much the same way as would the teachers who first gave Virgil lessons in poetry, or Cicero his first instruction in rhetoric, or first taught Archimedes mathematics. But with all due respect to everybody's capacities and without wishing to denigrate anyone – for what interest would I have in that? – these two owe nothing to their masters and everything to their own gifts. Had they never had a training, but had been left to their own fate, and had they at some chance moment come to painting through their own disposition, then I am convinced they would have achieved the same heights as they have now. It would be a mistake to think that they have been brought to this level through the teaching of others.»[38]

In what follows I shall argue the plausibility of the view that Rembrandt had reason to be grateful to his teachers.[39] Does that mean that Huygens' judgement should be considered wrong or highly exaggerated, at best an overstated rhetorical means of asserting what he saw as the exceptional talent of these two youths? That is one possibility. But one should also bear in mind

that at the time Huygens met the two young painters in 1628 – when they would undoubtedly have spoken of their training – they were both of them far beyond their last master, Pieter Lastman. By then they would no longer have seen themselves as disciples of Lastman, precisely because, as will become apparent, they emphatically – and most probably critically – distanced themselves from what they had learned from him.

In art historical literature it is often stated that there is no trace of Rembrandt's sojourn with van Swanenburg to be found in his œuvre. In some respects this is an empty assertion. It was customary for young painters to learn their profession with more than one master and for the second master to be the one whose specialism (and style) one wanted to acquire oneself. Rembrandt's own later pupils, in almost all cases, came to him after having undergone a preliminary training elsewhere. But that is not to say that the first training period was of no importance.

In those first years of training the foundations were laid for the later mastery. At that time, the aspiring painter was drilled in the techniques and the endless series of tricks and formulae that had to be mastered before one was able to represent reality on a flat surface. During these years, forms, specifically those of the human figure, were practised over and over again in all possible positions with the optical distortions associated with foreshortening and rounding, drawing on insight into the anatomical structure of the various parts of the body (fig. 13). In this early training period, the role of light and shadow in the depiction of forms was studied, first from drawn and engraved examples, then from plaster casts (fig. 14), and finally from living models who were, as a rule, clothed. (Drawing nudes was much less frequent in those days than in later academies of fine arts). During this stage of the training, drapery was rendered from printed examples or from nature to master the problems of the pleats and folding of fabric; prints with dogs and horses, landscapes, weapons, costumes etc.

were also copied. Paramount, however, was that whoever could not completely master the complex grammar of form, light and space would always remain a second-rate painter.[40]

If Orlers and Huygens are to be believed, two important conditions for a successful future were already satisfied very early on in Rembrandt's career: he had a strong talent and proved himself exceptionally hard-working. Almost all seventeenth-century sources on Rembrandt refer to his diligence,[41] but his œuvre as draughtsman, etcher and painter is no less witness. Such industry was apparently no mere product of some sense of duty – «nulla dies sine linea» (never a day without a line) – but, as Rembrandt showed throughout his career, it was fed by an unremitting curiosity and a need to experiment that is characteristic of all great artists.

The apprentice was to a certain extent servant and assistant as well as pupil. Sometimes, for example, he was used, or exploited to do chores or run errands for the mistress of the house. If this happened at the expense of his training, he or his parents could resist this on the basis of verbal agreements or a written contract. Payment for training was one of the ways of compensating the master for the time devoted to the pupil, but in addition to this the apprentice usually had to work off his apprenticeship by assisting his master with various routine operations. Assisting the master was self-evidently a sensible way of being initiated into the profession.

As well as we understand the place of drawing in the seventeenth-century artist's training, we have very little idea of the way a pupil was educated as a painter. We can assume that Rembrandt would also have had an introduction to painting under van Swanenburg. The mere preparation of the master's palette which, various sources inform us, was one of the apprentice's tasks, in the seventeenth century demanded considerable knowledge that had to be passed on from master to pupil (fig. 15).[42] Beside this, watching his master at work would have shown him how a composition was sketched out on a prepared canvas or panel, how the desired distribution of light and shade was prepared in the under-painting, what pigments and mixtures of pigments would adequately represent different aspects of the real world in

different tints, and with the required kind of rendering of materials. The pupil must have seen from his master in daily practise how paint was prepared and what binding media were used for this (fig. 16), what brushes were used and for what purpose, and countless other matters that a painter needed to know about – and he will have assisted him in these tasks.

Copying the work of the master at this stage – following the latter's working procedures and

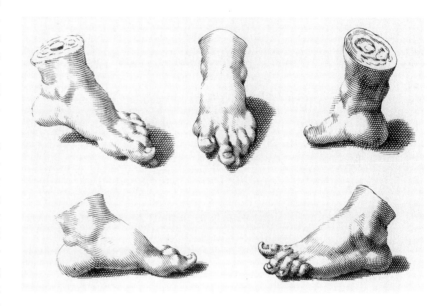

13
Engraved drawing model from Crispijn de Passe's *Van 't light der teken en schilderkonst*, Amsterdam 1643

14
Rembrandt Harmensz. van Rijn, *Apprentice Drawing from a Cast*, c. 1641
Etching, 94 x 64 mm
Bartsch 130, state II
Museum het Rembrandthuis, Amsterdam

15
Philips Galle after
Johannes Stradanus,
*Color Olivi* (detail),
c. 1590
Engraving,
Teil der Serie *Nova
Reperta*

16
Adriaen van Ostade,
*The Painter's Studio*
(detail), c. 1645
Panel, 37 x 36 cm
Rijksmuseum,
Amsterdam

Underworld (fig. 17; cf. cat. no. 1) did not make a permanent impression on Rembrandt, not so much because of the thematics of these paintings as through the confrontation with specific artistic challenges that painting fires in darkened surroundings present.

A brief digression on painting fires will bring us immediately to the heart of one of the most problems that have to be solved if we are to gain insight in the crucial problem of the relation between form and content. In view of Rembrandt's great narrative talent as a painter, etcher and draftsman, one would assume that the content of the work would have had an obvious priority for him; which would mean that, for Rembrandt, form would be subservient to content. The term ‹form› in this context has to be understood in the widest sense: including, for instance, such aspects as composition (in the plane of the image) and ordonnance (the spatial grouping of figures), colour, tone and the treatment of light and shade and their role in the suggestion of space and plasticity, the handling of paint and brushwork etc. To seventeenth-century eyes, which includes the eyes of the art-lover as well as painter, the mastery of the artist mainly consisted in the realisation of a convincing illusion of reality. As the painter Pierre Lebrun in 1635 wrote in his manual for lovers of the art of painting already quoted earlier:

> «when talking about fine paintings one should talk as if the things that are rendered are real, not painted ... one should deceive the eye; otherwise the painting is worthless.»[43]

In our discussion of form versus content, therefore, all those aspects which we include under the heading ‹form› have to be placed within the framework of the overriding quest for successful illusion. From the point of view of the seventeenth-century spectator, as will become evident, the life-like depiction of individual figures, even down to the expression in a posture or a figure's face, count as part of the illusion, quite apart from the narrative context in which these figures are situated.

Returning to Rembrandt's apprenticeship with Jacob Isaacsz. van Swanenburg, it is important to be aware that painting fire, apart from the context in which this occurs, must have ap-

style – served not only a pedagogical function but also expanded the production of the workshop, since such copies were saleable. In short, aside from the question of whether van Swanenburg was a painter of any importance, in the three years as his apprentice Rembrandt would have learned a great deal from him on which he could later build.

One wonders too whether the confrontation with van Swanenburg's scenes of Hell and the

17
Jacob Isaacsz. van
Swanenburg (attributed),
*The Last Judgement*
(detail), c. 1620
Panel, 28 x 88 cm
Rijksmuseum,
Amsterdam

pealed greatly to the imagination. Buchelius, the connoisseur whom we met earlier, noted in his *Res Pictoriae* as an apparently important detail for the art-lover that «It is an art to paint fires well.»[44] This note turns out to be a literal quotation of a summary that Karel van Mander had had printed in the margin of his didactic poem, in translation «The Essence of the Noble Art of Painting».[45] The part of the text to which this note referred is important for an understanding of Jacob Isaacsz. van Swanenburg's scenes of the hell and underworld. This is what Karel van Mander wrote:

> «An artist who can represent well in paint Vulcan's rage, such a terrible catastrophe, has a great mastery of the art of painting.»[46]

The text continues:

> «Not only the flames but also the smoke fills the air with different colours, so that it appears like the choking fumes of the Styx where, with many other ghastly spectres, Hydra and Cerberus shriek and roar. Painters must therefore pay heed to this, to make a fire look terrible, or to stoke the fires of the underworld described by the poets.»[47]

One gets the impression from this passage that the «art of painting fires well» took priority over the particular subject being depicted. This impression is further confirmed by a sixteenth cen-

tury northern Italian text from 1535, in which the despatch of three hundred paintings of Dutch origin is mentioned. An eyewitness relates:

> «Among them are twenty which represent nothing but landscapes on fire, which seem to burn one's hands if one goes to touch them.»[48]

The fact that one could almost «burn one's hands» on such paintings was apparently much more important than the question of whether, as undoubtedly would have been the case with such paintings, one was dealing with a destruction of Sodom and Gomorra after Lucas van Leyden, a Last Judgement in the style of Bosch or an Underworld with Charon Crossing the Styx by Patinir. One simply has to give full weight to the fact that Jacob Isaacsz. van Swanenburg in his scenes of Hell was in the first place playing to a fascination with convincingly painted fire, as would still exist later in the seventeenth century.[49]

One can apply this approach to the question of form and narrative content to the painting mentioned earlier, that Jacques de Gheyn III bought from Rembrandt around 1627/28, described in his dictated testament as

> «a painting by Rembrandt of two seated old men disputing, one with a large book on his lap, with sunlight entering.» (fig. 18)[50]

Rembrandt Harmensz.
van Rijn, *Peter and Paul
Disputing*, c. 1628
Panel, 72.3 x 59.5 cm
The National Gallery
of Victoria, Melbourne

Do we have to cudgel our brains over the question of who these old men might be on the basis that we could only settle the *raison d'être* of this painting if we could show, for instance, that this represents Peter and Paul in conversation?[51] Or might the *raison d'être* be simply be that Rembrandt was demonstrating how well he could paint «old men» and their «disputing», a «large book» and «entering sunlight»? Perhaps a comparable compartmentalisation of the challenge of illusionism and with it the various technical challenges of the painter's art relates to the purport of that advice quoted above, that art-lovers should go to the studio to study

«the magic effects of the pencil and the unerring judgement with which <u>the details</u> [underlining E.v.d.W.] are worked out.»[52]

In the painting with the old men and the «entering sunlight», certainly if one compares it with the *Tobit and Anna* (cat. no. 28) done two years earlier, one can see how much Rembrandt immediately began to concentrate on the problems of representing light and what astonishingly rapid progress he made in this. The representation of situations of highly complex illumination must surely have been one of the most important «compartments» in his own view of the *raison d'être* of his paintings. Who knows whether this interest in the working of light, which emerged in full force shortly after his period of training with Lastman and persisted till his death, was perhaps the most important result of Rembrandt's earlier apprenticeship, in his most impressionable years, with van Swanenburg. He must have been fascinated by what he saw his first master doing as a painter when he painted those scenes of Hell and Underworld «on which you could burn your hands.» It is obvious that the young Rembrandt very soon absorbed other important trends in this area of painting the light, in particular those of the Caravaggists (see cat. no. 29) – but his basic responsiveness to this aspect of the art of painting may already have been developed with Jacob Isaacsz. van Swanenburg.

In one other respect too, it can hardly have been otherwise than that his first master should have made a particular impression on Rembrandt: Jacob had lived for 24 years in Italy (from 1591 to 1615). We know for certain that he spent the last 15 years of this time in Naples. I referred above to Huygens' criticism of Rembrandt and Lievens' lack of interest in making the study trip to Italy, but of course in one sense Rembrandt had already spent three years in Italy. The van Swanenburg family must have been seen by their fellow citizens in Leiden as a small Italian enclave. Not so long before Rembrandt began his apprenticeship with Jacob Isaacsz. van Swanenburg, the latter had brought his wife and their three children of 15, 10 and 4 back from Italy to live with him in Leiden. Not only would the atmosphere of an Italian family have dominated his master's household; the master himself would have had countless stories to tell about Italian art. One only needs read Karel van Mander's biography of his master, Pieter Vlerick, to realise how the oral tradition functioned in the painter's workshop.[53]

## Rembrandt and Lievens
## 1620 to 1624?

An intriguing question associated with this attempt to understand Rembrandt's apprentice years is at what stage Jan Lievens appeared on the scene.

If Orlers' biography of Lievens is accurate, this child prodigy in the art of painting returned to Leiden after a second apprenticeship, which lasted two years, with Pieter Lastman. He was then twelve or thirteen years old. During the roughly four year period between Lievens' return and Rembrandt's departure for Amsterdam Lievens may already have had a certain impact on Rembrandt's early development as an artist. Like any young apprentice, Rembrandt must have worked daily with Jacob Isaacsz. van Swanenburg; but at the same time living a few streets further up was the 13-year-old Jan Lievens, who astonished everyone with this precocity, and over whom Orlers would write:

> «After leaving the aforesaid Lastman, he had no further teachers, and started working in his father's house, spending all his time diligently and industriously painting many and varied subjects from life.»[54]

There can be no doubt that Rembrandt and Lievens must have already known each other. Rembrandt attended the Latin school with Lievens' brother. Moreover, in a city which around 1620 had such a small population of painters and apprentices (see p. 17ff.) it would be hard to imagine that two young, up-and-coming painters, apparently much discussed, should not have known each other. They must have already exchanged knowledge – an exchange in which the more experienced, independent Lievens would have been the dispenser, and the apprentice painter Rembrandt rather the recipient.

It is clear that an apprentice painter such as Rembrandt could have worked not only with his master during the period of his apprenticeship, but also at home or elsewhere. The case of Isack Jouderville, the orphan who was a pupil of Rembrandt in 1629 and '30 and who probably accompanied him later to Amsterdam, possibly as his assistant, is a demonstration in point (see p. 60, fig. 3).[55] The unusually rich dossier on this boy kept by his guardians to account for their

20
Rembrandt
Harmensz. van Rijn,
*Christ Driving the
Money-changers from
the Temple*, 1626
43.1 x 32 cm
Cat. no. 12

19
Rembrandt, *The
Operation (Touch)*,
c. 1624/25
21.5 x 17.7 cm
Cat. no. 10

custodial performance to the authorities contains not only expenses for peat for the stove in his lodgings or the cost of clothing repairs, but also gives expenses for painting materials. According to several surviving contracts of apprenticeship, a painter's apprentice could expect to get his materials from his master, unless, as one such contract stipulates, the pupil is also painting for himself.[56] According to the receipts, the young Jouderville had purchased painting materials for his own use outside Rembrandt's workplace.[57] Can one not also imagine the young, searching Rembrandt doing the same? And during his apprenticeship with van Swanenburg, would Rembrandt not have sometimes worked

closely together with the younger but much further advanced Lievens, as he certainly did after his own apprenticeship with Lastman? This could well explain the existence of the Senses series (cat. nos. 9–11; fig. 19), genre pieces whose conception and composition seem to have been influenced by Lievens (see cat. no. 8). But these paintings, in their range of colour and handling of paint, also seem to anticipate the first history pieces that we know from the period following Rembrandt's return from his six months with Pieter Lastman, *The Stoning of St Stephen* (see fig. 3) and the Moscow *Christ Driving the Money-changers from the Temple* (cat. no. 12; fig. 20). If these two paintings, dated 1625 and 1626 respectively, were indeed painted after Rembrandt's return from Amsterdam, and the Senses before his departure to Lastman, as argued by other authors in this catalogue, one is left asking what influence, exactly, is Lastman supposed to have had on Rembrandt?

## Rembrandt and Lastman

«When I ask about the masters they had in their childhood, I am confronted with individuals who are scarcely known beyond the lower social strata» was how Constantijn Huygens dismissed Rembrandt's and Lievens' apprenticeships.[58] Those art-lovers who had read Karel van Mander's *Lives*, however, would have known that Rembrandt's second master was described there as a c. 20-year-old painter who was already «highly promising».[59] Huygens himself also mentions Lastman in this passage:

> «there are nowadays those numerous and perhaps even successful painters that I would normally describe as history painters, although the term is not really apt. I am thinking here of the Amsterdamers Pieter Isaacsz, Lastman and Pijnas…»[60]

which is followed by a list of the Utrecht Caravaggists and other Dutch and Flemish painters. Lastman was certainly not an obscure figure but a painter who dominated history painting in Amsterdam during the first decades of the seventeenth century. The poet and art lover Joost van den Vondel (1587–1679) even compared him with Rubens.[61]

Pieter Lastman, born in 1583, was a pupil of Gerrit Pietersz., and spent a period in Rome from 1603 to 1608 where, among others, he knew Adam Elsheimer. He died in 1633. Lastman's œuvre of history paintings consisting of easel pieces of moderate size with full-length figures enacting scenes drawn from the Bible and from classical history and mythology.

Like Jacob Isaacsz. van Swanenburg, Lastman must have made a considerable impression on Rembrandt. The question, however, is whether, as Ed de Heer once so congenially put it, he was Rembrandt's «eternal master».[62] In the most recent essay on Rembrandt's relationship with Lastman, Christiaan Tümpel's article in the 1991 Lastman exhibition catalogue, Lastman was again represented as primarily the master

whom Rembrandt admired all his life and whose influence regularly reappears in Rembrandt's work.[63] We read of paintings by Lastman that «made a huge impression on Rembrandt», and of others «from which he borrowed»; elsewhere Tümpel writes again of paintings for which «Rembrandt had great admiration» or «which he referred back to.» To understand properly what motivated the young Rembrandt it is highly important that we get a correct picture of his relation to Lastman. We need therefore to look more closely into this question.

It is an old discussion, this vexed question of how significant Pieter Lastman actually was for Rembrandt. Freise, who wrote the first monograph on Lastman, can also be credited as the author of the theory that Lastman had a lasting influence on Rembrandt.[64] Authors such as Knuttel, Stechow and Guratsch and, as seen earlier, de Heer and Tümpel also shared this view,[65] whereas Bloch and Gerson, for example, argued that Lastman's significance for Rembrandt should not be overestimated.[66] It is important to bear in mind that no written source exists to throw light on the matter; it is solely the formal relationships between several works by both artists that have fuelled this discussion.

Broos, one of those who claim to recognize deep traces of Lastman's influence on Rembrandt's style, was the first to describe Rembrandt's response to Lastman as «critical» (in the sense of analytical).[67] He used the word in connection with the red and black chalk copies of several of Lastman's paintings – altered in certain respects – that Rembrandt drew in the 1630s. An example of such an allegedly critical commentary is Rembrandt's large drawing after Lastman's *Joseph Distributing Corn in Egypt*. Lastman's painting is dated 1612, Rembrandt's drawing is usually dated to around 1636/7 (figs. 21 and 22). Lastman's *Joseph* painting contains a highly complex scene with dozens of figures busy selling or exchanging cattle or other commodities for corn. Joseph, standing on a higher level, is leaning on a parapet. He looks down at several gesticulating figures who, like Joseph himself, are situated in the second plane of the pictorial space. In Lastman's painting, there are several subsidiary scenes to the right of Joseph, continuing diagonally to the top right of the composi-

21
Pieter Lastman, *Joseph
Distributing Corn in Egypt*,
1612
Panel, 57.6 x 88.2 cm
The National Gallery of
Ireland, Dublin

tion. Rembrandt moves these scenes so that Joseph's head is the high point in the figural composition. The figure of Joseph now immediately demands attention – even though he is on the second plane. Rembrandt enhances this effect by raising the height of the parapet, making the figure of Joseph taller and giving him a larger turban. Rembrandt would seem here to be putting into practise van Mander's advice:

> «The most important figures must emerge above the others by reason of their standing on an eminence or being seated in such a way that they rise above the crowd …»[68]

Another significant change introduced by Rembrandt has to do with the representation of space. The sense of space in Lastman's painting is realised through differences in scale between figures, and by overlap and by differences in the degree of detail between foreground, mid plane and background features. He makes rather little use of the possibilities of aerial perspective, the effects of «the thickness of the air» in seventeeth-century parlance. The distribution of tonal values, the role of light and shade in the composition, the differences in tonal values between foreground and background are more consistently thought through in Rembrandt's drawing. The separation between first and second planes

and subsequently from the background in this way becomes much clearer than with Lastman. The tonal differences in the drawing, lightly but decisively stated, play a crucial role with Rembrandt in what would become known in the seventeenth century as *houding*, the complex of means – above all tone and colour – by which space was suggested other than by means of perspective, overlapping and diminishing scale.[69]

A third class of changes has to do with the treatment of light – partly in relation to the suggestion of space. Whereas Lastman has the strongest light falling on the kneeling woman in the foreground, Rembrandt places her together with the figure with a shoulder bag at her left in more subdued light and lets the strongest light fall on the figure between them, seen from the back. The figure on the left with shepherd's staff, standing by the horse, has become a dark *repoussoir* starkly silhouetted against the background.

The transformation Rembrandt brings to this graphic variant of a Lastman prototype is witness to the essential differences in Rembrandt's concern for questions of composition, space and light. By comparison with the pictorial intentions evinced by Rembrandt's drawing, Lastman's painting has more the character of a *tableau vivant*. For him it is more a question of

22
Rembrandt Harmensz.
van Rijn after Pieter
Lastman, *Joseph
Distributing Corn in Egypt*,
c. 1637
Black chalk, 313 x 462 mm
Graphische Sammlung
Albertina, Wien

illusion evokes by the various parts than through the power of a planned coherence between the parts of a scene. Lastman's picture is the sum of its parts, whereas Rembrandt is in pursuit of a dynamic unity. Rembrandt is here visibly thinking about the art of his former master and demonstrating alternative solutions.

Broos did not really follow up the promising line of thought of Rembrandt's analytical – if not critical – involvement with Lastman. In earlier cases where Rembrandt also fundamentally distanced himself from Lastman's prototypes, he tried to explain the relationships by arguing the case that these were apprentice works originating in Lastman's studio and therefore made under his direct supervision.[70]

The cases that instantly catch the eye where Rembrandt took works by Lastman as a point of departure are the *Balaam* (figs. 23 and 24) and the *Baptism of the Eunuch* (see cat. nos. 2 and 3 and fig. 2a [in cat. no. 2]) from 1626. It is evident in these two paintings that the ordonnance of the figures and other elements from Lastman's prototypes was, so to speak, dismantled and reassembled in a radically different way.

We are by now familiar with the phenomenon of Rembrandt, once he had become an independent painter, throughout his career setting his own pupils the task of making variants on his own work.[71] When it comes to these variants, however, one is dealing with paintings (drawings and etchings too) that are so close to the master's prototype in style and conception that they were long considered to be works by Rembrandt himself and seen as steps in his development.[72] In Rembrandt's variants on works by Lastman from 1625/26 the situation is radically different. Both stylistically and technically, we are looking at works that are impossible to confuse with the work of Lastman. It is as if Rembrandt subjected Lastman's compositional solutions to a process of revision so drastic that it is hard to see that such paintings could have done under Lastman's gaze, as Broos so forcefully argues.[73] In his view, as said, the relation between Rembrandt's *Balaam* and the *Baptism of the Eunuch* and a number of other works from the same period with Lastman's prototypes can be seen as evidence that they originated in Lastman's studio. The room for the development of such a hypothesis is a consequence of our uncertainty over the exact time that Rembrandt's six-month apprenticeship with Lastman took place. This uncertainty is due to the fact that we do not know how long the period was between the end of his apprenticeship with van Swanenburg (the exact

time of which we also do not know) and Rembrandt's departure for Amsterdam. It is normally assumed that Rembrandt's apprenticeship with Lastman was in 1624 or '25. Broos moved this period forward to 1625/26, which meant that part of the œuvre previously assumed to have originated in Leiden would actually have been painted in Amsterdam. Broos even speaks of the «first Amsterdam period».

There are, however, several objections to Broos' idea. The first is that all the relevant works by Rembrandt are monogrammed and dated. From seventeenth-century Dutch guilds rules one can deduce that in principle only the signature of the master of a workshop was permitted.[74] Another argument relates to the panels used by Rembrandt for his variants on Lastman. The panels of the *Balaam* (fig. 24) and the *Baptism of the Eunuch* (see fig. 1) are particularly significant in the context of this question, since both panels can be assigned to the same batch on the basis of their identical construction and closely corresponding format. The third panel belonging to this batch was used for the *Music-making Company* (cat. no. 22) in the same year, 1626.[75] But this latter painting is self-evidently an early result of the communal technical and pictorial adventures of Rembrandt and Jan Lievens (cf.

Lievens *Pilate Washes his Hands in Innocence*, cat. no. 24, and Rembrandt *Music-making Company*, cat. no. 22). The latter, one takes it, remained in Leiden while Rembrandt was with Lastman. In addition, these panels, share a standard format which, with little variation, is apparent in a large group of panels, to which the *Samson and Delilah* in Berlin, dated to 1628, also belongs. That panel was derived from the same tree as another panel that was painted in the same period by Lievens.[76] We are talking about panels of a standard format that has never been encountered among paintings by Lastman. There is a significant difference in format and proportions between the early panels of Rembrandt, on the one hand, and Lastman's panels from the same period, on the other. Lastman's panels, furthermore, were made from wood unsuitable for panel-making, often knotted and with undulating splits (which was one of the reasons why Lastman's *Baptism of the Eunuch* in Karlsruhe (p. 129, fig. 2a) could not travel to this exhibition).[77] The two largest early panels, both of the same size (c. 120 x 90 cm) and identically constructed, of Rembrandt's *Stoning of St Stephen* (cf. fig. 3) from 1625 and the Leiden *History Painting* (cat. no. 7) are exceptionally even-grained and in this respect quite different from the panels

used by Lastman and that, one assumes, Rembrandt would have painted on while in Lastman's studio.

A more important argument against the Broos hypothesis that part of Rembrandt's work of 1625/26 originated in Lastman's studio comes from the significant differences in style and technique between these paintings and those by Lastman of the same period.

It has been long pointed out that, in the *Balaam*, Rembrandt chose a vertical rather than a horizontal composition such that the figures placed one behind the other are, as it were, stacked up (cf. figs 23, 24). When publishing the newly discovered *Baptism of the Eunuch*, Defoer pointed out that Rembrandt here must drawn on certain compositional solutions of Rubens. As an alternative to Lastman's frieze-like, loosely grouped figures, Rembrandt opted for a dynamic, rather spirally tapered grouping. Already at this early stage of Rembrandt's development, one sees in this dynamic ordering the quest for how to deploy colour and light as the means of organizing space and compositional structure in a way that is fundamentally different from Lastman's straightforwardly descriptive use of colour and light. The same is true of the use of paint in relation to the rendering of materials. The way Rembrandt differentiates and intensifies the surface texture of materials is incommensurable with the much more uniform handling of paint by Lastman (figs. 25 and 26). A comparison, for example, between the donkey's heads in the two paintings demonstrates at once how much more intensively and more intelligently than his master Rembrandt engaged with the problems of form, light and anatomical structure. The most important difference however is that Rembrandt, compared with Lastman, gives his figures an exceptionally strong and, for his narrative purpose, effective expression: the talking ass as well as the angry Balaam beating it. It is not only the facial expression, but also what one would now call the ‹body language› that shows a much greater empathy on the part of the artist than was the case with Lastman's *Balaam*. It was, as we shall see, precisely this ability of the young Rembrandt that sparked Huygens' admiration.

When one compares the handling of colour, the treatment of contours, indeed the whole *peinture* of the Leiden *History Painting* (cat. no. 7) by Rembrandt usually mentioned in relation to Lastman's *Coriolanus* (cf. cat. no. 6), one is again struck by how fundamental the differences are. As Vitale Bloch wrote in this connection:

> «It should not be overlooked that Lastman, despite his stay in Rome and his personal acquaintance with Elsheimer, remained a Mannerist, unable to absorb the accomplishments of the naturalist painting born in Rome at that time.»[78]

Rembrandt, on the contrary, is from the outset an arch-‹naturalist›. If one starts out with the assumption that, during his apprenticeship with Lastman, he must have subordinated himself to his master in stylistic and technical matters, as was normal for a pupil, then his early paintings would have been stylistically much closer to Lastman than is actually the case. The confrontation of the earliest Rembrandts with works by Lastman from roughly the same period actually raises the question of whether Rembrandt ever really was trained by Lastman and if so, what that training could have consisted of. The question is certainly a pressing one when comparing Lastman's *Coriolanus* with Rembrandt's Leiden *History Painting*. Broos, however, argued:

24
Rembrandt Harmensz.
van Rijn, *Balaam and the Ass*, 1626
Panel, 63.2 x 46.5 cm
Musée Cognacq-Jay,
Paris

25
Pieter Lastman, *Balaam and the Ass* (detail), 1622 (cf. fig. 23)

*ordonnantie* (ordonnance) as follows:

«There are also stories which are more easily ordered, and in these one sets to work like the stallholder who cunningly disposes his wares on high shelves, down either side, and across the bottom. Thus it is that one introduces the witnesses of an event, on hills, in trees, on stone stairways, or clinging to the pillars of a building together with others, in the foreground, on the ground below.»[80]

Broos himself points out that Lastman's placing of figures in the pictorial space of the *Coriolanus* could well have been inspired by Karel van Mander's market stall metaphor.[81]

The fact that these ideas were set out as early as 1604 in van Mander's treatise throws a very different light on Rembrandt's presumed dependence on Lastman's *Coriolanus*. Even if the Leiden *History Painting* were a variant based on Lastman's *Coriolanus*, the differences are so great in every respect that one has to ask whether we should not consider the Leiden *History Painting* and the other variants of Rembrandt based on Lastman's work as having been painted more in a spirit of rivalry, as critical alternatives to Lastman's solutions, rather than as gratefully executed pupillary exercises based on the works of Rembrandt's «eternal master».

The heart of the problem posed by the interpretation of the relationship between the works by Lastman and Rembrandt is what one understands as ‹influence›. When Tümpel, quoted earlier, characterises the relationship between Rembrandt and Lastman as one in which, in Tümpel's words, certain paintings of Lastman «made a huge impression on Rembrandt» or «to which he [Rembrandt] harked back», this clearly counts as influence. The concept of ‹influence› for a long time enjoyed great popularity in art historical thinking. The possibilities unlocked by this conceptual tool were as seductive as those offered by the idea of ‹evolution› or ‹development›. For generations of art historians these were magic words that seemed to enable them to grasp the succession of events in the history of art.

Of course, it is self-evident that an artist may betray an unconscious assimilation of the stylistic qualities of another artist's work. This assimila-

«It is my contention that the significance of the *Coriolanus* for Rembrandt's conceptions regarding composition was far greater than has generally been assumed, and furthermore, that its influence is manifest over a much longer time span, running from the years of his apprenticeship through the last decade of his life.»[79]

This allegedly profound influence in fact means little more than the placing of figures on different levels with still other, lower figures kneeling in the foreground. This manner of disposing figures in the pictorial space is hardly Lastman's discovery, however. As Broos himself has already remarked, it was developed during the sixteenth century and had its antecedents in classical antiquity. Van Mander described this type of

tion may in part be determined by the fashion of the day, but it may also be stimulated by larger movements underway at the time, for instance a development toward a more thoroughgoing illusionism, or in relation to particular tendencies in the direction of the decorative, etc.

On the other hand there are conscious, deliberate borrowings. Certain artists may take over the solutions of other artists. This may betray a lack of original ideas on the part of the borrowing artist, but borrowings can also evince respect; they can be taken as homage to an admired precursor or master. This latter type of borrowing was also earlier covered by the term ‹influence›; but this changed when, as a result of work on seventeenth-century Dutch art theory, it became evident that the term *rapen* (to collect, pick up, gather, or even steal)[82] provided a historically sounder account of many types of borrowing.[83] With the discovery of the term *rapen* it became possible to talk about this form of ‹influence› in the contemporary language. In fact, one encounters the term *rapen* in seventeenth-century art historical writings used both as criticism and as praise. One even finds advice on how to use the pictorial elements of predecessors in an honest fashion such that the initiated connoisseur could appreciate the quotation. One might interpret Rembrandt's re-assembling of Lastman's paintings in a similar way, but I do not believe that this is warranted.

A thoroughly different approach is to take the quotation from predecessors, in whatever form, as a particular form of ‹rivalry›. It is evident from any number of historical texts that rivalry has been an important factor in the interaction between artists dating back to classical antiquity. The many references to envy in both texts and the iconography related to art, and to the profession of art, show how far this rivalry went.[84] The idea of *aemulatio* (emulation) has come in for considerable attention in recent interpretations of historical art theory. It is essential to the idea of emulation that one needs not only to equal but also to surpass the admired precursor:

> «rivalry ... inspired Raphael Urbino to surpass the great Buonarroti: and Michelangelo to climb to an unapproachable height. See then, O Pupils, in the arts each regarding the other with, dare I say it, jealous eyes

but without departing from the courtesies of civil life.»[85]

Already in classical times, however, the realisation that ambitious rivalry with a measurable outcome is only possible – who has surpassed whom, and in what terms – when the contest is fought, as it were, with the same weapons. Virgil, to take a favourite seventeenth-century example, could only measure himself against Homer and try to surpass the latter by staying close to him in choice of both his subject and the form in which he cast that subject.[86] In his efforts to surpass Raphael's *Transfiguration*, Sebastiano del Piombo took an equally large panel to start with.[87]

Could Rembrandt's relation to Lastman – as far as we can read the mutually related works – have

26
Rembrandt, *Balaam and the Ass* (detail), 1626
(cf. fig. 24)

been characterised by rivalry rather than the more usually assumed admiration? Perhaps we should look for the answer to this question in the way his ambitions could have been fuelled by the connoisseurs of the art of painting surrounding him.

The reader will recall the less than generous reaction of the Utrecht art-lover Buchelius to what he had heard spoken of Rembrandt: «Also, the son of a miller in Leiden is esteemed highly, though prematurely.» The significance of this text, as said, is that it shows us how highly Rembrandt was regarded by others and, thanks to Constantijn Huygens' autobiography, we know the tone and the content of the praise that Buchelius found so premature. Huygens' praise was related to a painting that he saw in 1628, two years after the period we have been discussing (cf. cat. no. 33). Buchelius' reticent reaction to such praise was expressed that same year. But Rembrandt was apparently already highly admired in 1626; after all, had not Alfonse Lopez bought Rembrandt's *Balaam* (perhaps given the tip by Constantijn Huygens)(fig. 24)? If the above interpretation is correct, this was one of the very works painted in emulation of Pieter Lastman.

As we shall see, Huygens' words of praise are pervaded by the idea of emulation. According to Huygens, Rembrandt not only surpassed his Dutch contemporaries, among whom Lastman is explicitly mentioned, but also the Italian artists of the sixteenth century and the even greater, legendary, artists of classical antiquity. This seems so exaggerated that one is inclined to take such accolades as little more than conventional formulae, particularly given the fact that Samuel van Hoogstraten would later address similar remarks to young artists in general:

> «For encouragement: come now, my young painter, awakened to the honour and glory of the great Masters, let the sense of rivalry be freely kindled in you. Let ambition stir you from your slumbers, for virtue also is of such nature that it can arouse the spirit to a determination to surpass the foremost. *It is no Herezy to outlymn Apelles.* A bold heart lives not only to equal in fame those who live today: but even to run past those who were ever thought illustrious. To prick the spurs of rivalry and emulation such that

they awake the sleeping desire for honour, applying all one's might in order to exceed, even, one's own powers.»[88]

But what is primarily of interest in this context is that Huygens' written praise must have reflected the praises which, in whatever form or at whatever moment, would also have been verbally bestowed, first on Rembrandt and Lievens, later on Rembrandt alone.

In the longest section of his autobiography devoted to a single topic, the section on the art of painting, Huygens reviewed the state of the Dutch art of painting – mainly, though not exclusively – on the basis of the many painters he knew personally. He ended with his careful analysis of Rembrandt and Lievens, quoted earlier, which begins:

> «Were I to say that they are the only ones who can hold their own against the absolute geniuses among the [in the same text] aforesaid prodigies, I would even then not be doing these two justice. And were I to say that they will soon surpass those geniuses, I would merely be expressing what their astonishing beginning has led connoisseurs to expect.»[89]

After the following section in which he compares Lievens and Rembrandt, there comes the famous passage on Rembrandt's «painting of the repentant Judas, who returns the pieces of silver, the price of betraying Jesus, to the High Priest» (see Appendix). Huygens places the painting immediately in the context of the whole history of art with the words:

> «Set beside it the whole of Italy, yes, everything of beauty to admire that has survived from the very earliest antiquity.»[90]

After praising Rembrandt's ability to depict Judas' expression of utter despair, Huygens continues:

> «I would put this beside all the beauty that the centuries have brought forth. This would I hold up to the simpletons who claim (and I have rebuked them on this before) that nothing is being created nowadays, or expressed in words, that the ancients have not already expressed or created. I maintain that no Protogenes, Apelles or Parrhasisus has ever produced, nor ever could produce, even were they able to re-

turn to this world, all that a young man, a Dutchman, a miller still in his beardless youth, has realised in a single human figure and represented in its totality. I am amazed even as I say this. Bravo Rembrandt! To have carried Troy, yes, all Asia back to Italy would be a lesser feat than for a Dutchman who has hardly ventured beyond the walls of the city of his birth to capture for Holland the highest title of honour of all Greece and Italy.»[91]

Perhaps the most important aspect of this passage is Huygens' conviction that the art of classical antiquity could be surpassed. This standpoint, which has to be seen in the wider context of what, later in the century, would be known as the «the quarrel between the ancients and moderns», puts Rembrandt in open competition with his predecessors, with – according to Huygens – the possibility of becoming the greatest artist of all time. That Huygens was one of those who thought the creations of their own time could surpass the achievements of classical antiquity («it is no heresy to outlimn Apelles') is evident not only from the passage quoted, but also from his brief digression on graphic art which ends with the words:

«In this art, our Netherlanders at the present time have reached a standard that has yet to be matched by anyone, even by the ancients.»[92]

If Rembrandt was so early faced with the opinion of people like Huygens that he through emulation could hold his own against his precursors and that, moreover, he was given the impression that he was already on course to defeat them all, this must have had a tremendous impact on his self-consciousness and his self-esteem as an artist. It is worth remarking that the exceptionally high regard in which he was held by art-lovers and connoisseurs alike persisted to the end of his life. In 1664, presenting a list of the artists known to him, the German art-lover Gabriel Bucelinus, (1599–1681) described Rembrandt, the only one of this list to receive any praise, as «the miracle of this age.»[93]

That Rembrandt did indeed measure himself against the great figures of art history is evident from his drawn variations on a print after Leonardo's *Last Supper* in which, just as in his

drawing after Lastman (cf. fig. 22), he introduced ‹improvements› (figs. 27–29). In this case he introduced asymmetry in a frontal composition of figures – a problem that, from then on, would preoccupy him throughout his life. Undoubtedly this was a form of emulation where the contest was ‹fought with the same weapons›. This digression was necessary to present the idea convincingly that Rembrandt's early variants on works by Lastman are better understood in the context of rivalry than considered as the exercises of an admiring pupil. Had the latter been the case, Rembrandt would hardly have distanced himself so rapidly from Lastman immediately after what I take to be his measuring himself against his former master. For that is one of the mysteries of the young Rembrandt: the speed and the intelligence, but above all the drive with which, already by the end of 1626, and subsequently, he sought new paths.

## Rembrandt and Lievens 1625 to 1631

It is generally acknowledged that Rembrandt's search for new paths in the art of painting was undertaken in dialogue – but also in a spirit of rivalry – with Jan Lievens.[94] Their collaboration is one of the pivotal moments of art history that can perhaps best be compared with the meeting of Picasso and Braque that was to lead to the development of Cubism.

There is less certainty, however, when it comes to the precise nature of the relationship between Rembrandt and Lievens, and it is perhaps not insignificant that Huygens says nothing at all on this point. In the present context, rather than pursue these joint activities in all their various aspects, I shall try to establish Rembrandt's place in this artistic symbiosis. In the first section of this essay, on the basis of several quotations, it was shown that Huygens stressed primarily the common distinction of these two young painters. In what follows, it will become apparent just how much he also emphasized the differences between them. The possibility should not be overlooked that he may also have had literary reasons for stressing the contrast.

In the eyes of their contemporaries, it must have been mainly the similarities between the works produced by Rembrandt and Lievens that was given more weight. This is evident, for example,

27
Anonymous, 16th century
Engraved copy after
Leonardo's *Last Supper*
that was in Rembrandt's
collection.

28
Rembrandt Harmensz.
van Rijn, free copy after
fig. 27, c. 1635
Red chalk, 365 x 475 mm
Benesch 443
The Metropolitan
Museum of Art, New York
(Robert Lehman
Collection)

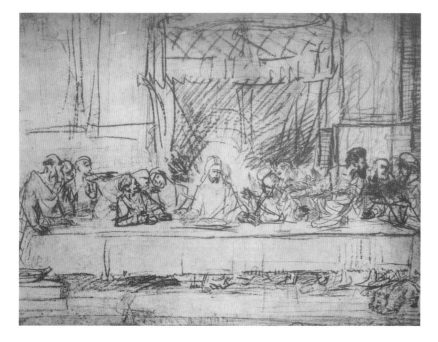

in the inventory of Frederik Hendrik's paintings drawn up in 1632, where we find listed «A painting in which Simeon in the Temple holds Christ in his arms» with the annotation that the painting was made by «Rembrandt or Jan Lievens».[95] It is not entirely certain which painting this refers to, but possibly it was the painting now in Hamburg (cat. no. 30).

The fact that Gerard de Lairesse brackets them together twice in *Groot Schilderboeck* of 1707 indicates that the two painters were regarded long afterwards as, in some sense, twins; not only artistically but more especially in terms of painting technique.[96] Both references are concerned with the painting technical qualities of their work, their use of impasto and the painting of shadows. It is necessary to be aware that Rembrandt's and Lievens' paths had already diverged

29
Rembrandt Harmensz.
van Rijn after Leonardo
da Vinci, *The Last Supper*,
1635
Pen in brown, wash,
heightened with white,
128 x 385 mm
Benesch 445
Staatliche Museen zu
Berlin, Preußischer
Kulturbesitz, Kupferstich-
kabinett

in 1631 both in the physical sense – Rembrandt went to Amsterdam, Lievens that same year to London – and in their stylistic and technical pre-occupations. When de Lairesse mentions the two painters in the same breath therefore he can only be referring to their shared time in Leiden. It says a great deal that the memory of their collaborative artistic adventure had lasted so long.

In the historiography of the relationship between Rembrandt and Lievens, sketched by Christiaan Vogelaar in the catalogue of the exhibition devoted to the two painters in 1991/92, one sees how completely Lievens drops out of sight in the eighteenth and early nineteenth century.[97] During that period many of his works were attributed to Rembrandt. Only gradually thereafter did the contours of Lievens as an artist once again become visible, a process in which his relationship with Rembrandt played no part. This situation changed dramatically with Worp's publication of part of Constantijn Huygens' autobiography in 1891, when Huygens' account of the «pair of painters» penetrated the world of art historians.[98] This text so appealed to the imagination that Neumann was able to write of Rembrandt and Lievens in 1905 that «they were like the *Dioscuri*, a pair with the unbridled courage of youth.»[99] In Neumann's time, this idea of profound artist friendship had acquired such common currency as a result of Romanticism's many legends of tempestuous artistic friendships that it was virtually inevitable that the Rembrandt-Lievens relationship would at first be seen in this way. As Klaus Lankheit sets out in his book on artistic friendships, this form of impassioned friendship has to be seen as one of the substitutes for lost religious belief following the Enlightenment. It is an image therefore that cannot without qualification be projected back on to the seventeenth century.[100]

Vogelaar points out in his historiographical sketch that – influenced by the echo of the cult of genius – Rembrandt was assumed without question to be the giver and Lievens the taker in their partnership; whereas in the modern art historical literature the relation is almost reversed. This happened not only under the influence of the realisation that the insight and skills of the child prodigy Jan Lievens must have matured much earlier than those of Rembrandt; he had also completed his apprenticeship before Rembrandt had even begun his. If one re-reads Huygens' text closely, one cannot escape the impression that the young Lievens pushed himself forward more forcefully, and that it was he who must have exuded the greater self-assurance. One of the most exciting passages in Huygens' text on Rembrandt and Lievens is his acute analysis of Lievens' attitude to matters of art:

«He is a young man of great mental powers, and if he is granted time, one can entertain for him the highest expectations. In various matters he has a penetrating and profound insight, more mature than a full-grown man, as I have more than once been able to ascertain in conversation. My one reservation in general concerns his inflexibility, which comes of excessive self-confidence. Any criticism is thus either rejected out of hand or, if he recognizes it as just, he takes it badly. This regrettable trait, damaging at any age, is simply disastrous in youth, for *a little leaven sours the whole dough*. And whoever is strongly cursed with the vice which so resembles this trait [Huygens probably means pride here] ‹deceives himself› in the words of the Scriptures. It is a sign of great wisdom to realise that God, as the poet said, ‹hath given with sparing hand to each a sufficiency›; that no one has ever been given everything; and that consequently one should approach anyone, whoever it may be, with open heart and mind, in the knowledge that there is always something to be learned from everyone.»[101]

It is striking that in Rembrandt's case, Huygens refrains from such remarks of psychological and moralistic kind. He is only positive in the tone with which he speaks of Rembrandt's art, while he avoids any comment specifically addressed to Rembrandt's personality traits. Lievens, on the other hand, he not only takes to task for his arrogant attitude, but also, as we have seen above, for a certain megalomanic tendency in his work. The passages that are crucial to his view of Rembrandt are those in which he characterises him as a painter and at the same time contrasts him with Lievens:

«Rembrandt, in contrast, will concentrate on a small painting with total dedication and achieves on a small scale a result that one might in vain seek in the largest pieces by others.»[102]

Or further on:

«In what we usually call history pieces the artist [Jan Lievens], wonderfully talented though he may be, will not so quickly match Rembrandt for imagination and vitality.»[103]

The image one has here of Rembrandt is, compared to Lievens, of a modest young man with powers of dedication and concentration that, in Huygens' eyes, appear to penetrate deeper than Lievens' gifts. Huygens stresses Rembrandt's power of imagination and his pursuit of a form of liveliness which Rembrandt would later describe, in a letter to Huygens, as the search for «die naetuereelste beweechgelickheijt» (the most lifelike emotion and liveliness [of his figures]).[104]

In retrospect, however, one has to conclude that Huygens' fears for Lievens were unjustified: that is, his fear that pride would be his downfall, that Lievens in his later career would become the victim of his own excessive self-confidence. In fact, Lievens had a rather successful career, first at the English Court, later in Antwerp and finally in Amsterdam. The facts that he was included in Anthony van Dyck's *Iconography*, that he (and not Rembrandt) was invited to contribute to the decoration of the *Oranjezaal* (the Orange Hall), and that he (and not Rembrandt) contributed a large painting to the decoration of the Amsterdam Town Hall, all point to a successful career, even though he fared no better financially than Rembrandt in the end (partly due to the general economic hardship associated with the Anglo-Dutch wars from 1650 onward).[105]

In artistic terms, too, he was certainly no failure in the eyes of his contemporaries. In particular, a number of paintings have survived from the late Leiden period that still belong with the very best of Dutch seventeenth-century art. One thinks of the *Job* in Ottawa and the *Young Man* in Edinburgh. He later painted the exceptional *Abraham and Isaac* in Braunschweig, the presumed sketch for which was so highly praised in a speech by Philips Angel in 1641.[106] There followed in his Amsterdam years, among other works, a series of exceptional portraits executed as either drawings or colored woodcuts, and

drawn and painted landscapes, all testifying that Lievens was a good and still-interesting artist. Nonetheless, Lievens' reasonably successful career ended in Rembrandt's shadow, and that can hardly be seen as an historical injustice. Insofar as we ever can have access to the secret of great art, those qualities that Huygens observed in Rembrandt, his extraordinary intensity and power of imagination and his exceptional ability to empathize with the figures he was representing, were to be the same qualities through which his fame so far outstripped that of Lievens.

In the Leiden years between 1625 and 1631, however, there must have been something extraordinary played out between the two young artists a joint and apparently unusually inspired search for new possibilities in the art of painting. Undoubtedly they would also have looked around them. In comparing Rembrandt's compositions from 1626 with the paintings of Lastman, the possibility has already been mentioned that the knowledge of Rubens' compositional approach could have played a role in Rembrandt's development of alternative solutions for Lastman's compositions. The rapidly developed tendency toward monochromy to be seen in the work of Rembrandt and Lievens from 1626/27 onwards also did not happen by itself. In this area, the ideas of Porcellis (1584–1632) («the great Raphael of marine painting» as Samuel van Hoogstaten would call him) and Haarlem painters like Pieter de Molijn (1595–1661) took hold in the various genres of painting around them with lightning speed, and had probably reached Leiden, specifically the Leiden still life painter Jan Davidsz. de Heem (1606–1683/84), before Rembrandt and Lievens committed themselves to this path. It must have been generally realised that the reduction of colour enhanced the credibility of the representation of light. As indicated above, the influence of the Utrecht Caravaggists also had a decisive effect on Lievens and Rembrandt with regard to the handling of light.

The two young painters must thus have looked about them avidly, without for an instant giving the impression that they ever risked becoming epigones. External impressions were immediately assimilated, just as critically as the lessons from Lastman had been; and the latter remark applies to Lievens as well as it did for Rembrandt, for also from Lievens' very earliest known work there is hardly a trace to be seen of his time with Lastman.

One of the advantages of their close relationship must have been that Rembrandt and Lievens were able to assimilate these external impulses so quickly and confidently into their own, constantly developing, pictorial language.

It is frustrating that we shall never know what conversations on such matters sounded like between the two young painters. As a rule, we can only try to reconstruct them on the basis of their work; just once or twice an echo of their conversations resonates down to us.

The sentence «Jan Lievens was courageously in his element seeking miracles in daubed paints, varnishes and oils» seems almost like a scrap of conversation washed up and deposited in Hoogstraten's book on the art of painting, where it has lain, preserved.[107] There is a good chance that this observation of Lievens' alchemical handling of paint was handed on by Rembrandt and along the way found its entry into his pupil's book. In another context I have argued that Lievens' technical experiments, in which Rembrandt must have participated, were initially aimed at a new form of rendering materials. The substance of the paint together with differentiation of the paint surface played an important part in this (see cat. no. 22).[108] But the pictorial results achieved through this alchemy with paint could be rapidly altered in nature. The locally, deliberately crudely finished surface of the paint enhanced in particular the atmospheric working of the painted image and at the same time contributed to a heightened effect of light and an almost palpable ‹presence› of forms (see cat. nos. 31 and 32). In the *Groot Schilderboeck*, which appeared 80 years later, de Lairesse cautions against a method of working «in the manner of Rembrandt and Lievens, whose colours run down the piece like dung.» In this same connection he speaks of daubing – «kladdery».[109] It is highly instructive to compare Lievens' and Rembrandt's later painting methods, for Rembrandt continued to explore the possibilities of a differentiated treatment of paint to the end of his career, whereas Lievens, who may well have been the instigator of this adventure in technique,

abandoned this route and succumbed to the influence of Anthony van Dyck.

In other areas too one has the feeling of witnessing the dialogue between the two young painters: for example, where for a while both painters are involved in a treatment of form where the contours tend to billow, thus suggesting a somewhat leathery plasticity (e. g. cat. nos. 23, 25–30, 59, 60). In a painting like *St Paul at His Desk* (cat. no. 32) the way of handling contours changes radically. Beside the flowing course of his contours, Rembrandt here introduces more angular interruptions that contribute to a sense of space.[110] If one follows Rembrandt's unflagging attention to the nature and quality of the contour, one is again struck by the relentlessness with which he pursues such an aspect of the art of painting (see also cat. no. 66).

As to etching, in the beginning Lievens was undoubtedly the more experienced and thus had an impact on Rembrandt's early efforts in this field (cf. cat. nos. 14 and 13). But his influence in this area was short-lived. It is significant that Rembrandt seems to have taken the struggle for his own style and technique into the art of etching on his own.

Erik Hinterding recently suggested that the group of very early, small etchings, including portrayals of Rembrandt's face, should be regarded as exercises in the art of etching. They must have been done after two of his very earliest etchings, as ambitious as they are clumsy, the *Rest on the Flight into Egypt* (cat. no. 13) and the *Circumcision* (fig. 30).[111] One can assume that Rembrandt did not learn etching during his apprenticeships with van Swanenburg and Lastman but that, once back in Leiden, he had begun to make the technique of etching his own. After these first two etched history pieces from 1625 or 1626 (cat. no. 13 and fig. 30), Rembrandt must have discovered that the successful production of a good etching required more than just drawing in the etching ground, putting the plate in the acid for the lines to be bitten, removing the etching ground, inking the plate and then taking off an impression. In the years between 1626 and 1630–31, virtually all the etchings have the character of experiments, whether they portray Rembrandt's face or that of young men from his circle of acquaintance, or the face

30
Rembrandt Harmensz.
van Rijn, *The Circumcision*,
c. 1626
214 x 160 mm
Cat. no. 40

31
Rembrandt Harmensz.
van Rijn, *The Circumcision*,
c. 1630
88 x 64 mm
Cat. no. 54

of the old woman usually taken to be his mother, or depict old beggars (cat. nos. 45, 46, 48, 49) or more or less miscarried history pieces, such as *The Small Lion Hunt* (cat. no. 51), *St Jerome Kneeling* (cat. no. 43) or *Peter and John at the Gate of the Temple* (cat. no. 44).

It is useful to be aware of the fact that in virtually all cases, as far as executing the drawing in the etching ground is concerned, this would seldom have taken more than an hour, often only a few minutes. In each relatively large etching from this period one can see what must have preoccupied the young Rembrandt and what in the meantime he was developing at amazing speed in his paintings and drawings: an ever increasing play between light and dark.

The gap between Rembrandt the etcher and Rembrandt the painter would only be closed around 1630–31. In the drawings executed in chalk, ink and wash, and in his paintings, it was relatively easy to realise the suggestion of light

and shade, but in etching Rembrandt had to develop a way of hatching that would create those rich, dark tones in the print that were to remain his lifelong goal as an etcher. The early unsigned etchings exhibit a carelessness of form compared with the searching concentration applied to contrasts of light and shade. It is little wonder he chose such a small format for these early etchings. In the larger etchings, such as the *St. Jerome* (cat. no. 43), one sees how Rembrandt's rather ineffectual hatching fails to achieve a satisfactory *chiaroscuro*; and in the «Self-portrait with the Double Needle» (cat. No. 78), as it is sometimes called, the broad, double hatchings seem to have been used as an attempt to find a shortcut to a solution.

Towards the end of the Leiden period, having succeeded with several small heads from 1628 onwards, Rembrandt produced a group of small etched histories in which he seems to have mastered the treatment of light and shade and concomitantly the coherent ordering of the pictorial space, just as well as in the paintings (cat. nos. 52–54). He seems to have resigned himself to the fact that this was only possible through the patient and immensely time-consuming work of hatching, an investment of time compensated by the fact that one could print a whole edition from the plate so produced (figs. 30, 31). It is of significance that of all the early etchings very few impressions exist. This is in accordance with the hypothesis that they were not intended to be saleable ‹products› but should be seen as experiments while getting to grips with the technique of etching.

Here, too, after the initial influence – and perhaps the decisive stimulus – from Jan Lievens, Rembrandt pursued his own path, once again following it to the end of his career. And once again it was this confidence in the early taken decision that made the essential difference between Rembrandt and the constantly shifting Lievens.

Any attempt to get a clear idea of the forces that drive a figure like Rembrandt is doomed to partial failure at best. In the end it remains a mystery. The same, of course, applies to every fellow human, past or present, even to ourselves; yet we have to go on making the attempt. What is special in the case of the young Rembrandt, compared with many of his contemporaries, is that there exist a surprising number of documents and an unusually rich and diverse œuvre of drawings, etchings and paintings from the years he spent as an independent young master in Leiden. What has been essayed in these pages, on the basis of these documents relating to himself and the figures surrounding him, and on the basis of his early œuvre, is an attempt to give an idea of the forces operating on him, but more importantly an idea of the possible inner motivation that is perhaps the core of the mystery of the young Rembrandt, the source, perhaps, of the artistic development of one of the greatest artists in human history.

* This essay and the next were written thanks to the support from the NWO (Netherlands Organisation for Scientific Research) and the University of Amsterdam for the *Rembrandt Research Project*. I am most grateful to Margaret Oomen as well as to Marieke de Winkel for their most valuable help, to the translator Murray Pearson and to the copyeditors Wanda Löwe and Deborah Cohen, who devoted so much care to this slowly growing essay.

1 Corpus, vol. 1, 1982, no. A 5; Defoer 1977, pp. 2–26; Wetering 1977b.

2 Corpus, vol. 1, 1982, no. A 1; Gerson 1962 and Gerson 1963.

3 On the life of Huygens see Strengholt 1987.

4 Worp 1891.

5 The quotes from Huygens' autobiography are translated on the basis of Huygens/Heesakkers 1987, pp. 70–90.

6 «excusare, aiunt, florentibus annis, quorum inprimis ratio habenda sit, non satis otii esse, quod peregrinatione perdant.»

7 «Testari cogor non vidisse me parem diligentiam aut assiduitatem ullo in hominum genere, studio vel aetate. Revera enim ἐξαγοραζόμενοι τὸν καιρὸν, hoc agunt unice nec, quo ad miraculum nihil desit, adolescentiae vel innoxiis oblectamentis, quia temporis dispendiis, afficiuntur magis, quam si annorum saturos senes videas et haec futilia quaeque praeexpertos. Quam improbi laboris indefessam, pertinaciam utcumque magnos subito profectus spondeat, moderari egregios adolescentes saepenumero optavi et corpusculorum, quibus a sedentaria vitâ iam nunc parum firmis aut robustis utuntur, suam quoque rationem habere.»

8 «Ego de singulis sic perfunctorie pronunciare audebo, Rembrantium iudicio et affectuum vivacitate Livio praestare, hunc alteri inventionis et quâdam audacium argumentorum formarumque superbiâ. Nam et animo iuvenile nihil hic nisi grande et magnificum spirans, obiectarum formarum magnitudinem non tam

adaequat libenter quam exsuperat; ille, suae se industriae involvens, in minorem tabulam conferre amat et compendio effectum dare, quod in amplissimis aliorum frustra quaeras.»

9 On the Dutch ‹art market› see Bok 1994 and recently Nederlands kunsthistorisch jaarboek 1999/2000.

10 Vasari 1550/1568. Mander 1604.

11 «… daerom rade ik dat men hare gronden in 't gros leere verstaen, haer grootste Meesters kennen, en desselfs handelingen onderscheyden. Ook in wat landen, Steden, en Paleysen de beste werken te zien zijn.» Hoogstraten 1657, p. 26.

12 «Hier toe zijn Vermander, Dureer en Junius dienstigh genoegh.» Hoogstraten 1657, p. 26. To van Mander's *Schilder-Boeck* that also contains *Den Grondt*, see Mander/Miedema 1973 and Miedema. The works of Dürer and Junius are: Albrecht Dürer, *Unterweisung der Messung*, 1525; Junius, *De pictura veterum*, Amsterdam 1637; Dutch translation, *De schilderkonst der oude begrepen in drie boeken*, Middelburg 1641.

13 Kind information by Annet van der Putten who studied such sources in view of these questions.

14 Vinne.

15 Scheller 1969; Amsterdam 1999/2000; Clark 1966; Broos 1977.

16 See Warnke 1996, pp. 202–223.

17 «Parine in pretio hodie pictura sit, οὐχ ὁρίζω. Sufficit ad honorem, quod summis terrarum dominis chara vel ab ingenuis tractetur, vel tales reddat a quibuscumque cum successu colitur. Utilitatis (siquidem hoc nomine lucri compendia aestimes) immensae semper fuit. Sed neutro horum intuitu patrem meum illexit. Viderat, quo et Graeci procul dubio collimarunt, et suâ, ut aiebat, imperitiâ didicerat fieri non posse, ut de pictura (nusquam non hodie obvia) quisquam non modice iudicaret, qui manu propriâ rudimenta artis quodammodo non tractasset. Viderat summos viros et ab omni maiore disciplinâ celeberrimos latis pro autoritate de picturâ sententiis inter peritos derisui

fuisse. Hinc illud propositi semper animo servârat, ut, quos omnium atrium callentes reddere non posset, eo perduceret, ut in iudicio praecipuarum citra contemptum essemus.»

[18] Pliny, Book 35; see also Wetering 1995, esp. p. 267.

[19] Huygens/Heesakkers 1987, p. 74.

[20] Hoogewerff/Regteren Altena 1928

[21] «Molitoris etiam Leidensis filius magni fit, send ante tempus.» Strauss/Meulen 1979, doc. 1628/1.

[22] Orlers 1641, pp. 375–377.

[23] «ende also hy gheduyrende den zelven tijt, zoo seer toegenomen hadde, dat de Const Lief-hebberen daerinne ten hoochsten verwondert waeren, ende datmen genoechsaem konde sien, dat hy metter tijdt een uytnemende Schilder soude werden». Strauss/Meulen 1979, doc. 1641/8.

[24] «… quos aequare solos si dixero quae in tot magnis mortalibus portenta designavi, aliquid adhuc infra merita istorum statuero, si superaturos brevi, nihil spei addidero, quam de stupendis initiis prudentissimi quique praeceperunt.»

[25] Strauss/Meulen 1979 (see note 21).

[26] Schwartz 1984/85/87, pp. 35ff.

[27] Strauss/Meulen 1979, doc. 1663/7.

[28] Strauss/Meulen 1979, doc. 1641/6.

[29] See Moes 1894, p. 240 and Baraude 1933.

[30] «Ea ego tantae spei ac felicitatis initia expendens, indignari non obscure soleo, fieri potuisse, ut incuriâ negligerentur, quemque inter homines Belgas aeterno patriae ornamento natum patet, condito talento sterili illaudabilique otio indormivisse. Sed hic, pene dixerim, non satis angustae rei domesticae fructus est.»

[31] «een out slapent manneken bij een vuijr sittende, sijn hant in de boesem hebbende». Strauss/Meulen 1979, doc. 1641/1; A. Bredius 1915, pp. 126–128.

[32] Hoogstraten 1678, pp. 316f.

[33] Castiglione 1528.

[34] Beck 1624, 29 February (p. 54): «Ik las des avonts wel 1 uijrken in van Manders Schilder-boeck»; 25 April, about his conversation with the cabinet-maker (p. 82): «met wien ick mennigerley praetie hadde van de Const».

[35] «zy is bemint in alle Hooven der werelt en van haer wel te kunne spreken verplicht dikwils Vorsten en Princen ons te hooren …» Hoogstraten 1657, p. 26.

[36] «pour scavoir donc parler de ce noble mestier, il faut avoir esté à la boutique disputé avec les maistres, veu le traint de pinceau, et le jugement asseuré pour espulcher toute chose …» Merrifield 1849, p. 769.

[37] «gants geen lust ofte genegentheyt» … «dewijle zijne natuyrlicke beweginghen alleen streckten tot de Schilder ende Teycken Conste». Orlers 1641, pp. 375.

[38] «Si praeceptores quaero, quibus usos puellos constat, vix vulgi supra laudem evectos homines invenio, quales nempe res tenuis parentum viliore pretio tironibus assignavit, quique, si in conspectum hodie discipulorum veniant, eodem rubore confundantur, quo confusos credo, qui ad poesin Virgilium, ad oratoriam Ciceronem, ad mathesin Archimedem primi instituerant. Ut suum cuique tribuam, nec alterum laedam tamen, (mea enim quid interest?) nihil praeceptoribus debent, ingenio omnia, vel, si nemine praeeunte relicti olim sibi fuissent et pingendi forte impetum cepissent, eodem evasuros fuisse persuadear, quo nunc, ut falso creditur, manu ducti adscenderunt.»

[39] For more literature on Jacob Isaacsz. van Swanenburg see Ekkart 1998, pp. 125–128. For Lastman see Amsterdam 1992 with further literature and the monography by Astrid Tümpel (forthcoming).

[40] Wetering 1997, pp. 48–58, for more sources and literature see there.

[41] Sandrart, Baldinucci, Houbraken: in Slive 1953.

[42] Wetering 1997, pp. 133–152, for more sources and literature see there.

[43] «Pour parler des riches peintures, il en faut parler comme si les choses etoient vrayes non pas peintes».…. «Mais il faut tromper

[44] «Het is const wel branden te schilderen». Hoogewerff/Regteren Altena 1928, p. 82.

[45] «Dat het const is, wel branden te schilderen». Mander/Miedema 1973, pp. 192f., VII 32 and VII 33.

[46]: «Sy hebben in de Const al groot impery/Die wel uytbeelden Vulcanus vergrammen/Met veruwe/sulck grouwelijck misery …» Mander/Miedema 1973.

[47] «Niet alleen de vlammen / maer oock de roocken / Van verscheyden verwen de Lucht vervullen / Jae t'schijnen d'afgrijselijcke smoocken Stygij, daer met veel leelijcke spoocken / Hydra, en Cerberus, tieren en brullen: Dus dan de Schilders hier op achten sullen / Om eenen brandt schrickelijck uyt te stellen / Oft t'vyer te stoken in Poeetsche Hellen.» Mander/-Miedema 1973.

[48] «et in tutti questi ci sono venti che non mostrano altro che paesi da foco, che pare che brusino le mani approximandosi per toccargli». Buscaroli 1935, p. 56 ; English quote taken from Gombrich 1971, p. 109.

[49] Verhoef 1994.

[50] Strauss/Meulen 1979, doc. 1641/1.

[51] Tümpel 1969, pp. 182–187.

[52] See Note 36.

[53] Mander 1604, fol. 252v, lines 34–40.

[54] «Van den voorschreven Lasman ghescheyden wesende, heeft hy daer nae sonder eenigen anderen Meester, hem zelven ten huyse van sijn Vader onthouden, ende alle sijnen tijt met vlijt ende naersticheydt toe gebracht, met veele ende verscheyden dingen naer het leven te schilderen…» Orlers 1641.

[55] Bredius, vol. 6, 1919; Corpus, vol. 2, 1986, pp. 76–88.

[56] For the analysis of apprentices-contracts see Jager 1990, pp. 51–56 and Corpus, vol. 2, 1986.

[57] Corpus, vol. 2, 1986, pp. 53–54.

[58] See note 38.

[59] Mander 1604, fol. 293v, 32–33.

[60] «Quos historiographos pictores, nescio an parum proprie, nuncupare soleo, nec pauciores neque adeo minores Belgium meo saeculo edidit, ut Petrum Isacium, Lasmannium, Pinassium, Amstelodamenses, …»

[61] Freise 1911, pp. 273f.

[62] Heer 1991.

[63] Tümpel 1991.

[64] Freise 1911, pp. 237–272.

[65] Knuttel 1955, p. 46; Stechow 1969; Guratsch 1975.

[66] Bloch 1937; Gerson 1962.

[67] Broos 1975, p. 210.

[68] «De heerlycke Beelden sullen uytsteken/ In hoocheyt staend' oft sittende gheresen/ Boven die ander …» Mander/Miedema 1973, chapter V, 36.

[69] Taylor 1992.

[70] Broos 2000.

[71] E. van de Wetering in: Corpus, vol. 2, 1986, p. 50; Bruyn 1989; Franken 1997; Franken.

[72] One among many examples is demonstrated when surveying the historiography of the two versions (Berlin, Washington) of *Joseph and Potiphar*.

[73] Broos 2000.

[74] Corpus, vol. 2, 1986, p. 57.

[75] Corpus, vol. 1, 1982, no. A 2, A 5, A 7, see under «Support».

[76] Kind information by Dr. Peter Klein, Ordinariat für Holzbiologie, Universität Hamburg. The Lievens painting concerned is cat. no. 32 in Braunschweig 1979.

[77] Kind information by Martin Bijl, former chief restorer of the Rijksmuseum Amsterdam.

[78] «Es darf nicht übersehen werden, dass Lastman ungeachtet seines Aufenthaltes in Rom und seines persönlichen Verkehrs mit Elsheimer, ein Manierist geblieben ist, unfähig die neuen Errungenschaften der naturalistischen Malerei wie sie damals in Rom geprägt worden sind, aufzunehmen.» Bloch 1937.

[79] Broos 1975, p. 199.

[80] «Oock zijnder om ordineren bequamer / Daer men mach doen ghelijck den Cramer / Daer zijn goet ten tooghe stelt schoon te wonder / Op hooghe borden / ter sijden und onder / Soo maeckt-men d'History beschouwers eenich / op heuvels / boomen / oft op trappen steenich. Oft houdend'aen colomnen der ghestich-ten. Oock ander voor aen op den grondt beneden.» Mander/ Miedema 1973, chapter V, 34–35.

[81] When Broos formulates the hypothesis: «Other such borrowings from the Coriolanus can be seen in Rembrandts famous Hund-red-guilder print (Bartsch 74, fig. 20), a work which once again is constructed on the market-stall principle etc. …» Broos 1975, p. 217.

[82] On theory of literature see Warners 1957, p. 87.

[83] Emmens 1968, pp. 111–115, Mander/Miedema 1973, vol. 2, pp. 388f.

[84] Pigler 1954.

[85] «Naeryver verwerkt. … ontstak Raphaël Urbijn, om den grooten Buonarot de loef af te snijden: En Michel Agnolo om een onge-naekbaere hoogte te beklauteren. Zie dan vry, ô Leerlingen, malkanderen in de konst met, dorst ik't zeggen, nijdige oogen aen, doch zonder van de heusheyt in het borgerlijk leeven te wijken.» Hoogstraten 1678, p. 215.

[86] Warners 1956/57, vol. 2, p. 2 ff.; Hoogstraten 1678, p. 193.

[87] Vasari 1550/1568, vol. 2, p. 143.

[88] «Tot Aenmoediging. Kom nu, mijn Schilderjeugt, die van de eer en glory der groote Meesters tot wakkerheyt wort aengeprikkelt, laet u vry dien naeryver ontsteeken. Laet d'eerzucht vry uw slaepen verhinderen, want de deugt heeft ook dien aert, datze't gemoet tot een yver verwekt om de voorste voorby te stappen. *It is no Herezy to outlymn Apelles.* Een grootmoedich harte staet niet alleen, om al die noch leven, in vermaertheyt in te loopen: maer zelfs, om al die oyt doorluchtich geacht wierden, voorby te rennen. Zoodanich prikkelen de spooren van naeryver en volgzucht, datze de slaepende eergiericheyt ontwaeken, en alle krachten doen inspannen, om zelfs boven vermogen te geraeken.» Hoogstraten 1678, S. 215.

[89] «…quos aequare solos si dixero quae in tot magnis mortalibus portenta designavi, aliquid adhuc infra merita istorum statuero, si superaturos brevi, nihil spei addidero, quam de stupendis ini-tiis prudentissimi quique praeceperunt.»

[90] «Accedat Italia omnis et quidquid ab ultimâ antiquitate speciosi superest aut mirandi.»

[91] «… omni saeculorum elegantiae oppono et scire inscitissimos mortales cupio, qui, quod alibi insectati sumus, nihil effici magis quam dici hodie autumant, quod non dictum prius et effectum vetustas viderit. Aio enim nulli aut Protogeni, aut Apelli, aut Parrhasio in mentem venisse, nec, si redeant, venire posse, quae (obstupesco referens) adolescens, Batavus, molitor, imberbis uno in homine collegit singula et universa expressit. Macte vero,

mi Rembranti, non Ilium in Italiam tanti, non omnem Asiam portasse fuit, quanti Graeciae et Italiae summam laudem in Batavos pertractam ab homine Batavo, urbis patriae vix adhuc pomoeria egresso.»

[92] «… quo nunc artificio, si quisquam (nec veteres hic excipio) Belgae mei praestant …»

[93] Schillemans 1987; see also Wetering 1997/98.

[94] On Rembrandt and Lievens see for instance Jan Białostocki 1979; Chr. Vogelaar in: Leiden 1991/92; Gutbrod 1996.

[95] Strauss/Meulen 1979, doc. 1632/3. «Een schilderij daerinnen Symeon sijn den in den Tempel, Christus in sijne armen heeft, door rembrants oft Jan Lievensz. gedaen».

[96] Lairesse 1707, Book V, pp. 323/24.

[97] Chr. Vogelaar in: Leiden 1991/92.

[98] See note 4. For an analysis of this text see Ekkart 1991/92.

[99] Neuman 1905, vol. 1, p. 55.

[100] Lankheit 1952, p. 89ff.

[101] «… magni animi puer et, si vitalis fuerit, a quo nescio quid non summi expectandum. Iudicio pollet in re quâlibet acri, pro-fundo et supra virilitatem maturo, cuius inter confabulandum periculo non semel facto, unum illud improbare soleo, quod, nimiâ quâdam sui fiduciâ rigidum, reprehensionem omnem aut plane recuset, aut admissam aegre patiatur; vitio, omni quidem aetati magnopere noxio, adolescentiae vere pernicio-so, ut fere μικρὰ ζύμη ὅλου τὸ φύραμα ζυμοῖ, et, qui huic vicino vitio tenentur ἐνεργικῶς, in sacris dicuntur ἑαυτοὺς φρεναπατᾶν. Magnum sapientiae compendium fecit, qui, tribuisse cuique deum ratus, parcâ quod satis est manu, omnium vero neminem compotem extitisse, cuivus mollem animum atque ingenium docile submittens, a nemine non doceri aliquid persuasum habet.»

[102] «… ille, suae se industriae involvens, in minorem tabulam conferre amat et compendio effectum dare, quod in amplissi-mis aliorum frustra quaeras.»

[103] «In historiis enim, ut vulgo loquimur, summus utique et mi-randus artifex vividam Rembrantii inventionem non facile as-sequetur.»

[104] Strauss/Meulen 1979, doc. 1639/2.

[105] Bok 1994, p. 25f.

[106] Angel 1642, pp. 48f.

[107] «In d'aengesmeerde verwen, vernissen und olyen wonderen te zoeken was Jan Lievens dapper t'huis». Hoogstraten 1678, p. 238.

[108] Wetering 1997, pp. 173–190.

[109] «op zijn Rembrands of Jan Lievensz., dat het sap gelijk drek langs het stuk neêr lope». Lairesse 1707, Book V, p. 324.

[110] Cf. Bruyn/Wetering 1982.

[111] Hinterding 2001, vol. 1, p. 73.

# Delimiting Rembrandt's Autograph Œuvre – an Insoluble Problem?

*Ernst van de Wetering*

Dedicated to Josua Bruyn, with whom I spent countless happy hours while searching for the boundaries of the young Rembrandt's painted œuvre.

1
Jan Lievens, Portrait of *Constantijn Huygens* (detail), 1629
Panel, 99 x 84 cm
Musée de la Chartreuse, Douai

Constantijn Huygens (fig. 1), with whom I have dealt at some length in my first essay in this catalogue, recalled in his autobiography that he had wanted to pass on some advice to Rembrandt and his friend and colleague Jan Lievens. Indeed, he may actually have given them this advice; and had they followed it, the art historical literature on Rembrandt (to stay with him for the time being) would now look very different. For instead of the mass of publications under which so many bookshelves these days groan, there would stand a single, well-thumbed and frequently-reprinted sourcebook, accompanied by a number of volumes of commentary and reproductions. But we would certainly have been spared the endless series of œuvre catalogues in which authors since the nineteenth century have contested each other's work on the extent and composition of Rembrandt's œuvre, not to mention innumerable other publications. Huygens' advice to Rembrandt and Lievens was:

«Just as with Rubens, what I would especially like these two to do is to keep an inventory of their work, a description of their paintings. What this should contain (for both the admiration and instruction of future generations), after a discreet account of their way of working, is an indication with each painting of how and why it had been planned, composed and executed.»[1]

One of the most important consequences of the fact that the young Rembrandt did not follow Huygens' advice is that for many years now we have been embroiled, and will probably remain embroiled for ages to come, in questions of the attribution of works that may well betray Rembrandt's style but where doubts yet persist as to whether they are actually his own work.

## The pupil as imitator

As we know by now, it is not the case that Rembrandt was faked on any significant scale in later centuries. The confusion that surrounds his œuvre is rather a consequence of his early and subsequently growing fame and, with it, the concomitant desire of many rising artists of his time to come and learn from him. It is this which, in conjunction with the seventeenth-century system of training, led to the enormity and complexity of the problem of authenticity associated with Rembrandt. One learned a craft, including that of a painter, by imitating one's master as faithfully as possible and only subsequently did one learn to develop one's own style. As Willem Goeree (1635–1711), one of the most informative seventeenth-century writers on matters of art, wrote:

«a pupil, out of a respectful willingness to learn, should so long have absolute faith in the teaching of his master, although he may not understand or endorse all of it, that after a period of working he sees its truth in all its clarity: and if then, but not before, he tries to gradually free himself from it.»[2]

It must have been already known in Rembrandt's time that his pupils learned to imitate his style so well that their work was sold as Rembrandt's autograph work. Rembrandt's first biographer, Arnold Houbraken (1660–1719), who partly got his information on Rembrandt from several painter friends who had served apprenticeships with Rembrandt, or from the children of deceased former pupils, refers to several cases, of which that of Govert Flinck (1615– 1660) is typical. Flinck, he says, had entered into an apprenticeship under Rembrandt

> «to the end of becoming familiar with his handling of paint and way of painting, which he duly learned in such short time that several of his pieces were taken for the actual brushwork of Rembrandt and sold as such.»[3]

Houbraken also writes of Arent de Gelder (1645–1727) that, after his first apprenticeship with Samuel van Hoogstraten, he

> «left for Amsterdam to learn to paint in the manner of Rembrandt, in which he succeeded so well that I have to say, to his fame, that no-one could come so close to his way of painting.»[4]

There are other witnesses, too, to the fact that Rembrandt's pupils made his working procedures completely their own. Therefore, as Flinck's case demonstrates, confusion over the question of whether a painting is actually an autograph Rembrandt had already arisen very early on. It probably happened soon after his first pupil set foot in Rembrandt's studio.

### ‹Phantom pupils›

It has usually been assumed that Gerard Dou (1613–1665) was Rembrandt's first pupil. Jan Orlers, the Leiden burgomaster and chronicler of his city, gives the exact date on which the fifteen-year-old Gerard Dou entered into his apprenticeship with Rembrandt: February 14, 1628 (it was a Thursday) (fig. 2).[5]

We are not entirely certain, however, that Dou was Rembrandt's first pupil. It is mere chance that the names of a number of Rembrandt's pupils have survived. In the case of Dou we only know that he was Rembrandt's pupil because Dou was to become as famous in his own lifetime as Rembrandt himself and therefore earned a place in Orlers' *Description of the City of Leiden*. Had Dou died only a few years after finishing his apprenticeship, however, it is doubtful whether we should ever have known that he was taught by Rembrandt; and yet paintings by the young Dou could well have entered into circulation that were for some time – possibly to this day – seen as works by the young Rembrandt.

Apart from their later achieving fame in their own right, there are other ways in which we have come to know of several painters who were apprenticed to Rembrandt in their youth. Isack Jouderville, the second and only other pupil whose name we know with certainty from Rembrandt's Leiden period, did not become famous and consequently is not mentioned in Orlers' chronicle of Leiden. Indeed, he would never have been identified as a pupil of Rembrandt's had he not been an orphan. The system of the ‹orphans court›, with its carefully-controlled procedure of fostering out the orphans in its care, entailed considerable administration; guardians had to account for the way they exercised their guardianship over their charges.

3
Isack Jouderville, *Self-portrait* (detail),c. 1629
Panel, 38 x 37 cm (oval)
The National Gallery of
Ireland, Dublin

drart (1606–1668), even spoke of the «innumerable» pupils who populated Rembrandt's workplaces.[8] This was in the Amsterdam years, admittedly, but there could well have been others in the Leiden period besides Dou and Jouderville, whose names alone happen to have survived.

The same Joachim von Sandrart, who, as we discover time and again, was very well informed, also wrote that Rembrandt derived considerable income from the sale of both paintings and etchings done by his pupils.[9] It was in no sense unusual for work done by pupils within the context of their training to be sold for the benefit of their master. Education and production went hand in hand in seventeenth-century workshops. If one adds to this the fact that one of the most important training methods, as already mentioned, was to imitate the master, it is obvious how confusion could arise over the question of who had painted what. In the light of the system of training referred to above, the relevance of the question of whose actual hand was responsible for a particular work is a matter that deserves consideration. One thing is certain: the more important the artist was perceived to be, both by contemporaries and subsequently, the more heated the debate over the question of authenticity. The historian Jaap van der Veen has demonstrated, on the basis of seventeenth-century documents, that it was certainly a matter of some concern to many of a painter's contemporaries whether they had bought a work by the master or by one of his pupils or assistants.[10] What makes the authenticity question particularly provoking in Rembrandt's case is that he is one of those artists considered to be exceptional and self-willed. In the past it was even thought that Rembrandt was a completely isolated figure. The influential eighteenth-century Swiss artist and theoretician Heinrich Füessli (1741–1825) – Henry Fuseli when he lived in England – could still write

> «if Rembrandt ever had a master, he certainly had no pupils. Holland was incapable of recognising his talents».[11]

The fact that Rembrandt, as it later emerged, was imitated by his pupils on such a grand scale has given rise to very different reactions. In Kenneth Clarke's view, the fact that the work of

In the case of Isack Jouderville, the administrative records were kept. Among the innumerable surviving documents relating to Isack are a number of receipts written and signed by Rembrandt, acknowledging receipt of payment for tuition because he had «taught him the art of painting» (fig. 3).[6]

It is, however, by no means impossible that Rembrandt had other pupils during his time in Leiden; young painters who, perhaps through force of circumstances, went on to become bakers or seamen, or who succumbed to one of the diseases that ravaged the population of Leiden. We do know that over his entire career, Rembrandt had many pupils. In the case of 31 young men, we know this for certain from various sources.[7] A contemporary of Rembrandt's (and between 1637 and 1643 a fellow Amsterdamer), the German painter Joachim von San-

Rembrandt and his pupils could be confused was explained once you allow that

«Rembrandt was the most inspiring teacher that had ever lived, and since almost every talented Netherlandish painter at the time worked in his studio, he could raise their talents to the point of genius. Thus mediocrities could paint masterpieces».[12]

Gary Schwartz, on the other hand, refers to ‹a cruel paradox that bedevils Rembrandt studies›:

«Whereas Rembrandt himself is considered as unique an artist as ever lived, his individual works are so lacking in uniqueness that they are constantly being assigned to other hands».[13]

For Svetlana Alpers, this paradox of uniqueness and mass production was sufficiently striking to devote an entire book to the matter: *Rembrandt's Enterprise: The Studio and the Market Place*.[14] Had these three authors been better informed about seventeenth-century studio practice, they would undoubtedly have taken a less inflated view of this perfectly normal phenomenon.

## The confusion of hands

In the case of Rembrandt, it was not only the accepted training practice of his time that caused confusion. There is also the fact that Rembrandt's and Lievens' work was (and sometimes still is) so difficult to distinguish; this has certainly played an important role in the whole problem surrounding the demarcation of Rembrandt's autograph œuvre from the Leiden period. In the 1632 inventory of paintings belonging to the Dutch stadholder Frederik Hendrik, two paintings from 1631, which are now generally regarded as works by Rembrandt, were recorded as works by Lievens (fig. 4).[15] On the other hand, two paintings from the collection of Charles I of England, described as works by Rembrandt in an inventory of 1639, are almost certainly incorrectly attributed and would seem to have been painted by Lievens. For one of the paintings concerned – the lost *Young Scholler Sitting uppon a Stoole … by a Seacole fire* the interchange can be demonstrated, because the same painting was described by a more reliable Leiden source as a work by Lievens.[16]

This confusion between Rembrandt and Lievens has persisted to the present day. In Abraham Bredius' 1935 œuvre catalogue that was long held to be authoritative, there are some seven paintings that are not by Rembrandt but by Jan Lievens or other anonymous painters who seem to have worked under the direct influence of Lievens (it is not known whether in his Leiden period Jan Lievens had pupils as Rembrandt did; it cannot be ruled out).

The confusion between Rembrandt and Lievens was still not resolved during work on the first volume of the series of RRP publications, *A Corpus of Rembrandt Paintings* (hereafter referred to as the *Corpus*), which was devoted to the Leiden period and appeared in 1982. At that time there were still heated debates over the question of whether, for example, the spectacular *Esther's Feast* in Raleigh (p. 194, fig. 24a) was by Rembrandt or Lievens. At the time, there was inadequate knowledge of Lievens' œuvre, but the extensive Lievens exhibition organized in 1979 in Braunschweig changed this situation. The complex succession of stages in the young Lievens' stylistic development became more clearly evident in this exhibition than ever before. There were also – and still are – differences of opinion concerning the so-called *Rembrandt's Mother* in Windsor Castle, which was still listed in the first volume of the *Corpus* as an authentic Rembrandt (no. A 32) (fig. 5). In the second volume, however, this painting was attributed to Lievens.[17] During work on the first volume, the Lievens characteristics of the painting had certainly already been noted, but the fact that in the above-mentioned 1639 inventory of Charles I it was listed as a work by Rembrandt initially outweighed the stylistic evidence to the contrary.

The gradual sorting out of the different ‹hands› of Rembrandt and Lievens, however, is relatively simple compared with the problems that arise in relation to Rembrandt's pupils. After all, sufficient works are known with certainty to be by Rembrandt and Lievens to allow us to gradually build up fairly reliable stylistic profiles of both painters, against which disputed paintings can be tested. When it comes to Rembrandt's pupils, however, this is far less possible. Since seventeenth-century pupils were not allowed to sign with their own name while still in their master's workshop, we have no handle there. Furthermore, it has proved exceptionally difficult to extrapolate backward from the œuvre they later created under their own name to their earlier period of apprenticeship. At first sight, this seems odd; but it becomes clearer when one recalls that the master's stamp during the apprenticeship period was, as Goeree's above-cited text attests, so strong that their own style could only emerge some time later. Often the only help in isolating the work of a pupil from the œuvre of the master might be a general idea of the quality of the artist concerned, or perhaps one should say an idea of the presumed inherent limits of his talent. In the case of Isack

Jouderville, which will be discussed later, the criterion of specific weaknesses in this painter's talent was a useful one.[18] In the case of Gerard Dou, this is theoretically much more difficult – theoretically, because it is still not possible with certainty to identify work from Dou's apprentice period. One can, however, conclude from Dou's later œuvre that he was uncommonly gifted. On this basis alone, it should in theory be more difficult than with Jouderville to distinguish his Rembrandt imitations, painted during his apprenticeship, from Rembrandt's own work. A further complication is that the earliest dated work of Gerard Dou is from 1636, fully five years after he had left Rembrandt's studio.

4
Rembrandt Harmensz.
van Rijn, *The Abduction of Proserpina*, c. 1631
Panel, 84.8 x 79.7 cm
Staatliche Museen zu
Berlin, Preußischer
Kulturbesitz,
Gemäldegalerie

This makes it virtually impossible to reconstruct a reliable chronology for works attributed to him that are thought to have been painted before 1636. And this, in turn, makes it absolutely impossible to extrapolate back to the style of the young Dou at the time that he was working in Rembrandt's studio. Yet one more added complication: once Dou was independent, he, like Rembrandt, must himself have begun taking on pupils at a relatively early age. The work of these hypothetical pupils could in turn confuse our picture of the young Gerard Dou. Indeed, in my opinion, this actually happened during the recent Dou exhibition, when what would appear to be the work of mediocre Dou disciples was presented as early work of Dou himself.[19] If one then assumes that more pupils who remain unknown to us could have worked in Rembrandt's studio, it becomes clear how difficult it is to bring order to that group of paintings which in general terms show the characteristics of the young Rembrandt and yet do not seem to be from his own hand. It might therefore be useful first of all to try to gain some insight into the nature of the system of studio production that could have developed in the context of Rembrandt's training. In so doing, it is important to realise that Rembrandt may have accepted no – or hardly any – beginners in his studio.

## Studio production

Seen over the course of Rembrandt's entire career, almost all of his known pupils had already completed their primary training when they came to him – just as Rembrandt himself had under Jacob Isaacsz. van Swanenburg.

In general, one can divide the products of a painting pupil into four categories, two of which probably involve graphic works:

- Drawn copies of works by the master. In the words of Goeree:

> «having pupils make drawings of good paintings will teach them how to reduce a large work to small proportions, through which they will immediately learn to estimate and to arrive at a firm positioning of the different forms»[20];

- Drawings in which the composition and ordonnance (the placing of the various protago-

nists) of history pieces were practised. In the words of Rembrandt's pupil Samuel van Hoogstraten (1627–1678):

> «the way to be sure and certain in ordination is to get used to making many sketches and drawing many histories on paper, for the theory will be of little use if it is not established through practice.»[21]

Pupils' ‹painted› works – as far as we can infer from surviving apprentice works, certainly those that can be traced back to Rembrandt's studio – include:

- the painted copy and
- the variation (to a greater or lesser degree) based on the master's work.

As far as this last group is concerned, it is important to note the following: Surveying the production of Rembrandt's studio, a pattern emerges whereby, parallel to Rembrandt's own production, there must have been a production of ‹satellites›, as we call them, of Rembrandt originals. These are of free variations painted by pupils, which, although produced in the context of their training, must also have been considered saleable products.

Just how easily painted studio copies can be confused with Rembrandt's originals can be seen in the case of three early self portraits. The

6
Rembrandt-Studio,
Copy after the painting
fig. 7
Panel, 23.4 x 17.2 cm
Staatliche Museen
Kassel, Gemäldegalerie
Alte Meister

7
Rembrandt Harmensz.
van Rijn, *Self-portrait*,
c. 1628
Panel, 22.5 x 18.6 cm
Amsterdam, Rijks-
museum

8
Rembrandt-Studio,
Copy after the painting
fig. 9
Panel, 37.9 x 28.9 cm
Royal Cabinet of
Paintings Mauritshuis,
The Hague

9
Rembrandt Harmensz.
van Rijn, *Self-portrait*,
c. 1629
Panel, 38.2 x 31 cm
Germanisches
Nationalmuseum,
Nuremburg

10
Rembrandt-Studio,
Copy after the painting
fig. 11
Panel, 49.7 x 37.3 cm
MOA Museum of Art,
Atami

11
Rembrandt Harmensz.
van Rijn, *Self-portrait*,
c. 1629
Panel, 42.8 x 33 cm
The Indianapolis
Museum of Art

Kassel early *Self-portrait* (fig. 6), long considered an original, was proven to be a copy of the painting that surfaced in 1959 and is now in the Rijksmuseum (fig. 7). The *Self-portrait* in The Hague (fig. 8), until recently considered to be an autograph Rembrandt, turned out to have been painted after the original in Nuremburg (fig. 9). Similar confusion has arisen between two versions of a self-portrait, of which the one in the MOA Museum in Japan (fig. 10) proves to be the copy, while the version in Indianapolis, long assumed to be the copy, has turned out to be the original (fig. 11).[22]

In these three cases, correction was possible because the prototypes still existed and could be investigated by means of X-rays. In other cases where a hypothetical prototype has been lost, studio copies could still be taken for original Rembrandts. This is even more likely to happen when it comes to free variations on Rembrandt's work. An interesting example of such a free variation that is easy to identify as the work of a pupil is the *Minerva* in Denver (fig. 12). This painting was nevertheless still considered by Bredius to be an autograph work by Rembrandt. In *Corpus I* it was argued on several counts that this is a work by Isack Jouderville.[23] On the basis of the quality alone, the possibility can definitively be ruled out that it could be an autograph work by Rembrandt. In fact, it is based on several works that are from his hand: The *Old Woman Reading* (fig. 13), the *Minerva* (fig. 14) and cat. no. 33 for the wall and the lighting of the head. The painting in Denver in fact is a composite of elements taken from these paintings.

## Connoisseurship

The fact that Jouderville's *Minerva* (cf. fig. 12) was long considered an original Rembrandt says a great deal. It demonstrates that the image of Rembrandt current at that time admitted this attribution to him. In our own time, we shall never know for certain what influence our contemporary image of Rembrandt has had on our view of Rembrandt's œuvre. In the end, there is but a single ‹method› for trying to isolate Rembrandt's own œuvre from the wider group of paintings in his style, and that is connoisseurship. Connoisseurship, one could say,

rests on ‹recognising› a ‹hand› and a ‹mind› which manifest themselves in a work, as well as specific characteristics of the painting concerned that relate to its ‹quality›. It will be made clear that such an approach involves a considerable degree of subjectivity.

Recognition normally occurs at a glance, as everyone knows who has ever recognised a former classmate in a busy street after many years. One does not rationally weigh up physiognomic or other features in the act of a specific recognition. That is unnecessary. With connoisseurship, however, it is not a simple matter of ‹recognising› a painting that one has seen before, but of recognising qualities of a painting that one thinks one knows from other paintings by a particular artist. The discerning of the kinship between these qualities is what leads to ‹recognition›.

The problem with connoisseurship in the field of art, however, is that those features that we have stored in our minds from the countless paintings we have seen are normally unreliable. Surveying the history of Rembrandt scholarship, it becomes evident that one's image of Rembrandt – even that of an experienced connoisseur – can be contaminated by the qualities of paintings which, it turns out, are not by Rembrandt at all. Paintings done more or less in Rembrandt's manner by ex-pupils such as Govert Flinck, Nicholaes Maes, Karel van de Pluym or Arent de Gelder, although signed by them, sometimes had this signature painted over and a bogus Rembrandt signature superimposed. Subsequently the underlying signatures of the authors have emerged, but for a long time and to a considerable degree these paintings fed the image of Rembrandt then current. This meant that the possibility of recognising Rembrandt's ‹hand› was seriously distorted – a glance at the *Minerva* of Jouderville (fig. 12) – see the hands and the face – is enough to see the unfortunate consequences.[24] This confusion is even greater in the case of Rembrandt because one cannot avoid the impression that he hardly ever fell back upon routine. As will become evident in the following section, the range of his artistic possibilities was exceptionally broad. Another great connoisseur, Bernard Berenson, proposed that «the greater the artist,

12
Isack Jouderville, *Minerva*,
c. 1631
Panel, 43.9 x 35.6 cm
The Denver Art Museum

the less possible it is for the connoisseur to rely on fixed criteria of authenticity and the more important the qualitative factor becomes.»[25]

If one speaks of bringing qualitative criteria to bear, this would inevitably seem to imply introducing academic criteria for correct drawing, etc. But precisely in the case of an artist like Rembrandt, the tendency has long existed to emphasise his anti-academicism.[26] Since the Romantic period, faults in the academic sense have actually been interpreted as signs of his genius.[27] But even if one departs from strict academic norms of correctness in matters of form, anatomy, etc., there are countless ways of applying qualitative criteria which, without drawing on an academic canon, also do not remain purely subjective.

Many such qualitative criteria of authenticity are concerned with the relation between pictorial elements and the logic of the spatial, plastic and anatomical structures of things, or the pictorial intelligence in matters of illumination and

tonal relations. At another level, there are the effects obtained in the rendering of materials, shadow-working and so on, which invoke rather different criteria of quality. In the end, however, one has to reckon with those intrinsic properties of a work and with our response to them, whereas the painter's power of imagination and concentration enter as seemingly imponderable criteria. At this level, the question of the connoisseur's judgement is key; and then the point is reached where one of those statements has to be uttered which, in our modern democratic society, are taboo: «either you see it or you don't». In this context, Rembrandt's pupil Samuel van Hoogstraten sketches the comical situation of art lovers who would make huge detours in order to see works of art in the original.

> «Which they habitually do with such great prejudice that they imagine they are seeing what is not there to be seen; of which I have ample enough experience: for I have also been amazed to see them gazing starry-eyed at vanities which they could have done better themselves.»[28]

We are touching here on the problem of being blinded by the aura of a particular work of art, a phenomenon that plays a more significant role than is normally assumed in discussions surrounding the authenticity of works in the style of Rembrandt.[29]

## An equation with too many unknown variables

What follows is more a demonstration of the problems facing the Rembrandt researcher than a triumphalist presentation of the solutions. The reader will probably soon get the feeling that he or she is wandering around in a ‹floating construction›. The problem one is confronted with when one begins to investigate the possible authenticity of a Rembrandtesque painting is rather like a mathematical equation with too many unknown variables. It might therefore be a good idea first to have a look at some examples of these.

As explained above, we do not know whether Dou and Jouderville were the only painters besides Rembrandt (and possibly Lievens) active in Rembrandt's studio in the period that is

13
Rembrandt Harmensz. van Rijn, *An Old Woman Reading (The Prophetess Anna?)*, 1631
Panel, 59.8 x 47.7 cm
Rijksmuseum, Amsterdam

14
Rembrandt Harmensz. van Rijn, *Minerva*, c. 1631
Panel, 60.5 x 49 cm
Staatliche Museen zu Berlin, Preußischer Kulturbesitz, Gemäldegalerie

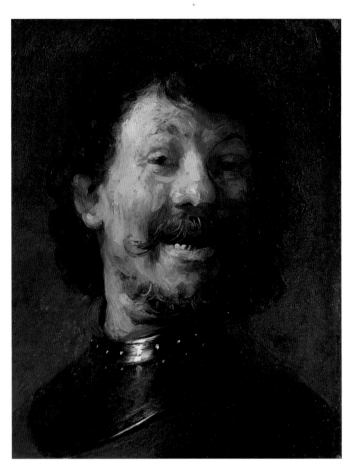

15
Rembrandt Harmensz.
van Rijn, *Bust of an Old
Man in a Fur Cap
(Rembrandt's Father?)*,
1630
Panel, 22.2 x 17.7 cm
Tiroler Landesmuseum
Ferdinandeum,
Innsbruck

16
Rembrandt Harmensz.
van Rijn, *Laughing Soldier*,
c. 1629/30
cat. no. 79

crucial to the following demonstration – from roughly 1627 to 1629 – or whether we have to take into account the presence of still other ‹hands› working in Rembrandt's style.

Moreover, we do not know the range of variation within Rembrandt's ‹own› style. As I have argued in my other essay in this catalogue, during those first years in Leiden, Rembrandt was feverishly searching for new possibilities in the art of painting. He experimented with various pictorial means and rapidly developed in several directions. Thus a painting whose authorship was once considered questionable – such as the *Baptism of the Eunuch* (cat. no. 3), discovered in 1974 – can turn out in the end to be an autograph Rembrandt , although initially it did not seem to fit into our idea of his work.

Another unknown variable in our equation is the fact that we know nothing of the possible function or preferences of those who commissioned his works. As a result, we do not know what external influences may have played a part in determining the appearance of different paintings.

We do not know what the significance may be of the fact that some works were signed with a Rembrandt monogram and dated while others were not. Nor do we know whether such inscriptions can serve as proof of authenticity. Indeed, there are powerful arguments against making this assumption.[30]

Furthermore, the material history of different paintings can also vary quite radically. One painting may have been subjected to more damage than another, either through the ravages of time or through being more or less drastically cleaned, and so on. The appearance of some paintings can be affected by a thick, yellowed layer of varnish, while others have been cleaned, making comparisons hazardous.

But the most oppressive uncertainty, time and again, is this question: which paintings give us a safe point of departure, a touchstone for those properties specific to Rembrandt that could be used to recognise his hand in other works, or could decide us to remove a work from Rembrandt's hypothetical œuvre? The number of reli-

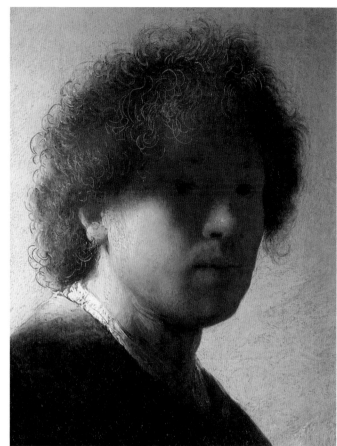

ably-documented early paintings by Rembrandt is small. On what, exactly, can we then base the process of ‹recognition› outlined above?

The fact that a painting should find itself listed in a document under Rembrandt's name relatively soon after its creation (if we are sure that we can identify the painting referred to) is no guarantee that it really is from Rembrandt's hand. The examples referred to above of the early switch in attribution between paintings by Rembrandt and Lievens bear witness to this (cf. figs. 4, 5).

## The hard core of authentic Rembrandts from 1627 to 1629

From the period 1627–1629, we know of only seven works that can, on the basis of documentary evidence, be linked to Rembrandt with a degree of probability verging on certainty – the ‹documents› here including several very early print reproductions. There is a quartet of *tronies* (two of them in this exhibition, cf. cat. no. 79, 80), reproduction prints that were made by Jan van Vliet (1600/10–1668), undoubtedly in consultation with Rembrandt, not long after they had been painted. This fact, coupled with information gained through technical and scientific research, means that we can safely accept these small paintings as works by Rembrandt (figs. 15, 16, 17, 18). It has become increasingly clear that Rembrandt collaborated very closely with van Vliet during the years between 1630 and 1634.[31] The striking differences in execution and conception between these four tronies illustrate how wide the range of the young Rembrandt's style already was. The stylistic range of the other three clearly-documented paintings from this period, 1627–1629, was even wider. One of them is the «painting done by Rembrandt, of two seated old men disputing, one with a large book on his lap, with sunlight entering» (fig. 19) discussed in my first essay.[32] The painting concerned is described in this way in the will of the artist and connoisseur Jacques de Gheyn III (c. 1596–1641), whom Rembrandt must have known well, since he painted his por-

17
Rembrandt Harmensz. van Rijn, *Bust of an Old Man with a Cap,* c. 1630 cat. no. 80

18
Rembrandt Harmensz. van Rijn, *Self Portrait,* c. 1628 Panel, 22.5 x 18.6 cm Rijksmuseum, Amsterdam

painting reveals such a highly complex artistic genesis (in which various drawings were also involved) (cat. no. 34) that we can be certain that what we are dealing with here is not just another old copy of the painting Huygens described but the original itself.

### ‹La main chaude›: a demonstration

Among the documented paintings, the *Judas* (as I shall refer to the painting for the sake of brevity) (cf. fig. 22) is our best point of reference for the following demonstration. The relatively small-scale figures in this painting are located in a wide space defined by a locally-entering light; their interaction is described through attitudes and gestures. This description would also do for a painting entitled ‹La main chaude› (cat. no. 62; figs. 23, 24) after the party game that it depicts. This very small painting cannot be connected to Rembrandt by means of documents, nor is it signed or monogrammed, as in the case of the *Judas*. It only surfaced with a London art dealer in 1896 and up till now the predominant view has been that it cannot be a work by Rembrandt, even though from the moment it reappeared it was generally recognised as showing many of the characteristics of Rembrandt's early style.

To answer the question of whether ‹La main

19
Rembrandt Harmensz.
van Rijn, *Peter and Paul Disputing*, c. 1628
Panel 72.3 x 59.5 cm
The National Gallery of Victoria, Melbourne

trait in 1632 (fig. 20). In the same will an entry appears for a painting of «a man sitting near a fire, asleep with a hand on his breast, made by Rembrandt» (fig. 21).[33] The descriptions in the will are so specific and the subjects so unusual that one can assume with confidence that two paintings, one presently in Melbourne (cf. fig. 19) and the other in Turin (cat. no. 31; cf. fig. 21), are identical with the paintings cited in Jacques de Gheyn III's inventory.

Equally clearly documented is the *Judas Repentant* (cat. no. 33; fig. 22). This has to be the painting mentioned by Huygens in his autobiography, whose portrayal of Judas he so penetratingly described after his visit to Rembrandt's studio (cf. cat. no. 33). Moreover, Jan van Vliet – again undoubtedly acting in consultation with Rembrandt – made a reproduction print of this figure of Judas in 1634 (cf. cat. no. 33, fig. 33b). What is more, X-ray analysis of the

20
Rembrandt Harmensz.
van Rijn, *Portrait of Jacques de Gheyn III*, 1632
Panel, 29.9 x 24.9 cm
Dulwich Picture Gallery, London

*chaude*› could or could not be from the hand of Rembrandt, it is not enough to compare it with the *Judas* alone. We need other paintings with which to compare it. But as with ‹*La main chaude*›, those other paintings that show comparable characteristics cannot be traced back to Rembrandt in the way that the *Judas* can; nevertheless we need them if we are to proceed with this comparative investigation. The reader will soon come to understand why in the introduction to this section, I talked of a ‹floating construction›.

The *Judas* remains our only really secure point of reference. However, this highly ambitious painting is much larger (79 x 102.3 cm) and more fully elaborated than ‹*La main chaude*›, which measures only 21 x 27 cm and is far more sketchily executed (cf. figs. 22, 23, 24). The correspondences between ‹*La main chaude*› and the *Judas* are striking in several respects. But against the similarities we should also weigh the differences. In the *Judas*, the entering light appears to be daylight, whereas in ‹*La main chaude*› the space is illuminated by a candle or another source of artificial light hidden behind a seated figure in the left foreground. This figure is seen in silhouette. In the *Judas*, too, a figure in the left-hand foreground is outlined as a dark repoussoir against a lighter background. He likewise sits on this side of a brightly-lit table. The silhouetted figure in the *Judas* still reveals some outline detail; in ‹*La main chaude*› there is none.

For every point of similarity that one can point to, there are also differences, of greater or lesser significance, that also need to be weighed and considered: what bearing do these differences have on the larger question of whether or not ‹*La main chaude*› is by Rembrandt? Karel van Mander's influential *Schilder-boeck* gives us an early-seventeenth-century text on painting candlelight, in which he advises that «it is good if one puts a figure in the foreground from head to foot in shadow, and allows only the outline of flesh, hair or clothing to be touched by light».[34] Is the absence of detail from the silhouette in the left-hand foreground of ‹*La main chaude*› significant, or is it simply explained by the cursory nature of this small painting?

In both the *Judas* and ‹*La main chaude*› the sil-

21
Rembrandt Harmensz. van Rijn, *Old Man Asleep (Acedia?),* 1629
cat. no. 31

houetted figure in the foreground casts a shadow on the ground, but once again this similarity is offset by a difference. The shadow in the *Judas* has a rather vague margin running parallel to the bottom of the painting, whereas in ‹*La main chaude*› it stands out against the illuminated floor with a sharp, undulating outline, across which cuts the bottom edge of the painting. These differences may seem to betray differences in style, but they can be explained in terms of the differences in the nature and source of the light in the two paintings. The daylight in the *Judas* that streams in through an opening invisible to the viewer produces parallel shadows with diffuse edges – diffuse because the light enters in a wide stream. Candlelight, or any other form of artificial light, for that matter, has a point source. As Karel van Mander continues after the passage already quoted on painting candlelight: «the shadow must everywhere seek its direction from the light as a point source»[35] What this initially rather strange-sounding statement means is that the light from a candle flame radiates out in straight lines in all directions from its point source, which, in ‹La main chaude›, is hidden behind the silhouetted figure. This of course explains why the shadow of the silhouetted foreground figure is cast to the bottom edge of the painting. Such feature was already noted by Caravaggio's followers.[36]

The stylistic differences between the *Judas* and ‹La main chaude› are so far not decisive. Is this also true of the difference in the content of the two compositions? In the *Judas Returning the Pieces of Silver,* Rembrandt has chosen one of the most dramatic moments of the New Testament, showing Judas' remorse over his betrayal of Christ and the total lack of pity shown by the High Priest and his entourage in highly gripping fashion. On the other hand, in ‹La main chaude›, one foolish figure is being slapped by one of two other foolish figures, while a musician and several other figures seated at a table look on. There is an aura of gravity and piety that clings to the idea of the «great Rembrandt», from whose œuvre one could assemble an illustrated Bible.[37] Certainly in the first half of the twentieth century, when the work of an artist was still primarily seen as a matter of self-expression, it was difficult to imagine that two such utterly different scenes could be produced by the same mind. This certainly, though unconsciously, played a role in the reservations expressed with regard to ‹La main chaude›.[38] In the more matter-of-fact approach of today's art historians, this can hardly be regarded as a serious reason for denying an attribution to Rembrandt. After all, Rembrandt certainly painted, drew and etched other genre pieces, even if they represent a small minority.

The viewer may be either intrigued or baffled by the rather grotesque headgear worn by the silhouetted figure in ‹La main chaude›. In fact, it reflects a particular stage (c. 1628) in the rapidly-evolving form of the hat in seventeenth-century men's fashion. As can clearly be seen on the man bending forward in this painting, it was a type of hat with an extremely wide brim, folded up at the front so that, behind, the brim fell onto the man's back. The painter in the Boston *Studio* (cat. no. 61) is wearing a similar hat (fig. 25).

In other respects, too, one can point to affinities between ‹La main chaude› and this latter painting. The painting in Boston is one of those works that are generally considered to be an autograph Rembrandt – although in light of the discussion above, one may well ask oneself whether unanimity in recognising Rembrandt's hand in this painting means all that much.

Of the many features of the Boston *Studio* that one might investigate for similarities or differences with comparable features in ‹La main chaude›, I have chosen to look first at the costumes. The manner in which the costumes are painted, with their pleated folds, seams and rows of buttons, can give an artist away. Precisely because these elements offer the painter considerable freedom in their execution, the individuality of his style can reveal itself in them.

It would seem an obvious step to compare the painter in the Boston *Studio*, illuminated and executed in some detail, with the equally strongly-illuminated principle figure in ‹La main chaude›: the player bending forward. To sharpen this comparison, a third painting can be introduced: an *Interior with Figures* done by the Amsterdam painter Pieter Codde (1599–1678) (fig. 26). On the basis of the outfit worn by the figure on the left in the latter painting, one can safely assume that this must have been painted at the same time as the Boston *Studio* and ‹La main chaude›. This figure is wearing a costume almost identical to that of the bending player in ‹La main chaude›.

The comparison of the Codde painting with the two others makes it clear at a glance how different this artist's manner of handling light and shade is. With Codde, forms are distinct throughout the painting, whether they are in light or in shade, whereas in the *Studio,* parts of the costume disappear into deep, interlocking shadows. In ‹La main chaude›, large parts of the composition almost dissolve into shadow in the same way as we see in the *Judas.*[39]

When we turn to the drapery, a comparison between the *Studio* and the Codde immediately makes one aware of the importance that Rembrandt attached to conveying the weight of the material. Looking at his entire œuvre, at every turn one is struck by how much attention he paid to this feature. With Rembrandt, without being able to quantify it, one might speak of a kind of ‹specific gravity› that his figures possess. This is a feeling that the viewer is given unconsciously, but the way the materials fall certainly contributes to it. Just how much the rendering of textiles can differ in this respect is evident when one compares the left-hand figure in the Codde painting with the man bending forward in ‹La main chaude›. The material of the latter figure's costume hangs in ballooning pleats from the man's body, whereas with Codde the cloth either clings to the shape of the figure or else is crumpled in a relatively random pattern of folds. Juxtaposing these two paintings also makes it immediately clear just how closely ‹La main chaude› resembles the Boston *Studio* in this respect, even though the artist's garment in the *Studio* seems at first sight to be more subtly executed than that of the figure in ‹La main chaude›. The figure in the *Studio*, small though he is, is twice as large as the bending figure in ‹La main chaude›, which, at a height of 7 cm, is on scarcely more than a miniature scale. With the painter's clothing in the *Studio*, the linear elements – the splits and seams – are given a certain plasticity by the subtle way the shadows accompanying such details vary in breadth. This is evident to a lesser degree in the man bending over, so that the details in his costume have a more linear character. The difference is one of degree, however, and would seem to be mainly the result of the difference in scale between the two figures.

There are countless other points that one could investigate for correspondences and differences: the hands, for example, in ‹La main chaude› could be compared with those in the *Judas* and the Boston *Studio*. In comparison with the *Judas*, the even greater difference in scale of course plays its part. The hands in that painting are much more modelled than the almost stenotypic hands in ‹La main chaude›. What is remarkable in this comparison is the fact that the dismissive gesture of the High Priest – one of the key motifs of the painting – bears a striking similarity to the slapping hand of the player in the dark costume in ‹La main chaude›. It is not so much the similarity in form that matters here but rather the stroke of introducing a strong dynamic into the composition through a similar gesture. This may seem a rather far-fetched argument to indicate a relationship between two paintings; waving aside and slapping are, after all, actions that are integral to the narrative context of the two paintings. What is at issue here, however, is the nature of the artist's choice in giving such a gesture a pictorially important role, both compositionally and dynamically. But here, too, the insistent question again raises its head: if ‹La main chaude› was painted by a hypothetical pupil, could the latter have arrived at this solution by referring to the prototype by his master?

More important here are the similarities with the hands of the painter in the Boston *Studio*. Here, too, one has to take into account the difference in scale. Whoever has tried knows that it is extremely difficult to draw or paint a hand that is convincing in form and gesture. It is striking that in both paintings the hands are represented by a simple division of light and shade such that they are highly effectively characterised in form, attitude and gesture. The device of freeing the little finger of the painter's hand (in this case to hold the maulstick) seems to be used in ‹La main chaude› as a means of drawing the eye to the bending man's hanging hand and giving it a stronger expressiveness. The gesture with which the violinist beside the stairs in ‹La main chaude› holds his violin is equally well done in its simplicity. One also finds this way of painting hands, for example, in the undocumented but generally accepted *Christ at Emmaus* in the Musée Jacquemart André (fig. 27). The manual gestures of the recoiling disciple in that painting are realised with the same economy and efficacy.

There are also several technical arguments, objective though they may appear to be at first sight, which constitute part of our ‹floating construction›. ‹La main chaude› is painted on a very small, thin panel whose format exactly corresponds to the panel on which the *Old Man with Turban* (cat. no. 75) is painted. This latter painting is also undocumented; it is considered by us to be Rembrandt's own work on the basis of a number of mutually reinforcing arguments. When two paintings share the same format, this can sometimes bear on the question of attribu-

The paintings on page 74 have all been reproduced in the same scale (c. 1:6).

73

22
Rembrandt Harmensz. van Rijn, *Judas Repentant, Returning the Thirty Pieces of Silver*, 1629, 79 x 102.3 cm, cat. no. 33

25
Rembrandt Harmensz. van Rijn, *The Artist in His Studio*, c. 1628
24.8 x 31.7 cm
cat. no. 61

23
Rembrandt Harmensz. van Rijn, *Interior with Figures, Called ‹La main chaude›*, c. 1628
21 x 27 cm
cat. no. 62

28
Rembrandt Harmensz. van Rijn, *The Flight into Egypt*, 1627
27.5 x 24.7 cm
cat. no. 60

29
Rembrandt Harmensz. van Rijn or Circle of Rembrandt, *Man Writing by Candlelight*, c. 1628/30
13.9 x 13.9 cm
cat. no. 59

24
Rembrandt Harmensz. van Rijn, *Interior with Figures, Called ‹La main chaude›*, c. 1628, cat. no. 62

27
Rembrandt Harmensz. van Rijn, *Christ in Emmaus*,
c. 1629, Paper on panel, 37.4 x 42.3 cm
Musée Jacquemart-André, Paris

26
Pieter Codde, *Interior with Figures*,
c. 1628, Panel, 36 x 50 cm
Private Collection

tion, though usually such a correspondence carries little weight, for substantial quantities of panels were produced in standard formats in the seventeenth century.[40] The panel's format in this case would scarcely be of interest, therefore, were it not for the fact that the panels of ‹La main chaude› and the *Old Man with the Turban* belong to no hitherto-known standard format. But on the other hand, it is highly likely that the master and any pupil he may have had would take their painting materials from the same stock. It would seem to be much more significant that both panels have been shown by X-ray analysis to have been previously painted on, as were the Boston *Studio* and several other small works on panel painted by Rembrandt. We get a glimpse here of an aspect of the studio practice from which these paintings derive. Is this then an argument in support of attributing ‹La main chaude› to Rembrandt? To a certain extent; but what then should one make of paintings which, on grounds of style and quality, are difficult to see as Rembrandt's own work and yet were painted on a previously-painted panel? The *Foot Operation* is just such a case in point (cat. no. 26). If our suspicion is correct that this is not an autograph work by Rembrandt, then unfortunately what had seemed to be an important argument for attributing ‹La main chaude› to Rembrandt – the argument of the twice-painted panel – collapses with it.

One could extend the analysis even further of the similarities and differences between various parts of ‹La main chaude› and other works that one attributes with more or less certainty to Rembrandt. But what contributes most of all to this sense of ‹recognition› is the control over the painting as a whole that is so characteristic of Rembrandt. Several aspects of this treatment of light have been analysed already. The great power of the painting – the aspect that makes an attribution to Rembrandt almost imperative – is due mainly to the treatment of light in the painting ‹as a whole›.

We tend to take a successful pictorial illusion for granted without wondering what means the painter has used to ‹deceive› us. With ‹La main chaude›, one only has to follow the course of the diminishing light values into the deep shadows to the right in order to see how much delibera-

tion, patience and above all control of the painterly resources were necessary to achieve this effect in a coherent manner. This is also true of the way the figures are placed in a candlelight that rapidly diminishes with increasing distance. Evidently, the colours of the costumes have been deliberately chosen to strengthen this effect. (This was usual for Rembrandt – and not only Rembrandt, one sees the same effect, for example, in paintings by Hendrick ter Brugghen). The main figure is thus given a pale blue-grey costume that is conspicuously lighter than that of the man who is about to slap him. The illuminated man at the table wears a light ochre jerkin so that he almost dissolves into the light, while the violin player, in his dark brown cloak, almost dissolves into the shadows. If one also follows the diminishing strength of the light on the faces, the degree of thought behind the creation of this small artistic jewel is once again evident. For this author, at least, all this leads to the ‹recognition› of Rembrandt's hand, his mind and his individuality as an artist.

## The attributed painting as a point of departure for further attributions

Once a work has been attributed to Rembrandt's œuvre (or better said to the attributor's conception of Rembrandt's œuvre) this can serve as a bridgehead for the further attribution or rejection of other paintings. The risk involved in this process, however, is that further paintings can be attributed to Rembrandt that are difficult to connect with the confirmed, documented nucleus of Rembrandt's œuvre for the relevant period. One runs the risk of lapsing into what was once described as ‹the attribution game›, a preoccupation that can lead to quite dizzying constructions. Nevertheless, I have no hesitation in drawing a connection between ‹La main chaude› and the *Flight into Egypt* in Tours (cat. no. 60; fig. 28), a painting which, having once been introduced by Otto Benesch into the Rembrandt literature as an early work by Rembrandt, was removed again in the *Corpus* vol. I and tentatively attributed to Gerard Dou.

This painting, which has virtually the same format as ‹La main chaude›, is similarly a nocturnal piece in which an invisible light-source illuminates the protagonists. The light casts sharp shadows just as in ‹La main chaude›, shadows that have the same tendency to undulate rhythmically. The figures have the billowing outlines characteristic of Rembrandt in this period, and even Joseph's little finger is freed from the rest of the hand in the same way as it was in the Boston *Studio* and ‹La main chaude›. There are also striking correspondences between Mary's head and that of the figure behind the table in ‹La main chaude›. With Mary, there was initially the impression that the head had been damaged, without it being clear how the head had originally been painted, but the solution is apparent when one turns to the head in ‹La main chaude›. In both cases, one is looking at a cursorily-indicated oval with the suggestion of a nose, spots for the two eyes and a mouth done in similar fashion. The colour schemes of the two paintings are also related: mainly cool blue-grey, ochre, flesh colour and brown. In the *Flight into Egypt,* the subdued orangey tints in the donkey's basket also add to this. For the question of attribution, one hardly need write about the relevance of the dark repoussoirs in the corner. This was at the time a widely-employed way of creating space in the image and strengthening the suggestion of light,[41] but there are a number of striking similarities in the details when one compares ‹La main chaude› and the *Flight into Egypt*. The rhythm of the half-drawn, half-painted strokes with which the sagging form of Joseph's bag is painted is so strongly reminiscent of the manner in which parts of the costume of the man about to strike in ‹La main chaude› have been executed that one can hardly imagine that two different hands were at work. The pointedly typical way, too, in which the pipe and spout of the wine jug are indicated, on the one hand, and that used in Joseph's hat, on the other, is strikingly similar. This is not merely a stylistic detail; it tells us something about the technique. Introducing such fine lines calls for a specific consistency of the paint, but it also demands a particular hand and specific brush. Rembrandt was a master of the free yet controlled introduction of such linear details (for example, compare the illuminated edge of the panel in the Boston *Studio*) (cat. no. 61).

There is yet another painting which, on the basis of a series of similarities would seem to be by the same hand as ‹La main chaude› and the *Flight into Egypt*: the *Man Writing by Candlelight* from the Bader collection (cat. no. 59; fig. 29), a small painting on copper of a scholar in a nocturnal room, lit by a candle that is obscured by a large, open book. Some of the ingredients that particularly characterise the *Flight into Egypt* are also in evidence here; the sharp, radiating, sometimes undulating shadows cast by the invisible candle flame, the simple range of colours – limited here to brown, yellowish-grey and the flesh tone of the man's face – and the sharply-drawn pen in the hand of the writing man are all related. In terms of quality, this small work, apparently intended merely as a study in candlelight, is scarcely the equal of the *Flight into Egypt*; yet it is not so inferior as to rule out serious consideration that it should be attributed to the same hand: that of Rembrandt. Our shifting of the bridgehead from ‹La main chaude› to the *Flight into Egypt* leads almost inevitably to this conclusion. But if one holds the *Man Writing by Candlelight* next to a painting on roughly the same subject and in which all the qualities of Rembrandt's youthful style come gloriously into their own – *The Parable of the Rich Man* from Berlin (cat. no. 29) – then notwithstanding the differences in scale, one gets the feeling that one is dealing with an entirely different hand, a different artistic mind and certainly an incomparably lower quality. What now? Have we been led too far into the ‹game› of attribution? Have we descended step by step to a level that is simply incommensurate with that of Rembrandt himself?

But if one denies the *Man Writing by Candlelight* a place in Rembrandt's œuvre, would this not also disqualify the *Flight into Egypt* and, in turn, ‹La main chaude›? The process of inflation inherent in ‹the attribution game› can thus also run in reverse. In the attempt to demarcate the boundaries of Rembrandt's autograph œuvre, inflation and deflation, expansion and reduction therefore represent diametrically opposed approaches. If one surveys the history of Rembrandt research as a history of ‹expansionism› and ‹reductionism›, it is clear that reductionism has for some time had the upper hand; but has this perhaps gone too far? It may well be that

only hanging the paintings mentioned here side by side on a single wall in this exhibition can help us to decide where, in this case, to draw the line of demarcation between Rembrandt and some of his followers.

### Mini-œuvres by other hands detached from Rembrandt's œuvre

Within Rembrandt studies, a cluster of paintings has sometimes been recognised as stemming from the same hand, but not that of Rembrandt. These are often paintings that have long been attributed to Rembrandt but have subsequently been detached from the Rembrandt canon as a mini-œuvre, evidently by a single hand and mind and with a recognisable quality .

One such mini-œuvre contains the *Scholar in a Lofty Room* in the London National Gallery (cat. no. 63; fig. 30), the so-called *Rembrandt's Mother* from a private collection (cat. no. 64; fig. 31), and a scene executed on paper which, at first sight, appears to show a rest on the flight to Egypt, but in view of the composition of the company is usually described as *Resting Travellers* (cat. no. 65; fig. 32). There are several reasons for attributing these paintings to the same hand, one of them being that they share the common feature of seeming to have dramatised Rembrandt's expressive language. All three correspondingly demonstrate a rather vacant pathos that is alien to Rembrandt. The large, slack forms of the silhouettes are striking in this

31
Circle of
Rembrandt
Harmensz.
van Rijn,
*Bust of an
Old Woman
(Rembrandt's
Mother?)*,
c. 1628/29
cat. no. 64

32
Circle of Rembrandt
Harmensz. van Rijn,
*Travellers resting (The Rest
on the Flight into Egypt?)*,
c. 1629/30
cat. no. 65

regard. In the technical sense it also striking that they have been worked with scratching into the paint in a manner unusual for Rembrandt. To the end of his life, Rembrandt used scratching with the brush handle into wet paint as a way of rapidly bringing structure to particular passages. In these three paintings, however, it appears that scratching has been used to draw various details: in the *Scholar in a Lofty Room*, hinges, individual bricks and cracks in the plasterwork; in the *Rembrandt's Mother*, eyelashes, wrinkles and the complex structure of the collar and the pleating of the shirt. In the *Resting Travellers* the planks of the lean-to under which the horse stands as well as the stones in the rustic arch under which the silhouetted figure is seated are all drawn by means of scratching. In the lighter sections, the painter uses the paint in simply, sometimes loosely-structured patches, which are rather cumbersome in style. The feeling for detail that is so characteristic of Rembrandt, and the concentration with which he executed the details is absent from all three paintings in a way that at the same time seems to confirm the relationship between the three works.

## Afterword

The demand for a clear demarcation of Rembrandt's œuvre is not new. Over the past two hundred years, dozens of connoisseurs and scholars have presented ‹their› Rembrandt œuvre. Countless polemics have been launched. Members of the public have lost cherished Rembrandts, either lamenting or rebelling against edicts from one authority or another when these paintings suddenly turned out to be no longer by Rembrandt. Many owners were disappointed, angry or embittered when their paintings were removed from the Rembrandt œuvre, while others found themselves unexpectedly to be owners of Rembrandts that had previously been attributed to other painters or had led a dormant existence in anonymity.

Rembrandt research takes place against a background of high emotions. Enormous sums of money are involved on the art market whenever Rembrandt is concerned. The specialist knows how speculative his knowledge is and yet, against his will, is used as an ‹authority› and expected to provide certainty. All too often this certainty is demanded to settle matters of a financial nature, concerning the inheritance of estates, the art trade, investment and other issues that have little or nothing to do with the enjoyment of art or art history.

Of course, the museum public wants to be rid of the continual doubts that surround their favorite Rembrandts, spoiling their enjoyment of the works. Unfortunately, the fact that doubts, which are inherent in any scientific endeavour, should in the case of Rembrandt time and again become front-page news is, as we have seen, unavoidable. This, too, influences the tone of the discussions between insiders; discussions that in themselves ought to be completely normal.

Is it actually worth the effort to clamber about amongst these ‹floating constructions›, often with no clear view or even prospect of certainty? The answer has to be yes! The question of the artistic identity of a great artist will always be there, after all, even if no definitive answer can be given. This question is by now part of our culture for the simple reason that this culture is largely formed by key historical figures such as Rembrandt. More knowledge about Rembrandt therefore means more knowledge about oneself. And new knowledge is certainly produced by investigations of authenticity, even if these are often conducted along different lines than anticipated.

Because we are constantly approaching the diffuse Rembrandt œuvre with different questions and research methods, the spin-off from this research is proving to have a wider significance than initially anticipated. On-going stylistic and formal analyses – these days, increasingly illuminated by seventeenth-century art theory – lead us to think more clearly about the aesthetics underlying Rembrandt's artistic goals and to approach his art with a keener eye. The results of sometimes apparently absurd research investigations on Rembrandt's works – such as X-ray studies of his paintings and etchings (with particular reference to watermarks), the categorising of drawing materials in relation to the function of drawings, the measurement of panels and canvases, the analysis of ground and paint layers, and the analysis of historical texts that at first sight seem to have almost no connection with works of art – can throw light on aspects of art history that previously had been scarcely explored. The knowledge of seventeenth-century studio practices that has been generated by these approaches – of the preparation and supply of materials and equipment, of particular mechanisms of the art market, of contemporary evaluations of specific artistic qualities, of seventeenth-century education methods in the painter's studio, of aspects of the artist's relations to his public, and even of certain sides of the painter's self-image – could all turn out to be of more general interest. The significance of such research may extend far beyond Rembrandt studies in themselves. It should certainly not to be ruled out that this knowledge will also in the long term penetrate to the educational side of museum work, influencing the gaze of the museum visitor, leading him to see better and enjoy more, even when Rembrandt is far from his mind.

[1] This text is translated from Huygens/Heesakkers 1987, p. 85. The Latin text reads: «Quod de Rubenio optabam, ab his praecipue quoque, usurpatum velim, opus operum suorum ut formarent, tabularum tabulam, quâ, artificii sui quisque modestâ mentione factâ, illud omnis aevi miraculo simul et compendio demonstraret, quâ ratione, quo iudicio singula construxisset, ordinasset, elaborasset.»

[2] «eenen leerling, uyt een leersame agtinge, de onderwijsinge van sijnen Meester soo lang volkomen geloof geven, schoon hyze niet geheel en mogte verstaan of goed keuren, tot dat hy na een wijle arbeidens, de waarheid daar van ten alderklaarsten ziet: en alsdan, maar ook niet eer, hemselven daar van van allengskens tragten te ontslaan.» Goeree 1697, 3rd edition, pp. 16f.

[3] «ten einde hy zig die behandeling der verwen en wyze van schilderen gewende, welke hy in dien korten tyd zodanig heeft weten na te bootzen dat verscheiden van zyne stukken voor egte penceel-werken van Rembrant [sic] wierden aangezien en verkogt». Houbraken, vol. 2, 1719, p. 21.

[4] «naer Amsterdam vertrok om Rembrants wyze van schilderen te leeren, 't geen hem zoodanig toeviel en gelukte, dat ik tot zynene roem zeggen moet, dat geen van alle hem zoo na gekomen is in die wyze van schilderen». Houbraken, vol. 3, 1721, p. 206.

[5] Orlers 1641, p. 377f.

[6] Strauss/Meulen 1979, docs. 1630/2 and 4, 1631/3, 7, 9, 10

[7] See survey of Ben Broos in: Amsterdam 1983, pp. 46f.

[8] Sandrart/Peltzer 1925, p. 203.

[9] Ibid.

[10] Jaap van der Veen, «By his own hand, the valuation of autograph paintings in the 17th century», in Corpus, vol. 4, forthcoming.

[11] «Wenn er je einen Meister hatte, so hatte er doch keine Schüler; Holland war nicht dazu gemacht seine Talente zu erkennen.» Füessli 1803, p. 146.

[12] Clark 1969, p. 116.

[13] Schwartz 1984/85/87, p. 10.

[14] Alpers 1988.

[15] Strauss/Meulen 1979, doc. 1632/3.

[16] Strauss/Meulen 1979, doc. 1639/11 and Orlers 1641, p. 377.

[17] Corpus, vol. 2, 1986, «Corrigenda & Addenda» to no. A 32.

[18] See for Jouderville Corpus, vol. 2, 1986, p. 76–86.

[19] Washington/The Hague 2000.

[20] «het na Teyckenen van goede Schilderyen, ende die sal men haer laten van groot in een kleyne proportie brengen, waer door sy terstont leeren gissen, ende een vaste stellinge krijgen.» Goeree 1670, pp. 14f. One still finds such graphic copies from time to time; see for example Wetering 1999/2001.

[21] «Den wegh, om zeker en gewis in het ordineeren te woorden, is, datmen zich gewenne veel Schetssen te maken, en veel Historyen op 't papier te teykenen; want de wetenschap zal u weynich dienen, zoo gy ze door geen oefening vast krijgt». Hoogstraten 1678, p. 191. Many such drawings have been preserved. They have led to numerous problems of attribution; see for example Amsterdam 1985.

[22] See Corpus, vol. 1, 1982, no. A 14; London/The Hague 1999/2000, no. 8; Corpus, vol. 4, «Corrigenda», forthcoming.

[23] Corpus, vol. 1, 1982, no. C 9.

[24] Friedländer 1942, p. 200.

[25] Berenson 1902, p. 147.

[26] Slive 1953.

[27] Heiland/Lüdicke 1960.

[28] «'t Welk ook gemeenlijk met zoo groot vooroordeel geschiet, dat zy zich zelfs inbeelden te zien 't geen'er niet en is; waer van ik proefs genoeg ervaren hebbe: want ik hebbe'er ook met verwondering zien staroogen op ydelheden, die zy zelfs konden verbeteren.» Hoogstraten 1678, p. 197.

[29] Benjamin 1963. For theoretical aspects concerning connoisseurship in relation to Rembrandt's work, see: Corpus, vol. 5, Chapter I, forthcoming.

[30] See cat. no. 58 and the discussion in Corpus, vol. 1, 1982, no. C 23, p. 584, under «Signature».

[31] Hinterding 2001.

[32] «schilderije van Rembrandt gedaen, daer twee oude mannekens sitten en disputeren, den eene heeft een groot bouck op sijn schoot, daer comt een sonnelicht in». Strauss/Meulen 1979, doc. 1641/1.

[33] «een out slapent manneken by een vuijr sittende, sijn hant in den boesem hebbende, mede van Rembrandt gemaeckt». Strauss/Meulen 1979, doc. 1641/1.

[34] «staet wel, als men voor aen in 't brune Eenich Beeldt van de voeten tot de crune overschaduwt/ t'licht latende gheraken slechts den omtreck van naeckte haer oft laaken», Mander/ Miedema 1973, chapter 7, 34.

[35] «oock moet van het Licht, / als een punct of steke / De schaduw' overal nemen haer streke».

[36] Wetering 1988.

[37] See the editions of the Rembrandt Bible compiled by Hofstede de Groot, Amsterdam 1906–10; E. W. Bredt, Munich 1927–28 and Amsterdam 1931; or Internet www.statenvertaling.net.

[38] See here the quotation from Kurt Bauch in cat. no. 62.

[39] It should be borne in mind that dark paint darkens more than light paint. But since this holds equally true for Codde's work, the above observation remains valid. See Wetering 1999/2001; see also Barasch 1978, p. 150 and Chapter 3, «The Venetian School».

[40] See Ernst van de Wetering, «Painting materials and working methods», Corpus, vol. 1, 1982, Chapter II, esp. pp. 16f. and Bruyn 1979.

[41] Hoogstraten 1678, pp. 306–309. See above, note 35.

# Portrait or Character Head?
## The Term *Tronie* and its Meaning in the Seventeenth Century*

*Dagmar Hirschfelder*

### The *tronie* as a subject in Rembrandt's work

Throughout his lifetime, Rembrandt was fascinated by the human face and the possibilities it offered the artist. This trait is already very much in evidence during his early years in Leiden, where he executed works showing busts of individuals dressed in fictive costumes whose facial features receive particular attention (fig. 1). Characteristic of many of these representations is the exceptionally free and rich brushwork and a particularly effective handling of light. In early scholarly research, these works were frequently considered to be self-portraits or depictions of Rembrandt's family, since neither would have bound the artist to the conventions normally applied to commissioned portraits.[1] However, in most cases the identity of the sitter cannot be verified.[2] Moreover, the fact that the same faces appear in comparable single-figure paintings by pupils and followers suggests that the models were professionals. It was only following his move to Amsterdam in 1631 that Rembrandt began to accept commissions for portraits. He nevertheless continued the practice he had begun in Leiden of depicting heads, busts and half-figures depicting old people, soldiers, Orientals, men, women and children in fantasy costumes (fig. 2). While most of these were painted using models, they cannot be classified as portraits in the strict sense of the term. Rather they are anonymous figures, fictive portraits of literary or historical persons, allegorical personifications or exemplary types such as ‹Turks›, ‹Poles› or ‹Russians›; the identity of the model plays no role in the interpretation of the subject. Rembrandt's handling of paint distinguishes these works from his conventional portraits, as in many cases does the posture, facial expressions and gestures of the figures, their relationship to the viewer and the emphasis on their emotions. It is only recently that the study of these works has been recognised as an important area of research, and as yet little attention has been paid to the question of what constitutes a convincing terminological description of the group as a whole. Since it is assumed that the vast majority of these paintings were finished, marketable works of art, the previously preferred term «head study» is problematic even though their execution is extremely free and sometimes even experimental.[3] A more satisfactory designation would be «character head»,[4] even though this does not completely encompass the qualities and scope of the group. More recent studies favour the word *tronie* (pl. *tronies*), which is found in contemporary Netherlandish sources and which in the seventeenth century was synonymous with ‹head›, ‹face› or ‹expression›.[5] It is striking how often the word *tronie* was used to describe works of art in seventeenth-century sales catalogues and inventories. Rembrandt's inventory of 1656, for example, lists over thirty *tronies*.[6] In Harlem in 1704, over a fifth of the 692 entries in the inventory of the estate of Cornelis Dusart were cited as *tronies*.[7] In view of this evidence, two interesting questions arise: which works were described by contemporaries as *tronies*, and to what extent is the term relevant to modern research?

Following an initial overview of how the word *tronie* is used in art historical research, I will undertake a short etymological analysis of the term and examine its usage by contemporaries by evaluating a number of seventeenth and early eighteenth-century artistic treatises, inventories and documented sales.[8]

### The term *tronie* in scholarly research

Up to the present day, it has been mainly Rembrandt scholars who have considered the *tronie* to be an independent art form.[9] Kurt Bauch prepared the way when in his Rembrandt monograph of 1960 he explicitly differentiated between the master's portraits and his «heads and faces», designating the latter as a separate group.[10] He assumed they were initially made for study purposes or as preliminary models for Rembrandt's history paintings but soon became works in their own right.[11] Albert Blankert introduced *tronie* as a scholarly term. In addition to the genres of history painting and portraiture, he recognised in the work of Rembrandt and his pupils «a third category, a sort of ‹in-between› form»,[12] which he called *tronie*. Blankert however failed to consider the extent to which contemporary usage of the word justifies its application to a particular type of picture. The term *tronie* was also used in the 1982 oeuvre-catalogue of the *Rembrandt Research Project* to refer to «heads or busts of interesting types – ‹têtes de caractère›».[13] In addition to busts of mostly anonymous models in fantasy costumes, the authors also considered a number of self-portraits by Rembrandt to be *tronies*.[14] It is however questionable whether it is possible to draw a clear distinction between self-representations where the artist's identity is not the primary interest and historiated self-portraits containing ‹autobiographical› reflections.[15] Another aspect which has not been sufficiently clarified is the necessity of distinguishing between *tronies* and *portraits historiés,* costume-portraits and other seventeenth-century single-figure paintings.

Another difficulty in establishing an exact definition of *tronie* as a technical term is that scholars use the word to describe both independent, marketable works of art and preparatory studies for genre and history paintings.[16] The situation is further complicated by the supposition that the common practice in the sixteenth century, and especially in Flanders, of painting differing views of heads on separate panels in preparation for many-figured compositions may have paved the way for the production and spread of *tronies* in the seventeenth century.[17] The Antwerp painter Frans Floris, for example, made studies of heads which pupils and members of his studio, or even he himself, subsequently transferred to history paintings. These studies were kept in the studio and were frequently re-used.[18] To-

wards the end of the sixteenth century a market for such studies developed, which according to Lyckle de Vries were valued as authentic, stylistically characteristic works of the master.[19] The popularity of the works among collectors may have led to the development of the genre as an independent art form.

### The etymology of the term and its use in the seventeenth century

Even though considerable differences in execution and function characterise those works which scholars refer to as *tronies*, one is frequently led to believe that today's technical term is precisely defined and that its meaning can be derived from the seventeenth-century usage of the word.[20] However, not only is a definition of *tronie* as a pictorial form still out-

2
Rembrandt Harmensz.
van Rijn, *Bust of a Man in
Oriental Costume*, 1633
Panel, 85 x 63.8 cm
Bayerische Staatsgemälde-
sammlungen, Alte
Pinakothek, Munich

*trwyn* (‹nose›). The same origin applies to the Old and Middle-French ‹entroigne› (‹nonsense›, ‹mockery›) and ‹entroignier› (‹to make fun of›, ‹to mock ›), both of which can be traced back to the thirteenth century.[25] The sources of the Netherlandish *tronie* thus clearly possess negative connotations, and only this derisory sense survives today. The numerous orthographic forms derive from two main types: *tronie* (*tro(o)ny, tro(o)ni, tronie*) and *tronje*, which is closer to the French pronunciation and known in many variants.[26]

The word *tronie* was used in relation to paintings in the seventeenth century to describe faces and heads of the most diverse appearance. Karel van Mander is one of the first to use the word in this way when discussing the faces of protagonists in genre and history paintings as well as in altar-pieces. He notes, for example, that in a peasant wedding by Pieter Brugel the Elder: «one sees the faces (*tronien*) and unclothed parts of the bodies of the peasants in yellow and brown as if tanned by the sun – and their skin is ugly [...],»[27] while in the Ghent Altarpiece by the Van Eyck brothers «about 330 complete faces (*tronien*) appear, not one of which resembles another».[28] As Samuel van Hoogstraten's *Inleyding tot de Hooge Schoole der Schilderkonst* of 1678 shows[29], the term continued to be used in a comparable manner throughout the seventeenth century. It is thus evident that when applied to works of art, *tronie* was understood as a neutral reference to the human face or head.[30] Such a generalised application makes it impossible to draw any conclusions about the type of work listed in inventories as *tronies*. Since it cannot be excluded that a painting said to show a ‹face› or ‹head› may simply be a conventional portrait, the next step is to examine whether contemporary sources make a distinction between portraits and those paintings that are today considered to be *tronies*.

While portraits were specifically commissioned works that served primarily memorial and representative purposes, *tronies* are seen as depicting anonymous models, having been produced in large numbers and offered for sale on the open market, often for relatively low prices.[31] In order to distinguish between these two

standing, but it is also necessary to investigate the extent to which contemporary usage of the term can in this respect provide clarification.

From the early sixteenth century *tronie* was synonymous in Netherlandish with ‹face›, ‹facial expression› or ‹head›.[21] In addition to this antiquated meaning, *tronie* could also be used disparagingly to describe a face which arouses disgust, fear or ridicule. Similar to today's usage it meant ‹ugly mug› or ‹wry face›.[22] The word derives from the Middle-French *trongne* (*trogne*), which first appears around 1400 in Christine de Pisan as meaning «fausse apparence d'une chose»,[23] although in the fifteenth century it also occurs as a general designation for ‹face›.[24] *Trongne* is believed to stem from the Gallic *trugna* (‹snout›), which may have been combined with the Cymric

functionally quite different categories, scholars have opted to use the documented terms *conterfeytsel* and *tronie*.[32] However it has not been taken into account that in the seventeenth century, neither referred to a clearly definable pictorial type or genre.[33] Instead they were used descriptively, with *tronie* referring, as outlined above, to the subject, and *conterfeytsel* to the process by which a painting is created. *Conterfeyten* was understood in the sense of copying or imitating.[34] Accordingly a *conterfeytsel* represented an imitation or exact copy of nature.[35] The term applied not just to persons, but also to objects, animals, landscapes, buildings and city views.[36] Nevertheless in seventeenth-century inventories the term *conterfeytsel* is mainly cited in conjunction with the name of the sitter, in which case there can be no doubt that the painting in question is a portrait.[37] But as portraits are often just of a head or bust, it is equally possible to find them listed as *tronies* and not as *conterfeytsels*.[38]

It is interesting to note that when van Mander uses the word *tronie* in relation to portraits, he does so by directly connecting it to the term *conterfeytsel*[39] in order to draw attention to the face of the sitter:

> «There is an especially beautiful, distinguished portrait (*Conterfeytsel*) by him in Leiden in the Breestraat, which is of a young girl called Sara Schuyrmans; it extends to below the knees. As well as the satins, the clothes and the hands playing upon a zither, which are all well executed, the face (*tronie*) is admirable above all; it is a very good likeness, very carefully done [...]».[40]

From van Manders usage it can be concluded that when they chose the word *tronie* for portraits cited in inventories, contemporaries were alluding to the reduced picture format showing a head or bust. Conversely, the identification of a *tronie* as a *conterfeytsel* is also easily explained. The ‹conterfeyten of a tronie› simply means the faithful representation of the face of any model. It was evidently common practice in the seventeenth century to paint *tronies* ‹naar het Leven›, from life; when Rembrandt and his circle painted *tronies* they used the same models time and again.[41] Thus descriptions such as «een conterfeytsel van een oude manstrony»[42] or «een contrefeytsel manstronie met witten baert van van Dyck»[43] do not necessarily refer to portraits, but could also mean character or head studies painted from life. An equally ambiguous application of *tronie* occurs when the word is followed by details concerning the sitter: «Noch een cleine oostersche vrouwen tronie het conterfeisel van H. Ulenburgs huijsvrouwe nae Rembrant».[44] Citing the model's name does not automatically imply that the work in question is a conventional portrait, nor that the painter intended the sitter to be recognisable. According to de Vries, the identity of a model was of particular interest to a collector, who could thus «demonstrate his direct contacts with a famous artist, and his intimate knowledge of the genesis of the painter's works.»[45]

From the above it is apparent that the function of paintings called *tronies* or *conterfeytsels* cannot be derived directly from the contemporary usage of the terms. Nevertheless, in most cases the choice of a particular nomenclature in the sources does, it would seem, seek to indicate different types of paintings. Van Mander appears to be making such a distinction when writing about Geldorp Gortzius in his *Schilder-boeck*: «His works, in particular the multitude of portraits (*Conterfeytselen*) and distinguished faces (*tronien*) made by him, are most abundant [...]».[46] It can be assumed that van Mander would not have used two different terms to refer to the same pictorial type, i.e. portraits. Instead he distinguishes the painting of *tronies* as an art form in its own right and quite separate from portraiture. And even if van Mander did not understand *tronies* in the same way we do today, but rather as depictions of saints or of Christ,[47] his terminological differentiation is still remarkable.

So while the terms *tronie* and *conterfeytsel* are not mutually exclusive, they are also not identical, as each emphasises a different aspect of a painting. Describing a work as a *conterfeytsel* is to convey that the exact imitation of nature was the foremost concern of the painter. Since the «goet ghelijcken»,[48] to quote van Mander, was an important goal of portraiture,[49] conter-

*feytsel* is obviously the more appropriate choice when describing a portrait. *Tronie,* by comparison, is more neutral, since it refers less to heads which must bear a recognisable resemblance to the sitters but rather to ones which could belong to any individual. When mentioned in inventories, *tronies* are frequently characterised as anonymous figures by certain additions, such as *(oude) manstronie, (oude) vrouwetronie, jongenstrony, meydetrony, kindertrony, Juffrouw trony,*[50] It is, of course, still possible that the work in question is a portrait, yet the statistics suggest otherwise. In the inventories published in the *Getty Provenance Index,* the term *tronie* is used 1084 times for paintings, but in only 50 (or 4.6%) of those cases is the sitter named or otherwise identified.[51] By comparison, of the 2727 *conterfeytsels* in the *GPI,* 1857 (68.1%) are unquestionably portraits, as the sitter is identified.[52] It is moreover notable that *tronie* is frequently applied to biblical, historical, mythological and genre characters, that is to figures where the identity of the model is usually of no consequence. The subjects of entries such as «een Cristus tronie van Rembrant»,[53] «een Lievrouwentronie naer Rubbens»,[54] «een satyrs troni van Jordaens»,[55] «een boere tronij van Brouwer»[56] or «1 Sotstronie naer Joerdanes»[57] clearly preclude their being *portraits historiés.* And even where this is not altogether clear, as in the following examples: «een Sinte-Pieterstronie, nae Jacob Adriaensz. Backer»,[58] «twe tronyen van Heraklites en Democritus»,[59] «een Diana's tronie van Moreelsz»[60] or «een trony synde een harderin van Hoogstraeten»,[61] there are in general no references to the sitter, which would lead us to conclude that the paintings were not considered portraits. By contrast, the title «een Conterfeytsel van de moeder van zalr Jan Boursse antijcqx gedaen»[62] is far more likely to mean a portrait in fantasy costume.

Even though in most cases the term *tronie* does not refer to portraits, it does embrace a very heterogeneous group of works. Among these are busts of anonymous and iconographically identifiable figures as well as studies[63] and sculpted works such as heads carved from stone and marble or moulded in plaster.[64] In addition, particularly detailed inventories mention characteristic features or attributes of *tronies* that indicate that not only heads and busts, but also half and possibly even three-quarter-length depictions were called *tronies:* «een studenten Tronie nae Rembrant halff lichaems met een Clapmuts»,[65] «een vrouwe tronij leunende met de hant op een stoel van Rembrant van Rijn»,[66] «noch een tronitge van een vrouw met ongevlechten haire met twee kinderen aen de borst».[67] Accordingly, it is probable that paintings termed *tronies* but not described in any great detail may have shown more than just the head of the sitter. It must also be borne in mind when evaluating inventory entries that even contemporaries may not have had knowledge of the circumstances surrounding the creation of a work so that it must have been very difficult to distinguish between anonymous models in fantasy costume, *portraits historiés* and experimental self-portraits.[68] Thus the term applied in the sources will not always tally with the artist's original intentions. Moreover, the different philological backgrounds of those drawing up inventories and valuations should be taken into account. For example, many of the portraits cited in the list of paintings belonging to Chrispiaen Colyn and auctioned in Amsterdam in 1612 are called *tronies,*[69] while the term *conterfeytsel*

3
Jan Lievens, Title: *Diverse Tronikens geetst van J. L., Jacobus Christianus Excudit*
Etching, 76 x 61 mm
Staatliche Museen zu Berlin, Preußischer Kulturbesitz, Kupferstichkabinett

is not used at all. On the other hand, the inventory of Cornelis Dusart's collection, drawn up in 1704, mentions both *portretten*,[70] in many cases including details about the sitter, and a number of *tronies*. The latter were certainly not portraits, as they are attributed to genre painters such as Adriaen Brouwer, Adriaen and Isaak van Ostade or other ‹*tronie* painters›.[71] Thus, before drawing any conclusions about the meaning of *tronie* in an inventory, it is necessary to consider the collection's structure and – where possible – to determine the specific linguistic background of the person responsible for drawing up the inventory.

**Pictorial examples**

I wish to conclude by looking at some extant works which contemporaries identified as *tronies*. This is the case for a large number of etched busts by Jan Lievens, which were often bound together in series. A title page of such a series in Berlin shows a cartouche bearing the inscription *Diverse Tronikens geetst von J. L., Jacobus Christianus Excudit* (fig. 3).[72] Lievens's etched *tronies* show interesting character heads with very individual physiognomies and wearing a variety of costumes, including oriental ones (fig. 4).[73] In 1658 Jan C. Visscher brought out a series comprising seventy-two peasant heads which are organised in pairs and attributed by the publisher to Pieter Bruegel the Elder.[74] The series is entitled «snaeckse Tronjen», and the accompanying satirical inscriptions identify the figures as foolish and lewd characters.[75] This suggests that at least in this context the word *tronie* has a rather negative connotation suggesting ‹ugly mug› or ‹grimace›.[76]

Only rarely can entries in seventeenth-century inventories and sale catalogues be linked with known works of art. One interesting exception is the correlation between the *Bust of an Old Woman* (fig. 5) at Windsor Castle and the description of a painting in Jacques de Gheyn III's testament of 1641: «A painting of an old *tronie*, with violet velvet lined with gold cloth over the head, done life-size with a frame around it».[77] Since the *tronie* in Windsor had entered the English royal collection at some point prior to 1641, it could not have figured

4
Jan Lievens, *Bust of an Old Man in a Fur Cap*
Etching, 164 x 144 mm
State III (5)
Museum het Rembrandthuis, Amsterdam

in de Gheyn's inventory. However, according to the authors of the *Corpus*, the entry in the testament suggests that de Gheyn's painting was an exact copy of the one at Windsor.[78]

Even though it is often difficult to establish with certainty a connection between existing works and inventory entries, it is obvious that specific designations – a «turcxe tronij van Rembrant»,[79] «een laggende tronie van Reynbrant»,[80] «een Moriaens tronie»,[81] or «een krijgsmanstroonij»[82] – provide convincing titles for a number of those works which are today considered to be *tronies*. Perhaps the «turcxe tronij» identified a painting like Rembrandt's *Oriental* of 1633 in Munich (cf. fig. 2), while «een laggende tronie» may have referred to a work such as the *Bust of a Laughing Man in a Gorget* (cat. no. 79) in the Mauritshuis, The Hague.[83]

5
Jan Lievens, *Bust of an
Old Woman (so-called
Rembrandt's Mother)*
Panel, 61 x 47.4 cm
The Royal Collection,
Her Majesty Queen
Elizabeth II,
Windsor Castle

## Summary

In summary, we can conclude that the term *tronie* in the seventeenth century was not applied to a certain pictorial type and certainly did not describe a particular genre. The evaluation of the sources does, however, show that in the first instance *tronies* referred to heads and busts of anonymous, fictive and literary figures. For portraits the term *conterfeytsel* was usually used, while in the late seventeenth and early eighteenth centuries the word *portret* became increasingly common. Describing a painting as a *tronie* generally implied that the sitter's face is the main focus, although the possibility cannot be excluded that it also encompassed half-figure paintings. The fact that many of those works listed in the sources as *tronies* are not described in any detail suggests that the term may have been chosen where a more exact iconographical identification proved difficult.

The analysis of the philological history of the term *tronie* justifies its use for single-figure paintings of the type most commonly associated with Rembrandt in so far as a distinction from portraiture is intended. Nevertheless the seventeenth-century usage of the word does not provide a suitable basis for a general definition of *tronie* as a particular pictorial form or exercise. Instead, it is the extant works themselves which must be taken as the point of departure for any such endeavour, and it is here that the enormous potential of Rembrandt's early works is evident. His early *tronies* were created within the context of his history paintings and not, as one might expect, in relation to portraiture, and indeed they are formally quite different from his early portraits. They are thus easily recognisable as a distinct group within his oeuvre and one for which the word *tronie* is a most suitable term.

* The following essay is based on a lecture given at the symposium ‹Tronies› in de Italiaanse, Vlaamse en Nederlandse schilderkunst van de 16de en 17de eeuw (The Hague, October 19–20, 2000). I am grateful to Professor Hans-Joachim Raupp for valuable suggestions and a critical reading of my manuscript.

1 Cf. Bredius 1935; Münz 1953; Bredius/Gerson 1969.

2 Cf. Blankert 1997/98, pp. 45–46.

3 Cf. Bauch 1960, pp. 175–180.

4 Cf. already Valentiner, p. 37; Bruyn 1982, p. 40.

5 Cf. WNT, vol. 17/2, 1979, column 3209–3221.

6 Strauss/Meulen 1979, doc. 1656/12. For the frequency of *tronies* in Amsterdam inventories cf. Montias 1991, tab. 2–4, pp. 350ff.

7 Inv. Cornelis Dusart, Haarlem 1704, in: GPI 2000, N-5636.

8 The evaluated works include: Miedema, vol. 1, 1994; Hoogstraten 1678; Bredius; Denucé; Strauss/Meulen 1979; Antwerpse Kunstinventarissen; GPI 2000. The hitherto most extensive studies of the term *tronie* are by Pauw-de Veen 1969, pp. 190–193, and Schwartz 1989, pp. 112–114. Cf. in addition Müller Hofstede 1968, pp. 226; Held 1970, pp. 285f., 291f.

9 Cf. Blankert 1982, pp. 26–28, 57–59; Bruyn 1982, esp. p. 40; Bruyn/Wetering 1982, p. 8; Tümpel 1986, pp. 57–61, 187, 299; Bruyn 1989, esp. pp. 22–26; Schwartz 1989; Vries 1989; Kobayashi-Sato 1994; Vries 1995; Raupp 1995, pp. 13f.; Veen 1997/98; Wetering 1999/2000, pp. 21f., 36. In recent times paintings by artists who do not belong to the immediate circle of Rembrandt have also been described as *tronies*, e.g. Frans Hals's heads of children, merry drinkers and musicians, as well

as isolated half-figure paintings by the Utrecht Caravaggists. Bruyn 1988; Stukenbrock 1993, esp. p. 36. For Abraham Bloemaert's *tronies*, see Seelig 1997, pp. 120–126.

[10] Bauch 1960, p. 168.

[11] Bauch 1960, p. 178. Cf. also Tümpel 1986, pp. 57–61, 187.

[12] Blankert 1982, p. 26.

[13] Bruyn 1982, p. 40.

[14] Corpus, passim; Bruyn/Wetering 1982, p. 8; Bruyn 1989, p. 25. Cf. also London/The Hague 1999/2000, nos. 5, 8, 10, 14a, 18, 40, 42, 49, 52.

[15] Cf. Vries 1989, p. 194; Wetering 1999/2000, pp. 21, 36.

[16] Cf. Müller Hofstede 1968; Held 1970; Velde 1975, pp. 65–74; Held 1980, vol. 1, pp. 599–614; Urbach 1983, esp. pp. 6f., 19; Müller Hofstede 1987/88; Thiel 1999, pp. 105f., 125f., 142f.

[17] Vries 1989, p. 191. Cf. already Bauch 1960, p. 178.

[18] Cf. Velde 1975, pp. 65–74. In the 17th. century, artists such as Peter Paul Rubens, Anthonis van Dyck and Jacob Jordaens still used preparatory head studies, cf. note 16. These *tronies* were last discussed at the symposium ‹Tronies› *in de Italiaanse, Vlaamse en Nederlandse schilderkunst van de 16de en 17de eeuw*, The Hague, Royal Library, October 19–20, 2000. Cf. Hirschfelder/Raupp 2001.

[19] Vries 1989, p. 191.

[20] Sumowski 1983ff., vol. 1, p. 23, note 68, writes that the term *tronie* was «in Holland already in the 17th century a common term to describe a genre» («in Holland schon im 17. Jahrhundert als Gattungsbezeichnung [...] üblich»). Cf. Tümpel 1986, p. 299.

[21] Cf. note 5.

[22] WNT, vol. 17/2, 1979, column 3212–14, I.1.b. It is assumed that the Middle Dutch form *troenie*, which was first recorded in 1468 and appears to have had a meaning close to ‹drollery› or ‹joke›, is the same as *tronie*. WNT, vol. 17/2, 1979, column 3216, I.4.; MW, vol. 8, 1916, column 701

[23] Wartburg, vol. 13/1, 1966, p. 332f. Cf. Christine de Pisan, *Le Livre de la Mutacion de Fortune*, 2 vols, ed. Suzanne Solente, Paris 1959, vol. 1, p. 62, 6093.

[24] Cf. Wartburg, vol. 13/1, 1966, pp. 332f.; Trésor de la langue française, vol. 16, 1994, p. 653.

[25] Cf. Godefroy 1982, vol. 3, pp. 307f.

[26] WNT, vol. 17/2, 1979, column 3209. The common forms of *tronje* are: *troegne, troigne, trogni(e), troengne, trongne, trongnie, troenge, troengie(-ye), trong(h)e*. In the plural -n and -s were added. The most common form found in the sources is tronie/tronien: The singular *tronie* occurs in 224 of the 51020 Netherlandish inventory entries of the seventeenth and eighteenth centuries published in the GPI 2000; the plural *tronien* 88 times. By comparison the spelling *trony* is found in only 82 entries, the plural *tronies* in just 14. Moreover, both Karel van Mander and Samuel van Hoogstraten normally used *tronie(n)*.

[27] «men siet der Boeren tronien en naeckten, gheel en bruyn, als van de Son verbrandt, en leelijck van huydt wesende». Miedema, vol. 1, 1994, fol. 233v, 30–32.

[28] «ontrent 330. gheheel tronien, daer niet een d'ander gelijck en is». Miedema, vol. 1, 1994, fol. 200v, 15–16.

[29] Hoogstraten 1678, p. 31: «Maer tot het teykenen van tronien, handen, of geheele naeckten na 't leven, moogt gy gesmijdich root krijt op wit papier gebruiken.»; p. 44: «Veele hebben zich 't na 't leeven schilderen van menschentronien onderwonden, [...]. Een goode trony te kunnen maken is wel prijsselijk, maar een welstandige figuer met een maer taemelijke trony te maken, is meer». Cf. also Goeree 1682, p. 210ff.; WNT, vol. 17/2, 1979, column 3217ff.

[30] The use of the word in its meaning as a «head» is particularly prevalent for sculpted works. Cf. Inv. Jeremias Wildens, Antwerp 1653/54, in: Antwerpse Kunstinventarissen, vol. 1/6, 1992, doc. 1902, pp. 477f., 488f.

[31] Cf. Vries 1989, pp. 191–194; Veen 1997/98, p. 71.

[32] Cf. Veen 1997/98. For the term *conterfeytsel*, see Pauw-de Veen 1969, pp. 193–199; Schwartz 1989, pp. 112–114. The word

*portret* (from French *portrait*) is found from about 1640, but is only common in inventories after 1690. Of the 655 published entries citing *portretten* in the GPI 2000 only 22 date from before 1680. For the term *portret*, see WNT, vol. 12/2, 1949, column 3545–3549; Pauw-de Veen 1969, pp. 193–197; Pommier 1998, pp. 15–18.

[33] Cf. Held 1970, pp. 285f.; Schwartz 1989, p. 113.

[34] Cf. WNT, vol. 7/2, 1941, column 5312–5314.

[35] Cf. van Mander's frequent use of the expression «conterfeytselen nae t'leven». Miedema, vol. 1, 1994, fol. 264v, 23; fol. 265r, 4; fol. 280r, 32–33.

[36] Pauw-de Veen 1969, pp. 193f. Cf. Inv. Isaack Jacobsz. van Hooren, Amsterdam 1652, in: Bredius, vol. 3, 1917, p. 768, no. 8: «een conterfeijtsel van schapen en een dito van een bock»; Inv. Eijtje Ipens, Amsterdam 1653, in: GPI 2000, N-2261, no. 17: «1 conterfeijtsel van Dordregt met een ebbe lijst».

[37] Cf. Inv. Reijncke Gerrits, Amsterdam 1647, in GPI 2000, N-2275, no. 19: «Het contrefeijtsel van Atje Jaricx, in een ovael met een ebben lijst, van Govert Flinck»; Inv. Maritge Dircxs, Haarlem 1664, in: GPI 2000, N-2489, no. 2: «Noch twee conterfeytsels vande overledenens vader en moeder sa»; Inv. Jan Miense Molenaer, Haarlem 1668, in: GPI 2000, N-5314, no. 156: «2 Conterfeytsels van Jan Molenaer ende sijn huysvrou van Frans Hals, sonder lijst».

[38] Cf. Inv. Albert Vinckenbrinck and Geertruyd Collaert, Amsterdam 1665, in: GPI 2000, N-2311, no. 112: «De trony off het conterfeijtsel van de voorszegde Geertruyd Collaert zaliger, geschildert door Hendrick van den Broeck».

[39] Cf. also Hoogstraten 1678, p. 87, writing about portrait painters: «Jae de konterfeyters, die al reedelijke gelijkenissen maeken, [...] wil ik zelfs niet buiten, of booven den eersten graet stellen, ten zyze haere tronyen der gemelde hoedanigheyt van de verstandelijke ziele overstorten».

[40] «Een besonder schoon heerlijck Conterfeytsel is van hem [Hans van Aken] te Leyden in de Bree-straet, wesende een jonghe dochter, genoemt Sara Schuyrmans, en comt groot tot beneden de knien: boven dat Satijnen, cleeren, en de spelende handen op een Cyter, wel ghedaen zyn, is boven al verwonderlijck de tronie, die wel gelijckende, heel suyver ghedaen, [...] is». Miedema, vol. 1, 1994, fol. 290v, 39–44. Cf. also Miedema, vol. 1, 1994, fol. 254r, 29–33.

[41] In Rembrandt's inventory of 1656 five *tronies* are described as painted from life. Cf. Strauss/Meulen 1979, doc. 1656/12, no. 66: «Een tronie nae 't leven van Rembrant».

[42] Inv. Johannes Beerstraten, Amsterdam 1667, in: Bredius, vol. 3, 1917, p. 814, no. 7. The word *conterfeytsel* could also refer to depictions of historical or fictive persons. Cf. e.g. Inv. Jan Lievens, Amsterdam 1674, in: Bredius, vol. 1, 1915, p. 188, no. 8: «Conterfeytsel van Venus en Adonis».

[43] Inv. Jan-Baptista Anthoine, Antwerp 1691, in: Denucé, vol. 2, 1932, doc. 118, p. 356, no. 58.

[44] Inv. Lambert Jacobsz., Leeuwarden 1637, in: Strauss/Meulen 1979, doc. 1637/4. Cf. also the invoice for paintings sold by Dirck van Cattenburgh to his sister, Amsterdam 1658, in: Strauss/Meulen 1979, doc. 1658/22: «een schilderij sijnde een tronye door Rembrant nae hem selven geschildert».

[45] Vries 1989, p. 197.

[46] «Sijn wercken, bysonder de menichte der Conterfeytselen, en heerlijcke tronien van hem ghedaen, zijn seer overloedigh [...]». Miedema, vol. 1, 1994, fol. 280v, 15–17. Cf. also Miedema, vol. 1, 1994, fol. 298v, 32–34.

[47] Further above, van Mander mentions «twee schoone tronien, van Christus, en Maria» by Gortzius, which were in Cologne. Miedema, vol. 1, 1994, fol. 280v, 7–8.

[48] Miedema, vol. 1, 1994, fol. 291r, 8–11; fol. 292v, 11–30, 20.

[49] Cf. Jongh 1986, pp. 20–25; Veen 1997/98, p. 73.

[50] Such an addition is found in about one-third of the 1084 inventory entries of *tronies* (sculpted works excluded) published in GPI 2000. Cf. esp. Inv. Aert Coninx, Amsterdam 1639, in: GPI 2000, N-2071; Inv. Cornelis Dusart, Haarlem 1704, in: GPI

2000, N-5636; cf. also Inv. Jeremias Wildens, Antwerp 1653/54, in: Antwerpse Kunstinventarissen, vol. 1/6, 1992, doc. 1902, pp. 494f.

51 Even if inventories do not name the sitter they frequently list his or her relationship to the deceased, thus making an identification possible. Cf. note 37.

52 No sculpted works have been included and only those paintings called *conterfeytsel* where no additional information is given that would exclude the possibility of their being portraits.

53 Inv. Rembrandt, Amsterdam 1656, in: Strauss/Meulen 1979, doc. 1656/12, no. 118.

54 Inv. Erasmus Quellinus, Antwerp 1679, in: Antwerpse Kunstinventarissen, vol. 1/10, 1999, doc. 3333, p. 355.

55 Inv. Abraham Peronneau, Amsterdam 1692, in: Bredius, vol. 3, 1917, p. 850, no. 30.

56 Inv. Cornelis Dusart, Haarlem 1704, in: GPI 2000, N-5636, no. 185.

57 Forchoudt Brothers, Sales Register (no. 170, fol. 1), Antwerp 1671/11/14, in: Denucé, vol. 1, 1931, p. 122, no. 32.

58 Inv. Aert Coninx, Amsterdam 1639, in: GPI 2000, N-2071, no. 126.

59 Inv. Pieter van der Voort, Amsterdam 1624, in: Bredius, vol. 4, 1917, p. 1179, no. 67.

60 Inv. Aert Coninx, Amsterdam 1639, in: GPI 2000, N-2071, no. 7.

61 Picture sale Abraham de Cooge, Delft 1680/03/28, in: Bredius, vol. 5, 1918, p. 1512, no. 10.

62 Inv. Jan Boursse, Amsterdam 1671, in: Bredius, vol. 1, 1915, p. 121, no. 2.

63 From the end of the 16th century *tronies* by Frans Floris which were certainly head studies were listed in Antwerp inventories. Cf. Velde 1975, p. 489, doc. 102, pp. 500–502, doc. 129–131. In many cases, drawn *tronies* probably also belonged to the category of studies. Cf. Inv. Cornelis van Loo/Dorothea Olijcan, Haarlem 1673, in: GPI 2000, N-4591, no. 31: «1 ditto tronij geteyckent van Hendr. Goltzius».

64 Cf. Inv. Frederick Alewijn, Amsterdam 1665, in: GPI 2000, N-2349, no. 45: «1 tronij van pleijster»; Inv. Lodewyck van der Helst, Amsterdam 1671, in: Bredius, vol. 2, 1916, p. 407, no. 10: «Een gebootseerde tronie»; Inv. Jeremias Wildens, Antwerp 1653/54, in: Antwerpse Kunstinventarissen, vol. 1/6, 1992, doc. 1902, no. 81: «Een marmore Manstronie».

65 Inv. Aert Conincx, Amsterdam 1639, in: Strauss/Meulen 1979, doc. 1639/9.

66 Inv. Herman Becker, Amsterdam 1678, in: GPI 2000, N-2288, no. 135.

67 Inv. Louis van den Queborn, The Hague 1658, in: Bredius, vol. 4, 1917, p. 1151.

68 Cf. Schwartz 1989, p. 114.

69 Auction of paintings belonging to Chrispiaen Colyn, Amsterdam 1612, in: Bredius, vol. 3, 1917, p. 1072, no. 124: «1 tronje van de Graef van Egmont»; p. 1073, no. 147: «1 tronje von Duc D'Alva».

70 Cf. note 32.

71 Inv. Cornelis Dusart, Haarlem 1704, in: GPI 2000, N-5636.

72 Schatborn assumes that this title relates to the etchings Hollstein 60, 64–68, 70, however noting that it is impossible to connect the title page and the series with absolute certainty. Amsterdam 1988/89, p. 6 and 9, note 4. Cf. also Bruyn 1982, p. 40, note 8.

73 That these works were intended as portraits is improbable, not least because Lievens used the same models in a number of other works, such as the so-called Rembrandt's Father (fig. 4). Cf. Münz 1953.

74 *Tooneel des Wereldts ontdeckende de Ongestuymigheden en Ydelheden in woorden ende wercken deser verdorvene Eeuwe. Op-gepronckt met aerdige, en zin-rijcke Versen, benevens twee-en-tseventigh snaeckse Tronjen, getekent door den Konstigen Schilder p. Bruegel. Weesp 1658.*

75 Cf. Raupp 1986, pp. 302–304; Muylle 1994, pp. 257f.

76 Cf. also the description of Quinten Metsijs's grotesque heads by Alexander van Fornenbergh, *Den Antwerpschen Protheus ofte Cyclopschen Apelles dat is: het leven ende konstrycke daden van Quinten Metsys [...]*, Antwerp 1658, p. 31: «Van hem sijn oock eenighe ouw-bollighe Monstreuse Tronyen te sien, Mans en Vrouwen [...]». Quoted in Muylle 1994, p. 258.

77 «een schilderije van een oude tronigne, die violet fluweel mit goude laecken gevoedert op het hooft heeft, wesende soe groot als het leven mit een lijst daerom». Inv. Jacques de Gheyn III, Utrecht 1641, in: GPI 2000, N-1677, no. 11.

78 Corpus, vol. 1, 1982, p. 321. Cf. also White 1982, no. 58, pp. 101ff. Whereas the painting is considered to be by Rembrandt in the first volume of the *Corpus*, in the second a possible attribution to Jan Lievens is discussed. Corpus, vol. 1, 1982, no. A 32; Corpus, vol. 2, 1986, p. 839.

79 Inv. Frederick Alewijn, Amsterdam 1665, in: Strauss/Meulen 1979, doc. 1665/23.

80 Inv. Harmanus van der Ceel, Delft 1656, in: Strauss/Meulen 1979, doc. 1656/21.

81 Inv. Edo Quiter, Amsterdam 1694, in: Bredius, vol. 5, 1918, p. 1525, no. 37.

82 Inv. Aeltge Velthuysen (Widow of Carel Fabritius), Amsterdam 1634, in: Brown 1981, p. 147, doc. 6.

83 In Corpus, vol. 1, 1982, p. 633 the identification of the *Bust of a Laughing Man* (no. C 34) in the Rijksmuseum (Amsterdam) with the laughing *tronie* in Harmanus van der Ceel's inventory (cf. note 80) is considered possible.

# Young Rembrandt's «Rough Manner»
## A Painting Style and its Sources[*]

*Bernhard Schnackenburg*

### «Various sorts» of Rembrandt paintings

On December 8, 1750, Landgrave Wilhelm VIII of Hesse-Kassel wrote an enthusiastic account to his friend Baron Häckel in Frankfurt of his acquisition from Valerius Röver's widow of the famous Delft collection of paintings, founded by Valerius Röver senior in Amsterdam in the seventeenth century: «Among them [the paintings] are eight Rembrandts of such perfection that has never been seen before and of every sort and of the best manners of this master. Some are painted in the rough, thickly applied manner, while others are as fine as hardly seems possible for a Gerard Dou and Mieris.»[1] For the latter «sort», the founder of the Kassel Gallery may have been thinking of the very ornate *Portrait of Saskia van Uylenburgh in Profile in a Rich Costume* (fig. 1) with its finely painted pearls, while the broad brushstrokes and striking relief-like layers of colour in the *Bust of an Old Man with Golden Chain* (cat. no. 81) may

have been an example of the former (fig. 2; alongside, for comparative purposes, a work by a student of Rembrandt's, to be discussed below). These works are indeed astonishingly diverse in execution, a fact that no one could fail to notice since their comparatively small size (99.5 x 78.8 cm and 59.6 x 49.3 cm) demands close-up viewing. The manual act of painting is negated in the *Saskia* as minute brushstrokes invisibly merge with one another to capture form in space and light, whereas each of the broad isolated strokes of the loaded brush in the *Old Man with Golden Chain* creates its own pictorial structure and thereby renders visible the dynamics of painting and the physical presence of the painting's creator. A particularly good example of this process can be seen in the area of the forehead just above the base of the nose. There, single lines of thick flesh colour have their own plasticity with edges formed by the start and finish of each application of the brush. As these strokes run contrary to the horizontal wrinkles of the brow, they appear to have detached themselves and hover just above the surface of the old man's face. Further above, on his forehead, brightly illuminated dabs of whitish pigments form a relief.

Wilhelm VIII's account is of historical interest because he was resident in the Netherlands from 1703 to 1727. Known as «Prins Willem» of Hesse, he served as military commander of the citadel in the border town of Breda and later on in Maastricht. He enjoyed close ties with the court, since his sister Marie Luise was married to Johann Wilhelm Friso of Orange-Nassau, and as such is an ancestor of the present Dutch Royal Family. But Wilhelm was also in contact with artists, collectors and dealers, and was actively involved in discussions about art in the epoch that immediately followed the «Golden Age», the age of Rembrandt.[2] The very diverse nature of Rembrandt's painting is one of the principle aspects addressed in the first detailed Dutch biography of the artist, which appeared in the first volume of

1
Rembrandt Harmensz. van Rijn, *Portrait of Saskia van Uylenburgh in Profile in a Rich Costume* (detail: pearls on her left arm), c. 1634–42
Oak panel, 99.5 x 78.8 cm
Staatliche Museen Kassel, Gemäldegalerie Alte Meister

Arnold Houbraken's *Groote Schouburgh*, a biography of Netherlandish artists published in 1718.[3] Houbraken was himself a painter and a follower of the by then firmly established school of pure classicism. From his point of view, the differences in Rembrandt's work were the result of diminishing diligence, lack of meticulousness or simply careless daubing with paint. Rembrandt sought to prevent visitors to his studio from getting too close to his freshly painted works by warning that they would be overcome by paint fumes. Houbraken did not, however, accuse his famous compatriot of ineptitude, but rather of obstinacy and a disregard for generally accepted rules of art. The phenomenal success of Rembrandt's painting remained something of a mystery, but one that was indisputable and willingly acknowledged by Houbraken. Despite all his theoretical remonstrations, he concedes at the end of the book that even those works of the old master in which paint was applied «as if with a trowel» were so in demand that art lovers had to request such works repeatedly, exercise patience and pay high prices. Finally he cited a portrait which in strength and artistic mastery exceeded anything by van Dyck or Rubens.

At the very moment when this standard work appeared in print, the founder of the Kassel Gallery was in Holland. Of all that had been written about Rembrandt, Houbraken's portrayal of this disputed outsider, this mysterious genius, must have impressed him the most. His fascination was so great that he became one of the most obsessive collectors of Rembrandt of his age.[4] Yet it was only natural that he also sought works by the other great Dutch painters of the «rough manner»; indeed, he established the first collection of works by Frans Hals outside of Holland.[5] The diversity in execution of the Rembrandt paintings from the Röver collection quite clearly captivated him; so much so, in fact, that he failed to mention anything about their subjects in his letter to Baron Häckel.[6] The acquisition confirmed his belief that Rembrandt was unusually versatile and capable of creating

2
Rembrandt Harmensz. van Rijn, *Bust of an Old Man with Golden Chain* (detail of the face), 1632
Cat. no. 81

3
Rembrandt-Studio, *Bust of a Man with Unkempt Hair* (detail of the face), 1635
Oak panel, 66.6 x 52.6 cm
Private Collection, New York

paintings of «various sorts». Such a talent possessed a value all its own and one which he did not attempt to justify by speculating, for example, if the two paintings belonged to different creative phases. Such a question would in this case have been fruitless. Wilhelm VIII does not appear to have noticed or even cared that the dates 1642 and 1632 inscribed next to Rembrandt's signatures on the *Saskia* and the *Old Man with Golden Chain,* respectively, are relatively close, since they are not cited in the entries in the 1749 inventory of the painting collection.[7] Today we know that most parts of the Kassel *Saskia* had already been painted c. 1634.

## The «rough manner»: development, dissemination and the reaction of art critics

In seventeenth-century Holland, «rough manner» was a common technical designation[8] for a rough, free and highly autographic style of painting in which the paint is perceived as matter. As such, the «rough manner» was the direct opposite of the «fine manner», which was characterised by eliminating all signs of transition and creating a smooth surface which negated both paint as matter and the manual act of painting. Since the beginnings of oil painting in the fifteenth century, the «fine manner» was both the norm and standard, whereas the «rough manner», though known in ancient times and referred to in antique literary sources, only re-entered the art world in the middle of the sixteenth century, in Venice, where Tintoretto, Jacopo Bassano and Titian (in his later years) became its most influential proponents.[9] It was subsequently taken up by Italian Baroque painters such as Strozzi, Preti and Giordano, to name but a few. Spain produced two of the greatest painters in the «rough manner»: El Greco, who was trained in Venice, and Velazquez; while in Flanders, Rubens, van Dyck and Jordaens introduced new vitality using a broad impasto. In Holland, by comparison, Karel van Mander upheld, in his influential *Grondt der edel vry schilder-const* of 1604, the age of such artists as van Eyck, Dürer and Lucas van Leyden, while criticising his contemporaries: «The pigments today lie so rough and uneven that one could take them for a relief hewn from hard stone». This surprising statement must surely be read an exaggeration designed to serve an educational purpose and not as a description of reality.[10] Holland was and re-

mained almost entirely a land of fine painting, so it is no surprise that Rembrandt and Frans Hals, the two principal proponents of the «rough manner», should have stood out. Van Mander did, however, recommend the «rough manner» – at least as a theoretical possibility.[11] In this, he displayed greater openness and interest in experimentation than the majority of art critics before or after him, who regarded the painting style of even the best-known masters with ambivalence and open scepticism.[12] Only one later treatise, Marco Boschini's *La Carta del navegar pitoresco* (The Map of Pictorial Navigation), published in Venice in 1660, lavished unconditional praise on the «painterly» style of the Venetians and elevated it to the quintessence of painting.[13] In the minds of sixteenth-century Italian theoreticians, an individual, sketchy style denoted youthful impatience or the weakness of old age, or even worse, a labour-saving method of realising a quick profit. A brilliantly wild style, it placed excessive demands on the viewer's imagination and ability to assemble the blobs and rough brushstrokes into a finished composition.[14]

The extent to which such a radical view retained its validity during the seventeenth century remains to be seen. What is certain, however, is that texts continued to give advice on viewing and interpreting such paintings based on the principle that they could best be understood by ignoring the actual phenomenon. Houbraken offered the most important tip when he had Rembrandt himself suggest that when viewed from a certain distance, the negative features of the rough manner could be transformed into positive ones.[15] Significantly, even the style of late Titian received only indirect praise, since, so the argument, he understood how to disguise his industriousness and labour as a seemingly effortless exercise.[16] Painting that appeared haphazard, disorderly and vague threatened the validity of the existing system of objective and teachable rules of art. Especially Classicism, which brought forth numerous theoretical texts, strove to defend existing principles, and picked out one outstanding genius to set an example: Rembrandt. He was the «first heretic of art».[17] The following text and the last section of the exhibition will discuss the roots and beginnings of his rough manner, which in its mature and late form produced this drastic judgement.

## ‹Manner› and ‹style›

When Wilhelm VIII, writing some 250 years ago, referred to the « manners» of Rembrandt's painting, he chose a term seldom used today and certainly not as it was understood then. When discussing differences in painting such as those described above, we are accustomed to identifying the ‹style› of the artist. The terms ‹manner› and ‹style› are not, however, synonymous, and to clarify this it is necessary to give a short summary of their original meaning. *Manner*, in Italian *maniera,* is the oldest identification of the individual hand of a painter; it is already used in this way in Cennino Cennini's *The Craftsman's Handbook* from around 1390.[18] As of the sixteenth century, the word was also employed to denote certain painterly processes not confined to an individual artist.[19] Two centuries later, Lomazzo introduced the term *stile* in his 1584 treatise on painting.[20] Having begun with an historical citation, it is surely permissible to continue in the same vein by comparing two passages from texts contemporaneous with Rembrandt, a comparison which reveals a surprisingly different contextual emphasis.

In the introduction to his 1604 book on painting, *Den Grondt der edel vry schilder-const,* in the section dealing with the art of painting, Karel van Mander concludes his discussion of Titian's fine and rough manner with the following advice: «Here, oh noble painting apprentice, I have placed before your eyes in the most understandable fashion two types of *manner,* both good and promising success, in which each according to the disposition of his intellect and senses can follow».[21] An earlier definition of the term *style* is found in Agostino Mascardi's art treatise of 1636: «When one asks [an author] in which *style* he writes, he reacts with confusion, since he can write in no other style than his own, that which is dictated to him by his own genius [*ingenium*]».[22] Thus, in its original meaning, *manner* is an acquired and deliberately chosen artistic skill, while *style* is an unconscious quality of form guided by an innate predisposition and natural talent. The term *style* is used today in a broader sense, as the personal style which is the sum of intentional and unintentional formal characteristics; however, the original meaning of the word still retains strong associations.[23] The consequences of emphasising either *manner* or *style* are considerable, since the notion that the conscious decision in favour of one form is related to freedom of choice and flexibility in decision-making, while the idea that an unconsciously influenced choice of form is tied to a certain disposition and its development. The latter model makes it difficult to accept not only deviations from pre-defined parameters but also obvious contradictions in contemporaneous works of an artist.

## Young Rembrandt's «rough manner» in the light of art historical research

This is clearly evident in the conclusions of the team of Amsterdam specialists (Josua Bruyn, Bob Haark, Simon S. Levie, Pieter van Thiel, Ernst van de Wetering) who founded the *Rembrandt Research Project* (hereafter *RRP*). Since the late 1960s, it has been the project's goal to take a fresh look at Rembrandt's paintings and ‹clean up› his œuvre, using the latest technical and art historical methods. The results of its examination of the artist's early work, published between 1982 and 1989 in three large volumes as *A Corpus of Rembrandt Paintings,* are indeed impressive. The diverse and rigorously applied methods have brought an immense amount of new information to light, making the volumes an invaluable reference tool both for the study of painting in general and as a standard work on research into Rembrandt. They are the essential point of departure for all further analysis, and indeed for this study. Its exemplary attention to detail and extensive discussion of the most diverse aspects makes a repetition of the *Corpus* in the foreseeable future impossible. Subsequent œuvre catalogues by Gary Schwartz, Christian Tümpel, Werner Sumowski and Claus Grimm[24] had little choice but to follow the example of the *Corpus,* although they have not always accepted its conclusions.

But what were the foundations upon which the standards were set? In hardly any case did the technical information – age of the panels, structure of the colour pigments and the binding medium – give reason to change the hitherto accepted attribution. More often it was subtly-argued evaluations of quality that were decisive, and of course style played an important role. General comments on this can be found in the introduction to the first *Corpus* volume of 1982 as well as in the chapter «The Stylistic Development».[25] The question was: how can a representative framework comprising features from works of undisputed quality together with signed and documented works be established that could serve as a reliable standard for evaluating the body of material as a whole? It is here that general and theoretical considerations would have been a necessary precondition to establish how such a basis could be developed incorporating all variants of the work. For the first time one would have had to raise the difficult question of how much importance young Rembrandt placed on the different categories of sketch, study, modello and ‹finished› work intended for sale. But instead of reflecting on this, the team of authors followed a preconception which evolved from a series of generally-accepted major works whose style was described and analysed. Only within this narrow spectrum was discussion permitted about the limitation that should be set for the work of a single artist, and how much variation was to be allowed. One can only speak of variation if one has a basic concept.[26] The explanations of this reveal a clear association with Mascardi's historical definition of style. He talks of «... what could be called the artistic vision that one feels sets certain margins to what the artist makes or allows his hand to do, and his eye to see, while painting».[27] The answer, according to the RRP, is «fine painting», one that permitted only a limited degree of transgression. Although of considerable importance for understanding the painter and his development, these limitations were not clearly formulated but rather become evident through the attributions and especially through the de-attributions, and through the reasoning behind the decision. When it came to allocating Rembrandt's rough early painting to the different Corpus categories of A (autograph works), B (questionable attribution) or C (not authentic), the RRP came to very different conclusions. With one exception all were removed from the artist's accepted œuvre purely on the basis of the manner of painting, which was considered to have sprung the self-defined boundaries. Under such preconditions, the issue of quality was of secondary importance. Three genre scenes from a series of the Five Senses belonging to private collectors (cat. no. 9–11) were entered into the category of uncertain attribution (Corpus B 1–3),

whereby ‹beginner's pains› were taken into consideration. The Bust of a Laughing Man in a Gorget (cat. no. 79) in the Mauritshuis, The Hague, was also placed in the same category (Corpus B 6) because it was recognised that it formed part of a group of three paintings executed with a very unusual technique – gold-leaf on copper – of which one was considered to be unquestionably authentic.[28] The Old Man with a Cap from the Bader Collection (cat. no. 80, Corpus C 22) was firmly rejected, despite the documentary value of a reproductive print etched by Jan van Vliet in 1634, which even affirmed the invention of Rembrandt in its inscription, RH jnventor. The same fate befell the signed and dated Bust of an Old Man with Golden Chain of 1632 in Kassel (cat. no. 81, Corpus C 53) on the grounds that its elaborate execution was uneconomical and exaggerated.[29] Only the dated painting of 1627 in the Kunstmuseum Basle showing David with the Head of Goliath before Saul, which unfortunately is not exhibited, was accepted (Corpus A 9). The RRP was in this case completely convinced that the work was a sketch for a larger painting that was never executed. The diversity of the RRP's assessment allows a glimpse into the originality and uniqueness of each and every one of the group of «rough-manner» paintings that were executed between 1624/25 and 1632.

As early as 1979 the issue of errors of judgement was addressed when a member of the RRP team, Ernst van de Wetering, published an opinion which, when previously voted upon, had been rejected by the majority of the group. It concerned the rejection of the Bader Head (Corpus C 22, cat. no. 80) on the grounds of its «astonishingly coarse» and allegedly incoherent painting: «The coarseness of its execution should not be entirely excluded from our conception of Rembrandt's [early] manner of painting, as it was part of the image that quite a few of his followers had of this».[30] That this idea found no resonance up to the appearance of the third volume of the Corpus in 1989 must be seen as a symptom of the failure of the idealised concept of teamwork. Van de Wetering subsequently became sole leader of the RRP. In 1991, following a suggestion by Jan Emmens, he laid out the principles for further research using a new historical-theoretical basis in his extensive contribution to the catalogue of the exhibition in Berlin, Amsterdam and London.[31] In his – unfortunately unpublished – lecture, delivered at the Rembrandt congress in Amsterdam on January 16, 1991, van de Wetering once again returned to the topic of the «rough manner» in Rembrandt's early work, first raised in 1979, and so inspired the author of this contribution to conduct a new study of the rich collection of early works by the artist in Kassel.

## The rehabilitation of the 1632 *Bust of an Old Man with Golden Chain* in Kassel

None of the five character heads (*tronies*) from around 1630 and belonging to the collection of the Gemäldegalerie at Schloss Wilhelmshöhe was recognised in the *Corpus* as being by Rembrandt. In most cases the arguments were convincing: obvious discrepancies in quality were described and all references to previously expressed doubts were cited. Painful as the *RRP*'s ‹clean up› was for the museum, its documented reasoning appeared conclusive.[32] Only the *Bust of an Old Man with Golden Chain* of 1632 (cat. no. 81) remained immune to all attempts to condemn it as a simple imitation. The painting, which Horst Gerson, the most eminent Rembrandt specialist before the *RRP* team, considered a particularly rich and expressive work, stood its ground. Was not this powerful and expansive manner of painting executed with such confidence that each stroke of the brush possesses its own creative strength, and this in complete harmony with the sturdy robustness of the sitter? Was not this old man with his somewhat unfriendly but unforgettably intense look a new type, one that does not appear in the early works executed in Leiden but was discovered by Rembrandt in Amsterdam during his search for more monumental and emotional forms of expression? Do such details as the impressive swirl of a single hair scratched into the paint and yet so perfectly integrated in the overall mass of hair, or the white highlights in the lower lids of his watery eyes display any of the weaknesses or deviations from the methods of depiction which Ernst van de Wetering observed and described?[33] Does not the signature (fig. 4), rejected by the *RRP*, conform in every detail with the typical composition and form for the year 1632,[34] except that, in keeping with the overall style the artist, it was executed with an unusually

4
Rembrandt Harmensz. van Rijn, *Bust of an Old Man with Golden Chain* (signature), 1632
Cat. no. 81 (cf. fig. 2)

5
Rembrandt Harmensz. van Rijn, *Bust of an Old Man with Golden Chain* (X-ray), 1632
Cat. no. 81 (cf. fig. 2)

broad brush? It was most unfortunate that many years ago the *RRP* was given a completely inadequate and underexposed X-ray. The new one (fig. 5) shows a powerful and assured use of white lead that is comparable with other Rembrandt paintings of the same period.[35] As the painting of the old man in the Bader collection (cat. no. 80) had long been rejected as the work of Rembrandt, it was only after the *RRP*'s identification of the Kassel old man as a completely isolated example of an unknown but masterly imitator that the numerous similarities between the two were noticed. This is particularly evident in the rich, almost floating strokes of the brush and in the illumination of the contours of the left half of the face. The Bader painting, which has been exhibited on numerous occasions over the past years and has once again been generally accepted as being by the master himself,[36] is a study of light and facial expression painted in the small format that is typical for Rembrandt's work in Leiden. It is this kind of study that two or three years later the artist recalls when in Amsterdam he seeks to create a new type of work that will serve a number of different functions. All these arguments were incorporated into the entry on the Kassel painting in the 1996 catalogue of the Gemäldegalerie's collection.[37] This led Ernst van de Wetering to re-examine the painting in 1999, when he concluded that it was indeed by Rembrandt.[38] Our research has also yielded so many observations on other works by Rembrandt and his circle that a special section of this essay has been devoted to them. But the exhibition itself has also profited: in the third section, «Heads in a fine and rough manner», Rembrandt's *Bust of an Old Man with Golden Chain* takes centre stage, and is clearly related to the majority of the other paintings that surrounded it.

## Young Rembrandt and the art of «fine painting»

What distinguishes fine from rough painting is a question of definition and application. Characterising Rembrandt's early work as fine painting is perfectly acceptable when, as with van de Wetering,[39] it is compared with his late work. Rembrandt initially favoured a small format, small-scaled figures and a whole range of minutely-rendered details. But if one takes fine painting to mean the elimination of all visual signs of the manual act of painting, then Rembrandt was only occasionally a fine painter, such as in his 1642 portrait of Saskia wearing pearls (fig. 1) so finely executed that Wilhelm VIII was reminded of Frans van Mieris. Whereas Gerard Dou, the main proponent of the Leiden school of fine painting that was still in existence in the eighteenth century, sought to eliminate all traces of individual

brush strokes by blending together the layers of paint in a homogeneous polished surface, Rembrandt's interest, by contrast, lay in drawing attention to effectively accentuated elements. This emphasis was, of course, in part closely related to the demands of illusionism. Yet from the beginning one senses that this cannot be the sole reason; that for Rembrandt it served a greater purpose. The layers of paint are never completely smooth and can vary within a single picture from thick impasto to a thin translucent layer. The variation in the consistency and application of paint is enormous – gritty, rough, streaky or lumpy, with furrows or spirals made by the hairs or the end of the brush, interspersed with unfinished areas – but it is always understood and treated as tangible matter. Rembrandt avoids rendering larger areas of the surface in a smooth cohesive manner, but rather creates a dynamic structure through stippling or long lines of colour.[40] The *Bust of an Old Man with Turban* (cat. no. 75) of c. 1627 is an excellent example. Here the feather is attached to his turban by an agraffe, which is adorned by a ruby suggested by the most brilliant red blob of colour but with no apparent connection to its surroundings; the surface of his mantle is enlivened in the manner described above. Today, just as in the seventeenth century, no interested viewer can fail to notice such small abstract forms, not least because these often tiny panels be to held in one's hands and studied up close. There is nothing similar in Gerard Dou's early *tronie* in Kassel (cat. no. 76), for which, as van de Wetering observed, he used the same model as Rembrandt in the *Bust of an Old Man with Turban* (cat. no. 75). Whereas in the painting in Budapest (cat. no. 68) Dou emphasises the smooth continuity of the curved metal surface of a shield, Rembrandt uses small blobs of colour as highlights to draw attention to the relief decoration of a shield in his *Judas Repentant* (cat. no. 33). The fact that Dou, as Rembrandt's pupil, copied the motif from his master makes the very different ideals all the more obvious. Van de Wetering's comparison of details shows that the same phenomenon is present in portraiture.[41] When adding highlights to eyes Nicolaes Eliasz. called Pickenoy ensures they blend completely with the surrounding area, while Rembrandt favours white dots of colour which stand out quite clearly. Rembrandt, on the one hand, and Dou and Pickenoy, on the other, are worlds apart! Van de Wetering used convincing examples to interpret Rembrandt's technique as a means of characterising different textures. But in addition to this role, his technique must also be perceived as an element in its own right, as an expression of an artistic temperament which seeks to convey individuality and to differentiate between painterly and formal qualities. Seen from this angle, Rembrandt's painting is consistent in all stages of its development. There are no differences between a «fine» and «rough manner», but rather a «painterly» application of progressive graduations, of micro and macro-structures. This is all the easier to understand now that one of the principal testimonies to his «fine painting» has been de-attributed: the famous *Self-portrait with Gorget* from the Mauritshuis in The Hague. Executed in an unusually precise and linear manner, it is now considered a copy, possibly by Gerard Dou, after the far more complete and fluid version in the Germanisches Nationalmuseum in Nuremberg.[42]

It is thus possible to interpret Rembrandt's early manner of handling paint aesthetically; that is, as finely structured rough painting, adapted to suit the more or less small formats of his pictures. His teacher, Pieter Lastman, also preferred small supports, and a detailed study of his painting reveals similar forms though more schematic and less imaginative.[43] The most important forefather of this type of animated small-scale painting was Adam Elsheimer, who made a lasting impression on Lastman during his stay in Rome.[44] Rembrandt captures the very different characteristics of smooth and patterned materials by creating relief-like structures which give the contrast between raised and flat surfaces a particularly tactile quality. This technique of visual enrichment, which, according to van de Wetering, was inspired by late medieval painting,[45] was to prove especially important for his late work.

But irrespective of the typical features listed here, the small group of works discussed above is distinguished by an unquestionably broader, rougher and more forceful structuring of paint; by what can only be called a «rough manner» in the true sense of the word. Misunderstandings arose only because scholars have hitherto rarely considered these works in the wider context of this style of painting. The aura of Rembrandt's genius has led to studies which focus on specific, pictorially immanent aspects of a work, but all too often avoid raising such issues as outside influences or the function and sources of his style. With this in mind, the following will examine possible sources by looking beyond those that exerted direct influence on both Rembrandt and his fellow painter Lievens so as to trace the evolutionary line as far back as the Venetian painting of the late Renaissance.

### Rembrandt at the dawn of his career

Three genre paintings depicting the Five Senses in allegorical form (cat. nos. 9–11) mark the very beginning of Rembrandt's creativity. Up to a few years ago, the plumpness of the figures and the painterly execution of these unsigned works ensured they were considered unworthy of Rembrandt and therefore were hardly discussed in the context of his œuvre. They were first exhibited as early autograph works in the Stockholm exhibi-

6
Rembrandt Harmensz. van Rijn, *The Stoning of St Stephen* (detail), 1625
Oak panel,
89.5 x 123.6 cm
Musée des Beaux-Arts, Lyon

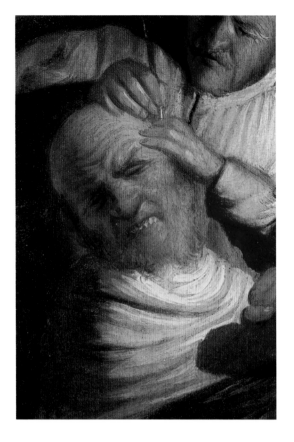

tion of 1992/93.[46] When the scene depicting an operation of the head (*Touch*, cat. no. 10) was sold at auction in 1995, the catalogue noted a positive opinion by Ernst van de Wetering.[47] Kurt Bauch saw in this group the work of an amateur whose streaky manner and wild brushstrokes failed to convince.[48] But it is impossible to ignore the similarities with Rembrandt's earliest signed paintings, such as his *Christ Driving the Money-changers from the Temple* of 1626 (cat. no. 12) and also the *Stoning of St Stephen* in Lyon, which bears the date 1625 and is thus his earliest dated work. A closer study of the painterly details in this key work is informative (fig. 6). The knotted white garment of one of the stone-throwing execution-ers is painted using exactly the same rich broad brushwork over a somewhat darker ground as is found in the cloth slung around the patient's neck in *Touch* (fig. 7). These strokes have little real val-ue in accentuating the actual folds of the cloth and so fail to convince. They are instead an ex-pression of an unrestrained artistic temperament, one in need of practice but willing to take a risk. The three allegorical paintings of the Five Senses are dominated by this style and are unrelated, contextually as well, to the work of Pieter Last-

man. Connections of a different sort are evident in the *Stoning of St Stephen*: the ornamental dal-matic of the martyr and the finely dappled render-ing of the walls of the ruins, both of which belong in the tradition of Elsheimer, are unthinkable without Lastman as mediator. These similarities and differences suggest the paintings were exe-cuted consecutively but were separated by a fun-damental experience: the conclusion of Rem-brandt's apprenticeship, when he spent about six months with Pieter Lastman in Amsterdam. There are indications that this may not have been until 1625, the year in which he painted the *Ston-ing of St Stephen*.[49]

### Lievens and Rembrandt: Learning together

If this late date for the apprenticeship is indeed correct, then the three allegories of the Senses be-long in Rembrandt's pre-Lastman era. They have never been considered in such a context and therefore testify to a completely different and im-portant influence on Rembrandt, one in which the use of an open and dynamic brushstroke comes to the fore. Since this manner of painting is so rare in Dutch art in that period, the choice of possible sources is not large. The dynamic brush-work which from the beginning Rembrandt sought to achieve was foreign to painters in Utrecht. Rembrandt's companion in Leiden was Jan Lievens, an artistic prodigy who, although a year younger than Rembrandt, had by 1620 a number of works to his credit.[50] Although he, too, completed an apprenticeship with Lastman in Amsterdam, no stylistic or contextual traces of this relationship are evident in Lieven's known œuvre. Instead he looked to the popular genre scenes depicted by artists in Haarlem and Utrecht for his large paintings of figures.[51] His earliest known painting, the *Tric Trac Players* (cat. no. 8), shows the influence of the Utrecht Cara-vaggisti in such features as the striped shirt of the servant and the ostrich feather. The loose and broad treatment of paint is, however, more typi-cal of the Haarlem school, in which, undoubtedly through contacts with Utrecht, similar genre scenes are found. Attention has already been drawn to depictions of musicians by Pieter de Grebber.[52] Lievens, however, goes one step fur-ther when he paints spot-like reflexes of light on hands and faces; this is particularly obvious in the way he attempts to enliven the face of the man smoking a pipe with broad unrelated lines of light on his forehead. Because Lievens is not altogether successful and the scene remains somewhat stiff, the probable source for his efforts has gone unnoticed. The work in question is a brilliant early work by Frans Hals: the *Merrymakers at Shrovetide*. It can be assumed that both Lievens and Rem-

brandt knew and admired this immensely popular painting, of which numerous copies and adaptations are known (Metropolitan Museum, New York, fig. 8).[53] Before the dusky background, the crowded gathering of common, burlesque carnival figures exudes an uncontrollable rowdiness that was beyond Lievens's artistic capabilities. But it is there that Rembrandt could have found

8
Frans Hals, *Merrymakers at Shrovetide*, c. 1615–20
Canvas, 131.5 x 99.6 cm
The Metropolitan Museum of Art, New York

9
Jan Lievens, *Allegory of Water and Old Age* (detail, picture with side-light), c. 1626
Cat. no. 73

his inspiration for the exaggerated, caricature-like figures of his unsophisticated satirical allegories of the Senses. In their early work, the two young Leiden painters were so dependent upon one another that these works must have been executed within a relatively short period in 1624 or early 1625. The composition of Rembrandt's allegory of Sight, the *Spectacles-Pedlar* (cat. no. 11), is an almost exact repetition of that of the *Tric Trac Players* (cat. no. 8): two figures in the foreground, the left one in half-profile, the right in profile, with two onlookers placed slightly to the right in the background.

Which of the two, Lievens or Rembrandt, should be given precedence? The answer to this question continues to elude us. Since the Lievens exhibi-

tion of 1979 in Braunschweig, which sought to free him from the overpowering presence of Rembrandt, it is generally considered that the more experienced Lievens preceded his colleague. According to Sumowski, Rembrandt put himself in the hands of his artistically superior friend.[54] But there is nothing to suggest this was the case with the *Spectacles-Pedlar*. The choice of a small format confirms Rembrandt's independence from Lievens and his depiction of the interaction and psychology of his figures is clearly more skilful. The provocative roughness of the execution can perhaps be understood as resulting not only from a lack of practice but also from a carefree desire to find a form of expression in keeping with the satirical character of the scene. It is notable that none of Lievens's documented works from the time before he began working with Rembrandt is known.[55] Were they perhaps nothing more than a testimony to a child prodigy? Taking the present state of research into account, it seems best to assume that the then seventeen and eighteen-year-old painters set out on their artistic careers together. It may have been that Lievens's unusual talent for absorbing inspiration of the most diverse nature was not matched by an equal ability to integrate it into his own work. It was his role as mediator that was more important for Rembrandt.

## The chronology of Jan Lievens' first period

Lieven's activity as an artist spans a period of over forty years. Yet within his œuvre it is quite clearly his early work and in particular his large depictions of single figures that is most significant. Werner Sumowski has collected a large body of material on the artist, and it is this which forms the basis for all further research.[56] Lievens differs from Rembrandt on two counts: firstly, almost all of Rembrandt's works from his early years bear a signature or date, and secondly, he undergoes a rapid development in quality and style. Neither holds true for Lievens, so that a chronology of the great majority of his works from the onset of his career has remained elusive. Sumowski understandably refrains from suggesting dates before the middle of the 1620s and generally opts for «around 1625». Here I wish, on the basis of style, to attempt a more exact chronology for the years 1625 to 1627. The *Tric Trac Players* (cat. no. 8) is followed around 1625 by two compositions showing a number of half-length figures, all of which are more advanced in the modelling of heads and hands: the allegories of the Five Senses and *Esther's Feast*.[57] One is immediately struck by the rich profusion of detail that may be an exaggeration of the characteristics of the painting by Frans Hals mentioned above (fig. 8). An obvious *horror vacui* dominates, the structure of folds is highlighted and rendered mechanically and there is a wealth of small-scale ornamental detail. A hitherto unknown painting of a *Youth Embracing a Young Woman* has recently surfaced[58] which must have been executed more or less contemporaneously, since the two figures have been «extracted» from the allegories of the Five Senses, where the central couple represents the sense of touch. The figures in this newly-discovered work are more lively and sensual and less doll-like, so that a date of 1625 seems plausible. Also belonging to this period are two paintings in Warsaw showing a *Young Man Blowing on a Glowing Coal* and a *Young Man Blowing on a Torch*, one of which is signed «J. Livius».[59] Common to all are the comparable treatment of folds and the noticeable similarity of the narrow squinting eyes. The open brushwork of the *Youth Embracing a Young Woman* flows in regular wavy lines. Here, as in his large, well-known *Esther's Feast* in Raleigh,[60] Lievens is more interested in a lively ornamental structuring of the surface than in capturing different textures.

But he departs from this approach in the Kassel group of the *Four Elements and the Ages of Man* (cat. nos. 72, 73). The initial impression of a homogeneous group of paintings is deceptive, for they testify to an interest in experimentation and a search for new possibilities. The middle two paintings, *Allegory of Air and Youth* and *Allegory of Earth and Manhood*, are distinguished by the powerful structuring of the figures through light and shadow, and the ensuing contrast with the sketchily-executed landscape. This technique is not particularly notable, something which cannot be said of the remaining two works. The first and last in the series, *Allegory of Fire and Childhood* and *Allegory of Water and Old Age*, show not only a heightened use of impasto but also greater subtly in its application so as to differentiate between the boy and the old man; this can be seen in reproductions made using raking light. The head of the old man (fig. 9) is painted in an open manner

and with a remarkable use of impasto. The pointed dab of colour on the nose, the brittle lines of wrinkles and the splinters of white highlights all combine to increase the impression of rigid old age. But although Lievens was clearly seeking an expressively sketchy manner of representation, the eighteen-year-old painter lacked the necessary confidence; he fails to present the wrinkled forehead as a cohesive physiognomic element. However, he accentuates the rounded form of the head of the youth (fig.10) with large amounts of white lead applied with flowing brushstrokes; the white shirt is sketched in a broad, self-assured manner. Here Lievens has clearly made progress compared with the pictures in Warsaw discussed above, so that a date of 1626 for the entire series

10
Jan Lievens, *Allegory of Fire and the Age of Childhood* (detail, picture with side-light), c. 1626
Cat. no. 72

seems the most plausible. The youth blowing into the fire (cat. no. 72) already shows the degree of maturity found in the series of the *Four Evangelists* in Bamberg, which must have been painted in 1627.[61] A principal work of the period of c. 1626 is the painting *Pilate Washes his Hands in Innocence* (cat. no. 24).

## Influences and stages of development in Rembrandt's early «rough manner»

«Jan Lievens was expert is seeking wonders in smeared pigments, varnishes and oils.» Ernst van de Wetering drew attention to this important note in Samuel van Hoogstraten's treatise of 1678.[62] A pupil of Rembrandt's, Hoogstraten credits Lievens with introducing a technical achievement which was then passed down in the studio tradition. The two paintings from the Kassel series of the allegories of the *Four Elements and the Ages of Man* testify to Lievens' experimenta-

11
Hendrick ter Brugghen, *St Jerome* (detail), 1621
Canvas, 125 x 106.6 cm
The Cleveland Museum of Art

tion with impasto and drying agents. Rembrandt was at that time chiefly preoccupied with the very different task of processing the innovations he had learned from Lastman in Amsterdam. The exhibition contains two works from 1626, the *Baptism of the Eunuch* (cat. no. 3) and the *History Painting* (cat. no. 7), which clearly show the extent to which Rembrandt took note of Lastman's compositions.[63] By this time he was already fascinated by the faces of old people, by the painterly challenge of a face covered in wrinkles, as his *Tobit and Anna* from the Rijksmuseum in Amsterdam (cat. no. 28) confirms. Caravaggism is here the focus of interest. Caravaggio himself favoured placing the emotionally-aroused faces of old people in compositionally important places. And just as he used impasto to emphasise raised eyebrows and wrinkled foreheads,[64] so too did Rembrandt accentuate Tobit's wrinkles by following the example of the Utrecht Caravaggist Hendrick ter Brugghen, whose *St Jerome* of 1621 in Cleveland (fig. 11) is cited here as an appropriate comparison.[65] It is only in the following year, 1627, that we find a picture in which Rembrandt could have adopted Lieven's method of using a thickened binding agent and a free sketchy handling of the brush – the latter, however, greatly transformed. In his *David with the Head of Goliath before Saul* in the Kunstmuseum, Basle, (fig. 12),[66] the variegated bright colours of thickened impasto are applied in an extremely broad manner that pulls the forms together, but they are also rubbed away so as to blend with the surroundings. The assured individuality and masterly quality of this small-scale work is astonishing and the entire composition is enlivened by contrasts in brushwork, such as between the horse and its rider, and between King Saul in the middle and the figures in the background. Rembrandt initially did not follow Lievens in employing the «rough manner» for entire figures but rather for small details in a many-figured scene. His success here seems effortless, especially as we know of nothing comparable preceding his *David* or, even more astounding, subsequent to it.

The next step in this development was to focus on the single-figure painting, and towards the end of the 1620s *tronies* showing the most diverse expressions and use of light assume a central role in Rembrandt's painting. With such works, the

12
Rembrandt Harmensz.
van Rijn, *David with the
Head of Goliath before Saul*,
1627
Oak panel, 27.5 x 39.5 cm
Kunstmuseum Basel

«rough manner» is not simply a matter of individual style; it is also a question of genre. The two are inseparable, making it indispensable to examine not just painting style but also the genre of head studies in the pre-Rembrandt era. To do this, it is necessary to look beyond the borders of the northern Netherlands and venture south.

The most revealing example of Rembrandt's interest in facial expression is the technically and stylistically unusual, etched *Self-portrait* of 1629 (cat. no. 78). It has the same experimental character as the contemporaneous series of three identically-sized small copper panels. These are overlaid with gold-leaf and on each Rembrandt painted a different type of *tronie* so as to display his virtuosity in different styles:[67] a *Self Portrait* of an especially soft, painterly quality; an *Old Woman at Prayer*, with fine, jewel-like spots of paint; and a *Bust of a Laughing Man in a Gorget* in the «rough manner» (cat. no. 79). He seems to have had numerous reasons for choosing this style for this particular subject: wearing a gorget, the soldier is an unkempt youth whose coarse laughter offers an unashamed view of his crooked and partly missing teeth. Such representations of a folkloristic and satirical nature and executed in a broad careless manner were already to be found

13
Frans Hals, *Peeckelhaering
(Merry Drinker)* (detail),
c. 1628–30
Canvas, 75 x 61.5 cm
Staatliche Museen Kassel,
Gemäldegalerie
Alte Meister

in Italian sixteenth-century painting.[68] When depicting such a figure, Rembrandt, as suggested above, must surely have looked to Frans Hals, the master of laughter and the «rough manner».[69] Hals' *Peeckelhaering (Merry Drinker)* (fig. 13) of ca. 1628–30 in Kassel was already famous in the

14
Rembrandt Harmensz.
van Rijn, *Old Man with a
Cap and Golden Chain*
(detail), 1631
Oak panel, 59.5 x 51.2 cm
Private Collection

ber of characteristics of Lievens' *Allegory of Water and Old Age* (cat. no. 73, fig. 9) of some three or four years earlier: the similarly inclined downward position of the head, the depiction of the eyes as black patches with no distinction between iris and pupil, the use of a fluid dark colour to shade the corner of the eye, painting dark shadows in the furrows on his wrinkled forehead to isolate the folds of flesh, and finally the broad loose dabs of light on his brow moving towards the sides of his face. Rembrandt paints all these elements with so much more assurance and conviction that one must perhaps overcome a certain reluctance about making the comparison. Rembrandt appears to have had an appreciative eye for the refined intentions in the early work of his friend and will almost certainly have had them explained to him by Lievens himself.

The small group of Rembrandt's heads in the «rough manner» mark a development towards monumentality and life-size depictions. From the start this was a matter of course for Lievens, but it was something Rembrandt had to achieve step by step. The *Bust of a Laughing Man in a Gorget* (cat. no. 79) is just 15.5 x 12.5 cm. The *Old Man with a Cap* (cat. no. 80), measuring 24.3 x 20.3 cm, was followed in 1631 by the similarly-dressed figure of an *Old Man with a Cap and Golden Chain* (fig. 14)[71] in the life-size format of 59.5 x 51.2 cm. The free brushwork of the earlier picture is not executed here with the same verve but is rather reduced and confined to the bridge of the nose and the lower part of the forehead, as if the artist shied away from his final goal. But this goal is clearly achieved in his Kassel *Bust of an Old Man with Golden Chain* of 1632 (cat. no. 81, figs. 2 and 33). It has no successor, nor is its manner intensified elsewhere. In this work Rembrandt combines the achievements of the two previous paintings: the sophisticated style of the *Old Man with a Cap* (cat. no. 80) and the presence, the outward looking gaze and the life-sized format of the painting of 1631 (cf. fig. 14).

## Jan Lievens' early contact with Antwerp

Accepting the suggestion that Lievens was a child prodigy but that his true career only began together with Rembrandt raises the following question: what did he do during 1625/26, when Rembrandt was in Amsterdam? Since he was ambi-

seventeenth century.[70] A comparison shows that although equal in quality, there are more differences than similarities. Hals conceives the head as a homogeneous plastic form and then loosely deploys spots of light and shadow to enliven and intensify the figure's sanguine character. Rembrandt's youth laughs in a less relaxed manner. He does not look out at us as much, and the subtle impasto brushwork plays a far greater role in modelling the face.

Quite different is the style of the somewhat larger *Old Man with a Cap* (cat. no. 80), which was probably painted around the same time. Whereas the face of the *Laughing Man in a Gorget* appears to have been uniformly kneaded with the brush, that of the old man shows greater variety. His smooth cheeks contrast strongly with his wrinkled brow. Despite having been painted at quite different times, Rembrandt seems to have adopted a num-

tious, curious, flexible, would have numerous places of residence in later life and was open to new sources, it is certainly imaginable that he also decided to use the break to further his own study outside of Leiden. While there is no documentary evidence to support an early interest in the important and very different mode of painting in nearby Antwerp, his work has long been seen as suggesting exactly this.[72] He was drawn at an early stage in his career to Flemish art; indeed much more so than Rembrandt, so that when Rembrandt moved to Amsterdam in 1631 Lievens immediately displayed this interest openly. Proof of this can be found in the competition between the two artists in 1631 to depict a rendering of *Christ on the Cross,* using as their source an engraving after Rubens. While Rembrandt sought his own solution for form and expression, Lievens follows his Flemish source much more closely.[73] A number of factors support Lievens' early contact with the south, not the least of which being that his father was born in Ghent.[74] J. Douglas Stewart's suggestion that Lievens may have been apprenticed in Antwerp already in 1620–21 is somewhat too daring,[75] but it is indeed plausible to see the eighteen-year old in the city, where he could visit the studios of Peter Paul Rubens and Jacob Jordaens and study their works and methods.

Douglas Stewart has already provided a piece of evidence for Lievens' special interest in Antwerp, where his youth and quest for (artistic) knowledge was surely met with openness and sympathy. He discovered a drawing with Lievens' monogram showing the head of a bearded man after a painted head study by Rubens.[76] It appears that whilst in Antwerp Lievens was less concerned with the famous compositions of the great master, which were known through prints, than with the studio practice, the study material and the recipes for paint. The head studies by Antwerp artists offered excellent examples of the technique and style of the «rough manner», and they provided the best impulses for his particular speciality: the single-figure *tronie.* Since this area of Antwerp painting has received little attention,[77] it is necessary to address it in a study devoted to Rembrandt.

It has been noted on different occasions that a formal relationship exists between the youth blowing into the fire in Kassel (cat. no. 72) and a

15
Peter Paul Rubens,
*Two Studies of the Head of a Young Man* (detail),
c. 1617
Oak panel, 46.3 x 63.5 cm
The Metropolitan Museum of Art, New York (on loan from Herman Shickman)

16
Peter Paul Rubens,
*Study for a Moorish King,*
1617/18
Oak panel, 65.5 x 50.5 cm
Rubenshuis, Antwerp

source from Utrecht: Honthorst's *Young Couple Igniting the Fire of Love* in Braunschweig.[78] This, however, does not apply to the manner of execution. The free-flowing forms of the shadows in the nostrils and even the less fluid white-lead highlights are not typical of Dutch models, nor even of

Hals; but the soft transition between forms is reminiscent of Rubens. A good comparison is a detail from Rubens' *Two Studies of the Head of a Young Man* from the New York collection of Herman Schickman and on loan to the Metropolitan Museum (fig. 15).[79] The sketchy execution of the white shirt using broad strokes of rich white lead is, however, closer to Rubens' *Study for a Black King* in the Rubens House, Antwerp (fig. 16).[80] The background of both the *Allegory of Fire* and the *Allegory of Water* (figs. 9, 10 and cat. nos. 72, 73) is unusual and has a Flemish flavour. Grey is applied in different directions in a stripy manner using a broad ‹dry› brush containing just a little colour. Consequently, the light brown imprimatura covering the white ground shimmers through. Apparently Lievens was impressed with the effect of the stripy imprimatura with which Rubens animated his oil sketches (fig. 17).[81]

### Van Dyck's early head studies and their influence

Lievens probably found the studio of Jacob Jordaens even more stimulating than Rubens'. Jordaens' initial emulation of Rubens' style of painting and use of relatively thin paint appears to have changed upon coming into contact with van Dyck. The works of the young artist's astonishing ‹rough period› may have prompted Jordaens to adopt a more vigorous style and emphatic use of

impasto. Various head studies point to close co-operation between the two artists in the years prior to van Dyck's departure for London in 1621 and for Italy shortly afterwards. Jordaens' greatest achievement in this area is his masterly study in an extremely rough manner of a man gazing upwards (cat. no. 70). A companion piece by van Dyck is in the Gemäldegalerie Berlin (fig. 18).[82] In both cases the model is Abraham Grapheus, a member of the St Luke's Guild, whose striking

facial features made him a very popular model. Since his pose is the same in both studies, it can be assumed that van Dyck and Jordaens worked side-by-side, the only difference being each chose a different type of illumination. Van Dyck portrays the face in full light, while Jordaens opted for greater differentiation between light and shadow, thereby optimising the effects of his relief-like application of paint. Van Dyck's sketchy impasto is more malleable in this work from the period around 1620. The head study was painted on paper but was subsequently cut out and pasted on a panel before being transformed into a figure praying. For good reasons these additions are attributed to Jordaens, who must have had van Dyck's work in his possession.[83] So in spite of van Dyck's absence, Lievens would still have had the opportunity to study his early work and take note of the Venetian elements which greatly enriched the art of painting in Antwerp. He may also have felt a special affinity for him as both were considered child prodigies who began their training before the age of ten, although van Dyck had already achieved a degree of fame to which Lievens still aspired. In any case, Lievens captured van Dyck's attention following the latter's return from Italy. The Flemish artist executed his colleague's portrait and included him in his *Iconography*, a series of etched portraits of famous artists and art lovers (fig. 19).

Were there other early studies by van Dyck in Jordaens' studio? This is certainly not implausible on two counts: van Dyck left no studio in Antwerp when he departed for Italy, and he had already undergone a radical change of style from a «rough manner» to a more elegant one, which looked to Venetian colouring more than brushwork. Accordingly, his earlier works lost a certain amount of their importance. When he painted his *Study of the Head of Abraham Grapheus* (cat. no. 70), Jordaens must have been familiar with at least one other, older head study by van Dyck (fig. 20).[84] A notable feature is the emphasis on the man's exposed neck and the deep folds of wrinkled skin.[85] The *Study of a Man* (fig. 20) belongs in a series of five studies of facial expressions in the collection of the Bayerische Staatsgemäldesammlungen, which van Dyck must have painted around 1616 when he was just seventeen years old.[86] From the series, the *Study Head* is shown in the exhibition (cat. no. 69). Having languished for decades in the storerooms of the Alte Pinakothek, the series

IOANNES LIVENS
PICTOR HVMANARVM FIGVRARVM MAIORVM LVGDVNI BATTAVORVM.
Ant: van Dyck pinxit.                                    Cum privilegio
Vosterman sculp.
G.H.

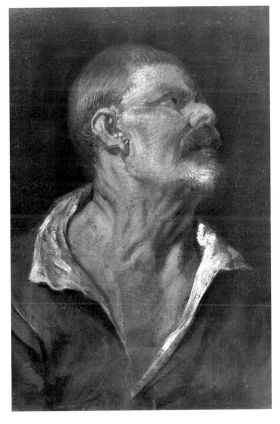

19
Lucas Vorsterman after Anthony van Dyck, *Portrait Jan Lievens*, c. 1630
Etching, 24.2 x 15.8 cm
Herzog Anton Ulrich-Museum, Braunschweig

20
Anthony van Dyck, *Study of a Man*, c. 1616
Paper on panel, 57 x 41 cm
Bayerische Staatsgemäldesammlungen, Munich

21
Jacopo Bassano the Elder,
*Crowning of Thorns* (detail
of right half), c. 1591
Canvas, 107 x 138.5 cm
Christ Church Picture
Gallery, Oxford

ry: Jacopo Tintoretto (1519–1594), Jacopo Bassano the Elder (ca. 1510–1592) and finally Palma il Giovane (1548–1628).[88] Around the middle of the sixteenth century, the former two were among the founders and main proponents of the style, and following their death the tradition was continued by the younger Palma. Apart from Titian, who possessed the most varied forms of expression, his contemporaries all had their own special techniques. Particular to Tintoretto is the ‹dry brush›, one which is so sparingly dipped in paint that when pressed against the canvas, individual hairs leave a clear trail, the areas of colour retain a veil-like transparency and the ensuing layering creates spatial structures. Bassano, on the other hand, avoids long sweeping strokes. His speciality is to break up the paint surface using abrupt thrusts of the brush, as well as dabs and splashes of colour which of themselves lack any structural value.[89] Both methods were important for the young van Dyck. The ‹dry brush› is a continually-used stylistic element until at least 1621. Already his earliest portrait, dated 1613 – when, as he proudly noted, he was just fourteen years old – displays elements of this in the dry gritty rendering of the old sitter's hair and beard.[90] Such an application of colour is evident in his head studies, particularly in the use of lead white for bright collars, as in his *Study Head* (cat. no. 69). On the other hand, the impasto slivers on his forehead are reminiscent of Bassano, whose late *Crowning of Thorns* in Oxford provides a good comparison (fig. 21).[91] Here one finds, especially in the head of the lower tormentor, a similar scattering of splintered forms. Equally, the depiction of the hard shadow which completely covers the man's left eye is also found in Bassano. A few head studies by Palma il Giovane have survived from what was presumably once a very rich collection. His *Head of a Bearded Old Man* (fig. 22) from the end of the sixteenth century is executed in the same technique that van Dyck favoured: oil on paper (later glued onto canvas).[92] Another example which Müller Hofstede has convincingly attributed to van Dyck, the *Study of a Bearded Man in Profile with a Band around His Head* (fig. 23), is stylistically similar in the use of brittle colour to model the loose folds of flesh on his brow.[93]

But since Anthony van Dyck only left Antwerp

has been rehabilitated by Justus Müller Hofstede, whose study pays tribute to its exceptional importance for the history of head studies, its powerful realism, intensity and expressive painting.[87] It only remains for me to make a suggestion that might explain the reckless, seemingly unprecedented manner of painting. Nothing similar to the broken and splintered impasto of the head (cat. no. 69) can be found in older Flemish painting, nor is it typical of Rubens; a point that needs emphasising here, as van Dyck is still ranked – undeservedly – amongst his followers and is thus overshadowed by the Flemish prince of painters.

**Van Dyck's Venetian roots**

In order to set us on the right track I intend to follow up a suggestion by Horst Vey, who proposed that van Dyck's «rough» style may have been inspired by Venetian models – not the late works of the famous Titian, but rather those of younger painters who were still active at the end of the sixteenth or the beginning of the seventeenth centu-

years after his apprenticeship had finished, where could he have come in contact with this type of Venetian painting, which so clearly made such an impression on him? The most plausible possibility is through his teacher, Hendrick van Balen, whose studio he entered in 1609. There he learned the necessary skills of the trade but did not follow his master in executing small-scale cabinet paintings. But what exactly prompted van Dyck to remain there for a number of years? The answer, it would seem, is that van Balen offered his pupil stimuli that coincided with his interests. For a long period, from about 1592 to 1598, van Balen was in Venice,[94] where he developed his style chiefly through an artistic exchange with Johann Rottenhammer. He, in turn, was a friend of Palma il Giovane, the leading painter in the city following the death of Tintoretto.[95] Hendrick van Balen's role in transmitting knowledge of modern Venetian painting to Antwerp has been underestimated, chiefly because his work is not monumental in scale. As with Rottenhammer, this limitation in size may not have been simply a matter of preference but rather one of economic necessity.[96] Van Balen probably knew far more about Venetian styles and techniques than his painting suggests, and even though no documents exist to prove it, he could easily have brought back to Antwerp drawings and oil studies about which he could tell his pupils a great deal.

## Lievens as the go-between

To return to Lievens: his recently discovered *Study of a Bearded Man in Profile* (cat. no. 71) has been included in the exhibition because it is clearly derived from van Dyck's head study (fig. 23). On account of its stylistic affinity to the Kassel cycle of the *Four Elements and the Ages of Man* (cat. nos. 72, 73), it can also be dated to c. 1626. Compared with van Dyck's study, Lievens has transposed the direction, and the forms appear somewhat rougher. Nevertheless, Lievens clearly tried to imitate the broad sketchy execution of the loose folds of skin on the brow, the wavy contour of the forehead and the stylised shape of the ear. But in extending the area around the head, indicating the presence of a shoulder, working on panel and applying a more painterly finish, Lievens was following a very different goal: instead of painting studies, for which there was already a circle of connoisseurs, the Dutchman created fully-fledged marketable paintings.

The wide-ranging studies of this essay seek to clarify the preconditions of Rembrandt's roughly-painted character studies (cat. nos. 79, 80, 81). As a type they are derived from Italian-Flemish head studies of the late sixteenth and early seven-

22
Jacopo Palma il Giovane, *Head of a Bearded Old Man*, c. 1600
Paper (41 x 27) on canvas, 45 x 32 cm
Private Collection, Italy

23
Anthony van Dyck, *Study of a Bearded Man in Profile with a Band around his Head*, c. 1618
Paper on Panel, 44.5 x 33 cm
Previously The Earl of Spencer, Althorp House

teen centuries.[97] Accordingly, the specific Netherlandish tradition of the *tronie*, especially the work of Dutch mannerists, played no part in Rembrandt's studies.[98] Their sketchy manner of execution, the interest in realism and in expressing emotions are features found in Flemish models. These characteristics are especially prevalent in Rembrandt and van Dyck. Moreover, Palma's melancholic old man (fig. 22) can be seen as an ancestor of Rembrandt's *Old Man with a Cap* (cat. no. 80). But no direct connection can be traced from Rembrandt to these models; Lievens is the go-between. As Hubert von Sonnenburg already established, there is nothing in Rembrandt's painting to suggest that he concerned himself directly with Italian painting. Whereas Rubens imitated the techniques of painters like Titian and other masters when copying their pictures, Rembrandt confined himself to drawings and beyond that sought inspiration from prints after Italian artists.[99] Given this, the conclusions of a survey conducted by Bert W. Meijer showing that the number of Italian works available for study in Holland in the 1620s was not large is of little importance for Rembrandt.[100]

### Expressive tronie and costume tronie: Types and functions in Rembrandt's early work

Among Rembrandt's early *tronies*, the four paintings described above (including that of 1631, *Corpus* 40a) form a sub-group executed in the years from 1629 to 1632.[101] The etched self-portrait in the «rough manner» of 1629 (cat. no. 78) is an absolute exception, as Rembrandt did not apply such a radical manner of execution in his early painted self-portraits. A more common type of *tronie* produced by Rembrandt over a longer period of time does not form part of this study, but the two earliest known examples are represented in the exhibition: the *Bust of a Man in a Gorget and Cap* and the *Old Man with Turban* from the years between 1626 and 1628 (cat. no. 74, 75). These can be augmented by other examples from 1629 to 1631, including the *Bust of an Old Man in a Fur Cap* in Innsbruck[102] and the *Old Woman at Prayer* in Salzburg,[103] and figures dressed mainly in oriental and Polish costumes executed between 1632 and 1639 in New York, Munich,[104] Prague, Amsterdam,[105] Washington

and Chatsworth.[106] Characteristic of the first type is a particular concentration on the face and the painterly depiction of wrinkled skin cast in strong contrasts of light or moved by laughter. There are no or almost no unnecessary details. This reduction is also evident in the work process and appears quite clearly in X-ray pictures, such as that of the Kassel *Bust of an Old Man with Golden Chain* (cat. no. 81). Compare the massive layers of lead white of the face with the thin painting of the bust (fig. 5), which is treated as a simple adjunct.[107] Taking into consideration the great variety of meanings given to the term *tronie* during Rembrandt's time (on this see the essay by Dagmar Hirschfelder in this catalogue), it would seem that the first type belongs to the core group – *tronies* in the true sense of the word; that is, depictions of exemplary and interesting «heads» and «faces». The second type is by comparison narrative and full of detail, with heads and bodies – sometimes shown as knee-pieces – dressed in elaborate headdresses, old-fashioned or exotic costumes and jewellery.[108] The manner of painting is comparable to contemporary many-figured compositions. The two types differ considerably from one another and vary both in their manner of evolution and function, and therefore I propose to distinguish between them by using the new terms «expressive tronies» and «costume tronies». It is certain that the *costume tronies* were considered «finished» paintings intended for sale and public viewing. Determining the function of both *expressive tronies* and the composition *David with the Head of Goliath before Saul* (fig. 12) is, however, more difficult for a number of reasons. Can we justifiably consider them as studies?

Since the sixteenth century, pure preparatory works were technically simpler and less exacting than works destined for the market. They were usually executed on paper or cardboard.[109] In the proposed line of development from Palma il Giovane to Rembrandt, there is a marked change in the choice of support from paper, as favoured by the young van Dyck, to solid panel, as chosen by Jordaens and later Lievens and Rembrandt. Even when Jordaens used his head study (cat. no. 70) for a monumental painting, it is probable that it was not painted for this mere purpose, the degree of virtuosity suggesting that it was intended as a work in its own right. Symptomatic of the tendency to view head studies as independent works is Lievens' transformation, described above, of van Dyck's head study into an autonomous picture (cat. no. 69).

It was generally the case that artists did not sign sketches, modelli and studies, as these were not intended for public viewing. The presence of Rembrandt's monograms and signatures on all paintings discussed here, some of which even bear a date, is unusual and new. Of course the sixteenth-century artist Frans Floris added his monogram to some of his small panels depicting individual heads, but their style was in no way conspicuously different from his other works, and from the start they were probably intended for sale. When discussing Rembrandt's sketchily-executed painting in Basle, Kurt Bauch noted that since the artist had signed and dated it, it is therefore neither a design nor a sketch.[110] Contrary to the opinion of the *RRP*, which still considers the painting to be a modello for an unknown or unfinished large-scale work,[111] it must be noted that no other version of such a painting is known; indeed, in Rembrandt's case not a single painted design for a painting can be shown to have existed. It was only after 1631 that he developed a special type of modello painted in grisaille for his etchings.[112]

A study can be said to have fulfilled its function when it is used in another work. Julius Held has already noted how rarely direct citations occur in the work of Floris and Rubens, who instead favoured a free adaptation of a basic type.[113] This principle is taken to its extreme by Rembrandt; not a single study head is repeated exactly in another work. Only when one takes the possibility of adaptation into account is it possible to also discover certain relationships in his œuvre. Thus the source of the important head of *Jeremiah Lamenting* of 1630 in Amsterdam (fig. 24) would seem to lie in the *Old Man with a Cap* in the Bader Collection (cat. no. 80).[114] Accordingly, the conclusion is that this method allows the source to retain it uniqueness and it is not diminished through the relationship with another, more prominent work.

A logical question arising from this is whether Rembrandt systematically assembled a collection of basic head studies as a catalogue of types for his history paintings. The answer must surely be no, because the number of his roughly-painted *tronies* is much too small for such a purpose, and

the composition in Basle (fig. 12) is moreover an isolated example. This sporadic appearance also contradicts the idea of producing for the market. And those who would propose that a large number of this type may have been lost should remember that of the six etched prints made by Jan van Vliet after Rembrandt *tronies*, five of the original models are still extant! That Rembrandt should have had the Leiden engraver produce prints of two of his four known *expressive tronies* is surely testimony to their outstanding importance. Whether Rembrandt also expected van Vliet to reproduce his rough manner remains unknown; the era of true facsimile graphics began only in the eighteenth century.[115]

To sum up, it can be said that all indications suggest that Rembrandt's roughly-painted early works were not the usual studies or sketches, but rather had a special status. They were neither incorporated into the work process, nor commissioned or painted for the free market. Instead they were in all probability first and foremost demonstration pieces designed to impress the *virtuosi*,[116] erudite lovers of art, visitors to the studio and of course his pupils. The «rough manner» was especially well-suited to the purpose, as Karel van Mander had singled it out as the most difficult exercise; one that could only be mastered after pupils had «suffered learning a clean manner».[117]

Such exemplary pieces provided studio members with models for a rich and profitable production of *tronies* and gave lovers of art objects they could admire. Rembrandt took more risks when painting *tronies* than with those pictures destined to leave his studio. The praise of connoisseurs encouraged him in further experimentation, which he gradually transferred to his official art, as will be shown below.[118] Those early works executed in the «rough manner» and discussed above play a key role: they nurtured the seeds of the type of painting which guaranteed Rembrandt a special place in the history of painting.

### Excursus: Rembrandt's *Bust of an Old Man with Golden Chain* and its influence

Rembrandt's 1632 *Bust of an Old Man with Golden Chain* in the Gemäldegalerie Kassel (cat. no. 81) concludes his small series of *expressive tronies* and at the same time represents the pinnacle of his achievement in this particular area. Hardly any other of his paintings exercised such a long and intensive influence, both on the artist himself and on his circle. The reasons for this lie in the formal maturity of the work itself and the general validity of the motif. In place of the extreme wrin-

kled appearance of the *Old Man with a Cap* (cat. no. 80), one finds a more even rendering of facial features. The wealth of expressive detail is derived solely from a strict concentration on physiognomy without the addition of unusual gestures or lighting. The simple pose and the old man's gaze out of the picture are features reminiscent of portraits. The absence of a headdress, which invariably steers the interpretation in a certain direction, ensures that the old man exhudes the neutrality essential if he is to be subjected to a variety of transformations. Rembrandt apparently wished to conclude the series of *expressive tronies* with a versatile basic type – and for this he indeed chose a most impressive model.

In the same year, 1632, he used the type in two very different single-figure paintings: a *costume tronie* and a history painting. The large-scale and representative depiction of a *Noble Oriental* in the Metropolitan Museum, New York, (fig. 25)[119] has the same physiognomy and a similar expression in his eyes, but his head is turned more to the front and his gaze is directed upward. In the Stockholm *St Peter* (fig. 26),[120] the head is inclined a little more to the right. Rembrandt retained the use of impasto for the face, but as these two works

25
Rembrandt Harmensz. van Rijn, *Noble Oriental* (detail), 1632
Canvas, 152.5 x 124 cm
The Metropolitan Museum of Art, New York

26
Rembrandt Harmensz. van Rijn, *St Peter*, 1632
Canvas, 82 x 62 cm
Nationalmuseum, Stockholm

were intended for a larger audience, he made it smoother and paid greater attention to connecting individual forms. He also avoids depicting the dishevelled hair and beard of the Kassel *tronie* by omitting it altogether for the *Oriental* and by giving the apostle a tidier appearance.[121] A portrait from his early Amsterdam period is very different and much closer in execution to fine painting. Recent restoration of the commissioned *Portrait of a Man Trimming his Quill*, now in Kassel, made the already known date of 1632 visible (cat. no. 82). The following year Rembrandt risked using the decidedly stylised wrinkled features of the *Oriental* and the *Apostel Petrus* for a portrait commissioned by Jan Rijksen and showing him together with his wife Griet Jans (Buckingham Palace, London; fig. 27).[122] The emphasis on the forehead and the use of unusually strong reds and yellows for the head of the shipbuilder in this double portrait leaves little doubt that he is a pictorial descendant of the old man in Kassel. Just a short time later, in 1634, Rembrandt went even a step further. As if no longer satisfied with reducing

and smoothing over his originally free and open style, Rembrandt not only returned once again to the daringly-abstract individual forms of the Kassel *Bust of an Old Man with Golden Chain* but expanded them even further in his *Portrait of Aechje Claesdr. Pesser* from the National Gallery London (fig. 28), as can be seen from the direct comparison in the exhibition (cat. no. 83). In the *Bust of a Man with Golden Chain* (cat. no. 81, cf. fig. 2) of 1632 Rembrandt appears to have found a particularly painterly solution which was to remain im-

30
Govert Flinck, *Bearded Old Man with Beret and Golden Chains*, c. 1642
Oak panel, 57 x 47 cm
Sale Cat., Christie's London, December 11, 1992, lot 79

31
Rembrandt Studio, *Bust of a Man with Unkempt Hair*, 1635
(cf. fig. 3)

portant throughout his career and to which he was to return many years later. Such is the case with one of the best known and most treasured self-portraits: his 1659 *Self-portrait with Beret and Collar* in Washington (fig. 29).[123] The origin of the rendering of the wrinkled brow with short overlapping strokes of impasto can hardly be missed.

The reactions of independent artists within Rembrandt's circle and subordinate members of his studio to the piece were very divergent. Having completed his apprenticeship with Lambert Jacobsz., Jacob Adriaensz. Backer from Leeuwarden arrived in Amsterdam around 1633 and sought contact with Rembrandt.[124] The bold manner of painting and the powerful characters of the *expressive tronie*, which arrived in Kassel in the eighteenth century, must have caught his eye. Backer decided to take up the artistic challenge presented by the *Bust of an Old Man with Golden Chain* and paint a ‹companion› piece. He was, it would seem, aware of the extent of his talent, and to avoid the impression of pure imitation, he conceived his depiction as an allegory of sight (cat. no. 84), which he incorporated into a series of the Five Senses, each of which depicts a genre-like figure. This was not unlike the series of the *Four Elements and the Ages of Man* (cat. nos. 72, 73), which Jan Lievens had painted some years previously. Backer's old man is an actor who with difficulty studies his face in a tiny piece of broken glass and appears to reflect on his wretched state and the inevitability of death. Backer chose as his model the same old man with the noticeably broad skull, lumpy nose, heavy circles under his eyes, bushy eyebrows and grumpy expression who had already sat for Rembrandt. But whereas the latter chose to concentrate on the unbroken power of the old man's eyes, the former saw the realism of a weather-beaten figure weighed down by old age. Backer also impressively uses impasto to capture the relief-like quality of the wrinkled face cast in contrasting light. But his painting is more stodgy and curvy than Rembrandt's and it still contains features of the Rubens' style practised by his teacher Lambert Jacobsz. Around the same time, another Jacobsz. pupil from Leeuwarden arrived in Amsterdam. Govaert Flinck formed closer associations with Rembrandt and remained in his studio as an assistant until 1635. But long after his departure he continued to fol-

low Rembrandt's motifs and style of painting. Werner Sumowski attributed a variant of the Kassel old man to Flinck, and its quality stands out among the numerous adaptations and variations (fig. 30).[125] Its broad, soft manner is characteristic of Flinck's style of around 1640. In comparison with Rembrandt, this style is less concerned with the particular effect of the paint itself but with the actual motif. The decorative addition of a beret with a gold band and a second gold chain certainly appealed to the demands of the market. The popularity of this figure is attested to by the numerous copies, many of which are, in turn, new variations.[126]

The style of Rembrandt's *Bust of an Old Man with Golden Chain* is so individual and idiosyncratic that traces of it are not hard to find in a number of paintings by anonymous members of the studio. For example, the signs of old age in the 1635 *Portrait of a Seventy-Year-Old Woman*, today in the Metropolitan Museum, New York, were painted in a simpler if more schematic manner.[127] At the same time, another assistant took on the exacting task of expanding the small series of *expressive tronies* already executed by Rembrandt by adding

one of his own executed in the emotionally-charged Baroque style currently favoured by the master. The *Bust of a Man with Unkempt Hair* in a New York private collection (fig. 31) conspicuously bears Rembrandt's signature and the date 1635.[128] The figure is comparable to Abraham in Rembrandt's *Sacrifice of Abraham* from the same year.[129] With a spontaneous movement of his head and a questioning gaze full of expectation, the man turns to an imaginary counterpart on the left. Quite different in concept from Rembrandt, this expressive study presses the figure into a certain role, such as is the case with the unbelieving and questioning Apostle Thomas. The invention appears to be original and the brilliant rough manner of painting is a further development of the style of the *expressive tronie* of 1632. These points were emphasised by the *RRP*. However a comparison of detailed close-ups (figs. 2, 3) revealed uncertainties and weaknesses in execution as well as an uneconomical application of paint: an array of tiny dabs of paint on the forehead confuse more than clarify, the plasticity of the side of the nose cast in shadow remains undefined and the highlights on the pupils are irregular and uncertain.[130] Finally, another example is the painting showing *St Paul* in the Kunsthistorisches Museum in Vienna, which concludes the exhibition. Here the interest lies more in the type of head rather than the style. The catalogue text (cat. no. 87) shows that the figure is a combination of two models by Rembrandt. The later of the two, the *Bust of an Old Man with a Golden Chain*, which was executed in Amsterdam in 1632, contains traces of an extroverted Baroque characterisation that was particularly popular during the mid-1630s. A comparison of details of the two heads (figs. 32, 33) shows similarities in the ‹design› of the wrinkles on the forehead, but also differences. These were essential in order to turn Rembrandt's realistic old man into a suitably idealistic Apostle. The broad face became thinner and thus more noble, but only in the lower half. The upper half now carries the high forehead of a ‹thinker›, a transformation that is very appropriate for the most intellectual of the Apostles. The strong expression of the *tronie* becomes one of penetrating intensity, whereby the eyes, which in a large-scale painting must capture the attention of the viewer, have been clearly enlarged. This new look at the Kassel *Bust of an Old Man with a Golden Chain* as the work of Rembrandt allows for both new insights into the master's painting and also provides new insights in the work practices of his studio.

\* I would like to thank Professor Bernard Aikema, Nijmegen, and Professor Ernst van de Wetering, Amsterdam, for many stimulating exchanges and much valuable information

1 «Acht Rembrandts sind darunter, desgleichen in solcher perfektion niemahls gesehen und zwar von allerhand sorten und denen besten Manieren dieses Meisters, theils sind von der rauhen dick aufgetragenen Malereyen, ander aber wieder so fein als ein Gerard Dou und Mieris kaum sein kann.» Quoted in Herzog 1969, p. 27.

2 Both/Vogel 1964; Herzog 1969, pp. 15–19; Kassel 1996, pp. 14–17.

3 Houbraken, vol. 1, 1718, pp. 254–270.

4 The inventory of 1816 lists 44 paintings as being by Rembrandt. All were acquired by Wilhelm VIII and his heir, Friedrich (Landgrave Friedrich II), whom Wilhelm trained in the appreciation of the arts.

5 The seven paintings by Frans Hals in the Kassel Gemäldegalerie were all acquired by Wilhelm and Friedrich. Kassel 1996, pp. 17, 138–140.

6 This is further confirmation of van de Wetering's observation that it was initially Rembrandt's brushwork that generated such admiration in later generations, cf. Wetering 1997, p. 268.

7 *Haupt=Catalogus von Sr Hochfürstl: Durchlt. HERRN Landgrafens Wilhelm zu Heßen, sämtlichen Schilderÿen, und Porträts. Verfertiget in Anno 1749.* New acquisitions by the Landgrave continued to be registered in the inventory until the outbreak of the Seven Years War in 1756. The inventory is in the possession of the Staatliche Museen Kassel.

8 Wetering 1991/92a, p. 16; Wetering 1997, p. 160.

9 A detailed and perceptive study of the development of the «rough manner» in Venetian art and the history of its dissemination is given by Philip Sohm 1991. On the «rough manner» in ancient art, see Sohm 1991, pp. 32, 37; Wetering 1991/92a, p. 21.

10 Mander/Hoecker 1916, p. 273, verses 19, 20; Mander/Miedema 1973, p. 599.

11 Mander/Hoecker 1916, pp. 273–275, verses 22–26; Mander/Miedema 1973, p. 600.

12 Sohm 1991, p. 25; Emmens (1968, p. 38) talks of a «Tuscan-Roman negative».

13 On Boschini, see Sohm 1991, pp. 1f.

14 The Habsburgs experienced problems with Titian's painting, so that after 1550 they favoured the Netherlandish artist Anthonis Mor. Mary of Hungary, aunt of Emperor Charles V, complained of the difficulty in looking at Titian's portraits close up. See Bert W. Meijer in: Venice 1999, pp. 501–503 and note 54.

15 For the Florentine art critic Giorgio Vasari (*Le vite de' piu eccellenti pittori, scultori, e architettori*, 1568), the late painting of the Venetian Titian presented a real challenge. In the same breath, he criticises it as carelessness resulting from old age yet praises its masterly and elegant «sprezzatura», the apparent ease with which the artist disguises the actual toil of work. One cannot (or should not) view it close up; rather from a distance the patches and brushstrokes come together to form an harmonious entity. This passage was important for van Mander and other theorists. It has always been interpreted in an ambivalent way, as is evident from the different nuances in various translations of Vasari's text, when the passage is sometimes cited as a criticism of the «rough manner» and sometimes as a neutral rule of art (cf. Wetering 1991/92a, p. 21, Wetering 1997, p. 163). However, Philip Sohm cites the example of Tintoretto's ground-breaking *Miracle of St Mark* of 1548 to show that Vasari's understanding was hardly in keeping with the intentions of the artist, for the original, albeit disputed, location was the Scuola di San Marco, which did not permit viewing from a distance. Theorists adhering to the primacy of precise draughtsmanship sought to explain the patchy painting style of the Venetians into line by subsequently relating it to ancient theories (Horace) on the different requirements for viewing from near and far. The painters, at least originally, did not seek to distance the viewer, but rather sought recognition for their invention and placed importance on the contradictory nature of viewing close-up and from a distance; see Sohm 1991, pp. 7, 43, 53. It is from this understanding that Rembrandt's statement, recorded by Houbraken, should be interpreted: namely as a measure of self-protection against the unappreciative reactions of uneducated viewers. The true lover of art would hardly have been antagonistic towards Rembrandt. Sohm points out that viewing roughly-painted works up close was already normal practice in the 17th century; see Sohm 1991, p. 50.

16 So Karel van Mander in 1604, following Vasari; see Mander/Hoecker 1916, p. 275, verses 24, 25.

17 This judgement was made in 1681 by the Dutchman Andries Pels; see Emmens 1968, pp. 28ff.

18 Pochat 1986, p. 216.

19 Pochat 1986, p. 278.

[20] Białostocki 1981, p. 14.

[21] Cited in Mander/Hoecker 1916, p. 275, no. 26.

[22] Cited in Białostocki 1981, pp. 31f., note 4. On the term ‹ingenium›, see Raupp 1984, pp. 166ff.

[23] Białostocki 1981, p. 13.

[24] See Schwartz 1984/85/87; Sumowski 1983ff.; Tümpel 1986; Tümpel 1993; Grimm 1991.

[25] Corpus, vol. 1, 1982, «Preface, Some reflections on method», pp. XIII, XVII, «The Stylistic Development», pp. 3, 9.

[26] Corpus, vol. 1, 1982, p. 3.

[27] Corpus, vol. 1, p. XV.

[28] Schwartz (1984/85/87, pp. 60, 62, 66, no. 46, 49, 60) already condemned the different judgements as arbitrary and demanded that the entire series be considered authentic. According to London/The Hague 1999/2000, p. 250, note 68 «Both paintings [B 5–6] are now universally accepted as by Rembrandt».

[29] Before the publication of the 2nd. Corpus volume, but after Josua Bruyn (1974) expressed the opinion that it is a forgery, Gary Schwartz defended the attribution, citing as support the provenance from the Röver collection; see Schwartz 1984/85/87, p. 197, fig. 211.

[30] Corpus, vol. 1, 1982, p. 580.

[31] See Emmens 1968; Wetering 1991/92a.

[32] Corpus, vol. 1, 1982, copy under no. A 14, C 24, C 26, C 30. Kassel 1996, pp. 245f., nos. GK 229, GK 230, GK 231, GK 232.

[33] Wetering 1991/92a, p. 24, figs. 27–29; Wetering 1997, pp. 171f., figs. 216–220.

[34] Cf. Corpus, vol. 2, 1986, pp. 100f., fig. p. 575.

[35] Cf. the X-ray of the *Portrait of Aechje Claesdr. Pesser* in the National Gallery, London (no. 83), Corpus, vol. 2, 1986, fig. p. 575.

[36] Texts by Erik Hinterding (see Hinterding 1996) and Albert Blankert (Melbourne/Canberra 1997/1998, no. 4) have been instrumental in instigating this change in opinion.

[37] Kassel 1996, vol. 1, p. 229.

[38] The examination was undertaken together with the head of painting restoration, Hans Brammer, on April 17, 1999.

[39] Wetering 1991/92a, p. 16; Wetering 1997, p. 160.

[40] The *Self-portrait* of 1629 in the Isabella Stewart Gardner Museum, Boston, is somewhat of an exception, Corpus, vol. 1, 1982, no. A 20; Washington/London/The Hague 2000/01, no. 10. The painting was particularly important for the development of Gerard Dou's fine painting.

[41] Wetering 1991/92a, figs. 27, 32; Wetering 1997, figs. 217, 220.

[42] Grimm 1991, pp. 20, 28; Washington/London/The Hague 2000/01, nos. 14a, 14b, figs. pp. 114, 115.

[43] Cf. the detail from Lastman's *Triumph of Mordecai* of 1617 (on loan to the Museum het Rembrandthuis, Amsterdam) on the cover of the exhibition catalogue Amsterdam 1991, where the various types of brushwork and the fine differentiation in textures are clearly evident.

[44] Cf. Elsheimer's *Adoration of the Cross* from the altarpiece in the Städelsches Kunstinstitut, Frankfurt, Andrews 1985, no. 16.7, colour pl. 66. Ornamental lines were drawn in the wet impasto of the dalmatic of the figure in the foreground with his back turned. See also Bauch 1960, pp. 129–134.

[45] Wetering 1991/92a, pp. 26f., figs. 34, 35; Wetering 1997, p. 173, figs. 223, 224.

[46] Stockholm 1992/93, nos. 46–48 (Christopher Brown). Already in 1984 Gary Schwartz has argued in favour of an attribution to Rembrandt; see Schwartz 1984/85/87, p. 34, figs. 12–14.

[47] Sale catalogue, Christie's, London, July 7, 1995, lot 57.

[48] Bauch 1960, pp. 227f.: «strähnige Malweise, die wilden Pinselzüge (die zwar doch nicht treffen)».

[49] See Amsterdam 1991, no. 20; Ben Broos in: Amsterdam 1999/2000, p. 92; Broos 2000.

[50] Schneider/Ekkart 1973, pp. 2f.

[51] Bauch 1960, chapter «Haarlem und Lievens», pp. 112, 119; Sumowski 1983ff., vol. 3, p. 1765.

[52] Slatkes 1981/82, p. 175; Washington/London/Haarlem 1989/90, p. 171.

[53] Slive, vol. 2, 1970, p. 36, vol. 3, 1974, no. 5; Washington/London/Haarlem 1989/90, p. 1, colour pl. II.

[54] Sumowski 1983ff., vol. 3, p. 1765.

[55] This according to Jan Orlers in his description of the city of Leiden of 1641; see Braunschweig 1979, p. 35.

[56] Braunschweig 1979; Sumowski 1983ff., vol. 3, nos. 1214–1285, vol. 5, nos. 2124, 2127, vol. 6, nos. 2355, 2357a–2367 (without the portraits).

[57] Sumowski 1983ff., vol. 3, nos. 1179, 1181.

[58] Canvas, 112 x 89.8 cm, 97 x 84 cm without additions. Sale catalogue, Christie's, Amsterdam, May 6, 1998, lot 120 with colour pl. (previously unpublished).

[59] Braunschweig 1979, nos. 6, 7; Sumowski 1983ff., vol. 3, nos. 1225, 1226.

[60] For the discussion and reproduction of the detail, see Wetering 1991/92a, pp. 27f., fig. 36; Wetering 1997, pp. 173–175, fig. 225.

[61] Oak panel, each 91 x 78 cm. Braunschweig 1979, nos. 10–13; Sumowski 1983ff., vol. 3, nos. 1230–1233. Particularly noteworthy are the books with tattered pages done in a painterly manner in the pictures of the Evangelists. Comparable examples can be found in two Vanitas still-life paintings by Lievens in the Rijksmuseum, Amsterdam, and in the Hannema-de Stuers Foundation, Heino (Sumowski 1983ff., vol. 3, nos. 1300, 1299); the latter is dated 1627 (Braunschweig 1979, no. 14).

[62] Hoogstraten 1678, p. 238; Wetering 1991/92a, p. 30; Wetering 1997, p. 176. According to the most recent finding, an oil-egg emulsion was used, see Groen 1997 and Wetering 1997, pp. 224-243, esp. p. 239.

[63] A further example is the painting *Balaam and the Ass* of 1626 in the Musée Cognac-Jay, Paris; Corpus, vol. 1, 1982, no. A 2.

[64] See Roeber 1998, pp. 64f.

[65] Canvas, 124.5 x 101.6 cm, signed and dated *1621*. The Cleveland Museum of Art. Nicolson/Vertova 1990, vol. 1, p. 191, no. 1133, vol. 3, fig. 1133.

[66] Corpus, vol. 1, 1982, no. A 9; Basle 1987, no. 80; Basle 2000, no. 7.

[67] The *Self-portrait* of 1630 is in the Nationalmuseum Stockholm, the *Old Woman at Prayer* in the Residenzgalerie Salzburg. See the concise discussion in Stockholm 1992/93, nos. 49–51 and London/The Hague 1999/2000, under no. 18.

[68] Bernard Aikema in: Hirschfelder/Raupp 2001, p. 199 and Lugano 1998.

[69] Tümpel 1986, p. 405, commentary on no. 127; Mariët Westerman in: Boston 2000/2001, p. 37 in relation to the etched self-portraits showing a laughing expression.

[70] Washington/London/Haarlem 1989/90, no. 31.

[71] Oak panel, 59.5 x 51.2 cm. Private Collection, Switzerland. Corpus, vol. 2, 1985, no. 40a; Basle 1987, no. 81.

[72] To cite a few examples: Kurt Bauch talks of Lievens' schooling in Antwerp, see Bauch 1960, p. 266, note 185. Gary Schwartz demonstrates that by illustrating the engraving by Matham after Rubens' *Samson being taken Prisoner* it was Lievens and not Rembrandt who used the print, see Schwartz 1984/85/87, pp. 82f., figs. 68, 69, 71. Josua Bruyn emphasises the notable Flemish orientation of the Evangelist series in Bamberg, see Bruyn 1988b, p. 327. J. Douglas Stewart sees the *Singing Man* in the Bader Collection, Milwaukee (Sumowski 1983ff., vol. 4, no. 1224 with colour ill.) as being derived both compositionally and technically from Rubens, see Douglas Stewart 1990, p. 46. Peter C. Sutton considers a general Flemish influence in the monumental form and soft painting of the large Amsterdam version of *Samson and Delilah*, see Melbourne/Canberra 1997/98, p. 222. Grateful thanks to Stephanie Dickey for placing at my disposal the text of her lecture on «Van Dyck in Holland» given at the van Dyck colloquium in Antwerp on May 19, 1999, in which she shows that Lievens was already one of the closest followers of van Dyck in Holland before 1630.

[73] Corpus, vol. 1, 1982, no. A 35; Schwartz 1984/85/87, p. 89, figs. 79, 80; Leiden 1991/92, pp. 114, 117; Sumowski 1983ff., vol. 3, no. 1245.

[74] See Schneider/Ekkart 1973, p. 1.

75 Douglas Stewart 1990, p. 45.

76 Douglas Stewart 1990, p. 46, figs. 4, 5; Sumowski, vol. 7, 1983, no. 1638x, pp. 3652f.

77 Characteristic for the situation is Julius Held's catalogue of Ruben's oil sketches, where he confines his examination to individual examples of head studies, see Held 1980, p. 595, and the explicit exclusion of head studies in the important exhibition of oil sketches in 1984, see Rotterdam/Braunschweig 1984, p. 14. The detailed research carried out by Justus Müller Hofstede on Rubens and van Dyck have provided the most inspiration, see Müller Hofstede 1968 and 1987/88. On van Dyck, see also the general overview by Held 1990/91.

78 Tümpel 1993, p. 26; Wetering 1997, p. 175f., fig. 229.

79 Panel, 46.3 x 63.5 cm. Held 1980 no. 446, pl. 433: executed c. 1617.

80 Panel, 65.5 x 50.5 cm, Rubens House, Antwerp, inv. no. p. 80. Jaffé 1989, p. 246, no. 318; Padua/Rome/Milan 1990, no. 39: executed c. 1617/18.

81 On the technique and aesthetic of Rubens' streaky imprimatura, see Sonnenburg 1979, pp. 11–18. In the *Miracle of St Frances of Paula* (illustrated; Munich 1986, pp. 451f.) the streaky painting in the upper-right corner can, according to Held (1980, no. 406), only have been added at a later date, so that it lies above the imprimatura, just as it does with Lievens.

82 Paper on panel, 57 x 45 cm. Glück 1931, fig. 32 right, p. 521; Antwerp 1993, p. 98, note 4; Berlin 1996, p. 43, fig. 933.

83 Ottawa 1968/69, p. 84 under no. 25; Berlin 1975, pp. 140f.; Antwerp 1993, p. 96, where it is also noted that van Dyck and Jordaens' studies were also executed *in paragone* (R.-A. d'Hulst).

84 Oil on paper on panel, 57 x 41 cm. Bayerische Staatsgemäldesammlungen, Munich, inv. no. 1240. Müller Hofstede 1987/88, pp. 147f., 152, fig. 22.

85 Regardless of how much the head studies of van Dyck and Jordens are based on emphatic realism, such a continuation of physiognomic characteristics from face to neck is a feature typical of ancient art. Bernard Aikema kindly drew my attention to the head of the *Old Fisherman*, a Hellenistic work known only through Roman marble copies (Zanker 1995, pp. 108–113, fig. 60), which in the seventeenth century was believed to depict the philosopher Seneca and which appears in numerous paintings, such as van Dyck's *Portrait of Justus van Meerstraten* in Kassel, see Kassel 1996, p. 111.

86 The use of impasto and strong red-brown tones for flesh are similar to the rendering of the hands and face of the *Crucified St Peter* in Brussels, which is dated 1615/16, see Antwerp/London 1999, no. 5.

87 See Müller Hofstede 1987/88.

88 Vey 1962, p. 20. He is followed by Müller Hofstede who compares the head of an old man by Tintoretto with van Dyck's, see Müller Hofstede 1987/88, p. 158, figs. 28, 160. Hans Vlieghe also expressed similar ideas and proposed Rubens and Hendrick van Balen as possible conveyors of the Venetian style, see Vlieghe 1998, p. 36.

89 Sohm 1991, pp. 7, 9.

90 *Portrait of an Old Man*, canvas, 63 x 43.5 cm (oval). Musée des Beaux-Arts, Brussels. Müller Hofstede 1987/88, p. 143, figs. 14, 16.

91 Canvas, 107 x 138, 5 cm., executed after 1590. The Governing Body of Christ Church, Oxford. Bassano/Fort Worth 1992/93, no. 78; Venice 1999, no. 151.

92 45 x 32 cm, originally 41 x 27 cm. Private Collection, Italy. Mason Rinaldi 1984, no. 78; Venice 1990, no. 92. My thanks to Professor Stefania Mason Rinaldi for placing a photograph at my disposal.

93 Paper on panel, 44.5 x 33 cm. Whereabouts unknown, previously The Earl of Spencer, Althorp House. See Müller Hofstede 1987/88, p. 159, fig. 29 for the attribution as a work by van Dyck from around 1617 and p. 161, fig. 31 for the connection with the artist's *Healing the Lame* in Munich. I wish to thank him for placing a photograph at my disposal.

94 Information kindly supplied by Bettina Werche (Weimar), whose dissertation *Hendrick van Balen (1575–1632) – ein Antwerpener Kabinettmaler der Rubenszeit* is in print.

95 Philip Rylands in: Dict. of Art, vol. 23, pp. 878–880.

96 It is possible that Rottenhammer may have had difficulty in obtaining large-scale commissions such as those executed by Tintoretto and therefore decided to specialise in small cabinet pieces, see John Andrew Martin in: Venice 1999, p. 617.

97 An important example of the dissemination of Venetian painting within Italy is a *Male Head* painted about 1590 by Annibale Carracci, who according to Posner (1971, no. 60) was influenced by Tintoretto and Bassano (canvas, 46 x 73 cm, Palazzo Pitti, Florence; see also Cooney/Malafarina 1976, no. 56). For this extremely broadly painted *tronie* Carracci adopted the ideals of a *pensiero*, a melancholic artist, possibly using another artist as model, cf. Raupp 1984, pp. 226ff. Previously considered a portrait, it is today exhibited as a *testa virile*.

98 Comparable genres are the drawn fantasy portraits and partly grotesque head studies by Hendrick Goltzius (see Reznicek 1961, nos. 291, 292, 320, 228) and some painted studies of expressions and poses by Cornelis van Haarlem (Thiel 1999, nos. 197, 262, 263, WO1). Abraham Bloemaert also developed a notably rich production after 1630, when presumably *tronies* had become fashionable through Rembrandt (Roethlisberger 1993, no. 518–529).

99 Sonnenburg 1995/96, p. 73.

100 Meijer 2000, p. 379.

101 The *Bust of an Old Man* (Paper on panel, 10.6 x 7.2 cm. Private Collection, New York. Corpus, vol. 2, 1986, no. A 74) belongs to an album and can therefore be omitted here.

102 Corpus, vol. 1, 1982, no. A 29. Cf. the essay by Dagmar Hirschfelder, p. 83, fig. 1.

103 Corpus, vol. 1, 1982, no. A 27.

104 Corpus, vol. 2, 1986, no. A 73. Cf. the essay by Dagmar Hirschfelder, p. 84, fig. 2.

105 Corpus, vol. 3, 1989, no. C 101. Now this painting is again considered to be autograph, see Perth/Adelaide/Brisbane 1998, no. 28 (Norbert Middelkoop).

106 New York: Corpus, vol. 2, 1986, no. A 48. Prague: ibid., no. A 95. Washington: Corpus, vol. 3, 1989, no. A 122. Chatsworth: ibid., no. A 128.

107 The *RRP* criticised the «unarticulated treatment of the clothing», see Corpus, vol. 2, 1986, p. 653.

108 Mariecke de Winkel (1999/2000) was the first to examine these details in her study *Costume in Rembrandts Self Portraits*.

109 See Rotterdam/Braunschweig 1984, p. 15. Rubens painted his oil sketches on oak panel and is a notable exception.

110 Bauch 1960, p. 119: «Rembrandt hat das Werk bezeichnet und datiert, es is also nicht ein Entwurf oder eine Skizze.»

111 See Corpus, vol. 1, 1982, p. 130 under no. A 9, and Wetering 1997, p. 146. On the discussion, see also Basle 1987, p. 212. Gian Carlo Bott (Basle 2000, no. 7) also arrived at the same conclusion and calls the picture an experimental panel «experimentelle Tafel».

112 See Wetering 2000/01.

113 Held 1980, p. 597.

114 Corpus, vol. 1, 1982, no. A 28. The relationship of the two heads has already been noted by Claus Grimm, see Grimm 1991, pp. 92, 89, figs. 163, 164. Ernst van de Wetering pointed out a further variation in the only known second version of the *Baptism of the Eunuch* (see Corpus, vol. 1, 1982, p. 37f, with ill.; Tümpel 1993, no. K4, fig. p. 51).

115 Amsterdam 1996, pp. 51, 64, nos. 6, 11. Among the sources are the *Bust of a Laughing Man in a Gorget* and the *Old Man with a Cap*, cat. nos. 79, 80.

116 On the term *virtuoso*, see Raupp 1984, pp. 72–80; on the real meaning of ‹lovers of the art of painting› «Liebhaber der Malkunst » in Rembrandt's time, see Wetering 1999/2000, pp. 22–25.

117 Mander/Hoecker 1916, p. 275, verse 26. In verse 23 van Mander

warns that different painters have failed in their attempts to imitate Titian's *ultima maniera*.

[118] Sohm (1991, pp. 26f.) points out that the «rough manner» was acceptable to sixteenth century authors such as Vasari only for works of a private rather than public nature; this attitude changed in the 17th century.

[119] Canvas, 153 x 111 cm. Corpus, vol. 2, 1986, no. A 48; Berlin/Amsterdam/London 1991/92, no. 9; New York 1995/96, vol. 1, no. 2, vol. 2, pp. 38f. Hessel Miedema questioned the de-attribution by the *RRP* of the Kassel old man upon seeing these two paintings together, see Miedema 1989, pp. 49f.

[120] Canvas, 82 x 62 cm. Corpus, vol. 2, 1986, no. A 46; Stockholm 1992/93, no. 54; Melbourne/Canberra 1997/98, no. 7.

[121] Claus Grimm was the first to recognise the relationship between the three paintings and reproduce large-scale details of all three together, see Grimm 1991, pp. 90f., figs. 47, 49. He also very kindly placed his wonderful slides at my disposal.

[122] Canvas, 114.3 x 168.9 cm, The Royal Collection, Her Majesty Queen Elisabeth II, Windsor Castle. Corpus, vol. 2, 1986, no. A 77.

[123] Canvas, 84.4 x 66 cm. London/The Hague 1999/2000, no. 73. Detail of the head on the cover of the English edition of the catalogue.

[124] On this, see Sumowski 1983ff., vol. 1, pp. 133–141.

[125] Panel, 57 x 47 cm, with false signature: *Rembrandt.ft.* Sale Cat., Christie's London, December 11, 1992, lot 79, as G. Flinck; Sumowski 1983ff., vol. 6, p. 3708, no. 2279b as G. Flinck, executed c. 1642. Two small variations of the Kassel head are reproduced in the Corpus, vol. 2, 1986, under no. C 53, one of them being the *Study Head of an Old Man* in the Metropolitan Museum, New York (panel, 21 x 17.5 cm, New York 1995/96, vol. 2, no. 39 as «style of Rembrandt»).

[126] Two examples: an old copy, folded over to create an octagonal, is in the Kassel Gemäldegalerie, No. GK 1112, Kassel 1996, p. 247, pl. 126; an expanded half-figure copy in Providence, Rhode Island, R. I. S. D. Museum, Inv. No. 23.330, previously attributed to Aert de Gelder. On *tronie* production in Rembrandt's studio and its contemporary status, see Veen 1997/98, pp. 71f.

[127] Canvas, 128 x 99.4 cm. Corpus, vol. 3, 1989, no. C 112; New York 1995/96, vol. 2, no. 24 as Jacob Backer.

[128] Oak panel, 66.6 x 52.6 cm. Corpus, vol. 3, 1989, no. C 100.

[129] Canvas, 193.5 x 132.8 cm, Hermitage, St. Petersburg. Corpus, vol. 2, 1986, no. A 108; Berlin/Amsterdam/London 1991/92, no. 21.

[130] The conclusions of the comparison as outlined in the Corpus were reconfirmed by a further examination of the painting in Amsterdam undertaken together with Ernst van de Wetering on October 18, 2000.

## Catalogue I

# Beginnings

Authors:
Bob van den Boogert (B.v.d.B.)
Ed de Heer (E.d.H.)
Justus Lange (J.L.)
Beate Chr. Mirsch (B.C.M.)
Bernhard Schnackenburg (B.S.)
Christiaan Vogelaar (C.V.)
Ernst van de Wetering (E.v.d.W.)
Marieke de Winkel (M.d.W.)

# 1
## Jacob Isaacsz. van Swanenburg (Leiden 1571–1638 Utrecht)
# Underworld with Charon's Ferry, c. 1620/30

Oak panel, 93.5 x 124 cm
Stedelijk Museum De
Lakenhal, Leiden,
Inv. Nr. S 251

Regteren Altena 1936,
pp. XIII, 33–35, 114,
note 3; Leiden 1949,
pp. 279f.; Gelder 1953b,
p. 276; Haak 1968, p. 19;
Leiden 1983, p. 328;
Regteren Altena 1983,
vol. 1, p. 89; Ekkart 1998,
p. 127

The Leiden painter Jacob Isaacsz van Swanenburg is better known for having been Rembrandt's first teacher than he is for his own work. In the second edition of his *Beschrijvinghe der Stadt Leyden* of 1641, the burgomaster of Leiden and city chronicler Jan Jansz. Orlers relates that Rembrandt's parents «took him to the good painter Mr Iacob Isaacxcs. van Swanenburch to be taught and trained by him / with whom he then stayed for about three years / and during that same time / he improved so greatly / that the art lovers were truly amazed by this / and they could easily see / that in due course he would become an outstanding painter.»[1] Orlers' account is likely to be reliable because he would have known Swanenburg personally – and probably Rembrandt, too. His admiration for van Swanenburg is confirmed by the fact that he had a work by the master in his not inconsiderable collection of paintings. The young Rembrandt's apprenticeship with van Swanenburg cannot have begun before 1617, when van Swanenburg settled for good in his native city after many years spent living in Naples. Around 1624 Rembrandt left Leiden temporarily to study with Pieter Lastman in Amsterdam. Contrary to Orlers' view, van Swanenburg's influence on the young Rembrandt is generally regarded as of little significance. Van Gelder and Bauch, however, argue that van Swanenburg did have an influence be-

cause, after more than twenty years in Venice, Rome and particularly Naples, he would have been the first person to alert the young Rembrandt to relatively unknown names like Caravaggio and his pupil Finsonius, who moved from Naples to Amsterdam in 1617.[2]

Van Swanenburg's known œuvre is restricted to just a few works. A *View of St Peter's Square* of 1628 bears the Italianate signature «Iacomo Swanenburch» but, given the date, it must have been painted after his return to the Netherlands.[3] A previously unpublished *Battle of Bethulia* with the same Italianate signature was recently purchased by the Stedelijk Museum De Lakenhal in Leiden. A panel of a scene in Hell marked «IVS» in the Museum Podmorskie in Gdansk is also generally attributed to van Swanenburg. Typical of this and other works attributed to the master is the suggestion of infinite space with a great many figures full of movement and dynamism clustered in groups. The works betray the influence of painters like Filippo Napoletano and other masters who had continued to work in the late mannerist style in Naples around 1600.[4]

In all its pictorial elements, this panel is related to the much larger work in Gdansk. It is painted not on canvas, but on an oak panel, which indicates that it was painted in the Netherlands, and in any event after the master's return to the country in 1617.

A huge, gaping monster's mouth encloses the personifications of the Seven Deadly Sins. A recumbent woman figures as the personification of sloth and a couple making love stands for lust; in the centre, two ruffians represent wrath, a woman tearing her tongue out personifies calumny and a woman with a purse, avarice; at the extreme right stands an ostentatiously dressed woman holding a mirror as the personification of pride, while a man who sits gorging himself at a table represents gluttony. In the left foreground, numerous naked figures are roughly dragged off by demons; a fiercely burning tower in the background and a fantastic boat, Charon's ferry, contribute to the horror of the scene. Pluto, the god of the underworld, and his wife Proserpina drive through the firmament in a chariot drawn by black horses. In a mysterious tableau at the upper right, a soul rising out of a pot in the form

1a
Jacob Isaacsz. van
Swanenburg, *Underworld
with Charon's Ferry*
(detail), c. 1620/30

126

of a woman clad in white is saved by an angel, under the watchful eye of a man in seventeenth-century dress flanked by a praying nun and a bell-ringer.

Described by van Regteren Altena and van Gelder as a scene in Hell,[5] the panel is erroneously identified in the 1983 catalogue of the museum's holdings as *The Sibyl shows Aeneas the Underworld*.[6] The association with Book Six of Virgil's *Aeneid* would appear to be unlikely, given the absence of both the Sibyl of Cumae and the Greek hero. Furthermore, the presence of Pluto and Charon's ferry indicate that this is the Greek and not the Christian underworld, and in particular Tartarus where the doomed souls remained. The Seven Deadly Sins, however, imply a Christian theme which, following Dante's *Inferno*, had since the thirteenth century figured in scenes of the Last Judgement. Whereas in the Greek underworld thousands are condemned to eternal torment, the scene with Christian overtones at the top right refers to the salvation of a chosen individual. The central themes in van Swanenburg's visionary work would thus appear to be the antithesis of the profane beliefs of classical antiquity, on the one hand, and the Christian message of salvation, on the other. Van Regteren Altena saw a heretical tendency in the scene and linked this to an incident in 1608, while he was still living in Naples, when the painter ran into trouble with the Inquisition over a painting of a witches' sabbath.[7] However, the praying nun and the soul saved by an angel in this panel point not so much to a heretical element as to a decidedly Catholic religious viewpoint. Van Swanenburg had converted to Catholicism upon his marriage in Italy. Possibly for this reason he was barred from inheriting from the estate of his father, the Leiden painter Isaac Claesz. van Swanenburg. In any event, he did not return to his native city until after his father's death in 1615.[8]

C.V.

[1] Orlers 1641, p. 375: «... gebracht by den welschilderende Mr. Iacob Isaacxcs. van Swanenburch, omme vanden zelven geleert ende onder wesen te werden / by den welcken hy gebleven is omtrent de drie Jaeren / ende also hy gheduyrende den zelven tijt / zoo seer toegenomen hadde / dat de Const Lief-hebberen daerinne ten hoochsten verwondert waeren / ende dat men genoechsaem konde sein / dat hy metter tijdt een uytnemende Schilder soude werden.»

[2] Gelder 1953b, p. 276; Bauch 1960, p. 44f.

[3] Statens Museum for Konst, Copenhagen; there is an unsigned version dated 1632 in the Städtische Kunstsammlungen, Augsburg.

[4] See Longhi 1957.

[5] Regteren Altena 1936, p. 33–35; Van Gelder 1953, p. 276.

[6] Leiden 1983, p. 328.

[7] Regteren Altena 1936, p. 33–35.

[8] Ekkart 1998, pp. 126f.

## 2
Pieter Lastman (Amsterdam c. 1583–1633)
# The Baptism of the Eunuch, c. 1612

Oak panel, 62 x 100 cm
Collection Frits Lugt,
Institut Néerlandais,
Paris, Inv. Nr. 4886

Defoer 1977, pp. 9ff.;
Amsterdam 1991, pp. 58f.

Pieter Lastman was the leading figure in a group of Amsterdam history painters who are referred to in art historical literature as the pre-Rembrandtists. As the name suggests, the work of these artists was generally studied from the perspective of Rembrandt's art. It is only in recent decades that art historians have started to judge the work of the pre-Rembrandtist painters, which is characterised by a considerable homogeneity, on its own merits.[1] The similarities lie mainly in the choice of subjects, type of composition and narrative manner. The other main pre-Rembrandtists are Jan and Jacob Pynas, Claes Moeyaert, Jan Tengnagel and François Venant.

Lastman was without question the most inventive and influential of these artists. He introduced new subjects into painting – subjects that had previously only been dealt with in prints, he researched his work by studying historical sources, and his skill at making his history pieces telling and comprehensible was unrivalled.

The six months which, according to Orlers, the young Rembrandt spent in Lastman's studio[2] were important for his artistic development. Lastman's influence is particularly evident in Rembrandt's earliest paintings. Some of them, like *Balaam and the Ass* (Musée Cognac-Jay, Paris) (p. 45, fig. 24), *The Stoning of St Stephen* (Musée des Beaux-Arts, Lyon) (p. 23, fig. 3) and the *History Painting* (cat. no. 7), are actually variations on paintings by Lastman. Broos contends that these early works were painted not in Leiden, as has always been assumed, but in Amsterdam under Lastman's supervision.[3] Challenging orthodoxy, he refers to Rembrandt's first Amsterdam period.[4] He also considers Rembrandt's *The Baptism of the Eunuch* of 1626 (cat. no. 3) to be one of the works created under Lastman's tutelage.

The story of the baptism of the eunuch is told in Acts 8:26–40. The apostle Philip was instructed by the angel of the Lord to go from Jerusalem to Gaza. On the way he met a eunuch, treasurer to the Ethiopian queen, Candace. The man was sitting in his chariot reading the prophecies of Isaiah. When Philip, instructed by the Holy Spirit, asked the eunuch if he understood what he was reading, the man requested that Philip explain the significance of the text. Philip then preached the gospel of Christ. The eunuch was converted and Philip baptised him in a stretch of water that they happened to be passing.

The eunuch kneels before Philip, who sprinkles him with water from his left hand. Two servants hold his turban and cloak. A third holds a large book. The eunuch's chariot is just visible in the background. His entourage watches, fascinated.

It is assumed that *The Baptism of the Eunuch*, which is not dated, was painted in about 1612.[5] There are three other paintings by Lastman devoted to the baptism of the eunuch. The earliest dates from 1608.[6] Later versions were made in 1620[7] and 1623[8] (fig. 2a). The four paintings differ in composition, perspective and additional elements. Executing different variations of a particular subject was typical of Lastman and in this, too, Rembrandt was to follow his lead.

In his rendition (cat. no. 3) Rembrandt combined motifs from various versions, without slavishly copying any of them. From the painting in the Fondation Custodia he took the principal group of Philip, the kneeling eunuch and the servant with the book.        E.d.H.

1   See, for example, Tümpel 1974; Sacramento 1974; Amsterdam 1991.
2   Orlers 1641, p. 375.
3   Broos 2000, p. 3.
4   Ibid. Broos's conclusion that Rembrandt's stay with Lastman must be dated to 1625–1626 is less innovative (cf. Amsterdam 1991, p. 54).
5   Amsterdam 1991, p. 59.
6   Freise 1911, no. 84. Tümpel 1974, p. 42.
7   Freise 1911, no. 86. Defoer 1977, pp. 9f., fig. 7.
8   Freise 1911, no. 85. Defoer 1977, pp. 10f.

Fig. 2a
Pieter Lastman, *The Baptism of the Eunuch*, 1623
Oak panel, 85 x 115 cm
Staatliche Kunsthalle, Karlsruhe

# 3
## Rembrandt Harmensz. van Rijn
# The Baptism of the Eunuch, 1626

Oak panel, 63.5 x 48 cm
Signed bottom right:
*RH.1626*
Museum Catharijne-
convent, Utrecht,
Inv. Nr. SCH. 380

Leiden 1976, no. S25;
Defoer 1977; Wetering
1977; Wetering 1977a;
Corpus, vol. 1, 1982,
no. A 5; Schwartz
1984/85/87, fig. 20;
Tümpel 1986,
no. 35; Schillemans 1989,
no. 1; Leiden 1991/92,
fig. 49; Slatkes 1992,
no. 38; Wetering 1997,
fig. 29; Broos 2000

Since its discovery by H. Defoer in 1974, this monogrammed painting, which is dated 1626, has been generally accepted as an authentic early work by Rembrandt.[1] The piece, which Rembrandt must have painted shortly after his apprenticeship with Lastman, is a good illustration of the way in which he started to use what he had seen and learned when he was with his teacher in Amsterdam, immediately giving it his own individual interpretation.[2]

Rembrandt must have seen and drawn copies for and/or of at least three of Lastman's painted versions of the *Baptism of the Eunuch* during his apprenticeship in the latter's studio: the versions that are now in Paris (c. 1612; cat. no. 2), Munich (1620) and Karlsruhe (1623; cf. fig. 2a).[3] Rembrandt borrowed elements from all three of these works and used them in his own depiction of the subject.

Rembrandt took the placement of the central group of figures – Philip, the kneeling eunuch and the servant standing behind him holding the open book – from Lastman's painting in Paris (cat. no. 2). He borrowed the eunuch's pose from the version in Munich and that of the standing servant from the version in Karlsruhe. Rembrandt quoted several motifs from this latter painting, which was completed shortly before he came to study with Lastman,

including the horses and the chariot with the large wheels in the background. Rembrandt gave the chariot a quarter turn; he also reduced the size of the wheels, but only during the process of creating the work, as X-rays reveal.[4] Other traces of Lastman are concealed under the layers of paint. Infrared photographs show that Rembrandt had initially painted a broad-leafed tree and a parasol in the top left corner, just as in Lastman's painting in Karlsruhe. Evidently he was not happy with these elements, so he painted the parasol out and replaced the broad-leafed tree with a palm.

The vertical, ‹stacked› arrangement of watching background figures used by Rembrandt is typical of his earliest history pieces of 1625 and 1626, such as *The Stoning of St Stephen* (p. 23, fig. 3) and the Leiden *History Painting* (cat. no. 7). Rembrandt derived this method of ranking from Lastman's carefully conceived multi-figure composition schemes. We also find similar ‹stacked› compositions in Rubens's work during this same period. Rubens often arranged his figures in a curve, which runs sideways and downwards from the upper centre, before sweeping back to the main action in the foreground. There is a similar curve in *The Baptism of the Eunuch*, indicating that Rembrandt must have studied prints of Rubens's monumental

compositions at an early stage in his career. In Rembrandt's approach to composition he opted for solutions that differ fundamentally from his teacher's. While Lastman often worked up his panoramic compositions as lavishly and extensively as possible, with numerous secondary figures, and situated them in a landscape that occupies a large part of the area of the picture, Rembrandt elects to concentrate on the central action and focuses his ‹direction of the scene› entirely on this objective. The curved grouping of the figures in *The Baptism of the Eunuch* leads the viewer's eye directly to the central event – the baptism – placed at

the heart of the picture plane, upon which the gaze of all the figures depicted is also fixed. Rembrandt took the pose of the servant holding the eunuch's turban from Lastman's painting in Paris (cat. no. 2), but he deliberately moved the figure to the right so that the boy no longer looks out of the picture but follows the dramatic event attentively. The positioning of the central group in the foreground, the literal pushing of the landscape into the background, the limitation of the number of secondary figures and the vertical arrangement of the figures, which are placed as a closed group around the vertical axis of the scene, contribute to the concentration that Rembrandt was aiming to achieve.

Another essential difference between Rembrandt and his teacher is the greater attention he paid from the outset to rendering surface textures. Whereas Lastman, with his rather smooth and consistent application of paint, only occasionally manages to achieve a really convincing rendition of a surface, as early as 1626 Rembrandt was already experimenting extensively with ways of applying paint so as to imitate surface textures. Through the clever placement of highlights and by varying the way he applied the paint to mimic the surface in question – particularly in the fabric passages, such as the eunuch's fur cape and turban, but also in the areas of skin and in the dog's coat – Rembrandt succeeded in producing a much more convincing result than his teacher. Rembrandt's *chiaroscuro* effects are also subtler than Lastman's and do more to heighten the impression of plasticity and realism.

Rembrandt took the uniform lighting, the harmonious distribution of colour and the use of bright colours in the foreground passages, which stand out against the more subdued tones in the background, from Lastman's work of the 1620s, such as his *Coriolanus* of 1625 (cat. no. 6). We also find the same bright colours used in *The Baptism of the Eunuch* in a number of other paintings by Rembrandt dating from 1626, including the *History Painting* (cat. no. 7) and the *Music-making Company* (cat. no. 22).                                          B.v.d.B.

[1]  Defoer 1977, pp. 3–9; Wetering 1977a, p. 178; Corpus, vol. 1, 1982, pp. 99–101.
[2]  See cat. no. 2 for a description of the subject: the baptism of the eunuch by Philip the deacon.
[3]  Defoer 1977, pp. 9–14.
[4]  Defoer 1977, pp. 11f.; Wetering 1977, pp. 52f.; Corpus, vol. 1, 1982, pp. 95, 99; Wetering 1997, pp. 28f.

4

Pieter Lastman (Amsterdam c. 1583–1633)

# Mercury, c. 1620/25

Red and white chalk,
on orange-red prepared
paper
280 x 200 mm
Fondation Custodia,
Institut Néerlandais, Paris

Bauch 1960, p. 107;
Amsterdam 1991, no. 33

Only in Amsterdam

Lastman's drawings in red chalk occupy a special place in his œuvre of drawings. They make up a group of seven sketches – all drawn on orange-red prepared paper, all figure studies. We know that Lastman used three of these works as preliminary studies for his paintings.

It had been the custom in Italy since the Renaissance to execute figure studies in red chalk. It is generally assumed that Lastman saw examples of this practice when he was living in Italy between 1602 and 1607. However, it is also possible that Lastman had come across this tradition earlier through Gerrit Pietersz., his teacher in Amsterdam. Lastman's earliest drawing, *Hagar and the Angel in the Wilderness*[1], would seem to confirm this. On the back of this sheet there is a little sketch of a woman's face

Fig. 4a
Rembrandt Harmensz.
van Rijn, *Standing
Beggar with a Leather Bag*,
1629
Black chalk, 290 x 169 mm
Rijksmuseum, Amsterdam

done in red chalk. Gerrit Pietersz., a brother of the composer Jan Pietersz. Sweelinck, spent some time in Italy just before the turn of the century, and consequently it is quite likely that Lastman picked up this technique from him.

The figure of Mercury, viewed from below, is drawn with exceptional flair. Most striking, perhaps, is the great freedom and variety in the use of line. Emphatic hatching is interspersed with flowing lines. Areas of shade are indicated with hatching and a few powerful accents. Nevertheless, it is not entirely successful. The hatching of the left leg and the billowing cloak are stiff and ignore the curves of the forms, which consequently have insufficient plasticity. The recent suggestion that the drawing may be related to a painting that was exhibited at the Royal Academy in London in 1932 and 1952 under the title *Mercury and Argus*[2] has proved to be unfounded. The work in question, which is in any case now attributed to Jan Pynas, bears no relationship to cat. no. 4.[3]

Drawings like *Standing Beggar with a Leather Bag* (fig. 4a) and *Standing Man with Stick* (cat. no. 47) reveal that the way Lastman drew with chalk had a profound effect on the development of the young Rembrandt's drawing style.

E.d.H.

[1] Yale University Art Gallery, New Haven (see Amsterdam 1991, no. 23).
[2] Amsterdam 1991, p. 162.
[3] Memo of 31 May 2001 from Astrid Tümpel.

135

## 5
## Pieter Lastman (Amsterdam c. 1583–1633)
# Man Carrying a Chest, c. 1625

Red and white chalk,
252 x 199 mm
Private Collection

Sumowski 1970, p. 129;
Rotterdam 1976, no. 83;
Amsterdam 1991, no. 34

The œuvre catalogue of Lastman's drawings compiled by Kurt Freise in 1911 contains no fewer than 93 entries. According to our current understanding, however, only fourteen drawings can be attributed to him with certainty. They were drawn between 1602 and 1625, and almost none of them appears in Freise's catalogue.

Despite the limited size of the œuvre, Lastman's drawings are very diverse in terms of function, technique and subject. There are pen and ink drawings of biblical figures (in the manner of his teacher Gerrit Pietersz.), a Roman landscape (inspired by Paul Bril and Willem van Nieulandt), a small portrait (in the style of Jacques de Gheyn), a copy after a painting by Veronese, and a design for a stained-glass window in the Zuiderkerk in Amsterdam. The figure studies in red chalk are the only coherent group in the œuvre. They are closely related in style, are drawn on prepared paper and are all roughly the same size. They also appear to have had the same function: They were used as preliminary studies or as material that could be consulted as required.

The inventory of his possessions that Lastman had drawn up in 1632, a year before his death, lists no fewer than ten albums of drawings, including «een deel roô [krijt] teyckeningen van Pieter Lastman» (some red [chalk] drawings by Pieter Lastman).[1] In 1656 they appear in Rembrandt's inventory, which was compiled in that year because of his bankruptcy.[2] Evidently Rembrandt managed to acquire the drawings from Lastman's estate – an indication of the great value he attached to these works.

The figure of a man carrying a chest is set down on the paper with forceful lines. The outlines, which consist of individual short strokes, and the areas of shadow are heavily emphasized. Highlights are suggested with white chalk. This type of figure, with its clearly defined muscles, is typical of Lastman.

There is no known painting in which this figure is literally quoted. There are, however, works that include similar types, bent forward and carrying a load. A good example is Odysseus on the little panel *Odysseus and Athena*, painted in 1625, and now in the Museum het Rembrandthuis, Amsterdam. His pose broadly corresponds with that of the figure in the drawing. This might indicate that Lastman did not always need drawings of this kind when he was making his paintings, but that he would make free variations on earlier studies as he worked.

E.d.H.

[1] Freise 1911, p. 18–21.
[2] Strauss/Meulen 1979, p. 377, no. 264.

## 6
## Pieter Lastman (Amsterdam c. 1583–1633)
# Coriolanus and the Roman Women, 1625

Oak panel, 81 x 132 cm
Signed bottom left:
*PLastman fecit Ao 1625*
The Provost, Fellows and
Scholars of Trinity
College, Dublin

Amsterdam 1991, no. 20
(with extensive biblio-
graphy); Broos 2000

*Coriolanus and the Roman Women* of 1625 can without doubt be regarded as Lastman's *Night Watch*. The work is the prime example of the skill with which Lastman was able to assemble scenes with a great many figures while retaining complete coherence. The painting made a lasting impression on Rembrandt.

The story of Coriolanus is told by both Livy (II, 40) and Plutarch (XII, 34–36). Their versions vary only in minor details. Gnaeus Marcius Coriolanus was a Roman general who lived in the fifth century BC. The honorific ‹Coriolanus› derives from his heroic actions during the capture of the city of Corioli by the Romans. In 491 BC, his arrogant attitude towards the plebeians brought him into conflict with the Senate. Embittered, Coriolanus took refuge with the Volscians, people against whom he had previously conducted a campaign. Under his leadership, the Volscians achieved great victories over the Romans and finally laid siege to Rome. The desperate Romans begged Coriolanus to lift the siege. Initially he turned a deaf ear to their entreaties, but when his mother Veturia and his wife Volumnia came to the army camp and added their voices to the chorus, he allowed himself to be persuaded and withdrew his army. Livy ends the story here but, according to Plutarch, the Volscians executed Coriolanus as a traitor.

Lastman based his composition on *The Vision of Constantine*, a fresco after a design by Raphael in the Sala di Costantino in the Vatican. Coriolanus's pose and his position on a dais in front of a tent are both direct quotes from the fresco, which Lastman had in all likelihood seen for himself. Lastman placed the kneeling figures of Veturia, Volumnia and her children in the foreground. They beg Coriolanus to lift the siege of Rome. Despite the large number of figures, the scene has remarkable coherence and clarity.

The well-balanced composition conforms in all respects to the requirements for a history painting laid down in art theory textbooks.[1] The protagonist is clearly recognizable, while the other figures are grouped in clusters. There is also, as prescribed, a great diversity of figure types and facial expressions. Depth is achieved, according to the rules, by means of *repoussoirs*.

There is a surviving study for Veturia and the boy beside her in red chalk (fig. 6a).[2] The horseman with his leg raised and his hand on his hip appears almost identically in Lastman's monumental Crucifixion of 1616 in the Museum het Rembrandthuis, Amsterdam.[3] The study for this figure, likewise executed in red chalk, is now in the collection of the Niedersächsisches Landesmuseum in Hanover.[4]

Rembrandt must have greatly admired *Coriolanus and the Roman Women*. At least three of his early works reveal a significant dependence on Lastman's painting, which Rembrandt probably saw in his teacher's studio. It is even possible that Rembrandt was able to observe the progress of the work as it was painted, be-

Fig. 6a
Pieter Lastman, *A Kneeling Woman and a Boy*
Red chalk, heightened with white, on orange prepared paper,
285 x 196 mm
Hamburger Kunsthalle

cause it was made in the year when he spent six months with Lastman.

The influence of *Coriolanus and the Roman Women* on Rembrandt's work, which has been studied by the *Rembrandt Research Project*, can be seen in the figures on the left-hand side of *The Stoning of St Stephen*, the composition and depth effects of the *History Painting* (cat. no. 7) and the structure and detailing of *David before Saul*.[5]

*Coriolanus and the Roman Women* bears witness to Lastman's immense skill at organising crowd scenes. We can see that Rembrandt was particularly interested in this aspect of Lastman's artistry not only from his own original work, but also from two copies drawn after *Joseph Distributing Corn in Egypt* (fig. 6b, 6c) and *Paul and Barnabas at Lystra*,[6] two compositions with numerous figures that Lastman had painted in 1612 and 1614, respectively. Rembrandt cop-

Fig. 6b
Pieter Lastman, *Joseph Distributing Corn in Egypt*, 1612
Panel, 58.4 x 87.6 cm
National Gallery of Ireland, Dublin

Fig. 6c
Rembrandt Harmensz. van Rijn after Pieter Lastman, *Joseph Distributing Corn in Egypt*
Black chalk, 317 x 404 mm
Graphische Sammlung Albertina, Vienna

Fig. 6d
Rembrandt Harmensz.
van Rijn, *Coriolanus
and the Roman Women (?)*,
c. 1659/60
Pen in braun,
195 x 125 mm
British Museum,
London

ied the composition of the works fairly accurately, but without including all the details. He was apparently only interested in recording how Lastman distributed the various figures and groups of figures over the picture plane.

There is also a similar drawing of *Coriolanus and the Roman Women* (fig. 6d).[7] Tümpel regards this sheet, which has been dated to 1659/60, as a drawn copy after Lastman's painting.[8] This is unlikely, however, since the drawing follows the example far less closely than do other copies after Lastman that Rembrandt drew. There are certainly some marked similarities, such as the figure of the rider, the positioning of the protagonist and the group of kneeling figure, but the differences are perhaps even more striking. The most obvious difference is that the principal scene is shown from further to the side. There are also countless differences in the details. The canopy under which the central figure stands, the procession of elephants, the little buildings on the right and the high mountain peak in the background

do not appear in Lastman's painting. All in all, it does not give the impression of having been intended as a copy – one could even ask whether it actually depicts the same subject. It could be that Rembrandt drew the picture from memory, but it is more likely that this is a deliberate reworking of Lastman's composition. The drawing was probably a study for a painting that was never executed or that was subsequently lost.                    E.d.H.

1  Broos 1975, pp. 199–228. See also Amsterdam 1991, pp. 125f., and Amsterdam 1999/2000, p. 92.
2  Hamburger Kunsthalle, Inv. no. 23980. See Amsterdam 1991, no. 31.
3  Amsterdam 1991, no. 9; Heer 1992.
4  Inv. no. 102b. See Amsterdam 1991, no. 32.
5  Corpus, vol. 1, 1982, pp. 72, 112, 134–135.
6  Present whereabouts unknown. See Amsterdam 1991, p. 72. The drawing by Rembrandt (Benesch 449) is in Musée Bonnat, Bayonne.
7  Benesch 1045a.
8  Amsterdam 1991a, p. 82.

7

Rembrandt Harmensz. van Rijn

# History Painting (The Clemency of Charles V?), 1626

Oak panel,
90.1 x 121.3 cm
Signed bottom right:
*RH.1626*
Stedelijk Museum De
Lakenhal, Leiden (on loan
of the Instituut Collectie
Nederland),
Inv. Nr. S 814

Bredius/Gerson 1969,
no. 460; Broos 1975;
Leiden 1976, no. S26;
Washington/Amsterdam
1980, no. 25; Corpus,
vol. 1, 1982, no. A 6;
Leiden 1983, pp. 268–270;
Schwartz 1984/85/87,
fig. 17; Tümpel 1986,
no. 117; Bruyn 1987; Straten 1991; Leiden 1991/92,
fig. 37; Slatkes 1992, no. 2;
Wetering 1997, fig. 37;
B. Broos in: Amsterdam
1999/2000, pp. 90–92;
London/The Hague
1999/2000, no. 1;
Tuynman 1999; Stümpel
2000; Broos 2000

None of Rembrandt's paintings has so exercised the pens of art historians on the subject of its iconography as this panel discovered in 1924, which, since no satisfactory explanation of the subject has yet been offered, is known as the «Leiden History Painting». It depicts a solemn ceremony, witnessed by a large number of chiefly military onlookers. A ruler wearing an imperial crown and holding a sceptre aloft stands on a dais facing three men who have gathered before him. The man in the centre of this trio, armed with a spear, is shown standing with his hat held respectfully in his hand. Judging from his upraised hand, he is swearing an oath. The other two men kneel on either side of the standing figure, the man on the right in a supplicating pose with his open palms outstretched. The man on the left, armed with sword and shield, holds his right arm across his chest in a gesture of submission. The two kneeling men look fearfully at the ruler, evidently afraid of his judgement.

The ruler is flanked on the left by a richly dressed man wearing a plumed hat who holds a military commander's baton. Behind the ruler stands his entourage, amongst whom, next to two bearded old men and a boy carrying the ruler's train, we can recognise the head of the young Rembrandt (behind the sceptre). At a table to the right of the ruler sits a secretary, who looks up at him in tense expectation of his verdict. In the centre of the scene, in the middle ground, stands a man with features rendered portrait-style who looks at the viewer. In the background, against a setting of mediaeval (not classical!) buildings, spectators try to catch a glimpse of what is going on. Some of them stand on the base of a column-shaped monument topped by an animal resembling a sheep. In the background on the right a regiment of soldiers shouldering muskets and led by a man wearing a sash and a beret marches by. Weapons are stacked up in the foreground on the left.

At least a dozen – mostly far-fetched – suggestions have been advanced as to the subject of this picture, almost all located in classical or biblical antiquity.[1] Recently two articles appeared almost simultaneously, both of which interpreted the painting as «The Horatii before King Tullus», a subject supposedly drawn from a virtually unknown play dating from 1616.[2] The scene is said to represent the moment when the three Horatius brothers swear a solemn oath to King Tullus that they will fight for Rome in single combat.

On closer examination, however, this latest explanation is also unsatisfactory. It ignores, for instance, the unmistakable imperial crown worn by the ruler, his gesture with the sceptre, which is traditionally associated with dispensing justice, and the associated gestures of supplication and subjugation by the figures in the foreground. It also fails to account for the undoubtedly significant presence of the animal on the column or for the fact that the men in the background on the right are carrying muskets, while the barrel of a firearm is also clearly visible in the pile of weapons in the foreground.[3] Although seventeenth-century painters often played fast and loose with the historicity of the costumes and attributes in their history pieces, the presence of firearms makes it highly unlikely that a subject from classical antiquity is being depicted here. It seems almost indisputable that the painting is of an event in the much more recent past.

During Rembrandt's period of apprenticeship with Lastman, he must have come into contact with a great deal of pictorial material of all kinds. This will undoubtedly have included prints after designs by Maarten van Heemskerck. In terms of its subject, the Leiden *History Painting* appears to be derived from one of his prints (fig. 7a). The print is part of a series showing the triumphs of Emperor Charles V, which was published in 1556.[4] It depicts how, after Charles V's victory at the Battle of

1 5 4 7

AVDACI IAM HESSO, FORTI IAM SAXONE PVLSO,
MVLTÆ SE INVICTI DANT SVB IVGA CÆSARIS VRBES.

*Vencido ya Langraue el atreuido,*
*Preso el Duque de Saxa y su compaña,*
*Han sus llaues a Cesar ofrecido*
*Las ciudades de nombre de Alemaña.*

XI

Quant le Lantgraue & Duc de Saxe furent
Par Lempereur chaffez, bien efbays
Plufieurs alors tous d'un vouloir f'efmeurent
A luy rendre grant villes & pays.

Mühlberg in 1547 over the Protestant German Princes – the representatives of the rebellious German cities that until shortly before had been part of the Lutheran Schmalkaldic League – surrendered to the Emperor. The delegates from the cities swore allegiance and loyalty to Charles V, upon which he granted them clemency. Rembrandt seems to have depicted the moment when Emperor Charles extends his mercy to the German cities. The three men in the foreground represent all the stages of submission: demonstrating subjection, swearing loyalty and begging for mercy. Remarkably enough, the physiognomy of the ruler with the imperial crown and sceptre has never before been linked with that of Charles V, although the portraits of the elderly Charles V bear a strong resemblance to the face in the Leiden work (fig. 7b). The way in which the Emperor pronounces judgement with an outstretched sceptre and confers mercy corresponds to his gestures in van Heemskerck's print. The cloth-covered dais on which the Emperor stands also appears to have been taken from this print. The sheep-like animal on the column, for which no explanation has previously been given, must be a ram which, with its noticeably high back, bears a strong resemblance to the hanging ram's fleece in the arms of the Order of the Golden Fleece, the order of chivalry headed by Charles V.[5]

The richly dressed man with the feathered beret to the left of the emperor carries a striking commander's baton. This must be Henry III, Count of Nassau, Charles V's powerful commander-in-chief. We find his portrait in profile wearing the same beret and with the commander's baton held in the same way in one of Bernard van Orley's preliminary drawings for the monumental *Nassau Tapestries*, made around 1530, illustrating the genealogy of the Nassau family (fig. 7c).[6] In Rembrandt's day this renowned series of monumental tapestries, which was one of the most valued and valuable family possessions of the Orange dynasty, was kept in Dillenburg Castle. The life-sized cartoons, however, were owned by Prince Maurice who, as van Mander writes, had them copied in oils by the Antwerp-born painter Hans Jordaens, who was working in Delft.[7] Frederick Henry attached so much importance to the series that he spent a small fortune having the tapestries woven again after the original cartoons in 1632. The original tapestries, the cartoons, and the painted and woven copies were lost in the eighteenth century. Rembrandt must have seen the original cartoons or the painted copies in The Hague.

Henry III of Nassau was not present at the event depicted, since he died in 1538. But the prominent presence of this important ancestor of the Oranges in the painting, in conjunction with the date 1626, is the clue to the deeper significance of Rembrandt's history piece. After the death of the fanatically counter-Remonstrant Prince Maurice in 1625, his half-brother Frederick Henry was considerably more tolerant in his role as stadholder of religious dissidents.[8] The Remonstrants in the cities of Holland, who had suffered years of oppression, hoped that they could now profess their religious convictions freely and openly without fear of persecution. The analogy with the clemency that Charles V showed the Lutheran inhabitants of the German cities, who had

shortly before been pursued as heretics, is evident. The picture could also be seen as an allegory of the (hoped-for) clemency of Frederick Henry towards people of other religious views.

As in *The Baptism of the Eunuch* (cat. no. 3) Rembrandt took a work by Pieter Lastman as the model for this ambitious history piece – in this case his teacher's *Coriolanus and the Roman Women* of 1625, which he probably saw taking shape in Lastman's studio (cat. no. 6).[9] Lastman's *Coriolanus* also depicts a commander who, standing on a dais and surrounded by soldiers, shows mercy to a group of kneeling supplicants. The composition of Rembrandt's painting draws extensively on Lastman's work. And yet it is the marked differences from Lastman's *Coriolanus* that make the painting so convincing a testimony to Rembrandt's artistic intentions.

Compared with Lastman, Rembrandt again endeavoured to achieve greater concentration in the work by restricting the number of protagonists and placing the central action directly in the foreground. Here, too, Rembrandt's subordinating method of composition differs in essence from Lastman's unhierarchic ap-

Fig. 7b
Anonymous after Jan Cornelisz. Vermeyen, *Portrait of Charles V*, c. 1550
Panel, diameter 17.5 cm
Rijksmuseum, Amsterdam

Fig. 7c
Bernard van Orley,
*Design for a tapestry of
Henry III of Nassau and
his three wives*, c. 1530
Pen and coloured ink,
399 x 529 mm
Staatliche Graphische
Sammlung, Munich

proach. In his portrayal of emotions, too, Rembrandt immediately distinguishes himself from his teacher, who could not equal his skill in this respect. A good example of this is the tense face of the secretary beside the Emperor, whose pose, glance and wrinkled brow are very like the head of one of the money-changers in *Christ Driving the Money-changers from the Temple*, which dates from the same year (cat. no. 12). Through the more subtle use of *chiaroscuro* effects, Rembrandt also succeeds in achieving greater plasticity than Lastman, particularly in the objects and figures in the foreground.

But the main difference between Rembrandt's style and Lastman's is the much greater attention Rembrandt devotes to expressing surfaces and, allied to this, the greater differentiation in the way he applies the paint. Whereas Lastman's consistent, relatively unvaried manner of painting often leaves us unclear as to what material he is depicting, Rembrandt consciously gears his painting method to the texture he wants to achieve.[10] The iron weapons in the foreground are painted smoothly and this, in combination with the clever placing of highlights, makes the representation of gleaming metal extraordinarily successful. The pattern of gold threads in the brocade cloak worn by the man on the far left, in contrast, is painted with heavy impasto, with tiny lumps of light yellow paint on a layer of ochre, creating a paint surface that imitates the fabric in both colour and surface texture. The light yellow flecks of paint not only work as highlights, contributing to the convincing way in which the gleam of light falling on gold thread is suggested: their three-dimensionality also means that the light falling on the surface of the paint actually reflects in the same way as it does on the fabric itself. Experimentation with applying the paint so that it imitates the actual surface is characteristic of a group of works that Rembrandt and Lievens painted in 1626, during a period when they were familiar with each other's work (see cat. nos. 22, 24).

In comparison with Rembrandt's earliest history piece, the no less ambitious but rather clumsily executed *The Stoning of St Stephen* in Lyon, painted in 1625 (p. 23, fig. 3), we can see considerable progress in the Leiden piece in the way that light and colour are used to make sense of the spatial structure of the scene. The objects and figures in the foreground are painted in bright colours and also strongly modelled using thick layers of paint. The sharp outlines with which these passages stand out from the cooler shades and more diffuse outlines of the background, where the paint has been applied much more thinly, contribute in no small measure to a convincing illusion of depth in the scene.

It has been suggested that this history piece and *The Stoning of St Stephen*, which are the same size, should be regarded as pendants. They have been linked to the reference to «two large pieces by Rembrandt» (twee braave groote stukken van Rembrandt) in the 1663 sale catalogue of the property of the Remonstrant Leiden humanist Petrus Scriverius.[11] Extraordinary hypothetical conclusions have been drawn from this concerning the iconographic relationship between the two works.[12] Since we have no information about the subjects of the paintings in Scriverius's possession, all these hypotheses must be regarded as speculative.

The weapons in the foreground were popular props among the painters in Rembrandt's circle: the round shield with the sun's rays, for instance, occurs in several of Gerard Dou's paintings (see e. g. cat. no. 68).        B.v.d.B.

[1] For an overview of all the suggested subjects, see: Corpus, vol. 1, 1982, p. 112; Straten 1991; Stümpel 2000, p. 44.
[2] Tuynman 1999; Stümpel 2000.
[3] This problem is acknowledged by Tuynman and Stümpel, but does not prevent either of them from placing the scene in antiquity anyway. For van Straten (1991) this detail was reason enough to reject all classical or biblical interpretations.
[4] Hollstein, vol. 4, p. 231, nos. 216–227. Cf. Rosier 1990, esp. p. 33.
[5] Cf. Straten 1991, p. 94.
[6] See among others: Fock 1969, fig. 5; Klooster 1990, fig. 1.
[7] Mander 1604, fol. 211r, 24–30.
[8] See the essay by Gerbrand Korevaar, pp. 13–14.
[9] See among others Broos 1975; Broos in: Amsterdam 1999/200, p. 90–92; Broos 2000.
[10] See Wetering 1997, especially pp. 173ff.
[11] Leiden 1976, p. 68.
[12] Ibid., worked out in more detail in Schwartz 1984, pp. 35 ff.

## 8
### Jan Lievens (Leiden 1607–1674 Amsterdam)
### The Tric Trac Players, 1624/25

Canvas, 98 x 106 cm
Spier Collection

Sumowski 1983ff., vol. 3,
pp. 1765, 1775, no. 1178,
fig. p. 1817; Nicolson/
Vertova 1990, vol. 1, p.
138; Sale Cat. Christie's,
London, July 8, 1994,
lot 86; Gutbrod 1996,
pp. 93-95 (not by Lievens)

Since the Middle Ages the board game tric trac (backgammon), played with pieces or men and dice, was a popular pastime. A notorious game of chance, often involving large sums of money, it was considered a vice. In a sixteenth-century woodcut, the game is shown as an attribute of the allegorical female personification of «Sloth».[1] Numerous depictions from the seventeenth century emphasise the negative aspects of the game, as is the case with this painting by Jan Lievens. The opponent of the young soldier on the right is an older and more experienced player, whose eye-glasses, perched on his nose, are generally taken as an indication of cheating. The scene is completed by two onlookers with large mugs of beer and pipes. Heavy drinking and smoking were considered inextricably related vices, since the dryness of the throat caused by smoking could be relieved by a cool drink.

Werner Sumowski correctly located this painting, which has been known in the literature for quite some time but has never before been exhibited, at the beginning of Lievens' œuvre. It can be considered the earliest of his known paintings.[2] On the one hand the attribution is supported by stylistic features characteristic of the young Lievens. They include the figural type, especially the striking bald head of the player on the left,[3] and such anatomical details as hardly-discernible fingernails. The contrast between the purple-red and orange-red of the two players is an example of what Sumowski observed as Lievens' early interest in colouristic refinement.[4] The painting on the other hand displays uncertainties typical of a beginner. The anatomy of the left hand of the young player is completely incorrect, more so than in any other work by Lievens. The brushwork is insecure and hesitant, in some parts pedantic and detailed, in others broad and blurred. The result is a flat, unconvincing modelling of forms. But what is of interest is the unusual treatment of the light in the face of the youthful smoker, and it is here more than anywhere else that Lievens' interest

in the painting of Haarlem is evident. The extremely broad highlights can only have come from an awareness of Frans Hals,[5] although Lievens undoubtedly realised that that master's dynamic verve was beyond his reach and thus never repeated the experiment.

Such observations place in the proper context those works most frequently cited as Lievens' sources: half-figure depictions of similar themes by the Utrecht Caravaggisti. Their folkloristic renderings of musicians and gamblers were popular with painters from other cities, and indeed the striped shirt of the soldier in our painting is a feature typical of the Utrecht painters. But beyond this the painting has hardly anything in common with the works of Hendrick ter Brugghen or Dirck van Baburen.[6] However, the compositional strategy of placing two figures in the foreground – the one on the right in profile, the one on the left in half-profile – and two background figures located slightly to the right is also found in Rembrandt's *Spectacles Pedlar (Sight)* (cat. no. 11) from his early series of the Five Senses. So already in their earliest works, painted in 1624 or early 1625, one finds evidence of artistic exchange between Lievens and Rembrandt, and it is notable that neither assumes the role of leader. It may have been that in the artistic climate of the period Lievens had an advantage over the more barbaric crude style of his friend, but Rembrandt's lively and witty figural inventions more than make up for it.          B.S.

---

[1]  See Amsterdam 1976b, no. 22, fig. 22a, with further information on the subject.

[2]  *A Presentation in the Temple* (Oak panel, 83.5 x 60 cm. Cevat Collection, Amsterdam. Braunschweig 1979, no. 1; Rotterdam 2000/01, colour pl. p. 65) of an extremely archaic appearance requires further investigation; it was not discussed by Sumowski.

[3]  Cf. the *Singing Man* in Milwaukee, Bader Collection (Sumowski 1983ff., vol. 3, no. 1224) and the *Bald-headed Man* in Dublin, National Gallery of Ireland (Sumowski 1983ff., vol. 3, no. 1255).

[4]  Sumowski 1983ff., vol. 3, p. 1766.

[5]  Cf. the essay by Bernhard Schnackenburg, p. 101 and fig. 8.

[6]  Dirck van Baburen, *Tric Trac Players*, Stichting Wagner - de Wit, The Hague. Nicolson/Vertova 1990, no. 1042 with ill. Hendrick ter Brugghen, *Tric Trac Players*, Centraal Museum, Utrecht. Nicolson/Vertova 1990, no. 1141 with ill.

## 9

Rembrandt Harmensz. van Rijn

# The Three Singers (Hearing), c. 1624/25

Oak panel, 21.6 x 17.8 cm
W. Baron van Dedem

Bredius/Gerson 1969,
no. 421; Leiden 1976,
no. S28A; Corpus, vol. 1,
1982, no. B 1; Schwartz
1984/85/87, fig. 13;
Tümpel 1986, no. A27;
Stockholm 1992/93,
no. 46

An older man in a tabard, an old woman with a turban and a young man with a beret, who stands behind them, sing together from a song-book, while the older man beats time with his right hand. The figures are crammed rather tightly into the picture plane, in a sort of trian-gular composition. This is probably why this lit-tle painting was subsequently enlarged. It was inset in a larger panel, after which the scene was extended on all sides, and parts of the orig-inal picture, particularly in the background, were overpainted. A burning candle was added at the lower left and a curtain was put in at the top left. In a recent restoration by M. Dooijes, all these additions were removed and the paint-ing was restored to its original state.[1]

The panel was one of a series on the subject of the Five Senses. As well as this work, which de-picts Hearing, the paintings of Touch (cat. no. 10) and Sight (cat. no. 11) are also still extant. The series must have been kept together at least until the beginning of the eighteenth cen-tury, given that all three of the surviving panels were enlarged and painted over in the same way. Material research has revealed that this must have been done after 1700.[2] Remarkably enough, the panel of *Christ Driving the Money-changers from the Temple* of 1626 (cat. no. 12), in which the figures are similarly crowded into the picture plane, had been subjected to the same treatment – although this had been reversed much earlier – so it may be assumed that these four works had belonged to the same owner for a considerable time.

Allegorical series of the Five Senses were a popular theme in graphic art and painting from the sixteenth century onwards.[3] At the begin-ning of the seventeenth century, series on the senses in the form of simple genre scenes be-came increasingly popular. Whereas these works were originally more or less refined and polite in tone, as the seventeenth century pro-gressed there developed an extremely vulgar variant of these scenes, in which figures from squalid backgrounds were ridiculed in a very coarse way. The allegorical meaning of such scenes was often not recognized again until the twentieth century. Rembrandt's sensory series is on the cusp of the two categories: his figures are unmistakably common types, but they are depicted with only the mildest of mockery.

In the use of half-length figures positioned in the foreground, the tight framing of the scene and the flat space behind the figures, these

genre pieces are reminiscent of similar scenes from the early 1620s by such Utrecht Caravaggisti as Gerard Honthorst and Hendrick Terbrugghen. There are also clear similarities in the treatment of the light, the use of colour and the realistic rendition of skin tones. Rembrandt must have been very familiar with the work of the Utrecht painters, which was highly sought-after in the mid-1620s. Their influence, particularly that of Honthorst, is evident in Lievens's work at an early stage (see cat. nos. 8, 24, 72, 73), so that it would seem obvious to conclude that Rembrandt was encouraged to paint scenes of this type, primarily by Lievens's earliest work. And yet, the differences between Rembrandt's genre scenes and those by the Utrecht painters (and hence by Lievens) are at least as striking as the similarities. The Caravaggisti – like Lievens – worked on a larger scale, gave their half-length figures more gravitas and presence, used stronger *chiaroscuro* and, above all, painted in a much more precise and careful manner.

The broad brushstrokes with which the skin is rendered are very noticeable. Rembrandt tried to suggest the wrinkled skin of the elderly people by leaving the brushstroke visible. The way in which the white collar of the older man in *The Three Singers* is indicated with a couple of touches of paint also shows us how, even in his very earliest paintings, Rembrandt was experimenting with a rough painting style in order to achieve a realistic representation of fabric. In this work, however, he is still a very long way away from the refinement that he would soon attain in harnessing the painting style to the expression of the surface he wants to achieve. The rather syrupy application of the paint, which

9a
Rembrandt Harmensz.
van Rijn, *The Three Singers
(Hearing)* (detail),
c. 1624/25

can also be seen in the *Stoning of St Stephen* of 1625 (cf. p. 23, fig. 3) in Lyon and, to a lesser extent, in *Christ Driving the Money-changers from the Temple* of 1626 (cat. no. 12) in Moscow, is typical of the artist's earliest work. The Senses series is also closely related to the latter of these works in terms of the composition and the characterization of the heads. However, when one compares the expression of surfaces and textures, the plasticity, the effect of depth and the positioning of the figures in the space, one very soon sees that the quality of these little paintings comes nowhere near that of the Moscow work.

The bright colouring of the little paintings in the Senses series is eye-catching – particularly after the recent restoration. There is no sign here of the more subdued colours of Lastman's palette – nor his uniform lighting – that Rembrandt would use immediately after his apprenticeship in Amsterdam in works like *The Baptism of the Eunuch* (cat. no. 3) and the *History Painting* (cat. no. 7) of 1626. This could be an indication that the senses paintings were done before the period he spent studying with Lastman. If this is the case, it makes them the earliest surviving paintings by Rembrandt.

Various authors have cast doubt on the authenticity of the Senses series.[4] In view of the extensive overpainting – now removed by the recent restoration – and the lack of any contempora-

neous comparison material, the *Rembrandt Research Project* had not previously been able to establish the authenticity of the series. However, there has never been any doubt that the works were created in Rembrandt's immediate vicinity.

Since it is hard to imagine that Rembrandt would have had a pupil even before his apprenticeship with Lastman – a pupil moreover who was able to mimic his earliest style so accurately – and since by the mid-1620s Lievens was already using an individual and very different style (see cat. no. 8), Rembrandt himself is left as the only remaining candidate for painter of the series. It would therefore seem justified to restore the series to the artist's authentic œuvre.

B.v.d.B.

1 Corpus, vol. 1, 1982, pp. 399, 402f.; Stockholm 1992/93, pp. 176, 179, note 1.
2 Stockholm 1992/93, p. 179, note 1.
3 See e. g.: Amsterdam 1997, pp. 241–244.
4 See among others Tümpel 1986, nos. A27–A29. The authenticity was first questioned by Bauch 1960, pp. 227f., who attributed the series to a pupil of Rembrandt's. In Bredius/Gerson 1969, nos. 421–421A, the attribution to Rembrandt is described as uncertain, as it is in Leiden 1976, p. 70. Schwartz 1984/85/87, p. 34, accepts the series as authentic, while Tümpel 1986, p. 30–31, 423, attributes it to an early follower of Rembrandt. (In the corrigenda of the second edition [1993], p. 465, Tümpel even suggests a much later date for the work, namely 1626/29.) In Stockholm 1992/93, nos. 46–48, the series, which had meanwhile been restored, is listed as authentic early work.

Rembrandt Harmensz. van Rijn
# The Operation (Touch), c. 1624/25

Oak panel, 21,5 x 17,7 cm
Private Collection

Bredius/Gerson 1969,
no. 421A; Leiden 1976,
no. S28B; Corpus, vol. 1,
1982, no. B 2; Schwartz
1984/85/87, fig. 14;
Tümpel 1986, no. A28;
Stockholm 1992/93,
no. 47

Not in the exhibition

Convulsed with the pain and with clenched fists, an old man with a barber's cape around his shoulders undergoes an operation being performed on his head by a barber who stands behind him wielding a lancet. An old man in oriental dress holds a candle to illuminate the surgical procedure and watches attentively. What is depicted here is the ‹removal of the stone›, a motif that occurs in art from the fifteenth century onwards. ‹Having a stone in one's head› essentially meant ‹being out of one's mind›. The ‹removal of the stone› was a popular device for illustrating human folly. In the Senses series, the painful operation is a telling representation of Touch.

*The Operation* was enlarged in the eighteenth century in the same way as *The Three Singers* (cat. no. 9). The areas that were added, which showed more of the barber's shop, were removed in a recent restoration. Here again, the bright local colours that the restoration revealed are arresting. The striking combination of pink and light blue shades in the barber's clothes was often used by the Utrecht Caravaggisti. The burning candle and the wrinkled faces, particularly that of the man with the candle, quote Utrecht examples. The caricatured head of the man with the candle, in profile and with a hooked nose, is a type that was often used at the beginning of the sixteenth century by Antwerp painters and artists like Lucas van Leyden to characterize unreliable or malicious people. The type probably originates in the caricatures by Leonardo da Vinci.

The same syrupy application of the paint can be seen in *The Operation*, particularly in the areas of skin and the clothes, as in *The Three Singers* (cat. no. 9). This manner of smearing on the paint is used to the greatest extreme in the barber's cape around the old man's shoulders, without, however, achieving a convincing plasticity or rendition of the fabric. The barber's head is the least caricatured of the three and is the most successful in terms of plasticity. As in the other panels in the Senses series, the hands are among the most crudely painted passages. Although hands were never to be Rembrandt's strongest point, they really are very clumsily painted here.

The characterization of the heads is similar to that in other early paintings, particularly *Christ Driving the Money-changers from the Temple* in Moscow (cat. no. 12). The way in which the wrinkled foreheads of the figures in *The Operation* are rendered is virtually identical to that in the painting in Moscow, although the expression of the surfaces and the modelling are much more successful in the Moscow work. As far as the authenticity is concerned, the same arguments apply here as apply to the other paintings in the series (cat. nos. 9, 11).

B.v.d.B.

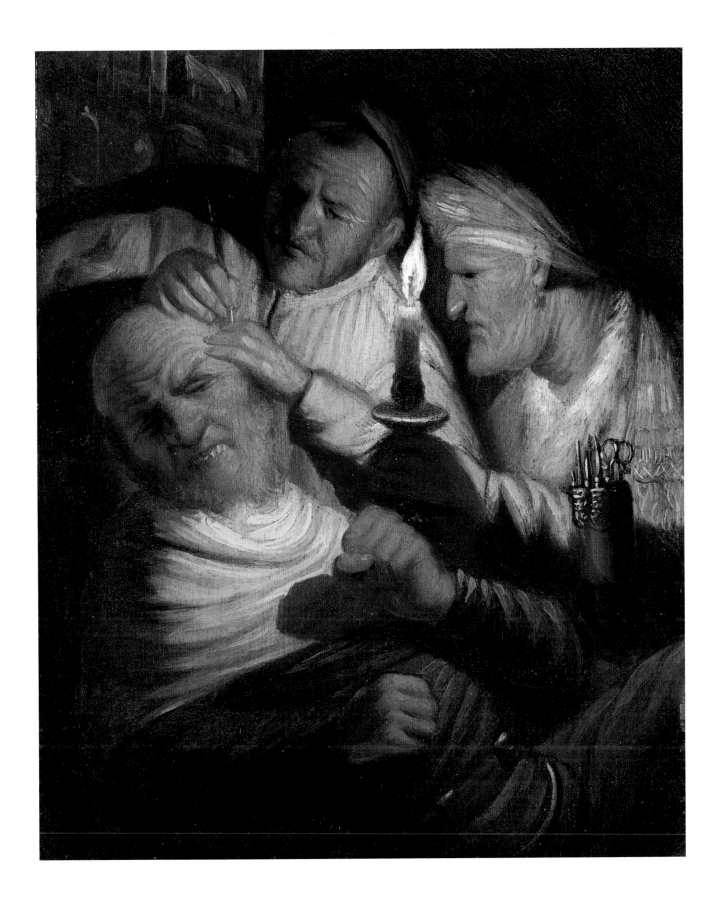

## 11
### Rembrandt Harmensz. van Rijn
# The Spectacles Pedlar (Sight), c. 1624/25

Oak panel, 21 x 17.8 cm
Private Collection

Corpus, vol. 1, 1982,
no. B 3; Schwartz
1984/85/87, fig. 12;
Tümpel 1986, no. A29;
Stockholm 1992/93,
cat. no. 48

A pedlar wearing a turban, with a purse promi-nently displayed on his hip, tries to sell a pair of glasses to an old man in a fur cap. He carries his wares in a box resting on his belly. The old man points to his eyes and is presented with a pince-nez by the spectacles seller. In the centre, be-hind the two men, stands an old woman with the same sort of spectacles perched on her nose. On the right in the background we glimpse the turned head of a man in a hat, who is just walking away.

*The Spectacles Pedlar* was enlarged and over-painted in the eighteenth century in the same way as the other little panels in the Senses se-ries (cat. nos. 9, 10). This painting, too, was re-stored recently and all the later additions were removed. Contrary to what had previously been thought, the head of the man in the hat, walking away on the right, is part of the original work. His disapproving look immediately tells us that there is something crooked about the transaction that is taking place. In the seven-teenth century, ‹selling someone spectacles› had a negative connotation: it was synonymous with ‹cheating someone› or ‹making a fool of someone›.[1]

The costume worn by the spectacles pedlar, with its slashed puff sleeves, is sixteenth centu-ry, and in Rembrandt's time only actors and fairground entertainers still wore it. The same is true of the clothes worn by the characters in *The Three Singers* (cat. no. 9) and *The Opera-tion* (cat. no. 10). Old-fashioned garments like these heightened the satirical and caricaturing effect of the piece. The pedlar's gypsy-style ear-ring, which we also find in the ear of the man holding the candle in *The Operation*, undoubt-edly denotes untrustworthiness and fraud in both works.

*The Spectacles Pedlar* is the most accomplished painting in the Senses series as far as the detail-ing and rendering of surfaces is concerned. Al-though the same coarse manner of painting used in the other panels in the series can also be seen here and there in this painting, there are some passages in the *Spectacles Pedlar* that have been executed with great precision. The box of wares in the foreground is rendered as a still life with many details and, thanks mainly to the sharp light accents, the representation of textures achieved here is of surprisingly high quality. The more tonal use of colour is also

noticeable in the *Spectacles Pedlar* in comparison with the local colours in the other two works. In this painting Rembrandt has made a much better fist of bringing unity to the picture by means of colour and tone.

The caricature head of the bearded old man is painted very roughly with broad red and yellow streaks of paint. The same crudely modelled head with the deep-set eyes and the wrinkled forehead can also be seen immediately under the feet of Saul in the background to the signed *Stoning of St Stephen*, now in Lyon, which dates from 1625 (cf. p. 23, fig. 3). In that painting the head is startlingly different in characterisation and technique from the other heads, which, with their more regular lighting and modelling, already display Lastman's influence. What this head does have in common with the other heads in the *Stoning of St Stephen* is the way in which the nose is rendered. The broad, red, shiny nose, with a striking white highlight is one of the most characteristic features of Rembrandt's very earliest works. We see this nose in the *Stoning of St Stephen* of 1625 and in *Christ Driving the Money-changers from the Temple* of

1626 (cat. no. 12), but never again after this. In the Senses series we find almost exclusively this early type of nose, so that the series can be placed right at the beginning of this development.

There are marked compositional similarities between the little paintings in the Senses series, particularly *The Spectacles Pedlar*, and *The Tric Trac Players* by Jan Lievens, a genre piece that was probably painted around 1624/25 (cat. no. 8). It is evident from the almost identical placement of the figures, the analogous poses, sometimes reversed, of the central figure in all the works in the series, the identical position in the picture plane of a head in profile in *The Spectacles Pedlar* and in *The Operation* (cat. no. 10) and also the similar way in which the gesticulating hands are placed in the scene that

11a
Rembrandt Harmensz.
van Rijn, *The Spectacles Pedlar (Sight)* (detail),
c. 1624/25

158

Rembrandt must have been very familiar with Lievens's painting. All the hands in *The Spectacles Pedlar* appear to have been borrowed directly from *The Tric Trac Players* and are, moreover, modelled in a similar way. The hands of the old man in *The Spectacles Pedlar*, for instance, are derived respectively from the left hand of the tric trac player on the right and the right hand of the tric trac player on the left. The old woman's hand, in mirror image, is taken from the left hand of the player on the left, while the spectacles pedlar's hand is borrowed from the right hand of the player on the right. The fact that Rembrandt used a composition by Lievens as the starting point for his own earliest paintings is an indication that the two Leiden painters were in close contact with each other in about 1624, probably before Rembrandt's apprenticeship with Pieter Lastman.[2]

X-ray photographs have revealed that *The Spectacles Pedlar* is painted over another picture.[3] The X-ray shows a seated female nude in a mannerist pose. It is possible that what we are seeing here are the remains of a painting from the studio of Jacob Isaacsz. van Swanenburg,

Rembrandt's first teacher, who made frequent use of the mannerist idiom in depicting nudes (see cat. no. 1).

A small painting with the same subject by Rembrandt is referred to in an anonymous archive document dating from 1640: «In 1640 bought a little piece, showing a spectacles seller by Rembrant, numbered 56 for 31 guilders 10 stuyvers.»[4] If this description does refer to the panel in question, it would mean that it was regarded as an authentic work by Rembrandt in 1640. The fact that the work described was sold separately in 1640 makes this identification less likely, however, given that, as we have explained (see cat. no. 9), the three little paintings probably remained together until the eighteenth century, when they were all enlarged in the same way.[5]                           B.v.d.B.

[1]  Corpus, vol. 1, 1982, p. 412–415.
[2]  Cf. the essay by Bernhard Schnackenburg, pp. 100ff.
[3]  Corpus, vol. 1, 1982, pp. 411f.
[4]  «Anno 1640 ghecoft een Stucxken, daerin een brilleman van Rembrant, geteykent N. 56 for f. 31–10.» Corpus, vol. 1, 1982, pp. 414f.
[5]  Ibid., adopted by Tümpel 1986, no. A29.

## 12
## Rembrandt Harmensz. van Rijn
# Christ Driving the Money-changers from the Temple, 1626

Panel, 43.1 x 32 cm
Signed (on the column):
*RH.1626*
The State Pushkin
Museum of Fine Arts,
Moscow

Bredius/Gerson 1969,
no. 532; Corpus, vol. 1,
1982, no. A 4; Schwartz
1984/85/87, fig. 22;
Tümpel 1986, no. 34;
Slatkes 1992, no. 37

The event that is the subject of the painting is narrated by all four of the Evangelists, in greatest detail by John (2:13–16): When Jesus went to the temple in Jerusalem at the time of the Jewish Passover, he found traders dealing in livestock, and money-changers sitting at tables and counting their money. Enraged, he drove them from the temple with a whip made from cords, with the words «do not make my Father's house a house of merchandise», and he overturned the money-changers' tables so that their money fell to the ground.

Rembrandt illustrated this biblical passage quite literally. With a furious glare and a face reddened with rage, Jesus raises his arm, on the point of bringing down the whip with great force on a merchant in a turban, with a money pouch on his back. The obviously terrified man tries to barge his way out and in so doing knocks over a table at which two money-changers and a soldier sit. The shocked money-changers grab for their coins, which slide from the edge of the tipped-up table in the foreground. The money-changer on the left, dressed in a fur-trimmed tabard, looks askance at Jesus.

The soldier on the right raises his arms, screaming, to ward off the blows of the whip. The scene of the action is indicated by the massive base of a column in the background. On this, in the form of an inscription, Rembrandt has put his monogram and the date 1626.

The painting, which was not recognized as a work by Rembrandt until the twentieth century, is now generally accepted as authentic.[1] It was enlarged in the eighteenth century in the same way as the three little paintings in the Five Senses series (cat. nos. 9–11). This intervention was reversed in 1930, so that the panel now looks as it did originally.

The reason for enlarging the painting must have been the extraordinarily tight space into which the group of figures is compressed. Like the similarly tightly-framed Senses series, the Moscow piece is directly related in terms of its composition, the use of half-length figures and the characterisation of the heads to Lievens's *Tric Trac Players* of c. 1624/25 (cat. no. 8). The right-hand money-changer's pose and the gesture with the arm correspond exactly with those of the tric trac player on the right. The

head of the tric trac player on the left is very similar to that of the left-hand money-changer. The secretary looking up at the imperial figure in the Leiden *History Painting*, which also dates from 1626 (cat. no. 7), has the same frowning face.

As far as the composition and the conveying of space are concerned, the difference between this little work and the *History Painting* could not be greater. In contrast to the immediately «legible» spatial construct of the scene achieved in the latter work with the aid of light, colour and a considered arrangement of the figures, the spatial structure in the Moscow painting is not at first glance obvious. This is primarily because of the positioning of the soldier with the upraised arms on the right. The suggested space does not seem deep enough for him to be there, and the gesture with his arms disturbs the clarity of the composition. This figure does, however, largely establish the drama of the scene, which must have been Rembrandt's main concern in this work.

Compared with the Senses series of c. 1624/25 and the *Stoning of St Stephen* of 1625 (p. 23, fig. 3), the plasticity of the figures, particularly the heads, has improved considerably. This was achieved not just by a more skilful treatment of the light, but above all by the expressive way in which the areas of skin were painted. The wrinkled, frowning faces are modelled with a restless pattern of fine impasto streaks of paint, giving them amazing vitality. In contrast, the fabric passages are painted much more coarsely. The folds in the clothes are indicated with broad, rapidly applied brushstrokes. The particularly convincing fur on the tabard of the money-changer on the left was painted in the same surface-imitating way as the eunuch's fur cape and the dog's coat in the *Baptism of the Eunuch* (cat. no. 3).

The shiny red noses, which we also find in the Senses series and the *Stoning of St Stephen*, are quite striking. The Moscow piece is the last work in which they occur. The presence of the «early noses» and the other similarities with these works indicate that this must be one of Rembrandt's earliest paintings from the year 1626.                                      B.v.d.B.

1 Corpus, vol. 1, 1982, pp. 91f.

## 13
Rembrandt Harmensz. van Rijn
# The Rest on the Flight into Egypt, c. 1626

Etching, 217 x 165 mm
Bartsch 59, state I (1)
Rijksmuseum,
Amsterdam,
Inv. No. RP-P-OB-120

White/Boon 1969, p. 31;
White 1969, pp. 23-27;
Corpus, vol. 1, 1982,
p. 482; Broos 1985,
nos. 25-26;
Amsterdam/London
2000/01, no. 1

It is generally assumed that *The Rest on the Flight into Egypt* was made immediately after *The Circumcision* (cat. no. 40). The two etchings are certainly very similar in terms of style and technique, and in both cases the authenticity of the works was questioned for many years. Now, however, they are universally accepted.

The differences between the two sheets are actually more striking than the similarities. A comparison reveals just how rapidly Rembrandt was developing. While the execution of *The Rest on the Flight into Egypt* is admittedly still rather unsure and crude, there is much greater variety in the use of line. The figures are defined with strong lines. Finer lines are used in the foliage, the landscape in the background and the hat, saw and basket beside Joseph. Hatching and cross-hatching are used to indicate the shadows. The use of fine, zigzag lines and the free, spontaneous drawing style reveal Lievens's influence. The way in which Rembrandt depicts the foliage actually seems to have been lifted straight from Lievens's *St John the Evangelist on Patmos* (cat. no. 14). Lievens's etching, however, possesses much greater clari-

ty and gives the impression of having been more carefully considered. Darker passages have been consciously used here to model forms and to make the protagonist stand out from the background more effectively. Rembrandt, in contrast, seems to be far more interested in the interplay of light and shade. He uses light and dark passages not to give figures volume or to clarify the composition, but as building blocks with which the picture is constructed – a task no artist had ever set himself before. On this occasion Rembrandt was unsuccessful. The alternation of dark and light areas is so diffuse that it compromises the legibility of the scene.

Joseph was warned in a dream that King Herod wanted to kill the newborn Christ child. To escape his vengeance, Joseph fled with Mary and the child to Egypt, where they remained until Herod's death (Mt 2:13–15). The ‹Rest on the Flight into Egypt›, which is referred to only in apocryphal writings and not in the Bible, was a particularly popular subject in Dutch art. Mary is generally shown breastfeeding Christ, but Rembrandt breaks with this tradition. In his

165

Fig. 13a
Lucas van Leyden, *The Rest on the Flight into Egypt*, c. 1506/08
Engraving, 159 x 139 mm
Rijksmuseum, Amsterdam

version Mary feeds the child with a spoon, while Joseph holds a bowl. There are several similarities between this etching and *The Flight into Egypt*, a small panel that Rembrandt painted around 1628 (cat. no. 60). The donkey and Mary's headdress are virtually identical, while Joseph's saw and broad-brimmed hat are very similar in type.

Rembrandt's composition quotes from an engraving by Lucas van Leyden (fig. 13a). The grouping of the figures, the way Joseph is offering the food, and the pose and position of the donkey have all been borrowed from van Leyden's engraving. The differences include the positioning of Joseph at a slightly lower level and the angle of Mary's head, which is now turned towards her husband. Making the figure of Joseph hold out the bowl of food has given him a more obvious function. Rembrandt's composition has greater unity as a result of these changes.

When an etching plate is printed, the impressions always appear on the paper in reverse. Artists often bear this in mind, as Rembrandt would appear to have done in this case. Rembrandt etched van Leyden's composition in mirror image on the plate. The reversal process that occurs during printing created a print that can be directly compared with van Leyden's

work. Rembrandt evidently wanted to remain as faithful to his model as possible.

The deliberate quotation of compositions and subjects from prints by famous artists is a recurrent phenomenon in Rembrandt's work. He was demonstrating his broad knowledge of the work of illustrious predecessors and contemporaries. Here, too, he may have been influenced by Pieter Lastman, whose work bears witness to a thorough knowledge of the graphic arts. Many subjects that Lastman introduced into painting had previously only appeared in prints. His paintings – Lastman did not make any prints – often include motifs or compositions derived from graphic arts.

*The Rest on the Flight into Egypt* is roughly the same size as *The Circumcision* (cat. no. 40). This has been read as an indication that both etchings were part of a series on the life of Christ that was never completed.[1] Although print series are arguably an important part of his graphic œuvre,[2] it is unlikely that Rembrandt, who had no experience whatsoever with printmaking, would have embarked on such an ambitious project at this stage in his career.

E.d.H.

[1] Bauch 1960, p. 104.
[2] Amsterdam/London 2000/01, pp. 36ff.

## 14
Jan Lievens (Leiden 1607–1674 Amsterdam)
# St John the Evangelist on Patmos, c. 1626

Etching, 156 x 141 mm
Hollstein 9, state II (4)
Museum het
Rembrandthuis,
Amsterdam, Inv. No. 342

Amsterdam 1988/89,
no. 4; Leiden 1991/92,
pp. 61f.

*St John the Evangelist on Patmos*, Lievens's first etching, comes across as far more mature than Rembrandt's *Circumcision* (cat. no. 40). The etchings date from the same period and were both published by Jan Beerendrecht of Haarlem. Everything indicates that Lievens and Rembrandt embarked on the technique of etching together.

Lievens placed the figure of John prominently in the composition, almost in the foreground. This lends the scene a certain monumentality, which is intensified because the Evangelist is viewed slightly from below. In contrast to Rembrandt's work, here the principal figure is clearly defined through the use of strongly emphasised outlines. The hatching and cross-hatching used to suggest shadows are drawn with care. The *chiaroscuro* effects are highly functional and contribute to the clarity of the composition. The use of a stippling technique, which probably derives from prints by Willem Buytewech, is typical of Lievens.[1]

The sturdy figure of St John and the use of a voluminous cloak with wide folds, which are characteristic of Lievens, reveal the influence of Lastman, who taught both Lievens and Rembrandt. The tight framing of the scene also seems to quote Lastman, who made a painting of the same subject in 1613.[2]

St John was Jesus's ‹beloved disciple›. After Christ's death he led the Christian community in Ephesus. During the reign of the Emperor Domitian, he was exiled to the island of Patmos, where he was inspired by visions to write his Revelation. John is identified by his writing implements and the eagle, which are also found in Lievens's etching.

In style and composition, *St John the Evangelist on Patmos* is closely akin to two other etchings by Lievens, which were made at the same time. They are *Jacob Anointing the Stone on Which He Has Slept*[3] and *Mercury Sends Argus to Sleep with His Flute*[4]. These etchings were published not by Beerendrecht, but by the Antwerp publisher Frans van den Wyngaerde.               E.d.H.

[1] Boston 1980, no. 70.
[2] Museum Boymans-Van Beuningen, Rotterdam (see: Amsterdam 1991, no. 4).
[3] Bartsch 9, Hollstein 4.
[4] Bartsch 10, Hollstein 18.

Jan Lievens fecit J Pietersse Berendr. e

## 15
### Jan Lievens (Leiden 1607–1674 Amsterdam)
# Mucius Scaevola and Porsenna, c. 1626

Pen in brown, brown and grey wash, over a sketch in black chalk, on two sheets of paper pasted together, 455 x 530 mm
Prentenkabinet van de Rijksuniversiteit, Leiden, Inv. No. AW 903

Sumowski, no. 1623x; Schneider/Ekkart 1973, no. SZ 412; Leiden 1976, no. T19; Braunschweig 1979, no. 49; Amsterdam 1988/89, no. 6

This monumental sheet is one of a group of ten related drawings, some of which were previously attributed to Rembrandt.[1] Bauch, however, attributed these works *en bloc* to Lievens, and this attribution is now generally accepted. These drawings were all made in the second half of the 1620s, in a period when Lievens's drawing style had not yet been influenced by Rembrandt's.[2]

The story of Mucius Scaevola is told by Livy and others. The Roman Gaius Mucius was given permission by the Senate to murder Porsenna, the king of the Etruscans. He made his way into the Etruscan army camp, but failed in his plan. He was captured and threatened with death by fire. To prove that no sacrifice was too great for him where the honour of Rome was concerned, he thrust his right hand into the flames. Porsenna, impressed by the Roman's patriotism and courage, then gave him his freedom. He owes his nickname Scaevola (the left-handed one) to this heroic act.

The drawing shows the hatching, cross-hatching and stippling that are characteristic of Lievens's early work. The strongly narrative style of drawing is also typical of Lievens's earliest period. The continuous outlines are strengthened in places by washes in grey and brown. The linear nature of the drawing is softened by the lavish use of the brush.

The crowded composition has much in common with two of Rembrandt's early history pieces – the Leiden *History Painting* (cat. no. 7) and *David with the Head of Goliath before Saul* (fig. 15a), dating from 1626 and 1627, respectively. The similarities are particularly marked in the latter work, which is also set in an army camp. The strong *repoussoir* as well as the framing, the type of army tent and the forest of lances and pikes held by the watching soldiers are found in both works. Sumowski argues that Rembrandt's painting was the starting point for Lievens's drawing and not vice versa, because at this time Rembrandt often painted history pieces with numerous figures, while Lievens concentrated on scenes with just a few figures.[3]

E.d.H.

[1] Sumowski, nos. 1622x-1631x.
[2] Amsterdam 1988/89, p. 29.
[3] Ibid.

Fig. 15a
Rembrandt Harmensz. van Rijn, *David with the Head of Goliath before Saul*, 1627
Panel, 27,2 x 30,6 cm
Kunstmuseum, Basle

## 16
## Rembrandt Harmensz. van Rijn
# Bust of an Old Man, c. 1629/30

Red chalk, heightened
with white, 114 x 91 mm
Benesch 39
Musée du Louvre,
Départements des Art
Graphiques, Paris,
Inv. No. 22 581

Paris 1933, no. 1165;
Paris 1988/89, no. 5

Only in Kassel

This rarely exhibited drawing of a bearded old man was previously attributed to Gerard Dou, but in 1933 it was rightly classified among the drawings by Rembrandt in the catalogue of the drawings in the Louvre. Before this, Michel had already drawn attention to the close kinship with *Christian Scholar in a Vaulted Room* in Stockholm,[1] a painting that is regarded by the *Rembrandt Research Project* as a copy after a lost original.[2]

By the end of the 1620s Rembrandt's drawing skills had developed to the full. His figure studies in chalk of this period are among the finest he ever produced. *Bust of an Old Man* is a representative example of these works. The drawing was made almost entirely in red chalk, with just the occasional touch of white chalk to heighten it.

The cloak and shoulder are set down with forceful, slightly sketchy lines and large areas of shadow. The old man's furrowed brow, in contrast, is drawn with great care and considerable attention to the fall of the light. This sophisticated combination of a varied use of line and strong contrasts between the deep dark shadow passages and the virtually unworked areas of the face results in convincing *chiaroscuro*. Rembrandt used this model on a number of occasions.[3] The same man, with his wrinkled face, balding head and magnificent beard, posed, for example, for several of his etchings, among them *Old Man with Flowing Beard*[4] and *Bust of an Old Man with Flowing Beard*[5] of 1630 and 1631, respectively. He appears in several of Rembrandt's drawings, including *Seated Old Man*[6], *Bearded Old Man in Profile*[7] and the preliminary study for *St Paul at his Desk*, which must have been made around 1629 (cat. no. 85). And he was also the model for two of Rembrandt's paintings – *St Paul in Prison* in Stuttgart[8] and *St Paul at his Desk* in Nuremberg (cat. no. 32).

E.d.H.

1 Paris 1988/89, p. 20.
2 Corpus, vol. 1, 1982, no. C 17
3 See note 1.
4 Bartsch 309.
5 Bartsch 315.
6 Benesch 37.
7 Benesch 42.
8 Corpus, vol. 1, 1982, no. A 11.

## 17
## Rembrandt Harmensz. van Rijn
# Bust of an Old Man, c. 1630

Red and black chalk,
147 x 145 mm
Benesch 38
Nationalmuseum,
Stockholm

Amsterdam 1988/89,
no. 13; Leiden 1991/92,
p. 66; Stockholm 1992/93,
no. 131

Only in Amsterdam

Benesch counts Rembrandt's *Bust of an Old Man* among a group of red chalk drawings of old men that were made around 1630 as preliminary studies for his paintings of saints and prophets.[1] We know of no painting on which this greybeard appears, but there is a print in which the same model figures in a virtually identical pose.[2] This print bears Rembrandt's monogram and the date 1630, but it is not generally accepted as an authentic work.

Rembrandt used the same model in almost exactly the same pose as Lievens (cat. no. 18). He showed the old man slightly more frontally. The almost irresistible impression is that they drew from this model at the same time, with Rembrandt sitting to Lievens's left. Unlike Lievens, Rembrandt also included the arms.

The differences in conception are more considerable. Schatborn has demonstrated this in impressive style.[3] Rembrandt is more interested than Lievens in the effect of the light. The drawing is built up of areas of shadow in different gradations, contrasting with open or almost blank passages.

His use of line is also more varied than Lievens's careful, tentative drawing technique. In Rembrandt's drawing, fine, random lines of varying thickness and intensity are interspersed with powerful accents. The very darkest areas have actually been emphasized with black chalk. The forms are indicated in various gradations of tone and are less precisely defined than in Lievens's drawing.　　　　　E.d.H.

[1]　Benesch, no. 38.
[2]　Bartsch 325.
[3]　Amsterdam 1988/89, no. 18.

2651

## 18
## Jan Lievens (Leiden 1607–1674 Amsterdam)
# Bust of an Old Man (verso: Part of a Mantle), c. 1630

Red and black chalk
(verso: red chalk on pale-
yellow-tinted paper),
137 x 116 mm (an extra
piece added bottom right)
Private collection,
The Hague

Schneider/Ekkart 1973,
no. SZ LXXII; Amsterdam
1988/89, no. 12; Leiden
1991/92, p. 66

At the end of the 1620s, both Rembrandt and Lievens usually drew with red chalk, which they used in combination with black chalk for the shadow passages. *Bust of an Old Man* is a good example of this.

Bauch attributed this fine sheet to Rembrandt,[1] but Benesch recognized Lievens's hand in it. There are now no longer any doubts about his attribution.

The closed, continuous outlines, the linear representation of the beard and the hair, the relatively flat chest, the cross-hatching and the moderate *chiaroscuro* effects certainly point to Lievens, whose drawing style is strongly linear.[2] A comparison with Rembrandt's *Bust of an Old Man* (cat. no. 17), for which the same man was probably the model, speaks volumes in this respect. In Rembrandt's work the shadows are largely executed in tone. The rapid, sketchy drawing style also differs from that of Lievens.

The back of the drawing, on which there is a red chalk sketch of part of a cloak, has been prepared in pale yellow. Lievens and Rembrandt copied this use of tinted paper for figure studies from their Amsterdam teacher Pieter Lastman.

*Bust of an Old Man* was probably made in or shortly before 1630.                E.d.H.

---

[1]  Bauch 1960, pp.176f.
[2]  Cf. Schatborn 1989, p.123.

## 19

Rembrandt Harmensz. van Rijn
# Bust of a Woman in a Heavy Headdress, 1631

Etching, 59 x 53 mm
Bartsch 355, state I (7)
Rijksmuseum,
Amsterdam,
Inv. No. RP-P-1969-139

White/Boon 1969,
pp. 157f.; Hollstein,
vol. 41, pp. 219, 233;
Amsterdam 1996,
no. 33b

Until recently, the only known impressions of *Bust of a Woman in a Heavy Headdress* were of the later states that were reworked by Jan van Vliet. Before the first state shown here was acquired by the Rijksprentenkabinet from a private English collection in 1969, its existence was known only from written sources.[1] The rediscovery of this unique example was extremely important, because it was at last possible to confirm the suspicion that the etching was started by Rembrandt. In only one other case does a surviving unfinished first state survive of a print begun by Rembrandt and reworked by van Vliet (cat. no. 55).

Art historians disagree about the number of Rembrandt's etching plates that were reworked by van Vliet. Earlier scholars, among them Rovinski and Münz, believed that there was a group of 27, but the current view is that no more than 12 prints were involved.[2] The grounds on which this assumption is based are not, however, entirely clear. One of the most intractable problems facing researchers is establishing precisely when specific things were done. Many of the alterations now attributed to van Vliet on stylistic grounds could very well be of a later date. More research into watermarks could throw new light on this matter.

Rembrandt's etching displays an immense variety in the use of line. The woman's head is composed of a complex web of heavy strokes, wavy lines, zigzag lines, cross-hatching and parallel lines. There is also tremendous variation in line

thickness. There is no other print in which Rembrandt has made such a concerted effort to achieve the effect of a pen drawing.

Little of the original etching work can be recognised in the states reworked by van Vliet – a total of seven of this print are known. He left only the face virtually untouched. Van Vliet's interventions are far removed from Rembrandt's intentions. In contrast to Rembrandt, who built his picture up out of light and dark zones, van Vliet's alterations were intended to give the work structure by clearly defining the separate forms, such as the headdress and the fur collar. This narrative style of drawing, although less subtle in execution, is vaguely reminiscent of the work of Jan Lievens, to whom the alterations have also been attributed. In the second state van Vliet added the monogram «RHL» and the date «1631». In the later states various elements, such as the cloak, the forehead, the headdress, the neck and the collar, have been covered with fine lines of shading (fig. 19a).

*Bust of a Woman in a Heavy Headdress*, together with the very similar *tronie, Bust of an Old Man* (cat. no. 55), is one of the small group of prints etched in the rough manner. It is easy to see how the public would have regarded these sketchy-looking works as unfinished and requiring further work before they could be sold.

E.d.H.

[1] White/Boon 1969, p. 158.
[2] Hollstein, vol. 41, p. 219.

Fig. 19a
Rembrandt Harmensz.
van Rijn, plate reworked
by Jan van Vliet, *Bust of
a Woman in a Heavy
Headdress*, 1631
Etching, 59 x 53 mm
Bartsch 355, state III (7)
Rijksmuseum,
Amsterdam

## 20
## Jan Lievens (Leiden 1607–1674 Amsterdam)
# Bust of an Old Woman, c. 1628/30

Red and black chalk, on pale-yellow-tinted paper, 108 x 83 mm
Mw. M. P. Klaver-Hienkens

Sumowski, no. 539xx (as Dou); Amsterdam 1988/89, no. 11; Leiden 1991/92, p. 66

This insightful drawing of an old woman was traditionally attributed to Nicolaes Maes. According to Sumowski, however, it is impossible on stylistic grounds to include this sheet in his œuvre.[1] The meticulous detailing that is particularly evident in the rendering of the wrinkled skin is certainly not very typical of Maes, whose drawings are much sketchier. On the basis of similarities with figure studies by Rembrandt dating from the late 1630s, Sumowski came to the conclusion that the work must have been made under his direct influence. He suggested that the drawing was probably by Gerard Dou, Rembrandt's first pupil.

In 1988 Schatborn pointed out the close relationship with the *Bust of an Old Man* (cat. no. 18) and attributed the drawing to Lievens.[2] The linear character dominates both drawings. The outlines are continuous and heavily emphasised in places. The way in which the eyes are drawn is also very similar. And the use of red chalk, in combination with black chalk for the shadows, is identical. Furthermore, *Bust of an Old Woman*, like the back of *Bust of an Old Man*, on which a fragment of a study of drapery can be seen, was prepared in pale yellow.

We can see just how differently Rembrandt himself set to work when we compare this *Bust of an Old Woman* with one of his studies of women (cat. no. 19). E.d.H.

[1] Sumowski, no. 539xx.
[2] Amsterdam 1988/89, no. 11.

## 21
### Jan Lievens (Leiden 1607–1674 Amsterdam)
# Bust of an Old Woman in Profile, c. 1629

Pen in brown,
147 x 132 mm
Inscribed top left: *Rem*
Maida and George
Abrams Collection,
Boston

Sumowski, no. 1639x;
Wellesley 1969, no. 2;
Amsterdam 1988/89,
no. 9; Schatborn 1989,
p. 122; Amsterdam/
Wien/New York/
Cambridge 1991/92,
no. 43

Robinson convincingly attributed this sheet, which for a long time was attributed to Rembrandt, to Lievens. The crux of his argument is its similarity to several etched *tronies* that Lievens made around 1630.[1] Although Robinson withdrew his attribution in 1970 and suggested Jan van Vliet as the possible artist, *Bust of an Old Woman in Profile* is now generally accepted as a work by Jan Lievens.[2]

*Bust of an Old Woman in Profile* is characteristic of Lievens in several respects. The strongly linear, descriptive manner of drawing is closely related to the style of his early drawings and prints (cf. cat. no. 14). The depiction of a head from the side is also typical of Lievens.

Schatborn was the first to point to the possible influence of Rembrandt, which can be seen chiefly in the contrasts between light and dark and the way in which the outline on the right is drawn.[3] Lievens' characteristic pen technique is in evidence on the shadow side. The shadow is suggested by means of heavily-thickened lines and hatching. The outlines are continuous. The lines on the light side are not continuous – they are made up of separate, sketchy little strokes. The random pattern of the hatching at the bottom may also have been influenced by Rembrandt.

On the basis of a comparison with a related drawing by Rembrandt, Schatborn arrives at a dating of 1628. According to Robinson, Lievens' drawing must have been made in 1629 or 1630. *Bust of an Old Woman in Profile* is one of only fifteen surviving drawings from Lievens' Leiden years (1625–1631).[4]          E.d.H.

[1]  Wellesley 1969, no. 2.
[2]  Sumowski, no. 1639x.
[3]  Amsterdam 1988, no. 9.
[4]  Amsterdam/Wien/New York/Cambridge 1991/92, no. 43.

## 22
Rembrandt Harmensz. van Rijn
# Music-making Company (Phyllis Seducing Two Men?), 1626

Oak panel, 63.4 x 47.6 cm
Signed left (on the cupboard): *RH.1626*
Rijksmuseum, Amsterdam, Inv. No. SK-A-4674

Bredius/Gerson 1969, Nr. 632; Amsterdam 1976a, p. 909; Amsterdam 1976b, no. 54; Leiden 1976, no. S28, p. 28; Bol 1977; Corpus, vol. 1, 1982, no. A 7; Schwartz 1984/85/87, fig. 23; Tümpel 1986, no. 118; Thiel 1989a; Leiden 1991/92, fig. 47; Straten 1992; Amsterdam 1992, pp. 76f.; Slatkes 1992, no. 103; Wetering 1997, fig. 16; Amsterdam 1999/2000, p. 53

In a room where the light falls from the upper left, a company is making music. The central figure is a young woman seated with her legs crossed, dressed very opulently in a brocade gown and striking red shoes, with a tiara-like ornament on her head. She sings from a music book on her lap, beating time with her raised right hand. Behind her chair stands an old woman with an oriental shawl over her head, looking on with her hand to her chin but not taking part in the music making. On the left behind the young woman sits a moustachioed man clad in a silk caftan and a turban, who plays a bass gamba.[1] On the right, on a table beside the young woman, stand a partly-gilded silver wine goblet and an open clavichord.[2] Old music books bound in leather and vellum are set out in front of the table in the foreground. A lute lies on the floor further to the left, and there is a viola da gamba on a small cabinet at the extreme left. In the background stands a young man wearing a large plumed hat who plays on a harp. On the panelled wall behind him hangs a painting depicting Lot and his daughters leaving Sodom, led by an angel, while Lot's wife changes into a pillar of salt in the background.[3]

The iconography of the *Music-making Company* of 1626 – like that of the Leiden *History Painting* (cat. no. 7) – has caused art historians a great many headaches. No wholly satisfactory explanation has yet been found for this scene, traditionally known as *The Music Lesson* and sometimes regarded in the past as a domestic group portrait of members of Rembrandt's family.[4] Scholars have pointed to similarities between this work and the popular tavern scenes by the Utrecht Caravaggisti dating from the early 1620s, which also often show musicians. More high-minded, allegorical interpretations, such as an allegory on Harmony or on Moderation, have been suggested. The scene has also been interpreted as a Vanitas allegory, specifically because of the books and musical instruments in the foreground, which are shown in exactly the same way in Leiden Vanitas still lifes of the 1620s. The *Rembrandt Research Project* did not arrive at a conclusive explanation and gave the painting the title of *Musical Allegory*, which had previously been introduced by Bauch, by which the piece has since been generally known.

Schwartz put forward a new interpretation – *The Music Lesson of Sensual Love* – which did not find acceptance because of its seemingly far-fetched nature.[5] He based his assertion on two emblems in an emblem book by Jacob Cats of 1632, whose significance he combined, it must be admitted, not altogether convincingly. Van Straten, who dismissed Schwartz's interpretation as «completely beside the point», countered with an explanation that differed funda-

185

Fig. 22a
Theodoor Matham after
Gerard van Honthorst,
*Violin Player*, 1626
Engraving, 217 x 169 mm
Rijksmuseum,
Amsterdam

mentally in both spirit and content.[6] He maintained that this «modest scene», as he saw it, was based on a passage from Paul's Letter to the Ephesians (5:18–19), which contains a warning about the dangers of wine – the cause of lewdness – and an exhortation to praise the Lord in song and music. The relevance of the wine goblet on the table and the picture of Lot on the wall is clear: Lot was reduced to impurity by the excessive consumption of wine and tempted into sexual intercourse with his two daughters. Van Straten explains the exotic clothes by pointing out that Paul was addressing a heathen audience.

Although this pious explanation does appear to explain several of the elements in this picture, it ignores a number of less virtuous details, which have attracted little if any attention so far and which throw an entirely different light on the scene – details that lead us to an extremely scabrous interpretation. In this respect Schwartz appears to have come closest to a possible solution.

In van Straten's interpretation, the young woman singer, who is clearly the central figure in the scene, is part of a pious company who «modestly» praise the Lord with song and music. The extraordinarily luxurious oriental clothes the young woman wears are enough in themselves to make this explanation completely untenable.[7] In terms of her clothes, she is but one in a long series of ‹worldly› women in sixteenth- and seventeenth-century art who, through the device of an ‹antique› court dress, were characterised as courtesans. The former prostitute Mary Magdalene is usually shown in such a costume, for instance, as is the allegorical ‹Woman of the World›. In the 17th century, the striking red shoes worn by the young woman must have had the same connotation of prostitution as red stockings. Moreover, the X-ray of the painting reveals that the woman was originally shown with bare breasts, something later concealed by the white veil that was rather clumsily painted over this part of her anatomy. The striking tiara, which, as we can see from the X-ray, only took on its eventual shape at a later stage, resembles the headdress worn by the equally sumptuously dressed «Mulier sine verecundia» (Woman without Shame) in the print from Cats' emblem book, to which Schwartz had already drawn attention.[8]

If the young woman is interpreted as a courtesan, the presence of the old woman on the right, who is not taking part in the music making, becomes understandable. As has been observed in the past, her physiognomy bears a marked resemblance to the type of the procuress who appears frequently in the work of Caravaggio and his Utrecht followers. The combination with the young courtesan makes it highly likely that she must indeed be interpreted as a procuress.[9]

In a print dated 1626 by Theodoor Matham after a painting by Gerard van Honthorst (fig. 22a) we see a young woman with her lips parted, playing the violin, dressed in an opulent décolleté dress and with a «creamy-white» type of face which is akin to that of the singing young woman in the *Music-making Company*.[10] What probably makes the print a key to the interpretation of Rembrandt's painting is the Latin inscription that the Leiden humanist Petrus Scriverius – as a «playful pastime» (Ludebat extempore) – added to it, which translates as «What, Pamphilus, do you think that the extravagant Phyllis is looking for with her face, voice, instrument and garb? A man!»[11] The philologist Scriverius, whom Rembrandt probably already knew in the 1620s,[12] was an extremely erudite scholar of classical literature, but he was also a lover of erotic poetry.[13] He must therefore have been very familiar with Martial's *Epigrams*, which at that time were considered to be «forbidden reading», in which the most diverse sexual exploits are described in explicit detail. One of these epigrams relates how Phyllis, who represented the prototypical temptress and courtesan, is visited by two men who both want to go to bed with her. She solves the problem by making love with the two men simultaneously.[14]

It is not surprising that this extremely improper poem has never previously been linked to this «modest scene». But if we identify the young woman as the Phyllis in Martial's epigram, we can explain not only the figures' ‹antique› dress, but also the presence of the two men. They fix their gaze on the hand, placed in the very heart of the picture, with which the young woman beats time. This apparently indicates that she has them both in her power. Her crossed legs, a ‹masculine› pose that was considered unseemly for women in public, is a sign of her dominance over the two men and reminds us that it was also Phyllis who succeeded in seducing Aristotle into allowing her to ride on his back, a subject that was extremely popular in fifteenth-century graphic art.

This erotic interpretation also elucidates other elements in the picture. The young man playing the harp not only plucks the strings of his instrument; he also makes a centuries-old copulation gesture with his hands.[15] He wears a very large (too large?) hat with a striking feather. A hat with a feather must have a sexual meaning in this titillating context, referring to the female genitalia.[16] We need only refer here to the plumed hat that hangs extremely suggestively on one of the bedposts in Rembrandt's etching *Le lit à la française*[17], and the feathered cap on the raised foot of one of the prostitutes in Nicolaus Knüpfer's *Scene in a Brothel* in the Rijksmuseum.[18] The playing of a stringed instrument also traditionally had a sexual connotation, as we learn, for instance, from the inscription on another print from the Matham studio, showing an old fiddler with a plumed hat, in which the taut strings are compared with the male erection.[19] The playing of the bass gamba, with its suggestive phallic shape, may therefore also be conceived as a fairly broad sexual pun in this context. And finally there is the striking «pictorial rhyme» with the picture of Lot on the wall – Lot who was, after all, seduced into intercourse with two women.

Elements from earlier interpretations can probably also be of significance here. The scene could very well be explained as a warning against the temptations and dangers of worldly pleasures. In this context the Vanitas symbolism of the musical instruments and the music books, which yield only fleeting sounds and transitory gratification, is certainly relevant. The reference to the consumption of strong drink as the cause of licentious behaviour in the shape of the wine goblet and the picture of Lot on the wall could be seen as an admonition against these sins. All the same, the work seems more likely to have been painted as a source of titillation for scholarly cognoscenti than as a moralising genre scene.

Although Rembrandt had spent seven years at the Latin School and was consequently capable of reading Latin verse, it is unlikely that he would have taken the initiative of painting such a scandalous subject himself. On the other hand, given his later delight in explicit scenes, this certainly cannot be ruled out. It is, however, more probable that his fellow-townsman Petrus Scriverius, who also provided the Phyllis inscription for Matham's print in the year this painting was made, presented him with the subject. It is even conceivable that he actually commissioned the painting.

In terms of its artistry, Rembrandt's *Music-making Company* is a tour de force in which he demonstrates the full extent of his virtuosity. None of his early paintings displays such diversity in painting technique or in the surface texture of the paint. Here again, Rembrandt's main concern seems to have been to achieve the most convincing possible expression of materials by applying the paint in a variety of ways so as to mimic the surface texture in question.[20] In places he actually used a painting technique and colours that were to be seized upon only by the impressionists centuries later.

Looked at from close up, the silk caftan of the bass gamba player proves to have been painted with countless tiny, irregularly applied touches of paint, while all these streaks and dots display a seemingly infinite variation in colour and light value. Using this ‹pointillist› technique, Rembrandt succeeds in creating an entirely convincing representation of gleaming silk. He demonstrates another astounding feat of painting technique in the young woman's gown. Using impasto, rapidly applied strokes and flecks of paint and a sophisticated pattern of pale yellow highlights, he is able to suggest with consummate realism the texture and lustre of brocade ornamented with gold thread. The lacquered wooden lute, whose texture and plasticity are rendered extraordinarily convincingly by the virtuoso placement of highlights, on the other hand, is painted very smoothly, although without pushing out the paint. The paint is opaque and Rembrandt has not used a glazing technique. The wood of the lute is rendered using unbelievably fine brushstrokes, in almost the same way as in the tempera technique of the early Italians. This enabled Rembrandt to reproduce even the grain of the wood – something that was not possible with the supposedly matchless glazing technique of the Flemish primitives. Rembrandt must have realised here that he was capable of emulating and even surpassing his illustrious predecessors when it came to rendering materials.

As proof of what he could do, Rembrandt seems to have deliberately focused on the contrasts between related materials. In the bindings of the books in the foreground, for instance, the difference in surface texture between worn leather and cockled vellum is very cleverly expressed. This comes not solely from the selection of the right colours, but above all from the precise positioning of the highlights and, perhaps even more importantly, from the painting technique: the leather is much more roughly painted than the vellum. This contrasting effect is achieved with precisely the same painterly means in the way the skin of the old woman's and the young woman's faces is rendered. As in the other paintings dating from 1626, Rembrandt suggests depth by allowing the strongly modelled passages with their sharp outlines that are towards the front to stand out against the background areas, which are rendered with less definition and in more subdued colours.

As Rembrandt was creating a temporary high point in his œuvre with this painting, we also see Lievens experimenting with the surface-imitation technique. In two monumental history pieces featuring half-length figures of around 1626, *Esther's Feast* in Raleigh (p. 194, fig. 24a) and *Pilate Washes His Hands in Innocence* (cat. no. 24), which was probably made shortly afterwards, Lievens likewise concentrated on the lifelike rendering of brocade, silk and other notoriously difficult-to-paint materials. The two painters must have tried to outdo one another and have experimented together with the consistency of the paint, the effects of colour combinations and of varying the manner of application, using a fine and a rough *peinture* alongside each other depending on the desired effect in that particular area of the painting.

Probably because the time-consuming surface mimicry-painting technique did not really lend itself to the large scale on which Lievens was accustomed to working, he switched to a different manner of painting after these two pieces, while Rembrandt's style was also to develop rapidly in a different direction. The tonal colour in the background of the *Music-making Company* and the light striking the wall are the precursors of the next phase in his artistic development.                                    B.v.d.B.

[1] Not a viola da gamba, as previously thought. There is a viola da gamba on the left in the foreground. See Amsterdam 1999/2000, p. 53.

[2] Not a jewel box, as previously thought. See Straten 1992, p. 160.

[3] Corpus, vol. 1, 1982, p. 122.

[4] See Corpus, vol. 1, 1982, pp. 120-123 for an overview of earlier interpretations.

[5] Schwartz 1984/85/87, pp. 42f.

[6] Straten 1992.

[7] Marieke de Winkel kindly informs us that this type of dress originates from Turkey.

[8] Schwartz 1984/85/87, fig. 25. Marieke de Winkel kindly informs us that in the seventeenth century, this type of headdress was considerd to be Persian.

[9] Schwartz 1984/85/87, p. 43, came to the same conclusion.

[10] Amsterdam 1997, no. 38.

[11] Amsterdam 1997, p. 202.

[12] Schwartz 1984/85/87, pp. 24-25, 37-40.

[13] Schwartz 1984/85/87, p. 42.

[14] Martial, Epigrams, X 81. Cf. the rhyming translation in Bruyn 1979a, p. 74.

[15] Cf. Amsterdam 1997, p. 363.

[16] Cf. Amsterdam 1997, p. 284.

[17] Bartsch 186.

[18] Amsterdam 1992, p. 61, no. A 4779.

[19] Amsterdam 1997, p. 201, fig. 4.

[20] Corpus, vol. 1, 1982, pp. 116-118; Wetering 1997, pp. 173-177.

## 23
## Jan Lievens (Leiden 1607–1674 Amsterdam)
# Christ in Gethsemane, c. 1627/28

Pen and brush in brown
and black, brown and grey
wash, 321 x 217 mm
Old inscription in brown
pen on bottom right:
*Livens.*
Staatliche Kunst-
sammlungen Dresden,
Kupferstichkabinett,
Inv. No. C 1437

Schneider/Ekkart 1973,
p. 359, no. Z 8; Sumowski,
vol. 7, 1983, pp. 361f.,
no. 1625x; Corpus, vol. 1,
1982, pp. 442f., fig. 3;
Amsterdam 1988/89,
no. 7

Only in Kassel

23a
Jan Lievens, *Trumpeter on
Horse*, c. 1627/28
Black chalk, pen in brown,
grey wash, 281 x 225 mm
Rijksmuseum,
Amsterdam

In the night on which he was to be taken prisoner, Jesus went to the Mount of Olives (Gethsemane) to pray and to submit himself in his hour of fear to the will of his Father. An angel then appeared and gave him strength. He had left the Apostles behind and urged them to pray, but they had fallen asleep (Lk 22:39–46). These are the details most often found in renderings of the scene in Gethsemane. Lievens, however, concentrates on the monumental figure of Jesus, who, seen slightly from above, kneels in the centre of the depiction. The strong fall of light from the right indicates the appearance of the angel. It is possible that the concept of this technically complex drawing was changed, for the initial sketch of a cowering Apostle on the left edge of the sheet appears in the end as an inconspicuous and fleeting brush sketch.

It has apparently gone unnoticed that the principal figure has been executed entirely with the brush. Only the plant in the lower-left corner has been done in pen and brown ink. For the lines of the figure, Lievens used black and grey with a grey-brown wash. The artist quite clearly has mastered the technique. The lines vary considerably, are broad in the shaded areas, fine for the face and in the lighter areas of the garment. Even the cross-hatching and dots, which in the first instance are reminiscent of engraving or a pointed pen, are done with the brush. This is evident in the swelling which occurs at the tip of each end of the lines. The use of the brush, which reacts to the slightest change in pressure, mellows the severity of the graphic vocabulary and brings it into line with the overall softness of the drawing. The dominating impression is of the wavy lines for the hair and outline of Jesus' garment and the soft and flabby folds of his wide cloak. Lievens rejects the *chiaroscuro* contrasts typical of strong modelling in favour of long flowing outlines and delicate graphic forms, which are reminiscent of the etchings by Willem Buytewech which Lievens had copied as a child.[1] The *Gethsemane* drawing is similar to one in the Rijksmuseum in Amsterdam showing a rider blowing a trumpet (fig. 23a).[2]

Sumowski convincingly dates both drawings to around 1627/28. They belong to the phase when Lievens appears to have been reacting to the increasing influence of Rembrandt on his art. Whereas in these years Rembrandt abandoned in his drawings and etchings all graphic systematic and formal precision in favour of a freer and more sketchy style (cf. cat. no. 41), Lievens is intent on exactly the opposite. A tendency to a more precise and refined individual form is also evident in his painting of the time. The naked angel, the attribute of the *Evangelist Matthew* of around 1627 (Bamberg),[3] shows remarkably long and rhythmic contours and smooth forms. The same beauty of line in conjunction with a greater refinement of modelling and a smoothness of the paint surface dominate the principal male figure in the large version of *Samson and Delilah*, probably painted in 1628, in the Rijksmuseum Amsterdam.[4]

B.S.

---

[1] See Schneider/Ekkart 1973, p. 2.
[2] Sumowski, vol. 7, 1983, no. 1626x; Amsterdam 1988/89, no. 8.
[3] Sumowski 1983ff., vol. 3, no. 1230, colour ill. p. 1869.
[4] Sumowski 1983ff., vol. 3, no. 1185; Leiden 1991/92, colour ill.
p. 81; Melbourne/Canberra 1997/98, no. 36 with colour ill.

191

## 24
## Jan Lievens (Leiden 1607–1674 Amsterdam)
# Pilate Washes His Hands in Innocence, 1626/27

Oak panel, 83.8 x 105 cm
Stedelijk Museum
De Lakenhal, Leiden,
Inv. No. 2195

Braunschweig 1979, no. 8;
Corpus, vol. 1, 1982,
pp. 442, 457; Sumowski
1983ff., vol. 3, pp. 1765f.,
1775, no. 1180, fig. p.
1819; Utrecht/Braun-
schweig 1986/87, p. 58
(J. R. Judson); Berlin/
Amsterdam/London
1991/92, no. 53; Leiden
1991/92, p. 91, no. 36;
Gutbrod 1996,
pp. 115–117

Jesus was brought to trial before Pontius Pilate, prefect of Judea under the Roman Emperor Tiberius. Convinced of Jesus' innocence, Pilate sought in vain to persuade the high priests and the Jewish people to free him: «But they shouted all the more, ‹Let him be crucified›. So when Pilate saw that he was gaining nothing, but rather that a riot was beginning, he took water and washed his hands before the crowd, saying, ‹I am innocent of this man's blood; see it yourselves›.» (Mt 27:23–24).

The painting of Pilate and *Esther's Feast* in Raleigh[1] (fig. 24a) are the only history paintings to have survived from Lievens' early years. Clearly the young painter invested all his skill in creating these two ambitious masterpieces. Lievens differs from Rembrandt in that his forté does not lie in depicting themes involving hectic action, such as the latter's turbulent *Christ Driving the Money-changers from the Temple* (cat. no. 12). Instead he prefers scenes which culminate in a moment of reflection. In the present case it is the moment when the authority of legitimate power concedes in the face of violence, and a symbolic act is invoked in an attempt to cast off responsibility. The depiction has a frequently-mentioned source: a composition by Hendrick ter Brugghen from around 1621 (fig. 24b).[2] A

small scene in the background of Lievens' picture makes it evident that he knew this work. It shows Jesus being led away by soldiers through a rounded door. It should also be noted that Lievens followed the biblical text more closely than ter Brugghen. He shows Pilate washing his hands, but not in a contemplative way but rather turning to the people. The mass of figures is actually too great for the composition, but such a claustrophobic crush serves to underline the beleaguered situation in which Pilate finds himself.

As in *Esther's Feast* Lievens places great emphasis on coloured and magnificent materials. Rembrandt competed with Lievens on this level, especially in his *Music-making Company* of 1626 (cat. no. 22). The two Lievens paintings are not, however, stylistically as close as hitherto has been assumed. The painting in Raleigh is dominated by a wealth of partly dissonant colours, decorative forms and small lively highlights. Lieven's *Pilate* is far less nervous in execution. Not so many isolated highlights are found on the faces, the figures are placed before a dark background instead of brightly-coloured lengths of fabric, the clothes are decorated with fewer clearly-delineated ornamental designs but instead the material falls in broad

193

24a
Jan Lievens, *Esther's Feast*,
c. 1625
Canvas, 130.8 x 163.2 cm
The North Carolina
Museum of Art, Raleigh

soft folds with lightly-sketched designs. Among the more informative details are both the head-dresses and fur wraps of Ahasverus and Pilate. Lievens' work is closer to achieving his desire to master a supple, flowing impasto in the Flem-ish manner. Pilate's turban is comparable in the broadly-sketched execution to that found in a sketch of the Moorish king by Rubens, which Lievens could have seen in Antwerp.[3] These characteristics bridge the gap to the de-pictions of the *Four Elements and Ages of Man* in Kassel (cat. nos. 72, 72), for which a date of 1626 is proposed in this catalogue. If *Esther's Feast* can be seen as Lievens' masterpiece of

1625, then his *Pilate Washes His Hands in Innocence* is the masterpiece of the following year, 1626. The comparison of the two paintings makes clear the speed with which the young Lievens, too, was making progress, still independent of Rembrandt. B.S.

24b
Copy after Hendrick ter Brugghen, *Pilate Washes His Hands in Innocence*
Canvas, 105.5 x 150 cm
Staatliche Museen Kassel,
Gemäldegalerie
Alte Meister

[1] Corpus, vol. 1, 1982, no. C 2 with ills. of details; Sumowski 1983ff., vol. 3, no. 1181, colour pl. p. 1820; Berlin/Amsterdam/London 1991/92, no. 52 with colour ill.

[2] The best known example is the well-preserved copy in the Gemäldegalerie Kassel, see Kassel 1996, p. 73, pl. 98 and Berlin/Amsterdam/London, p. 298, colour ill. 53a. The original, in which the background scene has been overpainted, is in the Museum of Lublin, Poland, see Schnackenburg 1987, pp. 174f., with ill.

[3] On the influence of Rubens on Lievens, cf. the essay by Bernhard Schnackenburg, pp. 106–108, fig. 16, 17.

## 25

Jan van Vliet (Leiden 1600/10–1668) after Jan Lievens (Leiden 1607–1674 Amsterdam)

# Isaac and Esau, c. 1633–35

Etching and burin,
472 x 389 mm
Inscribed: *J. Lieuius inv.
JG. v. vliet fecit*
Hollstein 52, state I (4)
Rijksmuseum, Amsterdam, Inv. No. RP-P-H-H-1385

Fraenger 1920, pp. XI,
78f.; Bauch 1960, p. 213;
Hollstein, vol. 11, p. 80,
no. 52; Bauch 1967a,
p. 164; Schneider/Ekkart
1973, p. 319; Amsterdam
1996, no. 34

Jan van Vliet not only reproduced paintings by Rembrandt in the form of prints; he also reproduced works by other artists – even if these remained the exception. This small group of prints includes *Isaac and Esau*, a reproduction of a painting by Jan Lievens that has since been lost.[1] The subject illustrates Lievens' interest in biblical scenes with a strong emotional charge, a predilection he shared with Rembrandt.

Isaac, the son of Abraham and Sara, is the second of the biblical patriarchs. Esau and his twin brother Jacob were born of Isaac's marriage to Rebecca. Jacob, the younger of the two, was the opposite of his brother in everything. He was shrewd, tenacious and enterprising; but he was also inclined to get his way by devious means. He succeeded, for example, in tricking Esau into giving up his birthright. Aided and abetted by Rebecca, he also deceived his nearly blind father. By passing himself off as Esau, he assured himself of his father's blessing. Once given, the blessing intended for Esau could not be undone.

In art it was customary to depict the moment when Jacob received the blessing from Isaac. Lievens, however, chose the moment at which the deception was discovered. This gave him the opportunity to portray a range of powerful emotions. Isaac has his arms crossed over his chest in impotent fury, because he knows that the blessing cannot be revoked. His fists are clenched. Esau, who has just returned from hunting, looks at his father in amazement. The game his father had ordered him to prepare lies on a table. Rebecca appears unmoved. With her left hand she pulls back the bed curtain, while she points to Esau with her right.

The motif of Rebecca pulling back the curtain is derived from an engraving by Maarten de Vos. Details like the bow, the quiver and the kneeling figure possibly refer back to a print by Maarten van Heemskerk.[2] But more important than these similarities is the resemblance to *Tobit and Anna* (cat. no. 28), a work that Rembrandt painted in 1626. Fraenger was the first to point this out. The figure types, the style, the composition, the way the fall of the folds is rendered and the lighting are clearly closely related.[3] This points not only to an interdependence, but also to a similar date.

Van Vliet published a second work by Lievens as a print. This was *Susanna and the Elders*, a painting dating from the mid-1620s that has also been lost. Watermark research has revealed that both reproductions were made between 1633 and 1635, in other words almost ten years after the paintings.[4]

Both prints are reproductions of paintings that are dated around 1625. There are no extant paintings of this period by Lievens in which several figures are shown at full length. Van Vliet's prints are consequently of inestimable value because they give us insight into Lievens' earliest development as a painter. At the same time they are evidence of the close relationship between Lievens' work and Rembrandt's.

E.d.H.

---

[1] *Christ and Nicodemus* (Hollstein 94), a reproductive print, which was discounted by Schuckman, is undoubtedly a work by van Vliet (see: Amsterdam 1996, no. 37).
[2] Amsterdam 1996, p. 90, note 1.
[3] Fraenger 1920, pp. 76ff.
[4] Amsterdam 1996, p. 33.

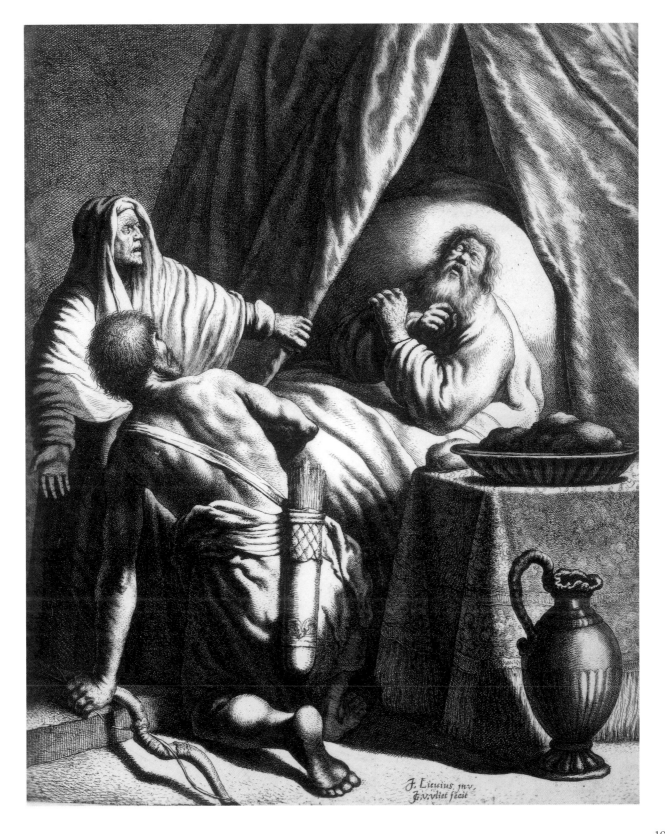

197

## 26

Circle of Jan Lievens (Leiden 1607–1674 Amsterdam) and Rembrandt Harmensz. van Rijn

# The Foot Operation, c. 1628–29

Oak panel, 31.8 x 24.4 cm
Inscribed left (on the
bench): *PHL 1628*
Private Collection,
Switzerland

Schneider 1932, p. 70;
Bauch 1960, pp. 213f.,
Corpus, vol. 1, 1982, no. C
11, Basle 1987, no. 78,
pp. 208f.

Only in Kassel

Seated in a low chair, a simply-dressed man is having his foot treated by an old man wearing spectacles. The patient's face is twisted in a grimace and both fists are tightly balled before his chest in reaction to an apparently painful foot operation. The surgeon, with his purse of instruments beside him on the bench, sits against a light wall on which hangs an unrolled map. A bowl and several bottles stand on the shelves above his head. The light entering from the left falls most intensely on the floor planking, the patient's shoe and a wicker basket in the foreground.

Bauch pointed out that in a series of prints of the Five Senses by Jan van Vliet the foot operation represents the sense of touch.[1] One of these prints is dated 1634, when there were still intensive contacts between van Vliet and Rembrandt's studio. This lends some weight to the supposition that the sense of touch could also have been the theme of the painting discussed here – not as part of any larger series of the Five Senses, however, but rather as an independent subject in its own right.[2]

At first sight, this small panel would seem to fit well into Rembrandt's œuvre of the period 1627 to 1628. Thus, in the handling of paint and the largely monochrome colour scheme there are similarities to the *St Paul in Prison* in Stuttgart (p. 216, fig. 30a) and the Boston *Artist in His Studio* (cat. no. 61) from 1627 respectively 1628. The handling of light with the illuminated foreground also puts one in mind of the latter painting, or of the *Simeon in the Temple* in Hamburg (cat. no. 30) from c. 1627. But it is precisely when one compares *The Foot Operation* with these paintings that striking differences become apparent, which virtually rule out the possibility that it was painted by Rembrandt. One important difference from Rembrandt's own paintings of this period (or at least those considered by us to be from his own hand) is that in its illuminated areas – and specifically the most strongly illuminated part: the floor in the foreground – the actual light intensity is rather low. Whereas in Rembrandt's own works the range of illumination extends from brightest light to deepest shade, the range

199

Fig. 26a
Jan Lievens, *The Foot Operation*, c. 1628
Chalk, pen and wash, 318 x 266 mm
Gabinetto Disegni e Stampe degli Uffizi, Florence

in this painting is compressed in a manner that betrays the painter's relative inexperience. This is also true of other aspects of the execution, which is in several respects rather hesitant. The chair, for example, whose shape is hardly convincingly rendered, is painted in countless streaks and with hesitantly-placed catch lights. Characteristic detail is missing from the heads and hands; and the same is true of the way the objects in the background are represented (cf., for example, the bottles with those in the background of the Boston *Studio* [cat. no. 61]).

The painting has often been linked with a drawing of the same subject in Florence that is usually attributed to Jan Lievens (fig. 26a).[3] Although the figures in this drawing are reversed in relation to those in the painting, the two works share a number of common motifs, such as the basket and shoe placed prominently in the foreground. It is therefore not unlikely that the panel was originally based on the drawing made by someone in Jan Lievens' circle, an idea that is certainly not contradicted by the rather bulky style that characterizes the painting. Compare, for example, the way Lievens in this period represents hands in the *Samson and Delilah* (cat. no. 27) as well as in the *Isaac and Esau* (cat. no. 25) that survives as a print reproduction by Jan van Vliet. As long as we do not know whether the young Lievens had pupils – or whether (which is not altogether unlikely) he influenced Rembrandt's pupils – the relation suggested here between the unknown painter of this work and Lievens or Rembrandt remains unclear.

The inscription «PHL.1628» on the left-hand side in lighter paint on the surgeon's bench only serve to deepen the puzzle. This writing was not added by a later hand, as the authors of the *Corpus* suspected.[4] Recent microscopic examination and analysis of a paint sample by the *Rembrandt Research Project* revealed that the monogram and date were added shortly after the painting was completed. The monogram, composed of rather wavy lines, shows a strong affinity with the RHL monograms on Rembrandt's own paintings from 1627–28 (see cat. nos. 29 and 75). However, what is remarkable is that there is no trace of any downward-sloping right foot of an R, nor does the state of that part of the painting allow the possibility that this has been rubbed off. One can always speculate that this might be the monogram of another painter; but it seems highly unlikely that a painter in Rembrandt's circle would have imitated Rembrandt's style of monogram so literally (apart from the foot of the R).

E.v.d.W./M.d.W.

---

[1] Hollstein, vol. 41, 1992, nos. 27–31, no. 30.

[2] See Schipper 2000 on the depiction of the Five Senses in Dutch art.

[3] See Corpus, vol. 1, 1982, p. 516, note 3, for the literature on the attribution of the drawing to Lievens.

[4] Corpus, vol. 1, 1982, p. 515.

## 27
Jan Lievens (Leiden 1607–1674 Amsterdam)
# Samson and Delilah, c. 1628

Oak panel, 27.5 x 23.7 cm
Rijksmuseum Amsterdam,
Inv. No. A 4096

Bauch 1960, p. 214–216;
Kahr 1973, p. 258f.;
Amsterdam 1976b, p. 472
(Rembrandt-School);
Braunschweig 1979,
no. 15; Corpus, vol. 1,
1982, no. C 1; Sumowski
1983ff., vol. 3, p. 1764f.,
1777, no. 1184, fig.
p. 1823; Leiden 1991/92,
p. 106–109, no. 61

The dramatic and tragic story of the hero Samson, who sacrificed himself after God had sent him to free the Israelites from the Philistines, (Judg 13–16) was one which deeply moved Rembrandt. It so captured his artistic interest that by the late 1630s he had depicted four different episodes from the story.[1] For the first of these works, all of which can be counted among his best, he chose to illustrate Samson's betrayal by the Philistine Delilah (fig. 27a). From the Middle Ages, this subject served as a moralising exemplum about the dangerous allure of women and the punishment that will be meted out to those who submit to illicit desire. Samson used his supernatural physical strength to wreak havoc amongst the Philistines. The source of this strength was his long hair, which he was forbidden to cut. To discover his secret, the Philistines bribed Delilah with a large sum of money, and it was not long before she was successful. Having informed the Philistines, she ordered one of them to cut Samson's locks after he had fallen asleep in her lap, thus making him powerless against his captors.

At the end of the 1620s it was not just Rembrandt who was interested in this subject but also his friend and rival Jan Lievens. Their three depictions are amongst the most important and most puzzling testimonies to their artistic co-operation. Lievens' small oil sketch, on loan from the Rijksmuseum, Amsterdam, was executed in reddish-brown and white tones and shows compositional similarities to Rembrandt's depiction in the Berlin Gemäldegalerie. The Rijksmuseum, Amsterdam, also owns Lievens' large-scale *Samson and Delilah,* in which the protagonists are shown as half and three-quarter-length figures (fig. 27b). All three works are closely related and focus on the same moment of dramatic tension: Delilah has summoned a man from amongst her people, and in the next instance he will rob the sleeping hero of his hair and thus his strength. The attribution of the unsigned and technically unique Amster-

dam oil sketch to Lievens and not Rembrandt has largely gone unchallenged since Kurt Bauch first proposed it.[2] There is, however, less of a consensus regarding the chronology and dating of the three works. Older research accepted without question that Lievens, working in Rembrandt's shadow, was inspired by the latter's Berlin painting, which bears the date 1628. Until today has generally been thought that Lievens first executed the sketch and then the large format, which Sumowski dates to around 1630.

The observations by members of the *Corpus* suggest exactly the opposite chronology. They dismiss Rembrandt's signature on the Berlin painting as inauthentic and date it on stylistic grounds to 1629/30,[3] while the two works by Lievens must have been executed before 1629. They emphasise that in this case Rembrandt must have used a pictorial invention by Lievens. This assessment of the situation can be fully endorsed and indeed further substantiated. As could be shown for Lievens' drawing *Christ in Gethsemane* (cat. no. 23), the large Amsterdam painting belongs to the category of works executed around 1627/28. It differs, however, from the *Evangelist Matthew,*[4] which can be dated with relative certainty to 1627, in the greater refinement of the modelling and its delicate yellow-orange colour combination. It is thus more likely to have been painted in 1628.[5] Even if no painting by Lievens is known which can be compared with the Amsterdam sketch, a few drawings, such as the *Gethsemane* sheet – which on the basis of its draughtsmanship belongs to the period 1627/28 – display flat, soft and flabby forms similar to those of the oil sketch. Consequently, both of Lievens' renderings of Samson and Delilah must have been executed within a short period.

But which came first? Taking into account the improvements in the oil sketch in mastering the dramatic challenges of the subject, the earlier work must be the large half-figure format

(fig. 27b), since it contains a number of obvious weaknesses. The lack of spatial depth gives the approaching Philistine insufficient room, his tense expression is grotesquely exaggerated and his gestures unclear, since it is Delilah who holds the scissors. Here Lievens depicts the story more as if it were a still life than a dramatic event; in Rembrandt's eyes this was indeed an artistic error of magnitude. Following his visit to the young painters in Leiden, Constantijn Huygens wrote that when depicting the so-called histories, the great and wonderful artist [Lievens] did not match the inventive liveliness of Rembrandt. It can be assumed that Lievens also had to listen to such criticism from others. Could it not be that the oil sketch was created as a spontaneous reaction to such comments? Taking as his point of departure a print by

Matthew Merian showing the scene populated by full-length figures, with a bed on the right and the Philistines pouring into the room,[6] Lievens quickly sketched a composition designed to prove his versatility and which indeed contains considerable improvements. The man holding the scissors in his hand stealthily approaches from behind while Delilah warns him to be silent by holding her finger to her lips is an excellent invention, although his features (those of Rembrandt?), with his wide staring eyes, still appear unnatural and exaggerated. Delilah's profile and the long line of Samson's neck are taken from Lievens' first version, while the hero's loosely hanging arm and the soldiers hiding behind the door are derived from Jacob Matham's engraving after Peter Paul Rubens' painting of the same subject, today in the

Fig. 27b
Rembrandt Harmensz.
van Rijn, *Samson and
Delilah*, c. 1628
Canvas, 129 x 110 cm
Rijksmuseum, Amsterdam

National Gallery in London.[7] Lievens' sketch impressed Rembrandt while simultaneously challenging him to make further improvements and to capture the mood of the moment. Rembrandt creates an atmospheric space of towering verticals in which unrelenting figures mark the stations of Samson's fate. Delilah casts a fearful glance at the Philistine who, holding the scissors like a sword, leans over to commit the deed as Samson lies peacefully asleep in his lover's lap. Rembrandt replaces Lievens' passive group of armed soldiers with a single soldier waiting behind the curtain of the bed for the moment when he can tie up Samson. Thus on the basis of a pictorial invention by Jan Lievens, Rembrandt executed his first «masterpiece of terror and tension».[8]                    B.S.

[1] *Samson and Delilah*, c. 1628–30, Staatliche Museen zu Berlin, Preußischer Kulturbesitz, Gemäldegalerie. Corpus, vol. 1, 1982, no. A 24. *Samson Threatens His Father-in-Law*, around 1635, Staatliche Museen zu Berlin, Preußischer Kulturbesitz, Gemäldegalerie. Corpus, vol. 2, 1986, no. A 109. *The Blinding of Samson*, 1636, Städelsches Kunstinstitut, Frankfurt am Main. Corpus, vol. 3, 1989, no. A 116. *Samson sets a Puzzle for his Wedding Guests*, 1638, Staatliche Kunstsammlungen Dresden, Gemäldegalerie Alte Meister. Corpus, vol. 3, 1989, no. A 123.

[2] Bauch 1960, pp. 210, 214f.

[3] The Gemäldegalerie Berlin has accepted the judgement concerning the signature but retained the date 1628, albeit with a question mark.

[4] The books belonging to the Evangelists in the series in Bamberg (Sumowski 1983ff., vol. 3, nos. 1230–1233, colour pl. p. 1869) have the same impressively tattered pages as seen in two contemporaneous Vanitas still-life paintings in the Rijksmuseum, Amsterdam (Sumowski 1983ff., no. 1300 with colour illustration) and in Kasteel Het Nijenhuis, Heino, dated 1627 (Braunschweig 1979, no. 14, Sumowski 1983ff., vol. 3, no. 1299).

[5] Helga Gutbrod convincingly pointed out differences in style in the comparative works cited by Sumowski to support his late date of around 1630, see Gutbrot 1996, p. 145.

[6] Tümpel 1993, fig. p. 388 under no. 4.

[7] Kahr 1973, fig. 19; Bartsch, vol. 4, p. 179, fig. 194.

[8] Gerson 1968/69, p. 176.

## 28
### Rembrandt Harmensz. van Rijn
# Tobit and Anna, 1626

Signed bottom left:
*RH.1626*
Panel, 40.1 x 29.9 cm
Rijksmuseum,
Amsterdam

Bredius/Gerson 1969,
no. 486; Amsterdam
1976b, p. 467; Leiden
1976, cat. no. S27;
Corpus, vol. 1, 1982,
no. A 3; Schwartz
1984/85/87, fig. 26;
Tümpel 1986, no. 2; Thiel
1989b; Berlin/Amster-
dam/London 1991/92,
no. 1; Slatkes 1992, no. 5

Only in Amsterdam

The scene is based on an episode in the apocryphal Book of Tobias (2:11–15, 3:1–6). It relates the story of how the old, blind Tobias, who has fallen on hard times, unjustly accuses his wife Anna of stealing a kid. Their impoverished circumstances have forced Anna to go out to work and earn a living from spinning, and she has been given the kid as a gift from her employer, but Tobias refuses to believe it. When he finally realises his mistake, he despairingly prays to God for forgiveness and begs to be allowed to die soon.

We see the couple in a wretched hut with a thatched roof, the light entering through a window top left. The old blind man sits on a rickety chair, his stick lying on the floor beside him. He wears a faded red, fur-lined tabard with darns and patches. This costly but wholly worn-out garment eloquently expresses both Tobias' former prosperity and his social downfall. Judging from the numerous holes, his jerkin and shoes are completely worn out after a lifetime's wear. With clasped hands, Tobias throws his head back and shows his sorrowful penitence. His wife Anna, an oriental shawl over her head, stands beside him with a kid under her arm and looks at him with an astonished gaze. Behind Tobias we see a rush chair on which lie a spindle and thread, indicating the nature of Anna's virtuous employment. In the semi-darkness of the background we can make out some domestic utensils on shelves against the wall. At the top left, next to the window, hang a birdcage and a bunch of garlic; above right in a niche over a wooden door there is a wicker basket. A little dog sits at Tobias' feet, warming itself at a small fire burning in the foreground on the right.

This is no doubt the last painting that Rembrandt made in 1626, since the artistic path he embarks on here continues into the work he was to paint in 1627. If we compare *Tobit and Anna* with the *Music-making Company* (cat. no. 22), which was painted slightly earlier, it is immediately clear that Rembrandt underwent an amazingly rapid development as a painter in a very short space of time. There are still examples of the surface-mimicking style of the earlier work here and there – in the fur lining of Tobias' cloak, for instance, in the old people's skin and in the fire burning in the foreground. But it seems as if even in these areas the paint has been applied more smoothly and evenly, with less relief. The painting of the draperies is also flatter, so that the forms have lost a degree of expressive force. This is not, however, to say that Rembrandt has not given thought to the expression of materials. Tobias' worn and dirty sandals, placed prominently in the foreground à la Caravaggio, are painted with extraordinary plasticity and realism. But the effect is achieved through an illusionistic manner of painting, not by applying the paint so as to imitate the texture of the material.

We can also see an important development taking place in the use of colour. Whereas Rembrandt had previously reserved the muted tones for the background, they now appear to be everywhere in the painting. Rembrandt is starting to break the colours here; in other words he starts to avoid strong colour contrasts and uses colours throughout the painting in tones that are close to one another in intensity. This creates a unity in the work and enables him, with the aid of lighting effects, to significantly increase the plasticity and the spatial values of the figures and objects he depicts by allowing them, as it were, to emerge from the semi-darkness. In *Tobit and Anna* the figures are consequently rendered with realistic plasticity in a credible spatial setting. Rembrandt very soon perfected this originally Caravaggist *chiaroscuro*, as we see in *An Old Usurer Examining a Coin* of 1627 (cat. no. 29). To this end, in Tobit and Anna Rembrandt introduces a second source of light into the scene in the shape of the fire below right, whose warm glow gleams on the dog's coat.

In *Tobit and Anna*, Rembrandt also devoted much more attention to the portrayal of deep human emotions – one of the other characteristics of his work that was to bring him such renown – than he had in his earlier paintings. His preference was for hard-to-express emotions like silent despair and misery, as the piteous figure of Tobias reveals. The point in the story that Rembrandt chose to illustrate is also important. Where many artists would have picked the moment of greatest drama, Rembrandt gives us the instant when the inner emotional tensions are at their height. This difference is evident when we compare Rembrandt's *Tobit and Anna* with the print of the same subject by Jan van de Velde after Willem Buytewech, which Rembrandt unquestionably used as his inspiration (fig. 28a). Whereas Buytewech has depicted the moment at which the indignant Anna scolds her mistrustful husband, Rembrandt chooses the moment of repentance and remorse that followed. In his gestures and facial expression, this Tobias can be regarded as a forerunner of the penitent figure of Judas in *Judas Returning the Thirty Pieces of Silver* of 1629 (cat. no. 33), the painting in which both the portrayal of human emotions and the use of *chiaroscuro* were to reach unprecedented heights.

During this period Lievens also concentrated more on the rendering of human emotions, but, probably influenced by Flemish examples, he opted for a manner of portrayal with more outward pathos, as his lost painting of *Isaac and Esau* (cat. no. 25) – now known only from a print – demonstrates. The way in which the figure of Isaac is depicted is similar in many ways to Rembrandt's Tobias, and the two works are also closely related in terms of composition, lighting and draperies. It tells us that at this stage in their careers, the two artists were still exploring new artistic possibilities together.

B.v.d.B.

## 29
Rembrandt Harmensz. van Rijn

# An Old Usurer Examining a Coin (The Rich Man from the Parable?), 1627

Oak panel, 31.9 x 42.5 cm
Signed left (on the book):
*RH.1627*
Staatliche Museen zu
Berlin, Preußischer
Kulturbesitz, Gemälde-
galerie, Cat. No. 828 D

Bredius/Gerson 1969,
no. 420; Berlin 1975,
pp. 347f.; Corpus, vol. 1,
1982, no. A 10; Schwartz
1984/85/87, fig. 30;
Tümpel 1986, no. 36;
Berlin/Amsterdam/
London 1991/92, no. 2;
Leiden 1991/92, fig. 41;
Slatkes 1992, no. 69;
Berlin 1996, p. 101,
fig. 1532

An old man with a pair of pince-nez perched on his nose sits at a table in a room largely shrouded in semi-darkness, in which we can make out a chair at the front on the left and a stove against the left wall. Against the back wall stands an open cupboard filled with bags of money. The single source of light in the room is a burning candle, so that only the man himself and the objects close to him are clearly lit. Lifting the candle slightly, the man intently studies a coin by the light of the candle, and the flame is concealed behind the hand in which he holds the coin. The man is surrounded by disorderly piles of old books, sealed documents and other papers. On the right beside the man is a strikingly large purse. Pseudo-Hebrew letters can be seen on one of the books and some of the papers. On the table in front of the man there is a gold-weigher's scale with a box of weights and more gold coins. In front on the left lies a large open ledger in which entries that have been crossed out can be seen.

We see here an old usurer, who is interested in nothing but his money and his account books. This painting was originally regarded as a genre piece, in which Rembrandt depicted a scene taken from everyday life.[1] Bauch suggested that this is a portrayal of Avaritia, or greed.[2] Others have countered by arguing that Avaritia is usually personified by an old woman, not by an old man.

Tümpel identified the painting as a biblical history piece, illustrating the rich fool in one of Christ's parables (Lk 12:13–21).[3] In this parable, which is a warning against avarice, Christ tells his listeners how a rich farmer intends to build larger barns to store all the fruits of his land so that he can take his ease, eat, drink and be merry for many years. Then God spoke to him, «Thou fool, this night thy soul shall be required of thee: then whose shall those things be, which thou hast provided? So is he that layeth up treasure for himself, and is not rich toward God».

This subject had never before been depicted in a painting, although it is found in sixteenth-century prints. They usually show a middle-aged man in a costly coat, surrounded by his treasures, while his prophesied end is represented very literally by a skeleton holding an hourglass at the open window.[4] There is often also a clock, as a symbol of transience. This iconography was followed by artists until late in the seventeenth century,[5] but not by Rembrandt: his work actually departs from it in a number of significant respects. The man is old and, unlike the rich man in the parable, he does not have many years of prosperity to look forward to. Aside from the books, promissory notes, gold coins and moneybags, which are unmistakably Vanitas symbols, there are no literal references to the man's approaching death (unless one interprets his age itself as such). There is also no clock: the object at the top left regarded by all authors, following Tümpel's lead, as a clock, is in fact a rectangular stove-pipe, similar to that in Rembrandt's etching of a half-clothed model of 1658.[6] The night-time setting of the scene is not in line with the iconographic tradition, although it does reflect the Bible passage, but it was probably chosen primarily for pictorial reasons.

Although the man's dress is old-fashioned (late 16th century, judging from the type of cap and the style of collar), this is not surprising in view of his advanced years. In any case the man's clothes do not seem to be intended to set the scene in antiquity, biblical or otherwise. Tümpel saw the pseudo-Hebrew script as an indication that Rembrandt had painted a biblical scene. It is far more likely, however, that this was to characterize the man as a usurer in a way that everyone would understand at that time: in the 17th century Jews were generally associated with speculation and money-trading, and the stereotype of the 'Jewish usurer', already common in the Middle Ages, was extraordinarily persistent.[7] It is certainly relevant in this

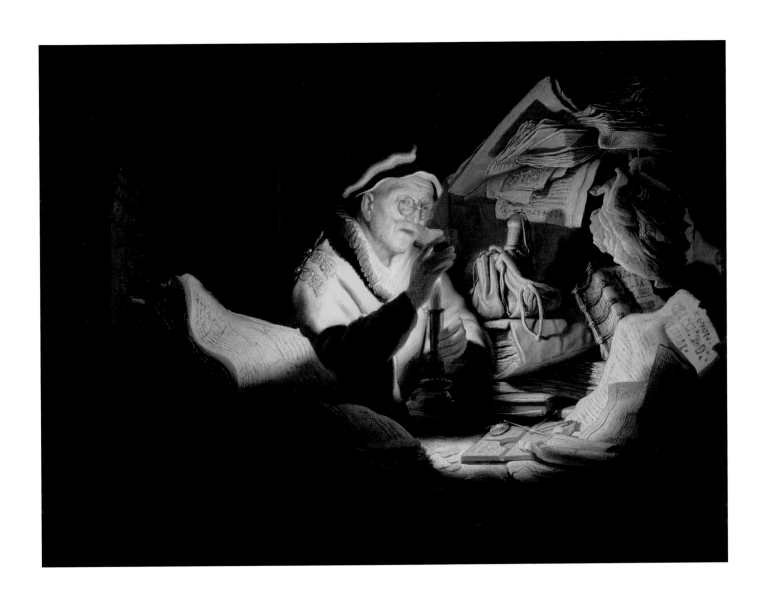

Fig. 29a
Gerard van
Honthorst, *An Old
Woman Examining
a Coin*, 1624
Canvas, Private
Collection

context that Rembrandt used the head type of the old man with spectacles a year earlier for one of the money-changers in *Christ Driving the Money-changers from the Temple* (cat. no. 12). We also find it in an equally negative, money-related context in Lievens' *Tric Trac Players* (cat. no. 8), from which Rembrandt probably derived it.

In terms of its iconography, the Berlin painting is very much akin to sixteenth-century scenes of greedy usurers and tax collectors painted by Quinten Metsijs, Marinus van Reymerswael and others. The usurers portrayed by them, who are surrounded by exactly the same attrib-

utes as the old man in Rembrandt's painting, are usually very definite caricatures. They have to be interpreted not only as a witty product of the eternal dislike of paying taxes, but also as an exhortation against greed and, in theological terms, the cardinal sin of avarice. The standard attribute of avarice is a purse,[8] just like the one displayed so prominently beside the old man in Rembrandt's painting. There is consequently much to be said for interpreting the painting as a representation of Avaritia and not as an illustration of the parable.

In this painting, Rembrandt for the first time uses the extreme chiaroscuro effects that were later to become a much-praised and enduring element of his style. The virtuoso play of light and shade that he demonstrates here is very like that in the night scenes by candlelight by the Utrecht Caravaggisti. A painting by Gerard van Honthorst dating from 1624, in which an old woman wearing spectacles holds a coin to the light in the same way as does Rembrandt's old man, may even be regarded as a direct source of inspiration for this work (fig. 29a).

Rembrandt seems, however, to be searching for something essentially different from the Caravaggisti. Where Honthorst tries to achieve a lifelike plasticity using spectacular light effects and realistic close-ups of striking areas of flesh, Rembrandt's objects owe their plasticity primarily to a convincing suggestion of the space that surrounds them. This space is made almost palpable by extremely subtle gradations of light and tone and marked variation in the sharpness of the outlines. The tonal unity of the scene contributes significantly to this suggestion of space. By limiting the colours used in the scene essentially to brown and grey tones, Rembrandt accentuates the extreme *chiaroscuro* effect around the burning candle even more forcefully. The application of the paint also appears to be directed towards this contrasting effect: while the *peinture* in the whole painting is noticeably even, impasto has been used only around the source of the light.

What Rembrandt himself would undoubtedly have regarded as his greatest achievement in this painting is not so much the rendition of the most brightly lit passages as that of the areas in semi-darkness in the background, where the light does not penetrate. This is something that Caravaggio and his followers never really succeeded in doing – in their work, where there is no light, there is darkness. Rembrandt is the first painter in the history of art who can depict a darkened room credibly, while maintaining the effect of depth.

Rembrandt did not confine his use of colour largely to browns and greys specifically for this night piece. As we see in *Tobit and Anna* (cat. no. 28), painted at the end of 1626, he is now introducing more tonal unity into the scene – in daylight scenes, too, like *Simeon in the Temple* (cat. no. 30), which was painted shortly thereafter. In his liking for broken colours and browns and greys, Rembrandt was following a trend that can be seen throughout all of Dutch painting from the middle of the 1620s onwards.                B.v.d.B.

[1] For an evaluation of the iconographic interpretations of the painting, see Corpus, vol. 1, 1982, pp. 139–141.
[2] Bauch 1960, p. 139.
[3] Tümpel 1971, pp. 27–30.
[4] Berlin/Amsterdam/London 1991/92, p. 128.
[5] Cf. Amsterdam 1997, no. 59.
[6] Bartsch 197.
[7] Schama 1987, pp. 587ff.
[8] Timmers 1947, p. 567.

## 30
## Rembrandt Harmensz. van Rijn
# Simeon in the Temple, c. 1627/28

Panel, 55.4 x 43.7 cm
Signed, by another hand,
lower right: *Rembrandt. f.*
Hamburger Kunsthalle,
Inv. No. 88

Bredius/Gerson 1969, no.
535; Braunschweig 1979,
no. U 5; Corpus, vol. 1,
1982, no. A 12; Schwartz
1984/85/87, fig. 29; Schatborn 1986b, pp. 56, 61;
Tümpel 1986, no. 39;
Warnke 1986; Leiden
1991/92, fig. 43; Slatkes
1992, no. 39; Melbourne/
Canberra 1997/98, no. 2;
The Hague 1997, no. 22

Only in Kassel

The treatment of the light, the use of colour and the representation of space make this painting one of Rembrandt's early masterpieces. The signature was added later, but the authenticity of the piece has never been called into question.[1] Stylistically and in terms of composition, the painting is closely related to *St Paul in Prison* in Stuttgart of 1627 (fig. 30a) and *Peter and Paul Disputing* in Melbourne, which dates from 1628 (p. 70, fig. 19).[2] It was probably painted not long after the former work, in about 1627/28.

As prescribed by Jewish Law, Joseph and Mary took their firstborn to the Temple in Jerusalem to present him to God (Lk 2:22–39). There they encounter the aged Simeon – one of the high priests of the Temple, according to a medieval tradition – of whom it had been prophesied that he would not die until he had seen the Messiah. When Simeon recognises the Christ child, he takes him in his arms and offers a prayer of thanks to God. He then blesses the surprised parents and says to Mary, «Behold, this child is set for the fall and rising again of many in Israel; and for a sign which shall be spoken against; (Yea, a sword shall pierce through thy own soul also,) that the thoughts of many hearts may be revealed» (Lk 2:34–35). The old prophetess Anna, who served God tirelessly in the Temple, also offers up a prayer at the sight of the Saviour.

Rembrandt depicts the moment when, after his prayer of thanksgiving, Simeon addresses Mary, while Anna recognises the Christ child. Bent down on one knee and with the Christ child on his arm, Simeon gestures as if in speech towards Mary. She and Joseph kneel in adoration, Mary with her hands folded, Joseph with his hat in his hand. Anna throws her hands up in awe and astonishment. The child has a halo around his head and appears to radiate light – a telling illustration of his description in Simeon's prayer as «a light to lighten the Gentiles» (Lk 2:32).

X-rays reveal that Rembrandt only decided on this specific moment in the Bible story as the painting was being created.[3] In the first sketch, Simeon holds his head thrown back with his face upturned, evidently offering up his prayer to God. This is also the way in which this passage is traditionally illustrated, among others by Rembrandt himself in his 1631 painting *Simeon in the Temple* in the Mauritshuis (p. 279, fig. 52a)[4] and in the later etchings Bartsch 49 (c. 1639) and Bartsch 50 (c. 1654) of the same subject. Another etching of 1630 (cat. no. 52), however, again shows us this specific moment in the story.

In this work Rembrandt sets the scene not, as he did in *Simeon in the Temple* in The Hague, in a monumental temple, but in a space that looks more like the whitewashed interior of a Gothic church. On the right behind a massive pillar, on which hangs a candlestick with an extinguished candle as a symbolic counterpart to the «light to lighten the Gentiles», wooden panelling – possibly a door or a wooden staircase – can just be discerned in the shadows. The place in the «church» where the scene appears to be set is possibly iconographically relevant: it is the first side chapel on the right, the traditional location of the baptistry.

In this painting Rembrandt again moved forward a further step in his use of muted, ‹broken› colours that are closely related in terms of tone. The palette is confined to shades of brown, yellow and grey, with only the occasional accent in another colour. (Mary's blue robe is an eighteenth century overpainting; it was originally light grey.[5]) This tonal palette, which brings unity to the scene and to the suggestion of the space, is in sharp contrast to the clear pale yellow of the passages that are illuminated by the light entering from the top left. The result is a lively composition with unprecedented spatial values.

The suggestion of space is largely dictated by the splashes of light on the wall and the pillar in

the background. We cannot see the window through which the light falls, but the bars of the frame are evoked by the grey shadows they cast on the wall. In a sense everything that is in front of this illuminated rear wall acts as a repoussoir, resulting in a powerful effect of depth throughout the scene. It is interesting to see how Rembrandt as it were reverses his previous method of suggesting space: whereas in the earlier works it was the background areas that were executed in the most muted shades and with the vaguest outlines, now it is the passages in shadow in the foreground that are painted in this way. The increased spatial values around

the central action that are created by this sophisticated manipulation of the depth definition are still further enhanced by chiaroscuro effects. In the chiaroscuro it is not so much extreme contrasts of light and shade that create a perception of depth and plasticity as the nuances of the light and the gradations of tone around the edges of passages in skimming light and areas that are backlit. The way in which the light passes behind the figure of Joseph to fall on Simeon's left foot is a superb example of this.

In the lightest passages (the Christ child, Simeon's garments and, above all, the sunlit areas of the wall and the pillar in the background) we also find the thickest layers of paint; in the shadowy passages the paint is applied much more thinly and evenly. The faces of Simeon and Anna are modelled very plastically, as is Simeon's robe, on which impasto touches and strokes create an extraordinarily convincing rendition of the fabric. But just as in *An Old Usurer Examining a Coin* (cat. no. 29), it is primarily the background that is a tour de force of painting technique. By painting the wall and the sunlight falling on it with impasto and fairly coarsely, with subtle variations in brown, yellow and grey indicating damp patches and other irregularities, Rembrandt approaches very closely the optical effect of a plastered wall. This might be conceived as a hangover from the surface-imitating manner that had produced such astonishingly lifelike results in 1626. But in this painting Rembrandt was not primarily concerned with the expression of materials. The lighting effects in the background are used first and foremost to intensify the feeling of space and to heighten the sense of drama. In this respect, *Simeon in the Temple* and the slightly earlier *St Paul in Prison* in Stuttgart (fig. 30a) mark the start of a development in the 1628–1629 period in which the form of the background was to become less and less clearly defined, and the lighting of the background increasingly

30a
Rembrandt Harmensz. van Rijn, *St Paul in Prison*, 1627
Oak panel, 72.8 x 60.2 cm
Staatsgalerie, Stuttgart

served to build up the dramatic effect around the protagonists.

In its pose and detailing, the figure of Joseph in the foreground, which acts as a repoussoir, is very like the figure of the Saint in Rembrandt's etching *St Jerome Kneeling* (cat. no. 43), which is dated slightly later – c. 1629 – on stylistic grounds. There are only two known impressions of this sketch-like print, executed in rapid hatching, which is among Rembrandt's largest etchings. It may be deduced from this rarity that Rembrandt made the etching solely for his own use, as a study for trying out particular effects. It is striking in this context that the two figures are almost the same size. Both works will have been made in the same year, probably 1628. In that year, too, Rembrandt painted the dated *Peter and Paul Disputing* in Melbourne (p. 70, fig. 19), in which the figure on the left is placed in the picture plane as a repoussoir in the same way as the figure of Joseph in *Simeon in the Temple*. One important difference, however, is that this figure has much sharper outlines than the figure of Joseph and that the «reversed depth definition» is barely used.

The heads of Simeon and Anna are types that derive from models Rembrandt and Lievens used a great deal in their Leiden years. The Anna head, often referred to as that of Rembrandt's mother, appears in a great many drawings, etchings and paintings by Rembrandt, Lievens, Dou and other studio members,

among them the painted *Bust of an Old Woman* in Essen (cat. no. 65), which also dates from c. 1628. The Simeon head with the characteristic long beard is found in, among other works, the painted *St Paul in Prison* in Stuttgart (fig. 30a) and in the drawn studies after this model by Rembrandt and Lievens (cat. nos. 16–18; for more examples, see cat. no. 16).

The Hamburg *Simeon in the Temple* has been linked with the reference in an inventory of the Stadholders Quarters of 1632 to «a painting in which Simeon, in the Temple, has Christ in his arms, done by Rembrandt or Jan Lievens.»[6] This description, however, applies equally well to the *Simeon in the Temple* in The Hague (p. 279, fig. 52a) or to a painting on this subject by Lievens. It is interesting that the piece in question was already causing problems of attribution so shortly after its completion. This illustrates yet again just how much their contemporaries saw Rembrandt and Lievens as a «painting duo» who worked in a very similar style.

B.v.d.B.

[1] Corpus, vol. 1, 1982, p. 152.
[2] Ibid., nos. A 11 and A 13.
[3] Ibid., p. 153.
[4] Ibid., no. A 34.
[5] Ibid., p. 152.
[6] «Een schilderije daerinne Symeon, sijnde in den tempel, Christ in sijne armen heeft, door Rembrants oft Jan Lievensz. gedaen.» Corpus, vol. 1, 1982, p. 157; cf. Warnke 1986 and The Hague 1997, no. 22.

## 31
## Rembrandt Harmensz. van Rijn
# Old Man Asleep (Acedia?), 1629

Panel, 51.9 x 40.8 cm
Signed bottom right:
*RL[..]29*
Galleria Sabauda, Turin

Bredius/Gerson 1969,
no. 428; Corpus I, 1982,
no. A 17; Schwartz
1984/85/87, fig. 84;
Tümpel 1986, no. 119;
Slatkes 1992, no. 105

An old man sits asleep in a room largely shrouded in semi-darkness. He is slumped in an armchair. His head rests on his left hand and his right hand is thrust into his jerkin. He is dressed in a light brown jerkin with buttons and a dark brown coat, which is thrown over his shoulders and falls over his knees. Under his right wrist we can see a sort of case, possibly a writing set. A small fire burns in the left foreground. Its glow catches an earthenware pitcher standing by the fire, a set of fire tongs leaning against the wall and a few sticks of wood. Top centre hang several dimly lit herrings on a string, hung up over what is apparently a fireplace, since one of the brackets of a mantelpiece can be vaguely distinguished above the man's head. Only the man's face is brightly lit, by a hidden light source coming from the front left.

Although in the past this painting, which is dated 1629, was attributed to Lievens and the attribution to Rembrandt has been questioned by Gerson and others,[1] it is now generally ac-cepted as an authentic Rembrandt.[2] In what is at first sight a simple little genre scene, Rembrandt has reduced the palette to a minimum and defined the space less clearly than ever before. We see only a wooden floor, what is probably a mantelpiece and a wall whose orientation is not entirely clear. The foreground and background are painted thinly and evenly, and it is only in the figure of the man that rather thicker layers of paint are used, with little touches of light paint here and there for the highlights. Nevertheless, in this almost monochrome painting, immense space and plasticity are achieved by the almost infinite shades of brown with which the forms are modelled. To achieve such convincing plasticity and, even more amazingly, such a convincing rendition of surface textures with such a limited palette requires a virtuosity that Rembrandt demonstrates here in full measure.

In this display of his ability, Rembrandt can hold his own with sixteenth-century painters like Antonis Mor, who in 1549 painted the

clothes in the portrait of his patron Granvelle in an almost infinite number of shades of black.[3] In the sixteenth and seventeenth centuries, pieces like this, in which showing off painterly virtuosity was an end in itself, were very much sought after by royal and other wealthy collectors, who kept them in their art cabinets among other curious and valuable objects. From a document dated 1641, it appears that Rembrandt's painting probably did indeed once have such a setting. In that year the painting was listed in the will of the well-to-do artist and collector Jacques de Gheyn III in The Hague.

In his will, De Gheyn left part of his collection of art and rarities to his relative Johannes Uyttenbogaert, a tax collector in Amsterdam, including «Noch een out slapent manneken bij een vuyr sittende, sijn hant inden bosem hebbende, mede van Rembrand gemaeckt» (Further, an old man asleep seated by a fire, with his hand in his bosom, made by Rembrandt).[4] He also bequeathed to his relative – whom Rembrandt knew very well and who was himself portrayed by the master in 1639[5] – another painting by Rembrandt, which can be identified as the *Peter and Paul Disputing* in Melbourne (p. 70, fig. 19), and his collection of valuable shells and other naturalia.[6]

If we assume that *Old Man Asleep* was intended primarily as a piece of painterly bravura, the question of its iconographic significance appears less relevant. And yet here, too, there proves to be an interesting context which throws light on the milieu with which Rembrandt came into contact in his Leiden years. The painting had long been regarded as a simple genre piece (although it was referred to as *A Philosopher* in the eighteenth century),[7] until Bauch suggested that it could be the sleeping Tobias.[8] Tümpel originally agreed, but later rejected the interpretation.[9] The *Rembrandt Research Project* came up with a very plausible explanation – that it is an image of the cardinal sin of Acedia, or sloth.[10] Sloth is often represented in art as a sleeping man or woman, and the hand in the bosom can also be linked with this personification.

The probable first owner of the painting, Jacques de Gheyn III, was the son of the distinguished artist Jacques de Gheyn II. He was a good friend of the poet Constantijn Huygens (who also served as secretary to the stadholder) and his older brother Maurits. Rembrandt knew them all.[11] In 1632 he painted pendant portraits of Maurits Huygens and Jacques de Gheyn III,[12] and from about 1628 onwards he and Lievens maintained contacts with Constantijn Huygens, who famously wrote about their work in terms of the highest praise. As Ernst van de Wetering explains in one of the essays in this book, the Huygens brothers and Jacques de Gheyn III belonged to a scholarly and art-loving elite of connoisseurs and art collectors who, among other things, went on studio visits together (they visited the young Rembrandt and Lievens, for instance), commissioned works from artists and made their mark on the artistic life of their times in many other ways.

According to his autobiography written around 1630, Constantijn Huygens regarded Jacques de Gheyn III as one of the most promising artists of his generation. However he also makes no secret of his considerable disapproval of the fact that De Gheyn, who, thanks to his family's wealth, was able to live the life of the leisured classes, did nothing. This Huygens saw as an unforgivable waste of talent. It is therefore by no means inconceivable that Constantijn Huygens commissioned the Acedia painting from Rembrandt and gave it to Jacques de Gheyn III as a pointedly appropriate gift.[13] This is precisely the sort of half-moralising, half-jesting token that the members of this intellectual elite were accustomed to give one another. If this interpretation is correct, it is the first painting that Rembrandt ever made for someone in the stadholder's circle.

B.v.d.B.

[1] Bredius/Gerson 1969, no. 428.
[2] Corpus, vol. 1, 1982, pp. 202, 204.
[3] Kunsthistorisches Museum, Vienna, Inv. No. 1028.
[4] Corpus, vol. 1, 1982, p. 206.
[5] In an etching, also known as *The Gold-weigher* (Bartsch 281).
[6] Amsterdam 1999, p. 64.
[7] Corpus, vol. 1, 1982, p. 205.
[8] Bauch 1960, pp. 148–150.
[9] Tümpel 1971, p. 20; Tümpel 1986, no. 119.
[10] Corpus, vol. 1, 1982, p. 206.
[11] Schwartz 1984/85/87, pp. 72ff., 91ff.
[12] Corpus, vol. 2, 1986, nos. A 56 and A 57.
[13] See the first essay by Ernst van de Wetering, p. 31.

## 32
## Rembrandt Harmensz. van Rijn
# St Paul at his Desk, c. 1629/30

Oak panel, 47.2 x 38.6 cm
Germanisches National-
museum, Nuremberg

Bredius/Gerson 1969, no.
602; Corpus, vol. 1, 1982,
no. A 26; Schwartz
1984/85/87, fig. 91;
Schatborn 1986b, p. 60;
Tümpel 1986, no. 74;
Berlin/Amsterdam/
London 1991/92, no. 5;
Slatkes 1992, no. 73;
Wetering 1997, fig. 232

Only in Kassel

In a room with plastered walls and exposed wooden beams visible on the right, an old man with a grey beard sits on a chair at his writing desk. His attributes – the sword hanging top right, the book in front of him and the pen in his hand – identify him as the Apostle Paul. Sunk in thought, he stares at an indefinable point somewhere in the space in the left foreground. His right arm hangs over the back of his chair and he leans on the table with his left fist clenched. He wears a light brown tabard, from which dark brown sleeves protrude, and an oriental shawl around his waist. The room is lit by daylight entering from the top left and a strong concealed light source behind the open book propped up on the table. The shadow this creates shrouds the whole foreground in darkness.

The painting shows an astoundingly clever treatment of the light, an extremely expressive application of the paint and matchless psychological insight. The combination of daylight and candlelight produces an extraordinary di-

versity of light effects, and Rembrandt has exploited the possibilities of chiaroscuro to the utmost. By placing the light source behind the book, Rembrandt gives the book a powerful repoussoir effect against the illuminated rear wall. The almost totally dark foreground also results in an immense sense of depth. Yet again, however, it is not the extreme contrasts of light and dark that establish the atmosphere and the sense of space in this picture so much as the wonderfully subtle gradations of tone which suggest the curves of the forms and the reflections of the light.

The painting is executed almost entirely in shades of brown and yellow, with a few colour accents in the shawl to indicate the pattern on it. The paint is applied thickly everywhere – both in the lightest areas and in the dark foreground and the other shadow passages. The brushstrokes have generally been left visible, particularly in the light passages. The illuminated walls are painted in a tangled pattern of rough strokes and dabs, which produces an ex-

traordinarily lifelike representation of the rough plaster surface and the rays of light falling on it. The face and clothes are modelled with great plasticity using short impasto touches and strokes, with less relief in the paint in the shaded area. The very varied *peinture*, the many light reflections and the variation in the outlines are very important aspects in creating the vitality and spatial values of the work.

The Rembrandt Research Project regards the unsigned and undated painting as an authentic work dating from c. 1629/30, in part on the grounds of similarities in the treatment of the light, the modelling and the *peinture* to the *Supper in Emmaus* in Paris, which was originally also dated c. 1629/30.[1] The *RRP's* proposed chronology for the group of paintings created at the end of the 1620s has met with criticism.[2] A slightly earlier date, c. 1628/29, is now being maintained for *Supper in Emmaus*. The expressive poses and gestures of the figures and their placement in the space in *Supper in Emmaus* are closely akin to those in *Judas Repentant, Returning the Thirty Pieces of Silver* (cat. no. 33). This

32a
Rembrandt Harmensz.
van Rijn, *St Paul at his Desk*
(detail), c. 1629/30

well-documented painting, which was made in 1628/29 and is dated 1629, is the most important point of reference for the dating of all the work produced in the late 1620s.

The painting in Nuremberg differs quite significantly from the *Judas* in the chiaroscuro effects and the positioning of the human figure in the space. It does, however, share the daring and virtuoso character of the *Old Man Asleep* in Turin (cat. no. 31), which is dated 1629. Rembrandt was trying out new artistic means at an amazing rate during this period, and there is consequently no question of any steady, measured stylistic development. In the modelling and the natural pose of the figure of St Paul, which has much more body and presence than the figures in earlier paintings, *St Paul at His Desk* looks forward to Rembrandt's work of a few years later.

The painting in Nuremberg has been linked with a drawing and an etching, likewise depicting *St Paul at His Desk*, both of which have been dated c. 1629 on stylistic grounds (cat. nos. 85 and 86).[3] The drawing clearly served as a preliminary study for the etching but, as the RRP rightly notes, not for the painting: despite the compositional similarities, the pose and the head of the figure of the saint are essentially different here. The etching, which is exceptionally rare and was therefore probably made solely for Rembrandt's own use, appears to have had the same function as the *St Jerome* etching had for *Simeon in the Temple* (see cat. no. 30) – it enabled Rembrandt to try out the effect of part of the composition. The model used for the head in the Nuremberg painting does not appear to be the same as the old man with the long beard in earlier works (see cat. nos. 16–18).

The striking oriental sword (yataghan) hanging with its sheath on the wall beside St Paul, was a popular prop in Rembrandt's studio. We also find it in a number of early paintings attributed to Gerard Dou, including *A Leiden Militia Member with an Arms Still-life* of c. 1630/35 (cat. no. 68).                    B.v.d.B.

---

[1]  Corpus, vol. 1, 1982, pp. 269f.
[2]  Schatborn 1986b, p. 60.
[3]  Corpus, vol. 1, 1982, p. 270.

## 33

Rembrandt Harmensz. van Rijn

# Judas Repentant, Returning the Thirty Pieces of Silver, 1629

Oak panel, 79 x 102.3 cm
Signed lower right:
*RL.1629.*
Private Collection

Bredius/Gerson 1969,
no. 539A; Corpus, vol. 1,
1982, no. A 15; Schwartz
1984/85/87, fig. 65;
Amsterdam 1985, no. 5;
Corpus, vol. 2, 1986,
p. 837; Schatborn 1986b,
p. 60; Tümpel 1986,
no. 40; London 1988/89,
no. 1; Leiden 1991/92,
pp. 122f., fig. 75; Slatkes
1992, no. 40; Amsterdam
1996, no. 9; Wetering
1997, fig. 103; Boston
2000/01, pp. 32–35, 60f.

In the Gospel according to St Matthew (27:3–5) we read how Judas is seized with remorse for his betrayal of Jesus and returns the thirty pieces of silver he had received in payment to the chief priests and elders in the Temple in Jerusalem. After his lament («I have sinned in that I have betrayed the innocent blood!»), the chief priests and elders distance themselves from him («What is that to us? See thou to that!»), whereupon Judas casts down the pieces of silver in the Temple, departs and hangs himself.

In an indistinctly defined space, identified for us as the Temple by a massive column in the rear wall, we see the repentant Judas on his knees in the foreground on the right. His clothes ripped open, his pose tormented, he wrings his hands in agony, his face contorted in remorse and sorrow. Tears streak his cheeks, and he has blood on his head to show that he has torn his hair out. In front of him on the wooden floor lie exactly thirty silver coins. Behind them, on a dais under a canopy, sits the high priest Caiaphas, the most fervent advocate of Jesus's arrest and execution. His opulent attire is in stark contrast to Judas's shabby garments. Dressed in a gold-embroidered maroon velvet tabard, a gold brocade cloak, gold-embroidered shoes and a silk turban, he makes a dismissive gesture towards Judas with his left hand, as he turns his head away. Behind Caia-

phas stands a chief priest in a tall cap, who looks down at Judas with a furious glare and clenched fists. To the left of him stand three elders, who lean forward and observe the scene with similarly unconcealed abhorrence, while the man in the middle makes a gesture of rejection. In the left foreground, with his back to the viewer, a scribe sits in a Savonarola chair at a table covered with a costly tablecloth on which lie, among other things, a large open book with Hebrew writing in it and a scroll. The overhang of the canopy is just visible at the top centre. The rear wall of the canopy consists of a green cloth trimmed with gold, on which a large gilded decorative shield hangs. In the archway on the right we see a hanging brass lamp and two figures coming up a flight of stairs. Judas's discarded cloak lies on the floor on the right.

The composition, the atmosphere and the effect of space are governed by a dazzling diversity of light effects, combined in an extremely ingenious manner. A beam of light, concentrated like a spotlight, falls from above left on to the table, the book and the coins on the floor. The surroundings are also illuminated by it; the most brightly lit areas being Judas's torso, Caiaphas's glittering garb and the clothes of the elder on the far left. The light also reflects off the shield on the right. The whirling interplay of light and shade, of reflections and nuances of light, lends the work a peerless vitality, spatial intensity and drama. Rembrandt has used extreme chiaroscuro effects – for instance around the scribe seated at the table, whose dark form acts as a powerful repoussoir against the brightly-lit book on the table – but it is the subtle passages against the light, like the cloth hanging over the table and Caiaphas's hand, that create this astonishing realism and plasticity.

The thickness and surface texture of the paint vary considerably.[1] The paint is mostly thinly applied in the shadow passages on the right-hand side, with impasto here and there for the

Fig. 33a
Rembrandt Harmensz.
van Rijn, *Study for «Judas
Repentant»*, c. 1628/29
Pen and wash,
115 x 145 mm
Private Collection

elements with the greatest plasticity, among them the cloth and the shield behind Caiaphas. On the left side the paint has a loose, irregular surface, which appears to be related in part to the changes that Rembrandt made to the composition in the course of the painting process. Because they have been painted over earlier passages – which can often be discerned in relief in the surface of the paint – some parts of the work were executed in a very thick layer of paint. The standing figure with the tall cap behind Caiaphas is one such area.

The most brightly lit passages are also painted with the greatest precision and detail. The most striking areas of flesh, like Judas's head, are modelled with fine impasto touches. The fabric passages, particularly in Caiaphas's clothes, are minutely detailed with fine stipples and tiny brushstrokes. The sophisticated placement of the highlights and the subtle colour nuances in the folds create an extraordinarily convincing representation of the material. The tablecloth on the left is painted with impasto dabs and streaks of paint, convincingly imitating the texture of the richly embroidered fabric and the way it catches the light. The colours used in this painting are more varied and less tonal than those in the works dating from 1627–28. The brown and grey tones are relieved by both cool and warm half shades, which are blended with the utmost harmony.

The authenticity of the monogrammed and dated painting has never been disputed since it was published in 1939 (prior to this it was known only from copies).[2] The many changes that the work underwent while it was in progress are an irrefutable argument in its favour. The history of its creation is a complex one, which can be largely reconstructed from X-ray photographs, observations of the surface of the paint and several surviving preliminary studies for earlier compositions (or parts of compositions).[3]

The X-rays reveal that in the first version of the painting there must have been a large curtain hanging on the left. At the upper centre there was originally a curved arch with vaulting – which can still be seen traced in the surface of the paint – that seems to have formed a sort of apse. In this, slightly to the left of centre, it is just possible to make out on the X-ray photographs the outlines of a high priest, seated high up on a throne, not dissimilar to the situation in the background of Rembrandt's etching *The Presentation in the Temple* of 1630 (cat. no. 52). This figure was originally the most brightly lit. The most important figures in the composition at this stage were the kneeling Judas and the high priest looking down on him from his throne.

This traditional composition, so reminiscent of Lastman, evidently did not please Rembrandt, since he painted out the arch and the high priest. He then proceeded to try out various compositions for the left side. His efforts can be traced on the preliminary studies that have survived. On one of them, a pen drawing with wash in Amsterdam (cat. no. 34), the curtain can still be seen at the upper left. It also shows, among other things, two scribes with tall caps by a table on which lies a book.[4] On a pen drawing in a private collection, which shows a subsequent stage, these scribes have been moved into the background and there is a man standing in the centre of the scene, viewed from behind, leaning over the back of a chair (fig. 33a).[5] The X-rays reveal that Rembrandt actually did put this figure with the chair in this place in the painting. In this version the beam of light was focused more on the seated figure of Caiaphas and a purse lay on the floor near Judas.

Eventually, Rembrandt painted all these passages out again; he focused the beam of light on the table to the left and on the coins on the floor, and he made the watching elders lean forward, so that attention is concentrated more strongly on the figure of Judas and the return of the blood money. As the painting progressed, so Rembrandt seems increasingly to have made Judas's personal drama the actual subject of the work. The successive phases in the genesis of the painting show Rembrandt searching for ever more effective means of putting this tragedy across.

The painting, probably the most ambitious history piece that Rembrandt painted during his Leiden years, was admired by his contemporaries primarily because of the powerful emotions he had succeeded in expressing in the tortured figure of Judas. This emerges clearly from the fulsome words of praise Constantijn Huygens devotes to this work in his autobiography, which was written in about 1630.[6] Huygens must have seen the painting at the end of 1628 or early in 1629 when it was still unfinished in Rembrandt's studio. Entirely in the spirit of the art theoreticians of his day, who attached great importance to the portrayal of human emotions, Huygens heaps praise upon the painting because of the pain and despair of the Judas figure. He uses Judas to argue that, with this work, Rembrandt has already surpassed his illustrious predecessors, including those of an-

tiquity – about the highest possible praise that this humanist could give. Thanks to Huygens's exalted description of the painting, *Judas* is one of Rembrandt's best-documented works.

This painting rapidly made a great impression on Rembrandt's contemporaries, as is evident from the many copies painted after it in the seventeenth century.[7] It also soon came to serve as a source of inspiration in their own work for artists in Rembrandt's circle, as *The Tribute Money* (cat. no. 34/I) in Ottawa, painted not long after the *Judas*, demonstrates. Some years later Jan van Vliet published the bust of the figure of Judas, with variations, as a print (fig. 33b).[8]

In the facial expression and the hand gesture, the figure of Judas is a descendant of the heartrending figures of Tobias and Isaac that Rembrandt and Lievens painted in 1626 (cat. nos. 25 and 28). B.v.d.B.

[1] Corpus, vol. 1, 1982, pp. 177–181.
[2] Corpus, vol. 1, 1982, p. 185.
[3] Corpus, vol. 1, 1982, pp. 181–191; Amsterdam 1985, p. 12; London 1988/89, no. 1; Wetering 1997, pp. 75 ff.
[4] Benesch 9 recto. Another preliminary study (Benesch 6 verso), a chalk drawing in Museum Boymans-van Beuningen, Rotterdam, has both scribes sitting on chairs. Cf. Corpus, vol. 1, 1982, pp. 186f.; Amsterdam 1985, pp. 12–15.
[5] Benesch 8. Cf. Corpus, vol. 1, 1982, p. 185; Amsterdam 1985, pp. 12–15.
[6] MS in Latin, entitled Vita, Koninklijke Bibliotheek, The Hague. See the translation of the integral text about Rembrandt and Lievens in the Appendix and the essays by Ernst van de Wetering. Translations of the Judas description in: Corpus, vol. 1, 1982, pp. 193f.; Schwartz 1984/85/87, p. 74; Huygens/ Heesakkers 1987, p. 86. The labelling of Huygens's description of the Judas painting as inaccurate has gradually become commonplace (cf. M. Westermann in Boston 2000/01, p. 34: «Huygens' ... misstatements»). Going by the most recent translation by C. L. Heesakkers 1987, however, I can discover no inaccuracies in the description. The less than faultless translation by P. Tuynman in Corpus, vol. 1, 1982 appears to be the cause of the confusion.
[7] Corpus, vol. 1, 1982, pp. 193–195.
[8] Bartsch 22. See Amsterdam 1996, no. 9.

Rembrandt Harmensz. van Rijn

# Three Scribes (Study for Judas Repentant) (verso: Study of a Woman's Legs), c. 1628/29

Pen and brush in brown, parts covered with white paint (verso: Red and white chalk), 226 x 176 mm
Benesch 9 recto
Rijksmuseum, Amsterdam,
Inv. No. RP-T-1930-54(v)

Corpus, vol. 1, 1982, no. A 15, fig. 8; Amsterdam 1985, no. 5 (verso); London 1988/89, no. 1, fig. 27; Leiden 1991/92, pp. 72f., 122f., fig. 73; Wetering 1997, fig. 25, pp. 25ff., 75ff.

There are very few surviving drawings by Rembrandt that can be identified as direct preliminary studies or composition sketches for paintings.[1] This scarcity is explained by Rembrandt's working method: he usually sketched out the initial layout for a composition on the painting itself, in the first phase of the painting process. This approach, which sixteenth and seventeenth-century art theoreticians regarded as the most virtuoso and the most courageous, required the artist to have a clear picture of the composition in his mind before he picked up his brush, to avoid having constantly to overpaint parts of the work during the creative process. Van de Wetering interpreted the self-portrait *The Painter in His Studio* in Boston of 1628 (cat. no. 61), in which we see the artist gazing musingly at his easel from a distance, as an illustration of this phase of ‹imagination› that precedes the actual application of the paint.[2]

Closer study has revealed that most of the drawings previously thought to be authentic preliminary studies for paintings by Rembrandt are in fact copies after paintings that were made by his pupils and followers. Authentic drawings by Rembrandt in which the composition of one of his paintings is set out usually prove to be either a sort of *vidimus* for the client, to which he could give his approval, or a rapid copy of the painting, possibly connected with positioning the work in a frame. The few drawings that can be regarded as true preliminary studies for a painting were not made prior to starting painting, but during the process of painting, when Rembrandt wanted to make radical changes to the composition, or parts of it, and tried out the effect on paper first. The present drawing is one of the finest examples of this. There are also some etchings (cat. nos. 43 and 86) – extremely few in number and consequently probably made solely for Rembrandt's own use – which must have been made for this specific purpose (cf. cat. nos. 30 and 32).

Rembrandt executed the drawing when he decided to make drastic changes to the composition of the principal work from his Leiden years, *Judas Repentant, Returning the Thirty Pieces of Silver*, which was painted in 1628–29 (cat. no. 33). After he painted out a high priest on a throne in the upper centre area of the painting, he had to alter the whole composition, particularly on the left-hand side. As the Amsterdam drawing shows, the large curtain at

the upper left, part of the original composition of the painting, had not yet been painted out. Rembrandt now wanted to enclose the left side of the scene with a group of two scribes by a table bearing an open book – the foremost man seated, the one behind standing and leaning forward over the book. To the right of these two scribes we can just make out the outlines of a standing man wearing a tall cap. This is the chief priest in the tall cap, whom Rembrandt was to shift to the right and position behind the seated Caiaphas in the final version of the painting. We can see that he decided to move this figure immediately after making the drawing from the fact that he blotted out this figure in the drawing with white paint. Wear to the surface of the drawing has revealed this figure again.[3]

The two scribes in the drawing do not appear in the painting in its final form. In their place we find a single scribe, slightly further to the right, who is shown from behind, sitting on a chair. The table and book were retained, however, and even became one of the main pictorial elements in the scene because of the bright shaft of light that falls on them.

The drawing was set down first using a pen and light brown ink and then broadly washed with a brush and the same ink. Rembrandt used this light brown ink, with grains of pigment visible here and there in the washes, primarily in his Leiden period. He used the same ink, for ex-ample, in his earliest landscape drawing, *Outskirts of a Town with Walls and a Gateway*, now in Cambridge (cat. no. 36). Another common feature of this drawing and the Amsterdam preliminary study is the coarse way in which the washes are applied, with rough, visible brushstrokes. The transparency of the washes allows the paper to show through in many places, and this contributes to the nuances of tone in these passages. There are unmistakable similarities between the loose manner of sketching and washing used in these drawings and the rough manner with which Rembrandt was experimenting in his paintings during this period.

A study of the legs of a seated woman (fig. 34a) has been drawn with red chalk on the back of the Amsterdam drawing.[4] This drawing has been linked as a preliminary study with the seated figure of Delilah in Rembrandt's *Samson and Delilah* in Berlin, which dates from 1629 (p. 204, fig. 27a).[5] Both sides of this sheet are thus a fascinating document of Rembrandt's working method in a year that was of such immense importance to his artistic development.

B.v.d.B.

[1]  Wetering 1997, pp. 25–27, 75–81.
[2]  Wetering 1997, pp. 87–89.
[3]  Amsterdam 1985, pp. 12f.
[4]  Ibid.
[5]  Corpus, vol. 1, 1982, no. A 24.

Circle of Rembrandt Harmensz. van Rijn
# The Tribute Money, c. 1631

Oak panel, 41.8 x 32.8 cm
Signed: *RHL 1629*
The National Gallery of
Canada, Ottawa

Corpus, vol. 1, 1982,
no. C 7; Ottawa 1987,
vol. 1, pp.241–244; Boston
2000/01, no. 11, pp.
106–108

Only in Amsterdam

Christ stands in a high, temple-like space with his back to a pillar. With his hand lifted high he addresses a group of four men in oriental dress, one of whom holds a coin between thumb and forefinger. Behind Christ, in the shadowed bottom right corner, four of his disciples are watching the scene and seem to be commenting on it amongst themselves. A sketchily-executed figure in a cap leans over the bannister of a staircase behind, while in the window above a darker arched opening stands a bearded man. In the background, two silhouetted figures are approaching from a lower level.

The subject of the painting is an episode from the New Testament (Mt 22:16–21, Mk 12:13–17 and Lk 20:20–26) in which Pharisees and Herodians seek out Christ in the Temple where he is teaching. They try to trap him by tempting him into speaking out on the question of whether a Jew is obliged to pay tribute to a heathen emperor. A positive answer would offend the Jews, but a negative answer would bring the Roman authorities down on him. Christ, who at once sees through this malevolent ploy, demands that they show him a penny and asks whose image it bears. On receiving the Pharisees' answer that it is Caesar's image, Christ silences them by saying: «Give unto Caesar the things that are Caesar's and to God the things that are God's.»

The monogram «RHL» is set in large yellow-brown letters together with the year «1629» in a cartouche above the arch, at the right of the painting (fig. 34/Ia). Compared with Rem-

Fig. 34/Ia
Detail of cat. no. 34a

Fig. 34/Ib
Rembrandt, *Oriental
Leaning on a Stick*, c. 1629
Pen in brown,
150 x 184 mm
Staatliche Museen zu
Berlin, Preußischer
Kulturbesitz,
Kupferstichkabinett

brandt's monograms, the prominent placing of the monogram and the large letters are highly unusual.

A dendrochronological investigation of the panel has shown that it is highly unlikely to have been painted in 1629, and that the painting's origin would be much more plausibly dated to after 1631, or even 1633.[1] Another strong indication that the painting could only have originated in or after 1632 is the fact that a number of elements seem to have been taken from other paintings by Rembrandt, such as the dark space with the pillar from the *Judas Repentant* of 1629 (cat. no. 33) and especially the *Presentation in the Temple* of 1631, now in The Hague[2] (p. 279, fig. 52a). Not only is the treatment of the floor very similar, but the capital has an almost identical form. The motif of the semi-shadowed man sitting in the foreground seems to have been borrowed from *Simeon in the Temple* in the Hague. The author of the painting could have made use of a drawing from Rembrandt's own hand portraying an *Oriental Leaning on a Stick,*[3] who (in mirror image) is closely related to the Oriental with the stick standing opposite Christ in the painting (fig. 34/Ib).

Cautious but not notably successful attempts have been made to connect the painting with works of Willem de Poorter (1608 – after 1648) or Paulus Lesire (1611 – after 1656).[4] Because this is a composite of elements drawn from earlier works by Rembrandt and in various respects shows characteristics of his working procedure, its author has to be sought in Rembrandt's immediate circle at the end of his Leiden period.                    M.d.W.

[1]  The dendrochronological research was conducted in 1981 by Dr. Peter Klein. See Corpus, vol. 1, 1982, p. 490 and Boston 2000/01, p. 107.
[2]  Corpus, vol. 1, 1982, Nr. A 34.
[3]  Benesch 10.
[4]  In the *Corpus* a connection was tentatively made with the work of Willem de Poorter. Volker Manuth, in a letter to the museum, suggested a connection with Paulus Lesire, and specifically with his *Widow's Mite* of 1632 in the Cevat collection (Sumowski 1983ff., vol. 3, no. 1137). See Boston 2000/01, p. 108.

## 35
## Rembrandt Harmensz. van Rijn
# Seated Scholar, c. 1630

Black chalk,
206 x 152 mm
Benesch 46
Musée du Louvre,
Département des Arts
Graphiques, Paris

Lugt 1929, no. 247; Bauch
1933, pp. 11f.; Sumowski
1980, vol. 3, p. 1160;
Paris 1988/89, no. 77

Only in Amsterdam

An old scholar sits slumped on the very edge of a large armchair placed beside a table laden with books and a globe. In a contemplative mood, the old man rests his head in his left hand while his right arm, on the armrest, supports his weight. His right leg is stretched out diagonally to the front. Whereas he is drawn with strong lines, the surrounding room is only lightly sketched. With just a few lines Rembrandt draws the contours of the man and uses thick hatching to create a dark tone. The depiction of the contemplative old man – be he a saint, an Apostle (e.g. cat. no. 32) or a secular scholar – appears frequently in the artist's œuvre. Equally, a number of paintings by members of the Rembrandt school betray knowledge of the drawing's composition and confirm the popularity of the subject.[1] The stooped posture of the man and his tired expression recall the toil of study, but also that of old age in general. The depiction of learning is simultaneously a metaphor for reflection on the passage of time.[2] His extended leg may also be a reference to Gabriel Rollhagen's emblem «Tamen discom» («Nevertheless I will learn»), in which the text reads: «And even when one foot is in the grave and (only) the other on this side of life, I will nevertheless remain busy in the study of the sciences.»[3] Rembrandt's seemingly fleeting sketch thus reveals a well thought-out composition which shows his intense preoccupation with the subject.

The attribution of this relatively large sheet has been the subject of much discussion. However it can now be regarded as being by Rembrandt, not least on account of the intellectual penetration of the subject. Frits Lugt published the drawing as the work of Gerard Dou from his time in Rembrandt's studio, with references to nineteenth-century attributions of sheets with similar subjects. But since no unquestioned drawings from Dou's early work are known,

Lugt's proposal fails to convince. The few drawings from the artist's later period are considerably different in style. As with his paintings of the period, they show a similar interest in the fine rendition of details. No sheet done in a sketchy style has been firmly identified.[4] Bauch, on the other hand, attributed the old man to Rembrandt on the basis of its relationship with other drawings in red chalk. Benesch followed this attribution and supported it by referring to comparable drawings.[5] Haverkamp-Begemann, however, questions Rembrandt's authorship and considers the attribution to Dou possible.[6] In the exhibition catalogue of the 1988/89 Paris exhibition, Starcky lists the drawing as being by an anonymous pupil and dates it to around 1630. Royalton-Kisch again proposed Rembrandt as the author and referred to the opinion of Schatborn.[7] A comparison with Rembrandt's 1633 drawing of *Lot Drunk* (cat. no. 38) can clarify both the attribution and the date. For both, Rembrandt worked using clear lines for the contours, such as the legs and arms. The details of the drawing in Paris are less finely executed, however, as the comparison between the body and the face shows. A dating of around 1630 thus seems appropriate.                                        J.L.

---

[1] Hofstede de Groot 1922, p. 47; Sumowski 1983ff., vol. 4, no. 1912 and 1960.

[2] Cf. the etching Chilon by Jacques de Gheyn III, 304 x 191 mm, inscribed: *HDG I.F. 1616*, showing a comparably slumped figure. See Braunschweig 1993/94, pp. 159–161.

[3] Gabriel Rollenhagen, *Nucleus emblematum selectissimorum, quae itali vulgo impresas*, Arnheim 1611, no. 75. See Henkel/Schöne 1967, col. 982.

[4] Sumowski 1980, vol. 3, pp. 1145–1183. There he supports the attribution of the exhibited sheet to Rembrandt.

[5] Benesch 1954, nos. 43–45.

[6] Haverkamp-Begemann 1961, p. 21.

[7] Based on the comparable treatment of the contours in an *Erection of the Cross* (Benesch 6), Schatborn dates the drawing to around 1629. Royalton-Kisch 1990, 133.

239

## 36
## Rembrandt Harmensz. van Rijn
# Outskirts of a Town with Walls and a Gateway, c. 1628/29

Pen and brown ink with
light and dark grey-brown
washes, 143 x 152 mm
Benesch 57a
Fitzwilliam Museum,
Cambridge

Schneider 1990 (with
extensive bibliography)

*Outskirts of a Town* is Rembrandt's earliest landscape and the only one we know of from his Leiden period. The precise location has never been identified and the question as to whether the drawing actually is of the outskirts of a town, as the traditional title suggests, remains open. It is, however, virtually certain that Rembrandt drew a real place. All the same, it would not appear that Rembrandt's prime concern was to provide a topographically accurate picture. His aim was to use washes to create a convincing image of the interplay of light and shade. He succeeded in masterly fashion.

The drawing is done in brown ink. The lines are jagged and seem rather awkward. The drawing of the dog in the foreground on the right is actually downright clumsy. The washes are applied in two gradations – deep grey-brown for the foreground and a lighter tone for the background – and give the drawing structure in the sense that they define the different spatial elements from which the drawing is constructed. The handling of the light is superb. The strong contrasts and the sparkling reflections in the darkest shadow passages lend the drawing an almost southern feel and call to mind the drawings of the Dutch italianate artists.

Technically and stylistically, *Outskirts of a Town* is closely related to *Three Scribes* (cat. no. 34) and *Woman Standing with a Candle* (cat. no. 37), which display a similar use of the pen and washes. In view of the similarity to *Three Scribes*, which is a preliminary study for *Judas Repentant, Returning the Thirty Pieces of Silver* of 1629 (cat. no. 33), *Outskirts of a Town* must have been drawn in that same year or shortly before.

E.d.H.

## 37

Rembrandt Harmensz. van Rijn

# Woman Standing with a Candle, c. 1630

Pen and brush in brown,
brown and grey wash,
heightened with white,
181 x 132 mm
Benesch 263a
British Museum, London

Berlin/Amsterdam/
London 1991/92, no. 6;
Edinburgh 2001, no. 8

Only in Amsterdam

For many years it was assumed that this remarkably fine and detailed drawing of a young woman with a candlestick must have been made around 1635 or even later. On stylistic grounds, however, Royalton Kisch came up with a date of c. 1631.[1] The angular, slightly uncontrolled use of the pen and the wash do indeed make this drawing very similar to several drawings dating from the latter years of Rembrandt's Leiden period, such as *Three Scribes* (cat. no. 34) and *Outskirts of a Town* (cat. no. 36). The similarities between these works also support the attribution of *Woman Standing with a Candle* to Rembrandt, even though in terms of character and conception this drawing is not entirely typical of his work.

The woman is shown almost full length. She leans on her left elbow on the edge of something that might be a well. Her gaze is directed to the left, searching the distance, as if someone might appear from that direction at any minute. She holds a candlestick in her left hand. The surroundings are shrouded in the darkness of the night. It is not inconceivable that the scene relates to a Bible story or some other written source. However, there is no iconographic relationship with any of Rembrandt's paintings or etchings.[2]

The use of an artificial light source in a scene places exceptional demands on an artist. Rembrandt tackled this problem not only in his paintings and etchings but also, as in this case, in his drawings. In *Woman Standing with a Candle* the forms are given volume by the effect of the light from the candle, which slants up from below. Rembrandt achieves this effect by using brown and grey washes of different intensities, applied very subtly but with rapid brushstrokes over the pen and brown ink drawing of the scene. The areas of the paper left unworked play a crucial role, since they are the lightest passages in the work. The strong contrast between these light passages and the dark background makes it appear that the woman is coming forward out of the semi-darkness, and this gives the figure extraordinarily powerful plasticity. This effect of space is reinforced by the many grey and brown nuances in the dark background, which create an absolutely convincing sense of depth in the darkness.

It is probably this outstandingly successful positioning of the figure in a convincing space that lends the drawing its appearance of being a more or less independent work of art. This has led various scholars not to regard the drawing as a study, although it certainly should be seen as such. As far as the experimentation with light effects is concerned, the drawing echoes Rembrandt's paintings and etchings of the same period, in which this quest for ever more convincing *chiaroscuro* can also be seen.

E.d.H.

[1] Berlin/Amsterdam/London 1991/92, p. 35.
[2] Ibid.

## 38
## Rembrandt Harmensz. van Rijn
# Lot Drunk, 1633

Black chalk, heightened with white, 251 x 189 mm
Signed (in black chalk):
*Rembrandt f 1633*
Benesch 82
Städelsches Kunstinstitut, Graphische Sammlung
Frankfurt am Main, Inv. No. 857

Frankfurt 1991, no. 22; Amsterdam 1996, pp. 40ff.; Frankfurt 2000, no. 55

Only in Amsterdam

In his Leiden years Rembrandt's drawings were, almost without exception, figure studies. We know of virtually no drawings of landscapes or biblical stories, of which he was to make so many in later life, that date from this period. The studies he made are usually only indirectly related to his painted works. They were exercises in drawing the human figure in various poses and emotional states, and in different light. This constant practice served to make him so proficient in drawing the human figure that he could ultimately put down any figure on paper, panel or copper plate from memory.[1]

In addition to this large group of figure drawings there are several surviving drawings that served specifically as preliminary studies for a painting. *Lot Drunk* is a fine example. This beautifully handled sheet was a study for the main protagonist in a lost painting, which we know from a print by Jan van Vliet (cat. no. 39). Van Vliet's etching, which is dated 1631, reproduces a work that was painted shortly before, possibly in 1629–30.[2]

It seems that, above all, Rembrandt wanted to portray the effects of alcohol on the human body. Lot, whose daughters have got him drunk, sits half-slumped. He holds an empty drinking vessel in his right hand. He is fuddled by the drink and stares blankly ahead.

Comparison with the engraving reveals that the clothes and the pose of the body – particularly the legs – correspond very closely, but that Rembrandt made drastic changes to the character of the figure of Lot. In the print, we see a depiction not of the lack of resistance caused by alcohol, but of the irrational exuberance that can accompany heavy drinking. Lot's open, shouting mouth and his outstretched hand holding the empty wine vessel give him a dynamism that is lacking in the drawing.

The drawing is a splendid illustration of the heights that Rembrandt's drawing skills had attained by the end of the 1630s. The clothes are set down with heavy chalk lines. The outlines, particularly those on the side in shadow, are accented here and there with deeper black. The lively use of line contrasts with the extremely sensitive and refined way in which the face is drawn. The consummate use of black chalk in varying gradations of tone convincingly suggests the forms and the effect of the light slanting down from behind.

The great sophistication with which the figure of Lot is worked out lends the drawing the character of a work of art in its own right. The signature and date, which were added several years after the study was drawn, reinforce this impression. *Lot Drunk* is one of the few drawings by Rembrandt to be signed with his full name.[3]

E.d.H.

---

[1] See Schatborn 1989, passim, and his contributions in Leiden 1991/92, pp. 60–79, esp. p. 72.
[2] Corpus, vol. 1, 1982, pp. 36f.
[3] Frankfurt 2000, p. 136.

## 39
### Jan van Vliet (Leiden 1600/10–1668) after Rembrandt Harmensz. van Rijn
## Lot and his Daughters, 1631

Etching, 275 x 223 mm
Hollstein 1, state II (5)
Museum het Rem-
brandthuis, Amsterdam,
Inv. No. 277

Amsterdam 1996, no. 1

Between 1631 and 1634 the Leiden engraver Jan Gillisz. van Vliet made prints of twelve paintings by Rembrandt. *Lot and his Daughters*, an etching dated 1631, reproduces a lost painting which, according to the *Rembrandt Research Project*, must have been painted in 1629 or 1630.[1]

The story of Lot and his daughters is told in Genesis 19:1–38: Lot, who was Abraham's nephew, lived in Sodom, a city whose inhabitants were sinful. God decided to destroy Sodom and neighbouring Gomorra because of the licentious behaviour of the citizens. As a result of Abraham's intercession, Lot and his family were spared. Three angels warned him of God's intentions and told him to escape with his wife and two daughters. However, they were forbidden to look back as they fled. Lot's wife ignored this prohibition, looked back and was turned into a pillar of salt. After the destruction of Sodom, Lot and his daughters sought shelter in a cave. Cut off from the world, the daughters feared that there would be no one to provide heirs, and so they plotted to get their father drunk and seduce him. They

each bore a son – Moab and Ben-Ammi, the ancestors of the Moabites and the Ammonites. The seduction of Lot had long been a popular subject in art. Many of the elements in Rembrandt's version come from the iconographic tradition: the burning city in the background, the fire raining down from the sky, the petrified form of Lot's wife and the meagre possessions they are taking with them on their flight. However, Rembrandt's work departs from tradition by depicting not the seduction itself but the moment before it. The manifest eroticism that usually characterises treatments of this subject is consequently less explicit here.

Jan van Vliet, a contemporary of Rembrandt's, lived in Leiden all his life. We do not know where or by whom he was educated. His career as an etcher was relatively brief. His earliest prints, illustrations for Cats' *Self-stryt* after designs by Adriaen Pietersz. van de Venne, date from 1629. After 1637, the year in which his monumental *Triumph of Frederick Henry* appeared, his output ceased. Only a copy after Rembrandt's *Beggar Family on the Tramp*[2] is of a later date. The abrupt end to his career proba-

Fig. 39a
Unknown artist after
Rembrandt Harmensz.
van Rijn, *Lot and
his Daughters*
Red and black chalk,
heightened with white,
292 x 231 mm
British Museum,
London

bly had to do with his marriage to Susanna van Campen in 1636, which brought him great prosperity. Evidently van Vliet no longer had to make a living from his graphic art. The fact that he was no longer working as an etcher is confirmed by a number of notarial deeds in which he is described as a wine merchant. His oeuvre, which consists of around a hundred prints, was consequently created in the space of only nine years. Van Vliet also painted. The only surviving painting by him, a kitchen scene now in the collection of the Hermitage in St Petersburg, bears absolutely no resemblance to Rembrandt's work. Van Vliet died a wealthy man in 1668, a year before Rembrandt.[3]

A red chalk drawing in the British Museum's collection shows the scene in reverse (fig. 39a). For a long time this drawing was erroneously thought to be by van Vliet. However, it cannot have served as the preliminary study for the etching, for it shows none of the usual traces left by the process of transferring a design to the etching plate: the lines have not been indented and there is no layer of black chalk on the back. The differences between them would also appear to confirm that there is no direct re-lationship between the two works. In the drawing, for example, there is a walking stick next to the figure of Lot that is absent from the etching. On the other hand, the loose shoelace on Lot's right foot only appears on the etching. It is now assumed that the drawing documents an earlier stage in the creation of the painting. There is a preliminary study for the figure of Lot in the Städelsches Kunstinstitut in Frankfurt (cat. no. 38).

Van Vliet produced an attractive etching, but it is not entirely successful in every respect. The shape and texture of the rock face remain unclear and it is not obvious where the rock ends and the sky begins. The reason probably lies in the strong contrasts between light and shade that were undoubtedly present in the painting. Large areas, like the rock face, were probably shrouded in deep shadow. Rendering passages like this, where the forms are suggested rather than defined, in an etching presented van Vliet with an almost impossible task.          E.d.H.

[1] Corpus, vol. 1, 1982, pp. 36f.
[2] Hollstein 96.
[3] Amsterdam 1996, pp. 6f.. See also: Prins/Smit 1997, pp. 213ff.

## 40
### Rembrandt Harmensz. van Rijn
# The Circumcision, c. 1626

Etching, 214 x 160 mm
Inscribed: *Rembrant fecit I.
P. Berendrech. ex.*
Seidlitz 398, state II (2)
Museum het
Rembrandthuis,
Amsterdam, Inv. No. 236

White/Boon 1969, p. 165;
Amsterdam 1988/89,
no. 5; Berlin/Amster-
dam/London 1991/92,
p. 161; Leiden 1991/92,
p. 61f.

A remarkable development in the graphic arts took place in the first quarter of the seventeenth century: engraving was gradually superseded by etching. At the same time, painters increasingly turned to the technique of etching, which was considerably easier to learn than engraving. They saw the etching as the ideal medium for disseminating their ideas and compositions. Rembrandt and Lievens must have been aware of this trend. Their first graphic experiments date from 1625 and, despite some characteristic differences, reveal a striking mutual dependency. This interaction can be seen until 1628.

The crude and clumsy technique used in Rembrandt's earliest etching, *The Circumcision*, led to longstanding doubts about its authenticity. Gersaint did include the etching in his catalogue of Rembrandt's graphic work published in 1751, but later scholars did not regard the work as autographic. In modern art-historical literature, however, the print is generally accepted as Rembrandt's work.

The subject is drawn from the New Testament. According to Luke's Gospel (2:21) Christ was circumcised when he was eight days old. The Bible says nothing about the place where the circumcision was performed, but in Western art the event is usually set in a temple. In another pictorial tradition, based on apocryphal writings, it takes place in a stable, because under Jewish law, a woman was considered unclean for forty days after giving birth and could consequently not enter a temple. We find both of these traditions represented in Rembrandt's oeuvre.

According to the inscription, *The Circumcision*, like Lievens's earliest etching (cat. no. 14), was published by Jan Pietersz. Beerendrecht, a bookseller in Haarlem. As a publisher of prints, Beerendrecht had a specialist list consisting primarily of small-format prints made by *peintre-graveurs*.[1] These were painters, like Rembrandt and Lievens, who had not originally trained as engravers. The collaboration between Rembrandt and Beerendrecht remained limited to this one etching. Rembrandt himself published almost all the other etchings that he produced during his long career. The care that he devoted to selecting the paper, the inking of the plate and the frequent reworking of his etching plates probably ruled out the possibility of contracting the print out to someone else as he had done in the case of *The Circumcision*.

With the numerous figures, *The Circumcision* is an ambitious work. It calls to mind Constantijn Huygens' comment that Rembrandt preferred to work on scenes with several figures. The main group with the high priest who performs the circumcision is contained in a triangular composition. Two figures on a raised platform observe the scene. A similar arrangement of figures is found on the right-hand side of *The Stoning of St Stephen*, Rembrandt's earliest dated painting.[2] The composition makes a rather disorganised and confused impression. The work lacks restfulness and – unlike Lievens's first etching – looks as though it was made by a beginner. Nevertheless the print contains a number of elements that would later characterise Rembrandt's manner, such as the attention paid to the effects of light and shade and the incredibly free and spontaneous style of drawing.

Although his technique was strongly influenced by Lievens, Rembrandt's hatching is freer and sketchier, while the outlines are looser and more open. This free and open etching style may have been inspired by the work of Willem Buytewech and Moses van Uyttenbroeck. This sketch-like manner may also be derived from the work of the Italian artist Antonio Tempesta, whose influence can be seen most clearly in Rembrandt's lion hunts of 1629 (cf. cat. no. 51) and of 1641.[3]

E.d.H.

[1] *Nederland naar't leven*, Museum het Rembrandthuis, Amsterdam, 1993, p. 36.
[2] Amsterdam, 1988/89, p. 27.
[3] Bartsch 114–116·

Rembrant fecit                    I. P. Berendrecht ex.

## 41
### Rembrandt Harmensz. van Rijn
# The Flight into Egypt, c. 1626

Etching, 146 x 122 mm
Bartsch 54, state I (6)
Rijksmuseum,
Amsterdam, Inv. No.
RP-P-OB-108

White/Boon 1969, p. 28;
White 1969, pp. 25ff.;
Chapman 1990, p. 21;
Leiden 1991/92, p. 63;
Amsterdam/London
2000/01, no. 2

In this early etching – his third – Rembrandt takes a huge leap forward. Many aspects of his late style can already be identified in *The Flight into Egypt*. Rembrandt has learned that forms can be rendered with broken lines and that the careful placement of dark accents can convincingly suggest plasticity. He has abandoned for good the use of continuous outlines, regular hatching and cross-hatching. The scene is built up entirely of a pattern of fine, random lines, drawn with great freedom. The shapes are indicated with just a few open lines. The broken outlines and the areas left unworked, contrasting with areas of shade and dark accents, are reminiscent of a washed pen-and-ink drawing. There can be no doubt that Rembrandt deliberately set out to achieve this effect.

This free manner of etching, which is without precedent, recalls the words of the Florentine artist Filippo Baldinucci. In his pamphlet on prints published in 1686, he writes admiringly of «Rembrandt's exceptional manner of etching ... which is characterized by a free and irregular use of line, without defined outlines, and which results in a deep, powerful chiaroscuro of painterly quality.»

Mary occupies an important position in the composition. She sits on a donkey, which is led by Joseph, and looks out at the viewer. She holds the tightly-swaddled Christ child in her arms. What strikes us is the prosaic nature, the almost secular character of the scene. Whereas in *The Rest on the Flight into Egypt* (cat. no. 13), which Rembrandt made not long before this, the elevated status of the infant Jesus was signalled with a halo, here there is nothing to remind us that this is the Holy Family.

Rembrandt made corrections in brown ink on

Fig. 41a
Rembrandt Harmensz.
van Rijn, *The Flight into
Egypt* (after reduction of
the etching plate), c. 1627
Etching, 79 x 51 mm
Bartsch 54, state II (6)
Rijksmuseum,
Amsterdam

Fig. 41b
Rembrandt Harmensz.
van Rijn, *Self-portrait
Leaning Forward*, c. 1628
Etching, 61 x 48 mm
Bartsch 5, state I (3)
Rijksmuseum,
Amsterdam

one of the two known impressions[1] of this etching. They reveal that he was particularly dissatisfied with the position of the donkey's hind legs. Evidently he had originally intended to make changes on the plate, but he seems to have decided on second thoughts that only the figure of Joseph was worth saving. Rembrandt resorted to a solution that was as daring as it was drastic. He cut the plate in such a way that only Joseph was left (fig. 41a). In the second and third states he worked the scene up further, concentrating mainly on intensifying the areas of shadow. Although part of the donkey's head still remains visible, there is no longer anything to indicate the Christian character of the original work. Joseph is reduced to an anonymous peasant. Later interventions, which added extra lines to the shading and replaced Joseph's tall hat with a flat cap, are not regarded as autographic.

After he had cut the plate, Rembrandt etched his first little self-portrait on the upper left portion. He did not take the trouble to remove Mary's head, and she can still be seen faintly in the earliest states, upside down, just above Rembrandt's head (fig. 41b). Cutting plates was typical of Rembrandt's approach. White argues that this shows that Rembrandt did not work according to a predetermined plan, but simply went with his intuition.

The style in which the print was executed has a parallel in drawing, but so too does the cutting of the plate. In the age before modern means of correction were available, artists often resorted to the scissors to remove less successful areas. Rembrandt himself corrected his drawings in this way.                                      E.d.H.

---

[1]  Bibliothèque Nationale, Paris.

## 42
## Rembrandt Harmensz. van Rijn
# Man in a High Cap Walking, c. 1627

Pen and ink, grey wash,
106 x 54 mm
Benesch 14
Musée du Louvre,
Département des Arts
Graphiques, Paris
(Bonnet Bequest)

Only in Amsterdam

Benesch regards this pen drawing of a man walking to the left with a stick and a tall hat as a preliminary study for the figure of Joseph in the *Flight into Egypt* (cat. no. 41), one of Rembrandt's earliest etchings. Just how closely Rembrandt's use of the pen resembles his etching technique becomes clear if we compare the figure in the drawing and the figure of Joseph in the etching. In both cases the outlines are indicated with the same broken lines, which, as White rightly observes in his stylistic analysis of the two works, suggest rather than define.[1] The grey wash on the drawing indicating the shadows also finds a parallel in the hatching in the print, while the two works display virtually identical *chiaroscuro* effects.

The technique and the format make it seem likely that the drawing was done from memory and not from a model.[2] Rembrandt needed a constant supply of the most diverse figures for his paintings and prints.[3] By continually practising drawing from the model or from memory, he not only built up enough knowledge and experience to draw any figure he wanted without a model in front of him, he also had an arsenal of sketches that he could use as the starting point for the figures in his paintings and etchings. *Man in a High Cap Walking* is probably one such sketch. It is in any event not a direct preliminary study for the figure of Joseph in the print: the differences between the two figures are quite simply too great for this to be the case. In all likelihood this is an older free sketch that Rembrandt worked up for the etching. This would explain the differences between the drawing and the etching.

Benesch follows Lugt in dating the drawing c. 1628/30.[4] He believes the print was made in c. 1629/30. In the light of the similarities in drawing technique between this piece and drawings like *Seated Old Man* and *Man Leaning on a Stick* (cat. no. 50) it is more probable that both works date from c. 1627.                E.d.H.

[1]  White 1999, p. 22.
[2]  Cf. the remarks to cat. no. 50.
[3]  Leiden 1991/92, p. 72.
[4]  Paris 1933, no. 1159.

## 43
## Rembrandt Harmensz. van Rijn
# St Jerome Kneeling, c. 1627

Etching, 389 x 332 mm
Bartsch 106, state I (1)
Rijksmuseum, Amster-
damm, Inv. No.
RP-P-OB-627

St Jerome – theologian and Bible translator – is one of the four western Church Fathers. In art he is portrayed as a penitent, as a scholar or as a Doctor of the Church. His attribute is a lion. Rembrandt must have had a particular fondness for the story of St Jerome, for he devoted no fewer than seven of his etchings to this saint.[1] The present sheet is the earliest of these. Rembrandt shows Jerome kneeling; he is lost in prayer. Before him lies an open book and a skull. The head of a lion can be seen in the semi-darkness on the left. The scene is situated in a cave-like setting.

The first thing that strikes one is the size of this print. Almost 40 cm tall by more than 30 cm wide, it is the most ambitious print Rembrandt had thus far attempted. It seems that Rembrandt wanted to adapt his style to the size of the plate. The scene is drawn with rough, powerful strokes. Only the saint's head and his clasped hands have been drawn with care and attention. And yet the manner in which Jerome is drawn does not convince. The body is oddly angular and this, like the strongly emphasised outlines, is not very typical of Rembrandt.

The space is barely defined. The wall on the right, Jerome's robe and the floor on which he kneels all have the same pattern of hatching and cross-hatching drawn in varying directions. The lack of structure and unity gives the whole thing the look of a patchwork quilt.

The drawing of the skull and the lion – which does not appear to have a body – can only be described as inept. The skirt of the robe, under which Jerome's legs are concealed, looks extremely primitive. The saint moreover appears to be floating somewhere above the floor, rather than kneeling on it.

What is typical of Rembrandt is the great attention he has devoted to the way the light falls. The centre of the scene is bathed in full light, which shows up the features of the saint. The effect of the light as it enters from the upper right is subtly indicated with a few fine lines of shading under the nose and on the hands. The saint's back, in deep shadow, contrasts sharply with the areas of his robe that have been left unworked, but the poorly-hatched shadow passages actually work counter to the desired effect.

Rembrandt clearly struggled with the large format. The rough manner of etching and the hatching method proved unsuitable for achieving the necessary gradations in tone and hence giving the work unity and structure. In technical terms, too, the etching cannot be described as a great success. The spots on Jerome's robe are signs that the etching ground detached here and there during the etching process. Given that there are only two known impressions of this print, it seems that Rembrandt must have recognised this. He evidently did not think it worthwhile working on the plate any further.

Among the very earliest etchings, *The Apostle Paul* (cat. no. 86) is most closely akin to *St Jerome Kneeling*. This etching displays a similar treatment of the light and the same unstructured manner of hatching. Schatborn dates *The Apostle Paul* and the associated preliminary study to c. 1627.[2] On the basis of the similarities between the two etchings, *St Jerome Kneeling* must also have been made in c. 1627.

E.d.H.

[1] Bartsch 100–106.
[2] Schatborn 1986a, p. 4.

259

## 44

Rembrandt Harmensz. van Rijn

# Peter and John at the Gate of the Temple, c. 1629

Etching, 221 x 169 cm
Bartsch 95, state I (1)
Rijksmuseum,
Amsterdam, Inv. No.
RP-P-OB-178

White/Boon 1969, p. 52;
White 1969, p. 13, 27–30,
98, 107, 152; Schatborn
1986a, p. 32f.; Boston
2000/01, no. 2

The subject of the print, Peter's miraculous cure of a crippled beggar, is taken from Acts 3:1–8. This passage describes how Peter and John were accosted at the gate of the Temple by a lame beggar, appealing for alms. Peter said to the man, «Silver and gold have I none, but such as I have, give I thee: in the name of Jesus Christ of Nazareth. Rise up and walk.» The beggar stood up, ran into the Temple leaping with joy, and praised God for his unexpected cure. Rembrandt stuck closely to the biblical account. The scene is set by a gate. The beggar holds out his hand while the two Apostles bend over him.

In Dresden there is a figure study in black chalk of a man standing with his arms outstretched (fig. 44a).[1] Rembrandt used this drawing, which must have been drawn from life in the studio, as the model for the figure of Peter. The sheet is one of a group of figure studies, all drawn on the same paper, which have been dated on stylistic grounds to c. 1629. Watermark research supports the date.

The precise relationship between the drawing and the etching is, however, unclear. The figure of Peter on the drawing has not been scored through, and is in any event larger than the figure on the etching. The figures correspond in broad terms, but there are also differences. The figure of Peter on the print is clearly older and more wrinkled. He also has a slightly longer beard and he is more stooped. It is not clear whether it was a self-contained study that was adapted and used for the purpose later. This approach, in which studies of individual figures drawn in chalk are used later in a larger composition, is very similar to the working methods of Lastman, Rembrandt's teacher, (cf. cat. no. 5). The free, spontaneous etching style is reminiscent of Rembrandt's earliest etchings, such as *The Flight into Egypt* (cat. no. 41). Now, however, the *chiaroscuro* has been used much more successfully and convincingly. The uncontrolled patchwork quilt of light and dark areas has evolved into a scene built up from just a few dark passages which stand out vividly against the almost unworked areas of the plate. This new approach is particularly evident in the figure of Peter.

From the technical point of view, the etching is closely related to *Self-portrait Bareheaded* (cat. no. 78). Rembrandt may have used the more aggressive nitric acid for etching in this case too.[2] And here again, the lines have been bitten so deeply that they cannot retain the ink properly. There are only three surviving impressions of this rare print.                    E.d.H.

[1] Benesch 12. For the relationship between drawing and etching, see: Schatborn 1986a.
[2] White 1969, p. 13.

Fig. 44a
Rembrandt Harmensz. van Rijn, *Old Man, Holding his Arms Extended*, c. 1629
Black chalk, 254 x 190 mm
Kupferstich-Kabinett, Staatliche Kunstsammlungen Dresden

261

## 45
### Rembrandt Harmensz. van Rijn
# Beggar Man and Woman, c. 1629

Etching, 122 x 96 mm
Bartsch 183, state I (1)
Rijksmuseum,
Amsterdam,
Inv. No. RP-P-OB-422

White 2000, p. 172

*Beggar Man and Woman* is one of the earliest etchings by Rembrandt that was inspired by the work of Jacques Callot (1592–1635). As is the case in his other prints of beggars, however, it is not possible to identify a specific model. Rembrandt adopted Callot's subject and certainly borrowed certain aspects of his compositions, such as the positioning of the figures against an unworked background, but he produced an entirely individual work, which manifestly differs from Callot's work in the sketchy lines and strong contrasts between light and dark.

The old couple are seen from the side. They are lit by strong sunlight that falls from the upper right. The woman's face is shrouded in deep shadow. The man's balding head, in contrast, is brightly lit. The figures are drawn with great freedom, but are scarcely modelled. The effect of the light is suggested by rough, bold hatching indicating the shadows. Stylistically the print is similar to the *Lion Hunt* of c. 1629 (cat. no. 51).

Technically speaking, the etching is a failure. The lines are roughly bitten and the etching ground has become detached in places during the etching process. All in all, the etching appears to be highly experimental. Rembrandt had evidently not yet mastered the technical process at this stage in his career. He took the decision as to whether or not to do further work on an etching after the first impression had been pulled.[1] In this case the result was so far from his intentions that he decided not to do any more work on the etching.

There are only two known impressions of this etching. One of them is printed on the back of a unique impression of the etching entitled *The Leper*.[2] Münz does not rule out the possibility that this latter impression of *Beggar Man and Woman* is an earlier state than the one shown here, but given the poor quality of both impressions it is impossible to reach a definite conclusion.[3]

The composition of *Beggar Man and Woman* may be based on Rembrandt's drawing *Beggar Couple with a Dog* (cat. no. 46).          E.d.H.

[1] White 2000, p. 172.
[2] Bartsch 171.
[3] Münz 1952, no. 99.

## 46
### Rembrandt Harmensz. van Rijn
# Beggar Couple with a Dog (verso: Sketch), c. 1628

Pen in brown (verso:
black chalk),
165 x 145 mm
Benesch 22
Private Collection

Rotterdam 1956, no. 3;
White 2000, p. 171

More than any other work by Rembrandt, this study of two beggars walking along reveals the influence of Jacques Callot. The almost continuous outlines of the figures and the strong, vertical hatching used in the shadow passages are so close to the technique of Callot's etchings that this sheet can be counted among the very earliest in this genre.[1]

The composition of the drawing is very similar to that of *Beggar Man and Woman* (cat. no. 45), an etching Rembrandt made in about 1629. White suggests that the drawing served as the starting point for the etching.[2] Stylistically, too, there are similarities between the two works. The use of line in the etching is freer and looser, however, and less reminiscent of Callot. On this basis, it is fairly safe to say that the drawing preceded the etching. The two works show a different phase in Rembrandt's handling of Callot's influence.

Fig. 46a
Rembrandt, *Beggar Man and Woman behind a Bank*, c. 1630
Etching, 116 x 85 mm
Bartsch 165, state I (9)
Rijksmuseum, Amsterdam

265

*Beggar Man and Woman behind a Bank* (fig. 46a), a print with a comparable composition, illustrates the next stage, in which Callot's ideas have been entirely absorbed and integrated into Rembrandt's work. The detailing has now been taken much further. The couple, who are partially concealed behind a bank, have acquired individual features and are drawn with great compassion. The etching is also an advance from the technical point of view. The etching needle has been wielded with much greater assurance. There is variation in the use of line, and some lines – such as those that go to make up the bank – are more deeply bitten than others. Rembrandt reworked this plate no fewer than nine times. He concentrated primarily on achieving a more gradual transition between the foreground and the two beggars, without ever actually arriving at a satisfactory solution.

*Beggar Couple with a Dog* is one of a group of drawings made on the same Italian paper. Four of them, including Benesch 22, have a watermark – a bird in a circle – which is found in dated paper from 1629 and 1630.[3] There is a further indication of the date of this work in the upper left-hand corner of the drawing. A piece of paper has been attached here, on the back of which can be seen part of a chalk drawing. The style in which this is executed, according to Schatborn,[4] is the same as that in the three sketches of beggars in the Rijksmuseum, Amsterdam (cf. cat. no. 47).[5] The dating of these works coincides with that of the drawings on Italian paper.

This could mean that *Beggar Couple with a Dog* must have been made around 1629. Stylistically, however, a rather earlier date would seem more likely. The relatively heavy reliance on Callot and the florid, meandering handling of the pen which, although less angular, can also be seen in *Man in a High Cap Walking* (cat. no. 42) of c. 1627 both point in this direction. All things considered, a date of c. 1628 seems to be the most probable.                E.d.H.

---

[1]  Rotterdam 1956, p. 35.
[2]  White 2000, p. 172.
[3]  Schatborn 1989, p. 125.
[4]  Memo, 27 June 2001.
[5]  Benesch 30, 31 and 32.

## 47

Rembrandt Harmensz. van Rijn

# Man Standing with a Stick, Facing Left (verso: A Cap), 1629/30

Black chalk, 294 x 170 mm
Inscribed bottom right:
*Rem*
Benesch 32
Rijksmuseum, Amsterdam, Inv. No. RP-T-1989-A-2047 (r)

Amsterdam 1985, no. 4 (with extensive bibliography)

The chalk drawings Rembrandt made in his Leiden years can be divided into two distinct groups.[1] The first group comprises three studies of old men drawn with red chalk, touched with black and white chalk.[2] The shadow passages in these figure studies, which were drawn around 1627, are almost completely worked up with chalk used in varying gradations of tone. The second group, which is of slightly later date and includes *Man Standing with a Stick*, consists of six figure studies drawn with black chalk.[3] All these drawings have strong *chiaroscuro*, with the most brightly lit passages left unworked – a technique that Rembrandt also used in his etchings.

*Man Standing with a Stick* is set down on the paper with broad, powerful lines. The way in which the shadow passages are rendered with thick parallel lines betrays the influence of the French engraver Jacques Callot, whose series of engravings of beggars (*Les Gueux*) Rembrandt must have greatly admired. Despite the sketchy indication of the forms, Rembrandt

has rendered the fall of the light, which gives the man volume, with great care. The combination of a rough representation of the forms and an accurately observed *chiaroscuro* effect is typical of this group of six chalk drawings.[4]

The similarities between the drawings in this group are not confined to stylistic details. Rembrandt used the same Italian paper for all six drawings – paper that we know he used in 1629/30. This corresponds closely with the traditional dating for these drawings based on stylistic considerations. There is also surviving work by Jan Lievens and Jan van Vliet that was made on this same paper.[5]

Thematically and stylistically, *Man Standing with a Stick* is closely related to Rembrandt's etched beggars. A comparison with one of these sheets, also a standing man with a stick (fig. 47a), clearly shows just how much he endeavoured to achieve the effect of drawings in his etchings. The etching has the same drawing-like character and the same strongly emphasized shadow passages, while – as is also the case in the drawing – the most brightly lit areas are left blank. It is evidence of the great importance of Rembrandt's drawings to his development as an etcher.

The monogram «Rem» in the lower right-hand corner is not in Rembrandt's hand.[6] There is a small sketch of a cap on the back (fig. 47b).

E.d.H.

Fig. 47a
Rembrandt Harmensz. van Rijn, *Man Standing with a Stick*, c. 1629
Etching, 156 120 mm
Bartsch 162, state I (1)
Museum het Rembrandthuis, Amsterdam

1  Leiden 1991/92, p. 69.
2  Benesch 20, 37 and 40; cf. Leiden 1991/92, p. 69, note 18.
3  Benesch 12, 30, 31, 32, 45 and 196; cf. Amsterdam 1991, p. 25, note 2.
4  Amsterdam 1985, p. 10.
5  Amsterdam 1985, p. 10; Schatborn 1989, p. 125.
6  Amsterdam 1985, p. 10.

Fig. 47b
Verso of cat. no. 48

## 48
### Rembrandt Harmensz. van Rijn
# Beggar with a Crippled Hand Leaning on a Stick, c. 1629

Etching, 99 x 42 mm
Bartsch 166, state I (5)
Teylers Museum,
Haarlem,
Inv. No. KG 3733

The resemblance between *Beggar with a Crippled Hand Leaning on a Stick* and the work of the French engraver Jacques Callot was remarked upon by Gersaint as early as 1751.[1] Callot was among the most productive printmakers of his day. He was one of the first artists to concentrate almost exclusively on making engravings and etchings. His œuvre runs to more than 1500 prints and is made up mainly of series, among other things of saints, famous people, the seasons, the horrors of war, court celebrations and sieges. *Les Gueux*, a series of beggars and other street figures published in Nancy in 1622, was the source of inspiration for several seventeenth-century Dutch artists, including Adriaen van de Venne, Jan van Vliet, Pieter Quast and Gillis van Scheyndel. Rembrandt's etchings of beggars also came about as a result of the influence of Callot's work. Although the debt to Callot's work is unmistakable, Rembrandt's borrowings are always indirect.[2]

It is consequently not possible to identify a direct model for *Beggar with a Crippled Hand Leaning on a Stick*, an early etching dating from c. 1629. The print is most like Callot's *Beggar Warming his Hands* (fig. 48a). Both prints portray a beggar shown in profile, leaning on a stick. The bold lines and the placing of the figure against an empty background are typical of Callot. Rembrandt's etching shows a similar concentration on the protagonist. There are just a few lines below right giving some sort of indication of the setting, but it is not clear whether they represent a hill or a cottage.

From the way that Rembrandt contrasts the shadow passages, which are set down with forceful vertical lines, with the light, unworked areas, we can see that he was not only interested in Callot's subjects and compositions, but that he had also made a thorough study of his technique. Rembrandt also used this suggestive and effective manner of rendering light and shade in his drawings (see cat. no. 47). The spontaneous manner of drawing, the open outlines and the strong *chiaroscuro*, which distinguish Rembrandt's etchings from Callot's, are likewise closely akin to the style of his drawings. This underlines yet again that for Rembrandt there was essentially no difference between drawing on an etching plate and drawing on paper.

There are five known states of *Beggar with a Crippled Hand Leaning on a Stick*. Some authors are of the opinion that only the first state is completely authentic.                    E.d.H.

[1]  Gersaint 1751, p. 152.
[2]  Amsterdam 1985, p. 28, nos. 12–15.

Fig. 48a
Jacques Callot, *Beggar
Warming his Hands*, 1622
Etching, 137 x 82 mm
Lieure 484
Rijksmuseum,
Amsterdam

## 49
### Rembrandt Harmensz. van Rijn
# Beggar with a Stick in a Tall Hat and Long Cloak, c. 1627

Etching, 119 x 88 mm
Seidlitz 376
Rijksmuseum,
Amsterdam

Hind 1923, p. 123; Münz
1952, p. 172; White/Boon
1969, p. 164; Hollstein,
vol. 16, p. 234

The extent to which the young Rembrandt can split the opinions of scholars is evident from the debate that surrounds the authorship of this picture of a beggar with a cottage and two figures in the background.

At first sight the etching differs so greatly, both stylistically and technically, from Rembrandt's other graphic work that there has never been unanimity about its authenticity. Adam Bartsch, who compiled the first authoritative catalogue of Rembrandt's prints at the end of the eighteenth century, did not include this etching. Hind likewise did not regard the print as authentic. Münz was the first to recognise the relationship with Rembrandt's early prints from the 1627–1628 period, but he was not prepared to commit himself to a definite attribution. He did not rule out the possibility that it might be an incomplete reworking of an etching started by Rembrandt. Seidlitz published the sheet, without further elucidation, as the work of an unknown pupil of Rembrandt's. In the most recent literature, the etching, of which only one impression is known, has been attributed to Jan van Vliet on stylistic grounds.[1] Only White and Boon unreservedly attribute the etching to Rembrandt. They suggest 1629, or perhaps even earlier, as its possible year of creation. The figures are contained in continuous outlines and are similar in style and character to Rembrandt's very earliest etchings. The strong *chiaroscuro* effects are also more reminiscent of Rembrandt than van Vliet, who admittedly produced various series of engravings of beggars and street figures but who, unlike Rembrandt, always depicted his figures in isolation and without any background. Given the rather crude execution of the figures, the dark outlines, the scratchy hatching with which they are surrounded and the similarity to Rembrandt's very earliest etchings, it would not be unreasonable to suppose that the etching was made well before 1629, possibly around 1627.

E.d.H.

[1]  Hollstein, vol. 16, p. 234·

## 50
## Rembrandt Harmensz. van Rijn
# Man Leaning on a Stick, c. 1626/27

Pen in brown,
144 x 86 mm
Benesch 27
Private Collection

Rembrandt's smaller figure studies, like *Man Leaning on a Stick*, are generally executed in pen and brown ink. The larger figure studies are drawn with red or black chalk on much bigger sheets of paper. Schatborn believes that there may be a connection between the selection of the size of paper (and hence of the technique) and the circumstances in which the drawing was made. Large chalk drawings would have been done from life, whereas the smaller pen and ink drawings were drawn from memory. This would mean that *Man Leaning on a Stick* was drawn from the imagination, without an actual model. It was only constant practice in drawing from the model that enabled Rembrandt to do this.

On the basis of the undulating lines, Benesch dates *Man Leaning on a Stick* to c. 1628/29. However, the pen technique is very like that in *Seated Old Man* of 1626. The sketchily drawn pen lines and, above all, the way the shadow is suggested with a few short, fine parallel lines are common to both drawings. The stylistic similarities between the two drawings are such that we may safely assume that *Man Leaning on a Stick* was made at the same time or slightly later.                    E.d.H.

## 51
Rembrandt Harmensz. van Rijn
# The Small Lion Hunt, c. 1629

Etching, 158 x 117 mm
Bartsch 116, state I (1)
Museum het Rembrandthuis, Amsterdam

White 1969, pp. 152f.;
White/Boon 1969, p. 61;
Paris 1986, no. 13; Boston 2000/01, no. 3

*The Small Lion Hunt* is one of the most dramatic of Rembrandt's early prints. It was based on an etching by the Italian artist Antonio Tempesta (1555–1630).[1] Rembrandt must have held his work in great admiration – the inventory of his possessions drawn up in 1656 lists no fewer than four albums containing prints by Tempesta.[2]

Tempesta, who produced a great many hunting scenes, shows us two horsemen in oriental costume using their spears in an attempt to rescue a third rider, who is being attacked by a lion (fig. 51a). The scene is set in an open landscape.

Rembrandt borrowed the motif of a fight between a few horsemen and a lion from Tempesta, but the only thing he took over almost literally was the pose of the fallen horse. Otherwise Rembrandt departed from his model in virtually every respect.

Rembrandt concentrated fully on the main action by drastically simplifying the scene. He left out one of the horsemen and the landscape. He also elected to use a portrait format, which enabled him to contain the scene in a more dynamic triangular composition. However, the differences are not confined to elements of the composition. Equally striking is the difference in the use of line. Rembrandt drew with matchless freedom. There is nothing to recall Tempesta's accurately drawn outlines and carefully detailed composition.

The strong, unpolished *chiaroscuro* and the loose drawing manner reinforce the dynamism and drama of the work. And yet the rapidity with which Rembrandt worked also has a down side: The forms of the horsemen and the lion lack volume and are poorly defined.

On the grounds of the swift drawing style, the large figures, the rough execution and the barely modelled forms, *The Small Lion Hunt* is dated to c. 1629. E.d.H.

[1] First recognized by Münz. See Münz 1952, no. 251.
[2] Strauss/Meulen 1979, doc. 1656/12.

Fig. 51a
Antonio Tempesta,
*Lion Hunt*, c. 1620
Etching, 130 x 197 mm.
Rijksmuseum,
Amsterdam

## 52
## Rembrandt Harmensz. van Rijn
# The Presentation in the Temple, 1630

Etching, 103 x 78 mm
Signed: *RHL 1630*
Bartsch 51, state II (2)
Museum het
Rembrandthuis,
Amsterdam, Inv. No. 37

Around 1630 Rembrandt made a few very small etchings of biblical subjects. They include *The Presentation in the Temple, Christ Disputing with the Doctors* (cat. no. 53) and *The Circumcision* (cat. no. 54). Despite their tiny size, these prints are minutely detailed and convey an amazing sense of monumentality.

*The Presentation in the Temple* depicts the moment when the prophetess Anna meets the pious Simeon (Lk 2:36ff.). The group of Simeon, who holds the Christ child, Mary, Joseph and Anna is placed in a soaring architectural space amidst a throng of visitors to the Temple. The angel pointing the child out to Anna is a charming detail.

Cat. no. 52 is the earliest of the three etchings that Rembrandt devoted to the presentation in the Temple. The two later versions date from 1640[1] and the 1650s[2], but we also encounter the subject in a painting dating from c. 1627/28 (cat. no. 30). In this print, however, the group is placed in a much loftier space. There are also similarities with the panel in the Mauritshuis, The Hague, which dates from 1631 (fig. 52a). Although some elements of the etching, such as the high staircase leading to the high priest's seat, can also be found in this impressive paint-

ing, Rembrandt created an entirely new composition for it. The grouping of the main protagonists was radically altered. One mystery is the figure viewed from behind in the Hague painting, who cannot readily be identified as the prophetess Anna.

In comparison with the etchings that he had made only a year or two previously, *The Presentation in the Temple* marks a huge step forward. The etching is built up of a carefully thought-out and refined system of lines of varying thickness, bitten out more or less deeply. The great variation in line, hatching, cross-hatching and line thickness gives the print a painterly quality. There are two known states of the print. The rare first state has a white border at the top, which Rembrandt removed in the second state by cutting 17 mm away from the top edge of the plate. The beggar limping away on the left, whose leg and part of whose back can just be seen, is so roughly bisected by the edge of the picture that one wonders whether the left side of the plate was also cut off in an earlier state.

E.d.H.

[1] Bartsch 49.
[2] Bartsch 50.

Fig. 52a
Rembrandt, *The Presen-
tation in the Temple*, 1631
Panel, 60 x 48 cm
Royal Cabinet of Paintings
Mauritshuis, The Hague

## 53
### Rembrandt Harmensz. van Rijn
# Christ Disputing with the Doctors in the Temple, 1630

Etching and burin,
89 x 68 mm
Monogrammed and dated
(states 1 and 2 only):
*RHL 1630*
Bartsch 66, state III (3)
Museum het
Rembrandthuis,
Amsterdam

Bauch 1960, p. 176;
White/Boon 1969, p. 13;
White 1969, pp. 28-29;
Tümpel 1970; Paris 1986,
no. 11; Boston 2000/01,
no. 9

Between 1628 and 1630 Rembrandt etched in two starkly contrasting ways: a rough manner and a more refined, restrained style. The first group includes such prints as *Self Portrait Bareheaded* (cat. no. 78), *The Small Lion Hunt* (cat. no. 51) and *Peter and John at the Gate of the Temple* (cat. no. 44). *Christ Disputing with the Doctors in the Temple,* like the two little portraits of Rembrandt's mother of 1628,[1] comes into the second category.

According to St Luke's Gospel (2:46-47), when Christ was twelve years old Joseph and Mary took him to Jerusalem to celebrate Passover. At the end of the festival they returned home. However, unbeknownst to them Jesus had remained behind in Jerusalem. When his parents missed him and realised that he was not among the relatives and friends who had travelled with them, they went back to Jerusalem. After three days they found him in the temple, engrossed in a debate with the teachers of the scriptures. Rembrandt shows us the moment just before Christ is reunited with his parents. The interior of the temple is shrouded in gloom. The space is more suggested than defined. Only the colossal dimensions of the pillar lead us to suppose that the scene is set in a huge building. Christ looks small and insignificant against the imposing figures of the learned doctors. And yet, arms outstretched, he argues his point with complete self-assurance. The astonishing knowledge of the twelve-year-old Christ that has astounded the doctors can be seen from the earnest attention with which they listen to him. The minuscule figures on the extreme right are Mary and Joseph, who enter the temple unaware of what they will find.

There are three known states of the etching. The changes Rembrandt made were intended to focus attention on the figure of Christ and strengthen the balance within the composition. In the first state (fig. 53a) the figures on the left are still illuminated by light entering the area from the left, but in the second state (fig. 53b) this group is shrouded in darkness. Rembrandt also intensified the shadow on the back of the

Fig. 53a
Rembrandt Harmensz.
van Rijn, *Christ Disputing
with the Doctors in the
Temple*, 1630
Etching, 108 x 78 mm
Bartsch 66, state I (3)
Rijksmuseum, Amsterdam

Fig. 53b
Rembrandt Harmensz.
van Rijn, *Christ Disputing
with the Doctors in the
Temple*, 1630
Etching, 108 x 78 mm
Bartsch 66, state II (3)
Rijksmuseum, Amsterdam

figure in the foreground, which consequently works as a stronger repoussoir. The curved steps, which are an important part of the composition, are now more strongly accentuated. This alteration served to give greater emphasis to the figure of Christ.

The changes Rembrandt made in the third state were even more drastic. They were needed because the composition had become somewhat unbalanced. To restore the balance, Rembrandt cut the plate down on three sides and added two men to the right of the reading figure. The group of figures on the left and the signature were lost in the reduction of the plate.

The composition of *Christ Disputing with the Doctors in the Temple* is very like that of Rembrandt's painting *Judas Repentant, Returning the Thirty Pieces of Silver* of 1629 (cat. no. 33). The types of figures, the costumes, the dramatic lighting and the use of a gigantic pillar are common to both works.

Despite the tiny format, Rembrandt clearly took considerable trouble to give the different figures individual features – in their pose, their dress and their facial expressions. The carefully constructed web of hatching and cross-hatching produces convincing chiaroscuro. These light and shade effects are not an end in itself, however, but a means of making a distinction between the main and the subsidiary issues, of bringing unity to the composition and of putting across the meaning of the scene.

*Christ Disputing with the Doctors* is the print described as «Christ as a child and disputing» (Christ jongh synde en disputeerend) listed in the 1679 inventory of the Amsterdam print dealer Clement de Jonghe, who owned a great many of Rembrandt's etching plates. The present whereabouts of this plate, which was for many years in the I. de Bruijn collection, are unknown.[2]

E.d.H.

---

[1] Bartsch 352 und Bartsch 354.
[2] Hinterding 1995, p. 63.

## 54
Rembrandt Harmensz. van Rijn
# The Circumcision, c. 1630

Etching and drypoint,
88 x 64 mm
Bartsch 48, state I (2)
Museum het
Rembrandthuis,
Amsterdam

Filedt Kok 1972, no. 48;
Paris 1986, no. 12;
Boston 2000/01, no. 10

*The Circumcision* is closely related to *The Presentation in the Temple* (cat. no. 52) and *Christ Disputing with the Doctors in the Temple* (cat. no. 53). There are similarities of style, the prints are all the same small format, and they all depict an episode from Christ's childhood.

There is only a brief reference to Christ's circumcision in the Bible: «And at the end of eight days, when he was circumcised, he was called Jesus, the name given by the angel before he was conceived in the womb» (Lk 2:21). The Bible makes no mention of where the circumcision took place, but the books of the Apocrypha set it in a stable, since according to Jewish law, women were not admitted to the Temple for the first forty days after the birth of a child. This notwithstanding, in western iconography the circumcision is usually set in a temple. Rembrandt's etching follows this tradition, as does an earlier etching he devoted to this subject,[1] but in a later version of this print – probably in response to criticism of his earlier interpretations – Rembrandt locates the event in a stable.[2]

It is assumed that *The Circumcision* was made shortly after *Christ Disputing with the Doctors in the Temple* (cat. no. 53), because the repertoire of pictorial resources is used to even greater effect.[3] The balanced composition and the carefully conceived fall of the light focus our attention on the wailing Christ child, face contorted in pain, as he is circumcised by the high priest. The architecture and the figures placed in the darkness to the right and left reinforce this effect. Despite the small size, Rembrandt has taken the trouble to give each figure individual features and clothes. Mary and Joseph, however, are effectively reduced to anonymous spectators. They watch, almost unrecognisable, from the right foreground.

The second state of the *Circumcision* was described for the first time by Burollet and de Bussière in 1986.[4] It differs from the first state shown here in that some fine lines of crosshatching have been added in places.

Some authors assert that Rembrandt made use of the composition of an engraving of the same subject by Hendrick Goltzius, dated 1594.[5] However, the relationship between the two prints is far from apparent.                E.d.H.

[1] Bartsch 47.
[2] Filedt Kok 1972, p. 53.
[3] Paris 1986, p. 12.
[4] Ibid.
[5] Bartsch 18.

Catalogue II

# Early Fame,
# Early Following

## 55-56
### Rembrandt Harmensz. van Rijn
# Bust of a Bearded Man with a High Forehead, c. 1629

### Jan van Vliet (Leiden 1600/10–1668)
# Bust of a Bearded Man with a High Forehead, c. 1631

55
Etching, 88 x 75 mm
Bartsch 314, state I (2)
Rijksmuseum, Amsterdam

56
Etching, 74 x 66 mm
Bartsch 314, state II (2)
Rijksmuseum, Amsterdam

White/Boon 1969, p. 145;
Amsterdam 1996,
nos. 25a and 25b

The collaboration between Rembrandt and van Vliet was not confined to making reproductions (cf. cat. nos. 39 and 78). There are also etchings on which they actually worked together. This approach is quite common in painting, but it is very unusual to find artists combining forces in printmaking. The prints created in this way include *The Descent from the Cross* and *Christ before Pilate*, which date from 1633 and 1635, respectively. Both were etched by van Vliet after a design by Rembrandt. Proofs reveal that Rembrandt followed the production process closely and did not hesitate to make his own corrections on the etching plate.[1]

A series of small etchings bears witness to a different form of collaboration. In this case Rembrandt started the etchings, and van Vliet worked them up. As far as we know at present, this is a group of twelve prints. *Bust of a Bearded Man with a High Forehead* is one of them. For centuries this was the only known sheet that also existed in a first state not yet worked by van Vliet. In 1969 a first, unworked state of *Bust of a Woman in a Heavy Headdress* (cat. no. 19) turned up at a sale in London. Until then the only known states of this sheet, for which Rembrandt etched the design, were later ones that had been worked on by van Vliet.

The first state of *Bust of a Bearded Man with a High Forehead*, like that of *Bust of a Woman in a Heavy Headdress*, shows Rembrandt's original etching work. One is struck by the rough, sketchy etching style. Rembrandt's powerful hatching is sometimes linked to the work of the Italian etcher Antonio Tempesta, who used a similar technique.[2] Tempesta wanted to imitate lines engraved with a burin, but in Rembrandt's case, the point of using this «rough manner» appears to have been to emulate the effect of a pen-and-ink drawing. This can be seen particularly clearly on *Bust of a Woman in a Heavy Head-*

*dress*. There is immense variation in the lines. Strong, regularly-drawn lines are combined with spontaneous, sometimes ragged strokes. The thickness of the lines also varies. It even seems as if here and there Rembrandt has actually tried to simulate the effect of a drying or freshly-dipped pen. These experiments are not isolated instances. The two *Lion Hunts* (cf. cat. no. 51)[3] and his *Self Portrait Bareheaded* (cat. no. 78) are other examples of prints in which Rembrandt used the rough manner of etching.

Very little by Rembrandt's hand can be identified in the second state of *Bust of a Bearded Man with a High Forehead*. The whole sheet has been rather crudely worked. The bust, which is only sketchily indicated in the first state, is now worked out in detail. The shadows and outlines have been strongly emphasised. The plate has been cut down all round, evidently with the intention of achieving a more pleasing harmony between the image and the size of the print. The way in which it was worked is typical of the whole group of twelve etchings.

For years, art historians have speculated about the artist to whom this work should be attributed. On stylistic grounds it is now assumed that van Vliet was responsible. The hard contrasts and rather crude lines are indeed characteristic of his method.

We might ask ourselves what van Vliet's purpose was in working up Rembrandt's etchings. It should be said first of all that, judging by the first states of *Bust of a Bearded Man with a High Forehead* and *Bust of a Woman in a Heavy Headdress*, the first states of these etchings were not finished pieces. They appear to have served above all as experiments, exploring the potential of the etching technique. Etchings like these were meant strictly for studio use and were not issued. This conclusion is supported by the extreme rarity of these prints. The purpose of van Vliet's ad-

ditions was almost certainly to make the etchings saleable. Given the relatively large number of extant impressions, we may conclude that there must have been quite keen interest in this sort of work among collectors.                    E.d.H.

[1] Royalton Kisch 1984; Royalton Kisch 1994; Amsterdam 1996, esp. nos. 16a, 16b and 17.
[2] Amsterdam 1996, p. 88.
[3] Bartsch 115–116.

## 57

Jan van Vliet (Leiden 1600/10–1668) (?) after Rembrandt Harmensz. van Rijn

# The Beheading of St John the Baptist, c. 1631–33

Etching, 157 x 124 mm
Bartsch 93, state II (5)
Museum het Rem-
brandthuis, Amsterdam

White/Boon 1969, p. 171;
Amsterdam 1996, no. 19

John the Baptist prepared the way for Christ, whose imminent coming he announced. In his preaching he called on his followers to repent, and he baptised converts in the River Jordan. John came into conflict with the tetrarch Herod Antipas, whom he had denounced for his illegitimate relationship with his sister-in-law Herodias. The King had John thrown into prison. An ill-considered promise made by Herod to his stepdaughter, Salome, led to John's death. At a feast in honour of Herod's birthday, she danced for him. He was so enraptured by this that he promised her on oath that he would give her whatever she asked for. At her mother's urging, Salome asked for John's head. John was executed in Herod's prison, and Salome was presented with his head on a platter.

The beheading of John the Baptist, which is recounted in Mark 6:21-28, is a recurrent theme in art. Artists traditionally depicted the moment just before the execution. Rembrandt de-parts from this convention. In his etching, the executioner has just done his work and is on the point of restoring his sword to its scabbard. In the foreground lies the body of John, hands tied behind his back. His reed-cross lies alongside him. To the left of the executioner is the platter on which John's head will be placed. The scene is observed from the background by three figures, a motif that we also encounter elsewhere in Rembrandt's work.

There are five known states of the *Beheading of St John the Baptist*. The steps to the left of the platter only appear in the first two states. Later interventions concentrate primarily on strengthening the shadows. The etching bears the monogram «RHL», but is clearly not Rembrandt's own work. *The Beheading of St John the Baptist* is consequently considered to belong to the group of Rembrandt etchings that were worked up by van Vliet (cf. cat. nos. 19 and 55). The strong contrasts between light and dark, the continuous outlines and the hatching of the

Fig. 57a
Rembrandt Harmensz.
van Rijn, *The Beheading
of St John The Baptist*,
c. 1627
Pen in brown,
137 x 112 mm
Musée du Louvre,
Département des Arts
Graphiques, Paris

walls all point to him. The figures in the background, on the other hand, are not typical of van Vliet's work, nor are the carefully thought out changes in the various states. The drawing style is also more restrained than one would expect of van Vliet. A possible explanation could be that van Vliet worked under Rembrandt's supervision and consciously tried to imitate his style. Royalton Kisch has noted, in connection with van Vliet's reproduction prints, that he was capable of adapting his own style and imitating those of other artists.[1]

The suggestion that Rembrandt and van Vliet worked together closely on the production of *The Beheading of St John* appears to be confirmed by recent watermark studies. A watermark has been found in the first state of the etching that is also found in etchings by van Vliet and Rembrandt. The findings of the same study also indicate that the etching was made between c. 1631 and 1633.[2]

A study for the figure of the executioner by Rembrandt has survived (fig. 57a).[3] On the basis of this drawing, which dates from c. 1627, it can be concluded that Rembrandt was in any event responsible for the invention of the picture, which – as is the case with van Vliet's reproduction prints – preceded the etching by several years. The sketch, which shows the executioner in van Vliet's etching in reverse, is also important for another reason. This sheet gives us an insight into the way Rembrandt worked. We can clearly see from the way he altered the executioner's pose of the how he searched for the most satisfactory solution as he drew.

In 1640 Rembrandt etched *The Beheading of John the Baptist* again. This time he followed the iconographic tradition: John kneels before the executioner who holds his sword aloft, poised to strike the fatal blow.                E.d.H.

[1]  Amsterdam 1996, pp. 11f.
[2]  Amsterdam 1996, p. 29.
[3]  Benesch 101.

## 58
### Gerard Dou (Leiden 1613–1675) (?)
# Fragment of a Nocturnal Biblical or Historical Composition, 1628

Copper, 21.5 x 16.5 cm
Monogrammed:
*RHL 162(8?)*
Bridgestone Museum
of Art, Ishibashi
FoundationTokyo

Bode 1881, p. 54; Bredius
1881, pp. 182f.; Hofstede
de Groot 1899, p. 159;
Bredius 1935, Nr. 533,
p. 24; Bauch 1960, pp.
119–121, 129f.; Bauch
1967b, pp. 143f.; Tümpel
1967, Nr. 8, pp. 75–80;
Corpus, vol. 1, 1982, no.
C 10; Tokyo 1989

A number of men in the dark are illuminated by an invisible campfire. On the right stands a figure recognisable as a soldier by his helmet and cuirass, which reflect the firelight. He appears to be in conversation with the man beside him with the beret and the sash. The two seated figures in the foreground seem to be following the conversation while a third, turbaned figure sleeps, upright, with his head supported by his hand. In the shadow at the extreme right of the foreground, a man in a beret lies, half-leaning, asleep under a blanket. He, too, supports his head with his hand.

In the background at the left several figures can be seen under a vaguely-indicated arch, round a burning candle. One of them is betrayed as a soldier by his helmet and gorget; another is visible only as a dark silhouette, behind whom a third figure appears to catch the light. A fourth, his cap aslant on his head, stands behind the candle.

The painting was executed on a thin copper plate, from the left side of which a piece of indeterminate width has been cut off.[1] As a result, several figures have probably disappeared. Because of this incompleteness of the composition it is impossible to decipher the painting's iconography; the key to its identification was probably on the missing left-hand fragment.

In the past it has often been assumed that this was a history piece. Attempts to interpret the painting have mainly referred to episodes from the lives of the New Testament figures, Peter and Paul.[2] Bredius, Bode and Bauch, none of whom realised that the painting was incomplete, assumed that it depicted St Peter among the soldiers in the palace of the high priest. The man looking around would be Peter.[3] Bredius later changed his mind, proposing the title «St Paul in the Roman Camp».[4] Bauch tried to find

an explanation for the fact that a number of figures are so busily engaged in conversation during Peter's denial by suggesting that the painting did not depict the moment of the denial but the episode where, according to Luke, the soldiers and the women said to each other: «This man also was with him» (Lk 22:59).[5] Tümpel, the first to suggest that part of the painting was missing, tentatively proposed that it could originally have depicted St Paul casting a viper into the fire on the Island of Malta.[6]

As Hofstede de Groot had already established in 1899, the absence of any clear iconographic key (and he took the painting in its current form to be complete) meant that not a single figure could be satisfactorily identified. He therefore proposed the title «Soldiers Round a Watch Fire», with the implication that it was not a history piece at all but a genre painting.[7] An important difference between a genre and a history painting, however, is that in the first type, the figures are always depicted in contemporary dress, whereas it was considered fitting to dress the protagonists of a history piece in oriental or classical attire. Therefore, *A Nocturnal Biblical or Historical Scene (Fragment)*, the title given to the painting in the *Corpus*, is – at least provisionally – the most satisfactory.

The painting was taken to be an early work by Rembrandt from its discovery by Bredius in 1881 until its ejection from the canon by the Rembrandt Research Project. A team of Japanese researchers, *The Bridgestone Painting Research Group*, then conducted an exemplary investigation using the complete arsenal of art historical and scientific methods, resulting in the publication in 1989 of a book with the title *In Darkness and Light. A Rembrandt in Tokyo Reconsidered*.[8] The group's findings confirmed Tümpel's suspicion that a piece of the painting

on the left-hand side was missing. Furthermore, an attempt was made by Yoriko Kobayashi to identify the painting's place within Rembrandt's early œuvre through a sophisticated stylistic analysis. It became clear that it could only be accepted as such if one assumed an extremely wide range of stylistic possibilities within Rembrandt's early work; the date of its execution might also have to be pushed back to an early point in the chronology. On the basis of its colourfulness, unusual for 1628, it was dated by Ms Kobayashi to c.1626/27. She also pointed out the peculiar weaknesses in the handling of the forms and the anatomy of the figures. One need only look closely at the hands – always a difficult part of the human body for a painter.[9] The right hand of the soldier in the cuirass, which ought to be resting on his knee, does not in fact appear to touch that knee, while the other floats oddly in front of the hip; the anatomically unsatisfactory hands of the man by the fire are also much too large and hesitantly executed.

Once one has noted the deficiencies in such details, one is also struck by how clumsily the arms of the cuirassier are joined to the body, and how the excessively long arms of the man looking back and the cuirassier's standing leg appear to

be. The minimally-differentiated treatment of drapery is also much inferior in quality to comparable details in autograph paintings by Rembrandt.

But what the painting lacks above all is the casual yet telling efficiency of brushwork that is so characteristic of Rembrandt's autograph works. These multiple weaknesses rule out the possibility that we are dealing here with a work from Rembrandt's hand. Understandably, the *Bridgestone Painting Research Group* attributed great significance to the monogram «RHL», executed in light grey paint, together with the date «162[8?]» that seems to have been placed immediately on completion of the painting. The last figure is not entirely legible, but given its surviving remains it can hardly be other than an «8». In this catalogue more works not considered to be autograph Rembrandts exhibit R(H)L monograms (that also differ from each other radically in form, see cat. nos. 27, 34/I, 67 and 68). In one case, it could be demonstrated on the basis of paint samples that the monogram was added to the still wet paint (cat. no. 26; see also *Corpus* no. C 23). Should one suppose that such monograms were placed by someone other than Rembrandt as seals of work done in his studio or, almost immediately after a painting had left his studio, introduced by others in order to pass it off as a work by Rembrandt?

What makes the painting special is that it is in several respects ambitious, remarkably daring even. In particular, the painter of the *Fragment of a Nocturnal Biblical or Historical Scene* has paid considerable attention to one aspect of Rembrandt's early investigations in the area of light – what Rembrandt's pupil Samuel van Hoogstraten later referred to as working with «kindred colours». The first painting in which Rembrandt applied this method of working, in an already highly sophisticated way, is the painting of the *Peter and Paul Disputing* in Melbourne (p. 70, fig. 19). Hoogstraten recommends this procedure as follows:

«I therefore advise you not to mix up lights and shades too much, but to combine them appropriately in groups; let your strong lights be accompanied by lesser lights, and I assure you that they will shine all the more beautifully; let your deepest darks be surrounded by lighter darks, so that they will make the power of the light stand out all the more powerfully. Rembrandt developed this virtue to a high degree, and he was a master in properly combining kindred colours.»[10]

Both in *Peter and Paul Disputing*, also painted in 1628, and in the painting discussed here, one can see how this procedure is applied and how the effects achieved by it are akin in the two paintings. In the brightly-lit parts, light brown, yellow, light blue and light flesh colours are combined such that the number of local dark shadows that break up these passages are kept to a minimum. The glow of the sunlight, or the campfire, as the case may be, is thus suggested in a highly convincing manner.

The sophistication in the treatment of light, taken in conjunction with the deficiencies in the handling of form and the rather inept hand, could well indicate that we are dealing here with a young but talented beginner. Could this perhaps be one of the earliest works by the youth Dou, who entered his apprenticeship with Rembrandt at the age of 15? Despite all stated reservations against this kind of suggestion the attempt has to be made. It may perhaps be significant that the distinctive modelling of the faces evokes association with Dou. The profiles show the remarkable characteristic that the bottom half of the face continues a line with the forehead, a characteristic possessed by many figures in Dou's later genre pieces (cf. the *Quack Doctor* in the Museum Boijmans Van Beuningen).

But also the handling of nocturnal light, which is very different from that in ‹La main chaude› (cat. no. 62) and *The Flight into Egypt* (cat. no. 60) could point to Dou. The emphatically-painted candle flame in the background with the figures grouped around it is strongly reminiscent of the night scenes of the mature Dou.[11] Strange though the idea may at first seem, might not this clumsily-executed but original and ambitious painting perhaps be the earliest forerunner of Dou's later famous *Night School* (fig. 58a)?                E.v.d.W./M.d.W.

1 Tokyo 1989, p. 86.

2 For a complete survey of the different interpretations see Corpus, vol. 1, 1982, p. 511 and Tokyo 1989, pp. 75–80.

3 Bredius 1881, pp.182f.; Bode 1881, p. 54; Bauch 1960, pp. 119–121, 129f.

4 Bredius 1935, no. 533, p. 24.

5 Bauch 1967, pp. 143f.

6 Tümpel 1967, no. 8, pp. 75–80; for a thorough analysis of the various options, see Tokyo 1989, pp. 75–80.

7 Hofstede de Groot 1899, p. 159.

8 Tokyo 1989.

9 Cf. the essay by Ernst van de Wetering, «Delimiting Rembrandt's Autograph Œuvre – an Insoluble Problem?», p. 73.

10 «Daerom beveele ik u [aan] niet te veel met lichten en schaduwen door een te haspelen, maer de zelve bequamelijk in groepen te vereenigen; laet uwe sterkste lichten met minder lichten minlijk verzelt zijn, ik verzeeker u, dat ze te heelijker zullen uitblinken; laet uwe diepste donkerheden met klaere bruintens omringt zijn, op dat ze met te meerder gewelt de kracht van het licht mogen doen aafsteeken. Rembrant heft deeze deugt hoog in top gevoert, en was volleert in 't wel byeenvoegen van bevriende verwen». Hoogstraten 1678, p. 305.

11 Baer 2000/01, nos. 27, 28, 31.

## 59
### Circle of Rembrandt Harmensz. van Rijn
# Man Writing by Candlelight, c. 1629/30

Copper, 13.9 x 13.9 cm
Dr & Mrs. Alfred Bader

Bredius/Gerson 1969,
no. 425; Corpus, vol. 1,
1982, no. C 18; Kingston
1984, no. 7; Kingston
1997, no. 14; Pelletier
1998

An old man with grey hair sits at a table and writes in a book with a pen. He is dressed in a grey tabard and wears a brown cap. The space is largely shrouded in semi-darkness. The man is lit by a light source concealed behind a book propped up on the table. This also illuminates part of the plastered wall in the background, on which is nailed a piece of paper with illegible writing on it. A bottle hangs on the wall at the upper right; below it stands a globe.

Like *Fragment of a Nocturnal Scene* in Tokyo (cat. no. 58), *Man Writing by Candlelight* is painted on a thin copper plate. From an etching that was made after the painting in 1790, we know that it was originally slightly taller.[1] It is not signed or dated, and opinions vary as to whether it is an authentic work by Rembrandt.

In the eighteenth century it was regarded as an autographic painting by Rembrandt, as we see from the inscription on the 1790 reproduction.[2] A false monogram, «GDF.» (Gerard Dou Fecit), was added to the paper on the wall – probably at the beginning of the 19th century. This monogram was removed during restoration work in 1958, when it was found to be on top of the varnish.[3] Although several twentieth-century art historians, including Benesch and Rosenberg, have described the painting as an authentic work by Rembrandt, this view has

not been generally accepted.[4] In his edition of Bredius, Gerson considered the painting not to be authentic.[5] The *Rembrandt Research Project* attributed the painting to an artist in Rembrandt's immediate circle, probably a pupil, possibly the young Gerard Dou.

The stylistic similarities with *The Flight into Egypt* in Tours of 1628 (cat. no. 60) and *Fragment of a Nocturnal Scene* in Tokyo – paintings that were attributed to the same artist in Rembrandt's circle, possibly Gerard Dou – were an important factor in the *RRP's* decision not to accept the painting as autographic. Now that the *RRP* has reinstated the attribution of the painting in Tours to Rembrandt (see cat. no. 60), the question as to whether *Man Writing by Candlelight* should also be restored to Rembrandt's authentic œuvre is justified.

Although it is possible to identify similarities in the treatment of the light between this work, *Supper in Emmaus* in Paris of c. 1629 (p. 75, fig. 27) and *St Paul at his Desk* in Nuremberg of c. 1629/30 (cat. no. 32), particularly in the use of backlighting and a hidden light source, the differences in the treatment of the light are no less striking. If one compares *Man Writing by Candlelight* with these two works, particularly the painting in Nuremberg, in which the diversity of the *chiaroscuro* effects is taken to the ex-

59a
Circle of Rembrandt
Harmensz. van Rijn, *Man
Writing by Candlelight*
(detail), c. 1629/30

59b
Rembrandt Harmensz.
van Rijn, *St Paul at His
Desk* (detail), c. 1629/30

treme – not only strong contrasts between light and shade but also supremely subtle nuances and reflections of the light – it is difficult to accept that *Man Writing by Candlelight*, with its much more simplistic treatment of the light, was made by the same artist. It is as if the maker of the little painting in question saw the Nuremberg painting – with which it has obvious compositional similarities – and simply borrowed the most spectacular chiaroscuro effect from it: the backlighting around the concealed light source behind the book. He evidently did this without realising that the mood, the sense of space and the plasticity in the work are governed not so much by the extreme *chiaroscuro* effects, as by the more subtle gradations of tone and nuances of light.

In the application of the paint and the modelling, too, the painting falls short of what one would expect in a work by Rembrandt dating from the end of the 1620s. The surface of the paint varies in thickness and texture, but this differentiation in no way contributes to a convincing plasticity or expression of materials. The head is painted with short strokes, in Rembrandtesque fashion, but lacks any expressiveness. The folds in the clothes are coarsely modelled and the shadow passages are all executed in the same dark shade, without any nuances, so that adjacent areas of shadow appear to run into each other and the spatial relationship between the various forms is not always clear. Maintaining the sense of space and plas-

ticity in semi-darkened rooms was one of the particular artistic problems on which Rembrandt was concentrating in the period from 1628 to 1630 and for which he found such diverse and virtuoso new solutions, for example in *Judas Repentant* (cat. no. 33) and *Old Man Asleep* (cat. no. 31) of 1629. It is as good as impossible for Rembrandt to be the maker of a painting that fairs so badly on these crucial points.

*Man Writing by Candlelight* which, in view of its reliance on the Nuremberg painting, can be dated to c. 1629/30, must have been painted by an artist – who for the time being remains anonymous – in Rembrandt's immediate circle. The likeliest candidate would seem to be a pupil in the studio of Rembrandt (and Lievens?), who witnessed the numerous artistic experiments that were being conducted there at breakneck speed, but was not yet able to understand the finer points and consequently only took the most superficial elements from them. On the basis of the comparative material presently available, it is not possible to establish whether this pupil was the young Gerard Dou.[6]                                        B.v.d.B.

[1]  Corpus, vol. 1, 1982, p. 555.
[2]  Corpus, vol. 1, 1982, pp. 557–558, fig. 2.
[3]  Corpus, vol. 1, 1982, p. 555; Pelletier 1998.
[4]  Corpus, vol. 1, 1982, p. 557; Pelletier 1998.
[5]  Bredius/Gerson 1969, no. 425.
[6]  Cf. V. Manuth in: Kingston 1997, p. 14, who rejects an attribution to Dou on stylistic grounds.

## 60
## Rembrandt Harmensz. van Rijn
# The Flight into Egypt, 1627

Oak panel, 27.5 x 24.7 cm
Signed lower right:
*RH 1627*
Musée des Beaux-Arts
de Tours

Benesch 1954;
Bredius/Gerson 1969,
no. 532A; Corpus, vol. 1,
1982, no. C 5; Tours 1998,
no. 31

As we read in Matthew 2:13–14, after the birth of Jesus, Joseph and Mary fled into Egypt to escape the massacre of the firstborn decreed by King Herod. On this little panel, the flight into Egypt is depicted entirely in accordance with the iconographic tradition: Mary, with the Christ child in her arms, sits on an ass led by Joseph, who is on foot. The group of figures and the sandy path on which they are travelling are lit from the upper left by a light source that creates deep shadows on the ground on the right. The fact that this scene is set at night could perhaps be traced back to Elsheimer's *Flight into Egypt* in the Alte Pinakothek in Munich, which was published as a print by Hendrick Goudt.

The group walks diagonally towards the viewer. Joseph, barefoot and clad in a simple tunic and a straw hat, carrying a travelling bag, leans on a stick as he walks. He turns his head slightly away from the viewer. Mary has wrapped herself and her child in a blanket and wears a cloth twisted into a turban around her head. All we can see of the Christ child is his head, which is surrounded by a bright halo – literally a «light to lighten the darkness». The travellers' baggage, amongst which we can make out Joseph's

saw, the tool of his trade, is roped on to the back of the ass. In its pose, the ass displays a striking resemblance to the animal in Rembrandt's second etching, *The Rest on the Flight into Egypt* of c. 1626 (cat. no. 13). In the foreground on the left, silhouetted against the light, there is a thistle which acts as a repoussoir. It undoubtedly symbolizes both the inhospitable nature of the surroundings and the hardships that the travellers have to undergo on this «thorny path».

The little painting, which was attributed to Rembrandt by Otto Benesch in 1954, has a barely legible monogram and an even less legible date, which is usually read as 1627.[1] In 1982 the *Rembrandt Research Project* demoted the piece from an autograph work by Rembrandt to the work of a pupil of Rembrandt's, possibly the young Gerard Dou. In the essay in this catalogue «Delimiting Rembrandt's Autograph Œuvre – an Insoluble Problem?» the painting is tentatively attributed to Rembrandt once again.[2]

E.v.d.W.

[1] Corpus, vol. 1, 1982, pp. 480f.
[2] See above, pp. 76ff.

## 61
Rembrandt Harmensz. van Rijn
# The Painter in His Studio, c. 1628

Oak panel, 24.8 x 31.7 cm
Museum of Fine Arts,
Boston (Zoë Oliver Sher-
man Collection; given in
memory of Lillie Oliver
Poor 38.1838)

Bredius/Gerson 1969,
no. 419; Wetering 1976;
Corpus, vol. 1, 1982, no.
A 18; Schwartz
1984/85/87, fig. 36;
Tümpel 1986, no. 157;
Berlin/Amsterdam/
London 1991/92, no. 3;
Wetering 1991/92a;
Couprie 1992; Slatkes
1992, no. 104; Wetering
1997, fig. 102, pp. 75–89;
London/The Hague
1999/2000, p. 66, no. 17;
Boston 2000/01, no. 4

A young painter is depicted full length, standing in an austere studio. He is dressed in a long blue-grey robe with a sash tied around the waist, a flat white ruff and a broad-brimmed black hat. With a palette, a bundle of brushes and a maulstick in his left hand and a brush poised for action in his right, he looks from a distance at a large panel on an easel in the right foreground. The easel, positioned diagonally in the space and viewed from the back, is illuminated from the upper left by sunlight entering the room and casts a shadow in the foreground on the right. To the right of the easel there is a door leading to the staircase. The studio, a room with bare wooden floorboards and cracked and flaking plastered walls, is remarkably sparsely furnished. On the left behind the painter we see a plain worktable on which stand a glass bottle, an earthenware jug and an earthenware pot, undoubtedly containing linseed oil and other materials for making paint. To the artist's right, balanced on a section of tree trunk, is half a boulder, used as a grinding slab for preparing paint. Above this grindstone two clean palettes hang on a nail in the wall.

Until it was discovered and restored in 1925, this little panel existed in an enlarged form, with additions at the top and bottom to turn it into portrait format. This was probably done in the eighteenth century to make the painting the same size as *Travellers Resting* (cat. no. 65), with which, according to old sale catalogues, it formed a pair until well into the nineteenth century.[1] Although the painting is neither signed nor dated, the attribution to Rembrandt is generally accepted.[2] There is also remarkable unanimity about dating it to 1629 (but see below). In the past, opinions on the question as to which painter is portrayed here – Rembrandt or someone else in his studio – were briefly divided.[3] Comparison of the painter's features – only roughly indicated here – with early self portraits by Rembrandt[4] make it highly likely that this is Rembrandt himself, but it is not entirely certain.

Only a limited number of colours are used in the painting – predominantly grey, yellow and brown – but in an extraordinarily broad range of shades. The use of colour is reminiscent of Rembrandt's paintings of 1627/28, particularly *Simeon in the Temple* in Hamburg (cat. no. 30). The application of the paint is extremely sure and tailored in each passage to the rendition of the surface concerned. As is usually the case, the covering of paint is thickest in the light passages, while the paint in the areas of shadow is applied much more thinly. The shadows on the plastered wall are painted with broad brushstrokes. Details like the cracks in the wooden floorboards, the door and the easel are painted in a transparent dark paint over the ochre ground.

The space is remarkably clearly defined – certainly when we compare it with paintings dating from 1629 and later, in which the background is usually much less distinct. In this, and in the way in which the light shining through a window and falling on the rear wall is used to enhance the effect of depth, the studio scene again bears a striking resemblance to paintings like *Simeon in the Temple* or ‹*La main chaude*› (cat. no. 62). Although Rembrandt was already using repoussoir figures in the foreground in his very earliest paintings, we find repoussoirs in the foreground that are strongly lit from behind primarily in works dating from c. 1628 and later, such as ‹*La main chaude*› (cat. no. 62), *The Flight into Egypt* (cat. no. 60) and *Supper in Emmaus* in Paris (s. p. 75, fig. 27). In view of the above similarities to Rembrandt's painted work of c. 1627/28 and the differences between this panel and work dating from 1629, the painting may be dated slightly earlier than has thus far been the case, namely c. 1628.

At first sight, the painter's costume raises questions about the level of reality of the scene. In addition to some extremely fashionable accessories, like the flat ruff and the broad-brimmed hat, both in vogue at the end of the 1620s, the painter also wears a tabard (which is slightly too large for him) of a type that looks rather old-fashioned. According to Marieke de Winkel, this type of tabard can be dated to around

61a
Rembrandt Harmensz.
van Rijn, *The Painter in His
Studio* (detail), c. 1628

1610 and, given the long useful life of an expensive item of clothing like this, it is not unlikely that Rembrandt bought it second-hand and – with the sash, which does not belong with this garment, tied around the middle – used it as his everyday working attire.[5] In later self-portraits, too, Rembrandt often wears a tabard-style coat with a sash tied round the waist as his working clothes (see for instance the ‹large› Vienna *Self-portrait*). It is therefore quite possible that Rembrandt faithfully portrays himself here just as he used to dress when he was at work in his studio.

The spartan studio also seems to have been depicted as it actually was. Whereas many studio scenes contain weapons, books, classical statues and other attributes that refer to various aspects of the painters' profession, such props are notable by their absence from Rembrandt's studio piece. In this respect it is all the more remarkable that there is no chair in front of the easel. In the seventeenth century painters sat down to work, and the fact that this was also the case in Rembrandt's studio is tellingly illustrated by the worn areas on the lower strut of the easel, where the painter rested his feet as he worked. However, the very bareness of the room could provide one of the keys to the interpretation of the painting.

Ernst van de Wetering has explained the absence of the chair and the great distance between the painter and his easel by suggesting that the artist is shown here *prior to* rather than *during* the work of painting, while he is engaged in forming a picture in his mind of the scene he wants to paint.[6] Seventeenth-century art theoreticians discussed the creative process that preceded the actual work of painting; they praised the painter who worked on the basis of a concept (*idea*) developed beforehand in his mind, as against the painter who was led by chance (*fortuna*) or by routine (*usus*). It was just at the time when Rembrandt painted this self portrait that he came into contact with learned connoisseurs like Constantijn Huygens, who must have been very familiar with art theoretical *concetti* of this kind and most probably discussed them with the artist. The fact that this studio scene, so down to earth and workmanlike at first sight, seems to conceal an elevated art theoretical conceit, creates a paradox that an erudite humanist like Huygens would certainly have been able to appreciate.

B.v.d.B.

1  Corpus, vol. 1, 1982, pp. 212f.
2  Corpus, vol. 1, 1982, p. 211.
3  Ibid.; Wetering 1991/92b.
4  Cf. London/The Hague 1999/2000, nos. 1–15.
5  Information kindly supplied by Marieke de Winkel in conversation. Cf. London/The Hague 1999/2000, pp. 65–67.
6  Wetering 1976; Wetering 1997, pp. 75–89.

## 62
## Rembrandt Harmensz. van Rijn
# Interior with Figures, called ‹La main chaude›, c. 1628

Oak panel, 21 x 27 cm
The National Gallery of
Ireland, Dublin,
Inv. No. 439

Bauch 1960, pp. 243–245;
Brown 1984, pp. 205, 211;
Potterton 1986, no. 439,
pp. 127–129

Several figures are seen in a dark space, illuminated by an artificial light source. The figure seated before a table on the left in the foreground shields the viewer from the light source, so that this figure with a large, loose hat is outlined as a dark silhouette. On the other side of the table is a second man who holds a pipe in his hand and has a jug of wine before him. On the right, by the staircase, a violin player sits against a pillar. In the background, two vaguely delineated figures can be recognised, possibly a man with his arm round a woman. Of the two clearly lit figures in the middle, one has turned his back to the other while this latter has raised his hand as though about to slap the first. A third figure can be made out as a dark silhouette to the right of the bending figure.

In 1904 the subject of the scene was identified as the game «La main chaude», and since then the panel has been known under this title.[1] The idea of the game (which in the Netherlands was called *handjeklap*) is that one of the players turns his back to the others and, with eyes shut, holds one hand behind his back, palm uppermost. At a given moment one of the other players has to slap his hand (or his backside). If the ‹victim› can guess who slapped him, the latter must take his place; if he fails to identify who slapped him he stays for another round. In the present painting, the victim is cheating; instead of shutting his eyes, he is trying to spy which of the two other players is going to hit him.

It is evident from the many paintings of such scenes by genre painters like Jan Miense Molenaer and Cornelis de Man that this party game enjoyed a certain popularity in the Netherlands of the seventeenth century (fig. 62a). Apparently, according to these paintings, the game was usually played rather differently from the Dublin panting. In most of these paintings, the player to be slapped lays his head in the lap of a woman. The deeper significance of the game when played in this manner is to be found in the caption of an emblem in Johannes de Brune's *Emblemata ofte Zinne-Werck* of 1624, which reads: «a whore's lap is the devil's vessel» (Een hoeren schoot is duyvels boot).[2] In the commentary to the emblem the woman's lap is associated with the seductive but deceitful Delilah, who brought Samson to his ruin by cutting off his hair, in which lay the secret of his strength, while he slept in her lap. Apparently the game and its depiction could be construed as a moralistic warning against the enticements of beautiful but loose women.

The question is whether seventeenth-century players would themselves have been aware of this connotation whilst playing the game. In one of the paintings by Jan Miense Molenaer, the game is played exclusively by women; while in another the (male) ‹victim› lays his head in the lap of another man. In this regard, there seem to have been no fixed rules; it was played more for the crude fun of slapping and guess-

ing who had slapped. The painter of the painting discussed here seems to have limited himself to this banal essence of the game.

Although the game is central in the Dublin painting, it is not the only action represented. Given the context of men smoking, drinking and making music, this painting is not so much about the seductions of loose women but more about depicting a certain social behaviour which, unchecked, could lead to excess. The game would then stand for a rather pointless way of spending time, which furthermore is itself being undermined by the peeping player who tries to see who is about to slap him.

The attribution of the painting, exhibited in the National Gallery of Ireland as a work from the «Rembrandt-School», has been disputed since its discovery. For Kurt Bauch, the fact that the subject of this painting deviated from what he took to be the tradition of a game that was already played in the Middle Ages was sufficient to exclude an attribution to Rembrandt.[3] It is interesting to read how Bauch in his 1960 book on the young Rembrandt refused to allow the painting into his Rembrandt image. Having described the composition, he wrote: «All this speaks decisively against the possibility of Rembrandt being the author of the painting. ‹Genre-like›, unclear, fewer main figures than subsidiary figures, and this pure *staffage*; all of this is unlike him [Rembrandt].»[4]

Although the work was bought in 1896 as a Willem de Poorter, Duncan had already written in 1906 that it «is so far above that painter's [De Poorter's] usual work in imagination and quality and has so much in common with the earliest works of Rembrandt, especially the *Reposo* [see cat. no. 65] at The Hague, that the possibility that it, too, should have the greater name below it lingers in the mind.»[5] Like Duncan, later scholars like Benesch, Naumann and Haverkamp-Begemann also pointed out that an attribution to Rembrandt should certainly not be excluded. Otto Benesch – in an article from 1940 that was hardly noted – already attributed the painting to Rembrandt.[6] In Ernst van de Wetering's essay «Delimiting Rembrandt's Autograph Œuvre – an Insoluble Problem?», he argues in favour of the attribution of ‹La main chaude› to Rembrandt. Not only on the basis of style but also in view of the male fashion displayed it seems likely that this sketchily executed work should be dated to 1628-29.[7]                                E.v.d.W./M.d.W.

[1]   Potterton 1986, p. 128.
[2]   Mentioned and illustrated in Bauch 1960, p. 244.
[3]   «Dies alles spricht entschieden gegen Rembrandt als Schöpfer des Bildes. ‹Genrehaft› unklar, weniger Haupt- als Nebenpersonen und diese reine Staffage, das gibt es bei ihm [Rembrandt] nicht.» Bauch 1960, p. 243, note 208.
[4]   Bauch 1960, p. 244.
[5]   Potterton 1986, p. 128.
[6]   Potterton 1986, p. 128. Haverkamp-Begemann communicated his view orally. Benesch 1940, esp. p. 6. Prof. Dr. Egbert Haverkamp-Begemann kindly informed the authors of this entry about Benesch's opinion when this text was ready for print.
[7]   See above, pp. 58–90.

## 63
## Circle of Rembrandt Harmensz. van Rijn
# Scholar in a Lofty Room, c. 1628/29

Oak panel, 55.1 x 46.5 cm
(Falsely) signed to the
right (on the staircase):
*Rem.randt*
The National Gallery,
London, Inv. No. 3214

Bredius/Gerson 1969, no.
427; Corpus, vol. 1, 1982,
no. C 14

On a dais towards the rear on the left of a very high-ceilinged room, with a tall window reaching to the ceiling on the left, a man sits at a writing table with a large book lying open on it. The space is largely shrouded in darkness and semi-darkness, particularly the foreground and the right side of the scene. The light of a lowering sun enters through the high casement window on the left. The left-hand shutter is closed. The light falls on the plastered rear wall of the room, on which the shadows of the window frame and the closed shutter are suggested very evocatively. The window and the illuminated area of the wall occupy more than a third of the total area of the picture. Because the man sits in front of the closed left shutter and is consequently lit from behind, he is shown in silhouette, as is the table with the book in front of him. On a wall on the right of the room there are shelves on which books, papers and globes – attributes that identify the man as a scholar – can be discerned. The curved outline of a spiral staircase leading upwards can just be made out on the right.

The use of colour is very limited: the painting is predominantly executed in shades of grey. The paint is thickly applied, with irregular brushstrokes that contribute little to the modelling of the forms. The lit area of the wall is painted with heavy impasto and rough streaks of paint, very successfully conveying the optical effect of a plastered wall. The edges of the plaster where it meets the window frame, like the hinges in the window, are indicated with deep incisions in the paint.

It is interesting to see how the artistic innovations that Rembrandt (to some extent in collaboration with Lievens) achieved at the end of the 1620s were rapidly adopted by artists in his immediate circle. It is noticeable that these artists – who, we may assume, were pupils in his studio – seem to have concentrated on the most eye-catching, but at the same time most superficial elements of these artistic advances. When, for example, we look at the subtle light effects that Rembrandt introduced to maintain plasticity and spatial values in the depiction of half-dark rooms and the carefully considered light effects to heighten the drama of the scene, it is very apparent that his pupils only tried out the most spectacular effects and had little understanding of the subtlety or the thought pro-

cesses behind these solutions. We therefore see them especially exploring the possibilities of extreme chiaroscuro, with backlit effects and dramatic silhouettes as repoussoir (cf. cat. nos. 59 and 65).

In *Scholar in a Lofty Room*, the silhouette effect is similarly used as an important pictorial device. The extreme to which this is taken – and the limited functionality – betray an imitator exploiting a manifestly successful effect to the utmost. Another Rembrandtesque light effect has also been very obviously used: the light entering from the upper left through a window and falling on a plastered wall – a device that Rembrandt introduced in paintings like *St Paul in Prison* in Stuttgart of 1627 (p. 216, fig. 30a) and *Simeon in the Temple* in Hamburg of

1627/28 (cat. no. 30). Rembrandt uses this effect with immense subtlety to enhance the sense of space and heighten the drama of the scene. The almost grotesque prominence of this effect in the London painting creates the impression that the piece was made for the sole purpose of demonstrating this effect in its most extreme form.

The attribution of this painting to Rembrandt had never seriously been called into question until the *Rembrandt Research Project* described the work as a late Rembrandt imitation.[1] Aside from stylistic considerations, the *RRP* regarded the unusual nature of the support as an important reason for not accepting the work as authentic. The panel is made up of three horizontal boards of unequal width and thickness,

63a
Circle of Rembrandt
Harmensz. van Rijn,
*Scholar in a Lofty Room*
(detail), c. 1628/29

314

which are moreover fastened together with a scarf joint – unusual for a Dutch panel.[2] Dendrochronological examination revealed that the timber is early seventeenth century and originates from the Southern Low Countries, where this particular joint is quite often found in paintings. The *RRP* concluded from this that the painting was probably made in the Southern Low Countries.[3] Since it is entirely possible that this was a Flemish panel that was reused, this argument cannot be regarded as conclusive as far as the origin of the painting is concerned. The *RRP* also suggests, without any real argumentation, a date at the end of the seventeenth or beginning of the eighteenth century.[4]

Although the *RRP* was very confident in placing the painting outside Rembrandt's circle and identifying it as a late pastiche,[5] the work does not appear to possess either stylistic or technical features that would rule out a date at the end of the 1620s. The ‹restless› manner of painting, although far less accomplished and effective in its execution, is very similar to that in Rembrandt's paintings of the 1628–29 period. We also find the light effects, used more subtly and – again – more effectively, in Rembrandt's paintings dating from these years. And although in terms of painting we can see all sort of things in the work, on the right-hand side we can identify the same endeavour to achieve a convincing expression of objects in a darkened room as can be seen in Rembrandt's paintings of this period. There is consequently a lot to be said for dating the painting to around 1628/29

and attributing it to a painter in Rembrandt's immediate circle.

Both the date and the likelihood that this painter was a pupil in Rembrandt's studio are supported by the remarkable similarities in pose, lighting and positioning in the space between the reading scholar in *Scholar in a Lofty Room* and the scribe on the left, who leans forward and likewise reads a book, in *Three Scribes* (cat. no. 34), one of the preliminary drawings for Rembrandt's principal work during his Leiden period, *Judas Repentant, Returning the Thirty Pieces of Silver* of 1628/29 (cat. no. 33). This scribe, leaning forward over the table and the book in front of him, was also actually painted by Rembrandt, but later transformed into the elder furthest to the left in the painting. This change meant that the table and the book, which originally occupied a more central place in the painting, were moved to the left. Given the similarities, the painter of *Scholar in a Lofty Room* must have seen this passage in *Judas Repentant* before the final changes to the painting were made. This makes it very probable that the maker of the painting was himself working in Rembrandt's studio in 1628/29.     B.v.d.B.

[1]  Corpus, vol. 1, 1982, pp. 529–532.
[2]  Corpus, vol. 1, 1982, p. 529.
[3]  Corpus, vol. 1, 1982, p. 532.
[4]  Ibid.
[5]  Ibid. «An imitation that must be placed well outside Rembrandt's own circle, and showing none of the marks of his school in either style or execution.»

## 64
## Circle of Rembrandt Harmensz. van Rijn
# Bust of an Old Woman (Rembrandt's Mother?), c. 1628/29

Oak panel, 35.4 x 28.9 cm
Private Collection

Bredius/Gerson 1969,
no. 64; Corpus, vol. 1,
1982, no. C 42

The old woman in this painting is traditionally referred to as ‹Rembrandt's mother›. She is a model whom Rembrandt and artists in his immediate circle like Lievens and Dou repeatedly portrayed in paintings, prints and drawings. The custom of interpreting women's heads of this type as ‹Rembrandt's mother› has been subjected to unusual critical evaluation in recent years. The result has been that pictures which have for centuries been known as ‹Rembrandt's mother› are now usually referred to as the neutral ‹An Old Woman›. On the other hand, one of Rembrandt's finest portrait etchings, which undoubtedly depicts the same woman[1] (fig. 64a), is listed as ‹Rembrandt's mother› in the 1679 inventory of the print dealer

Clement de Jonghe – who knew Rembrandt personally and owned no fewer than 74 of his etching plates. There are consequently compelling grounds for continuing to regard the old woman in this painting as Rembrandt's mother, Neeltgen Willemsdr. van Zuytbroeck.

The woman is dressed in a black, fur-trimmed cloak. Beneath it she wears a red bodice and a white shift with an upstanding embroidered collar. Her head is covered by a black shawl that falls to her shoulders. The old, wrinkled face is brightly lit from the left side, accentuating the unevenness of the skin. She is placed against a dull grey background. Details like the wrinkles in the face and the stitching of the collar are indicated with striking scratches in the paint.

Fig. 64a
Rembrandt Harmensz.
van Rijn, *Rembrandts
Mother, Sitting at a Table*,
c. 1631
Etching, 149 x 131 mm
Bartsch 343, state II (3)
Museum het
Rembrandthuis,
Amsterdam

The paint in the most strongly lit areas of the face is applied with heavy impasto and rather coarse, uncontrolled brushstrokes, which contribute little if anything to a convincing modelling of the physiognomic details. The surface-mimicking application of the paint that Rembrandt used for areas of wrinkled skin is absent or has been ineptly used. As a result, the head lacks the plasticity that we usually find in Rembrandt's paintings. The same is true of the modelling of the folds and the execution of the clothes. We will search in vain in Rembrandt's paintings for parallels for the many broad scratches in the paint with which details of the clothing and the face are drawn. Scratches do occur in Rembrandt's paintings from the very earliest onwards – for example in the foreground on the right in *The Baptism of the Eunuch* (cat. no. 3) and in the hair and beards in the Leiden *History Painting* (cat. no. 7). But

Abb. 64b
Anonymous after Rembrandt
Harmensz. van Rijn,
*Bust of an Old Woman*
Etching, 79 x 63 mm
Bartsch 353
Rijksmuseum,
Amsterdam

Abb. 64c
Rembrandt Harmensz.
van Rijn, *Rembrandts
Mutter (en face)*, 1628
Etching, 63 x 64 mm
Bartsch 352, state II (2)
Museum het Rembrandthuis,
Amsterdam

Rembrandt uses these marks, scored with the end of the brush so that the light brown ground is exposed, only to swiftly accentuate a detail (such as the highlights on the tips of hairs) or to make the expression of the surface of a material more convincing with a few rapid scratches. The linear way in which the details have been drawn in this painting with the aid of scratches is foreign to Rembrandt.

On the basis of these departures from Rembrandt's style and technique, the *Rembrandt Research Project* described the painting as a late seventeenth-century Rembrandt imitation.[2] The late date suggested by the *RRP* rests, among other things, on the assumption that the painting is based on an etching of the bust of an old woman, which was previously attributed to Rembrandt but is now regarded as the work of a late seventeenth-century follower (fig. 64b).[3] The *RRP* does not consider the possibility that this print, with which the painting does indeed share compositional elements, might actually be based on the painting. In terms of physiognomy, there is in any event a stronger similarity between the painting and an etching by Rembrandt dated 1628 with which the painting has often been linked[4] (fig. 64c).

Another consideration that led the *RRP* to the suggested late dating is the unusual style of a painting which X-rays have revealed is concealed under the present layer of paint.[5] We can see the bust of a man with mid-length hair and a beret with a feather. This picture displays strong similarities to Rembrandt's tronies of men in plumed caps from the 1620s, such as *Bust of a Man in a Gorget and a Cap* of c. 1626/27 (cat. no. 74).

The random, inconsistent application of the paint and the drawing-like way in which scratches in the paint are used for the details are common to *Bust of an Old Woman*, *Scholar in a Lofty Room* in London (cat. no. 63) and *Travellers Resting* (cat. no. 65). These three paintings, which can probably all be attributed to the same painter, have been ‹detached› as a group from Rembrandt's authentic œuvre, as Ernst van de Wetering puts it.[6] The *RRP* placed this group of three far outside Rembrandt's circle and even stated categorically that they must be late Rembrandt imitations. Since it can be plausibly argued that *Scholar in a Lofty Room* was made by a painter working in Rembrandt's studio around 1628/29 (see cat. no. 64), it is possible to trace back the history of the whole group to Rembrandt's studio at the end of the 1620s.          B.v.d.B.

[1]  Bartsch 343.
[2]  Corpus, vol. 1, 1982, p. 670.
[3]  Bartsch 353.
[4]  Ibid. Cf. White/Boon 1969, no. 352.
[5]  Corpus I, 1982, pp. 667–670, fig. 2.
[6]  Cf. the second essay by Ernst van de Wetering, p. 79.

## 65

Circle of Rembrandt
# Travellers Resting (The Rest on the Flight into Egypt?), c. 1629/30

Oil on paper, stuck on panel, 38 x 33.7 cm (Falsely) signed lower left: *Rembrandt.f* Royal Cabinet of Paintings Mauritshuis, The Hague, Cat. No. 579

Bredius/Gerson 1969, no. 556; The Hague 1977, p. 200, no. 579; Corpus, vol. 1, 1982, no. C 12

Seen through a stone arch at night, a small group of travellers sits by a fire at the foot of the walls of a city or castle. On the left to the rear we see the base of a round tower with a barred window and large cracks in the stonework. The fire, which is concealed by the silhouette of a figure with a stick on the right of the arch, is the only source of light in the scene. It casts deep shadows on the wall and the tower, while the right foreground is shrouded in darkness. The central group of figures, who are brightly lit by the fire, consists of a seated woman holding a swaddled baby in her arms and a man with a floppy travelling hat, half hidden behind her, who lies resting with his head pillowed on his hand. Behind this group, under a ramshackle wooden lean-to, stands a riding animal, probably a horse, and a sleeping man can be made out in the bundle of cloth lying against the wall. The meaning of this nocturnal scene is not entirely clear. The nineteenth-century title *The Rest on the Flight into Egypt* was replaced in the early twentieth century with the more neutral

*Travellers Resting*, because the number of figures depicted and the setting seemed irreconcilable with the traditional iconography of the apocryphal biblical subject – the Holy Family seated beside a donkey in a rural setting, without any supernumeraries (cf. cat. no. 13). The central group on which the majority of the light falls is, however, so very similar to one of the known pictorial types of the Holy Family that there are good grounds for supposing that this does after all represent the rest on the flight into Egypt. To this there appear to have been added various elements that traditionally belong to the iconography of the Adoration of the Shepherds, such as the way that all attention is focused on the child, the location in a stable-like setting and the figure with the stick in the opening of the arch, who closely resembles a shepherd with a crook entering the stable. Rather than a spot in the wilderness, Joseph and Mary appear to have chosen a more sheltered place to spend the night on their journey into Egypt, and in this, while it may depart

65a
Circle of Rembrandt
Harmensz. van Rijn,
*Travellers Resting (The Rest
on the Flight into Egypt?)*
(detail), c. 1629/30

from the traditional iconography, a certain travellers' logic cannot be denied. In terms of local colour, the painting has something in common with the picturesque genre pieces from the 1620s by painters working in Rome like Cornelis van Poelenburgh and Pieter van Laer, which likewise often show small groups of common people by a city wall or under the stone arches of ancient ruins.

The work is painted in oils on paper. This paper was subsequently stuck on to a panel, which probably dates from the mid seventeenth century.[1] The painting thus has the same sort of support as the *Supper in Emmaus* in Paris of

1628/29 (p. 75, fig. 27), with which it also shows remarkable similarities in the treatment of the light. As in the Paris piece, there is a figure in the right foreground in front of a concealed light source, who appears as a dramatic silhouette against the strong backlighting. Where this light has an obvious function in *Supper in Emmaus*, namely to emphasise the supernatural character of the risen Christ and thus make the strong reaction of his supper companions understandable to the viewer, the silhouetted figure in the Hague painting seems intended solely as a repoussoir to reinforce the effect of depth. This deliberate use of a proven light effect, but without the functionality that the use of such an effect always has in Rembrandt's work, is just one of the things that the painting has in common with *Scholar in a Lofty Room* in London (cat. no. 63).

There are several other stylistic and technical similarities between *Travellers Resting* and the London painting, such as the restricted palette (the painting is almost monochrome, in shades of grey, yellow and brown), the coarse modelling of the forms using irregular brushstrokes and, above all, the drawing-like use of scratches in the paint to render details like cracks in the wall or highlights. *Travellers Resting* also has this technique in common with *Bust of an Old Woman* (cat. no. 64), although the latter shows scratches which are broader and executed with less finesse than those in the Hague painting. As Ernst van de Wetering remarks elsewhere in this book, on technical and stylistic grounds these three paintings can be regarded as a group by one and the same artist – who for the moment remains anonymous – and this group has been as it were ‹detached› from Rembrandt's œuvre.[2] Although the *Rembrandt Research Project* identified similarities in the treatment of light and the handling of cracks in the stonework between this work and paintings by Rembrandt like *Supper in Emmaus* and *The Painter in His Studio* in Boston of c. 1628 (cat. no. 61), the painting, together with the other two in the group, is described as a late seventeenth-century imitation.[3] However, since it can be convincingly argued that *Scholar in a Lofty Room* was made in Rembrandt's studio in about 1629 (cf. cat. no. 63), *Travellers Resting* may be regarded as a work from the same year.

B.v.d.B.

[1] Corpus, vol. 1, 1982, p. 519.
[2] Cf. the second essay by Ernst van de Wetering, p. 79.
[3] Corpus, vol. 1, 1982, p. 522.

## 66
Rembrandt Harmensz. van Rijn and Gerard Dou (Leiden 1613–1675)(?)
## Prince Rupert of the Palatinate and his Tutor as Eli Instructing Samuel, c. 1631

Canvas, 102.9 x 88.2 cm
The J. Paul Getty
Museum, Los Angeles,
Inv. No. 84.PA.570

Schneider 1932, p. 32;
Gelder 1953a, p. 37;
Sumowski 1983ff., vol. 1,
no. 244; Brown 1983;
Baer 1990, pp. 26–28

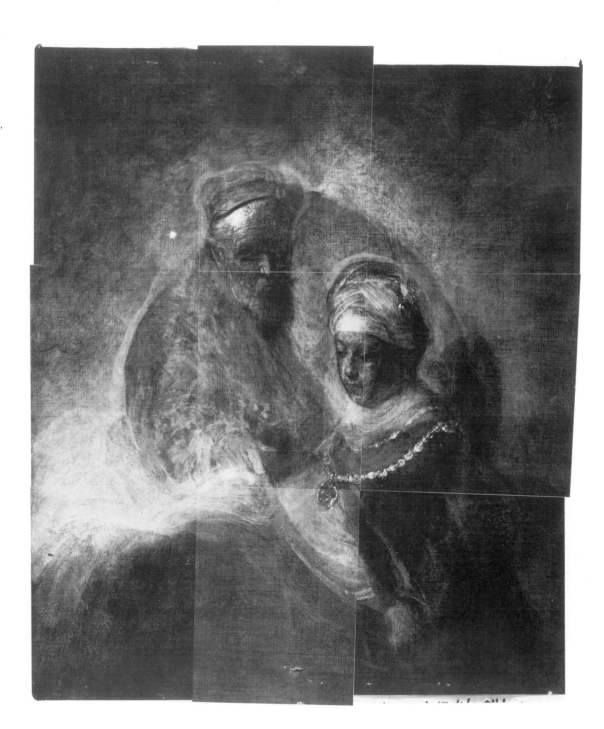

Fig. 66b
X-ray of cat. no. 66

A bearded old man in a velvet gown trimmed with fur and wearing a cap is teaching a boy. Together they are both gazing intently at a large folio. The older man appears to be pointing to a passage in the text. The youth is dressed in an oriental outfit consisting of a grey caftan with a sash and a purple velvet cloak. There are two chains around his neck on which hang a medal and a colourful scarf. On his head he wears a turban decorated with an *aigrette* of heron feathers and a jewel. The folio lies on a lectern covered with an oriental cloth. A reflection from the illuminated pages, invisible to the viewer, creates a sheen on the sleeve of the old man's velvet gown.

On the basis of the provenance and of an eighteenth-century description, this work was convincingly identified by Christopher Brown in 1983 as a portrait of Prince Rupert of the Palatinate (1619–1682) with a tutor, whose identity is unknown.[1] The pendant of the painting (of almost identical measurements) shows Rupert's elder brother Charles Louis of the Palatinate (1617–1680) together with his tutor Wolrad von Plessen (Fig. 66a). This second, closely comparable composition is by Jan Lievens and bears Lievens' monogram on the arm of the chair, together with the date 1631.

Rupert and Charles Louis were the two eldest surviving sons of the Elector Frederick V and Elizabeth Stuart, the deposed king and queen of Bohemia, who since 1619 had been living in exile at the Orange court in The Hague. Their many children were accommodated in the Prinsenhof in Leiden, where the eldest sons were enrolled in 1628 at Leiden University. Because neither prince is in contemporary dress but in oriental and classical costumes, respectively, it would seem an obvious assumption that these paintings are *portraits histories*. The painters seem to have complied with the taste of the princes' parents, who seemed to have prefer to have themselves and their children portrayed in this fashion.[2] Charles Louis, in his heavy gold satin tunic and laurel wreath, appears to have been painted as the young Alexander the Great with his tutor Aristotle, while Rupert's oriental turban puts one more in mind of a similar kind of subject from the Old Testament: the young prophet Samuel with his teacher Eli (1 Sam 1:24). For the sake of brevity, the painting will be referred to as *Eli Instructing Samuel*.

In the eighteenth century it was thought that the two pendants had to be attributed to Rembrandt; but once the Lievens monogram had been discovered on one of them, it was then assumed that they were both from Lievens' hand.[3] Following Schneider's rejection in 1932 of the attribution of *Eli Instructing Samuel* to Lievens, in 1953 Van Gelder tentatively described the work as a Rembrandtesque composition by either Dou or possibly Jan van Vliet.[4] At that time, the possibility was entertained that Jan van Vliet might have been trained by Rembrandt as a painter, even though we only know him as a graphic artist who collaborated closely with Rembrandt as the maker of repro-

Fig. 66a
Jan Lievens, *Portrait of Charles Louis of the Palatinate with his tutor Wolrad von Plessen as Aristotle instructing the young Alexander*, 1631
Canvas, 106 x 96 cm
The J. Paul Getty Museum, Los Angeles

duction prints after his early works.[5] The idea of Dou was undoubtedly suggested by the highly polished and meticulously detailed execution of the *Eli Instructing Samuel*. Only the illuminated side of the oriental cloth on which the book lies is painted differently, with the floral decoration indicated by very freely executed scratchings in the wet paint and additional free brushwork.

Until 1636, the year of his first dated painting, we have only an extremely vague image of the young Dou, and any attribution of this painting to him must therefore be tentative. This was also the reason that Ronni Baer entered clear reservations with regard to its attribution to

Gerard Dou in her œuvre catalogue.[6] Her most important arguments against the attribution were that Dou, throughout his entire career, painted small-scale figures on panel, whereas here, full-scale figures are painted on canvas.[7] Furthermore, she found it difficult to accept that this painting could have been the work of an 18-year-old youth. It seems obvious that the painting must have originated at the same time as the Lievens work considered to be its pendant, viz. 1631.

Baer's hesitation is understandable. The monumental conception of the painting with the complex torsion in the figure of Eli is not what one expects of a beginner. Van Gelder's surmise that one is dealing here with a Rembrandtesque work executed by Dou (or possibly by some other pupil) would seem to us nearest the mark. One can already see on the paint surface, in a long narrow gap between the background and the outline of Eli's back, a light paint of varying tone, indicating that the painting has undergone a complicated genesis. This is confirmed by X–ray analysis (fig. 66b), which shows a number of radical differences from what is visible at the paint surface. This underlying stage of the genesis of the work, as will become apparent, strongly evokes associations with Rembrandt's pictorial preoccupations between 1629 and 1632. Both the style and the temperament of the underlying brushstrokes show a strong affinity with those of Rembrandt. Thus there are grounds for suggesting the idea that Rembrandt began the work and that it was subsequently finished by someone from his studio, whose style is so reminiscent of Dou that Rembrandt's work, apart from the oriental cloth, was almost totally painted out.

This would not be the first painting from Rembrandt's studio, we believe, to have passed through a similar genesis.[8] The reasons why Rembrandt occasionally let others finish his work may differ from one instance to another; but certainly Rembrandt did have a tendency to leave work unfinished. Houbraken writes: «One thing is regrettable, that he was so liable to change, or driven towards something else, that he left many things only half finished.»[9] In this case, however, it must have been a commission, undoubtedly a commission from the circles of stadholder's court. It is therefore tempting to speculate on the reason why Rembrandt wanted or possibly had to stop working on this painting. From a later source, we know how irritable Rembrandt could be with his patrons when it came to portraits.[10] One of his rare portraits of children remained unfinished.[11] In other words, did portraits of children perhaps not suit him? Or was it the case with

this particular *portrait historié* that he pursued the history piece too far at the expense of the kind of decorum the portrait of a prince demanded? One can speculate endlessly over the reason why the work was completed by someone else in a markedly different form.

In the following analysis of this picture's genesis, the idea that we are dealing with a work begun by Rembrandt and very probably finished by the young Dou will serve as a point of departure in the hope that further observations may enhance the plausibility of this hypothesis.

First of all, one needs an idea of what Rembrandt's initial conception of this painting must have been. The X-ray shows a number of important differences from what is now to be seen. Firstly, the forehead of the old man was strongly lit. The cap, which is now pulled so far forward that it casts a shadow over the forehead and partially over the illuminated eye, was originally placed such that light fell on the front side of the skull. The paint, containing lead white, has apparently been laid on thickly. There are several paintings by Rembrandt from this period, including the *Jeremiah* of 1630 and the *Old Man with a Cap* from the Bader collection (cat. no. 80), where Rembrandt employed this particular means of locally heightening the illumination in a painting. It must have been one of the pictorial techniques with which he was preoccupied around 1630, which has to be seen in the context of Rembrandt's lifelong pursuit of a hierarchy in the values of light and tone in his paintings that would guide the viewer's gaze. It is interesting to speculate on the question of why Dou placed the cap such that the intensity of the light falling on the old man is much reduced. One possibility is that now, as a result of Dou's intervention, the strongest light falls on Prince Rupert, not on his tutor. Such an interpretation of this change could well indicate the interference of a patron, which, as suggested above, may at the same time explain why Rembrandt passed the work over to someone else.

A second radical difference with the painting in its current state is that both figures were originally placed in front of an arched bay. The boy's shadow was originally left reserved in this architectonic structure. Dou has replaced this with a more neutral background graduating from dark to light, with the boy's shadow vaguely indicated to his right. The choice of a background with indications of architecture is frequently seen in Rembrandt's early œuvre. He probably employed this often rather rustic architectural background to enable him to introduce steps in the hierarchy of light and tone mentioned above. Rembrandt's choice of such a background in this painting may also have to do with the *portrait historié* character of the painting. The demand for more decorum in the portrait, on the other hand, could have been the reason for the radical changes in the background.

The X-ray image also shows differences in the hand of the old man and a possible indication of Rupert's left hand. The tutor's hand was originally more foreshortened. The index finger pointed more to the fore, the thumb in the direction of the boy. If one compares the position of the earlier hand with the placing of the medal, the extent of the change becomes clear. The wrist has remained in the same place, but the hand has now been directed downwards by Dou. It also becomes clear that the corner of the folio was placed considerably higher than now. The gesture of pointing *into* the book must initially have been much clearer; now the old man merely points, as it were, along the book.

The light spot on the place where the armrest of Rupert's/Samuel's chair now is may be read as the illuminated back of the prince's hand with the base of the thumb that grips the armrest. The need to paint a hand there becomes obvious when one sees in the painting, in its present state, how odd it is that neither of the boy's hands is visible.

It will be clear that the aspects so far discussed of the underlying version of the composition already allow us to perceive a pictorial conception much more daring and spatially more interesting than is offered by the painting in its present form. The changes implemented by the final working of the painting diminish the more adventurous idea to a less baroque product. It would therefore not be surprising if these interventions were indeed the work of a still inexperienced though highly gifted painter such as the 18-year-old Dou.

The most Rembrandtesque element retained is the postural attitude of the old man with the splendid turning of the head relative to the trunk and the tilt of the body. This kind of attitude engaged Rembrandt both in early drawings and etchings and also, for example in a grisaille from 1633.[12] An etching from the same year that the painting is thought to have originated, 1631, shows the same carriage, though not so sophisticated as in the painting under discussion (fig. 66c). In the same etching Rembrandt also employs the flower motifs, executed in agitated, undulating scratches, that have been applied to the wet paint of the cloth on which the folio rests.

The passage in the X-ray left of the arm of the old man shows that characteristic quest pursued by Rembrandt for the relation between the form he presents and the illumination of the contiguous background. It is precisely in defining the role of light that one sees Rembrandt wrestling for the right solution, often tellingly documented in the X-ray image. In such passages one also sees how energetically Rembrandt pursued pictorial solutions. On the other hand, it is striking that in the X-ray image of Prince Rupert's head, only the lead white-containing highlights of the head as it now is can be seen. This would seem to indicate that Rembrandt had paid scarcely any attention to the prince's head when he passed the work over to Dou.

Some possible reasons have been suggested above that might explain why Rembrandt should have let the painting go. It is intriguing in this connection that these two important, closely-related commissions were not given to a single painter but to the two Leiden colleagues, possibly friends and rivals, Rembrandt and Lievens. It would not be the only time that they painted the same subject at the same time. Their *Christ on the Cross*[13] and their *Lazarus*[14] scenes are often thought to have originated in competition. This pair of *portraits histories* we are discussing could similarly have been painted as a contest. In the two other cited pairs of paintings, any such contest could have been proposed by the painters themselves, but here we are dealing with works undoubtedly done on commission. Should one speculate that perhaps the patron, or his representative, had conceived the idea of such a contest? It seems that connoisseurs of art were present at a painting contest held in Leiden or The Hague shortly before this, around 1629, between Jan van Goyen, François Knibbergen and Jan Porcellis[15], a contest described, though at second hand, by Samuel van Hoogstraten in 1678.[16] Constantijn Huygens, himself a connoisseur of

art, played Rembrandt and Lievens off against each other in his description of the two painters in his autobiography (see Appendix). It may be worth considering that he, as an important representative of the stadholder's Court, could well have been the one to transform the commission into a competition between Rembrandt and Lievens. It will always remain a mystery why Rembrandt gave up half way; but it must have been a charged moment when he did.                                          E.v.d.W.

[1] Brown 1983.
[2] See Judson/Ekkart 1999, nos. 343, 350, 244, 358, 365, 374, 380. In the same year, the electoral children were painted by Gerrit van Honthorst in classical dress in a group portrait as Diana with hunters, now in the Royal Collection in England. Judson/Ekkart 1999, no. 327.
[3] Brown 1983, p. 664.
[4] Schneider 1932, p. 32, note 1; Gelder 1953a, p. 37.
[5] Amsterdam 1996; Wetering 2000/01.
[6] Baer 1990, pp. 26–29.
[7] Baer 1990, p. 12.
[8] Ernst van de Wetering, «More than one hand in paintings by Rembrandt», Corpus, vol. 5, Chapter III, forthcoming.
[9] Houbraken, vol. 1, 1718, p. 258.
[10] See Strauss/Meulen 1979, doc. 1654/4.
[11] *Portrait of a Boy*, The Norton Simon Foundation, Pasadena, Bredius/Gerson 1969, no. 119.
[12] See Corpus, vol. 3, 1989, no. A 74.
[13] Lievens, *Christ on the Cross* 1631, Nancy. Sumowski 1983ff., vol. 3, no. 1245. Rembrandt, *Christ on the Cross*, Le Mas d'Agenais. Corpus, vol. 1, 1982, no. A 35.
[14] Lievens, *The Raising of Lazarus*, 1631, Brighton. Sumowski 1983ff., vol. 3, no. 1193. Rembrandt, *The Raising of Lazarus*, c. 1630, Los Angeles. Corpus, vol. 1, 1982, no. A 30.
[15] Wetering 1997, pp. 82–85.
[16] Hoogstraten 1678, pp. 237f.

## 67
### Circle of Gerard Dou (Leiden 1613–1675)
# The Return of Tobias and the Angel, c. 1635

Canvas, 108.5 x 143 cm
Signed with monogram
Private Collection, USA

Haak 1969, pp. 52f.;
Cevat 1973, pp. 83–88;
Corpus, vol 1, 1982, no.
C 4; Baer 1990, pp. 24–26

This painting depicts the apocryphal biblical story (Tob 11:9–10) of the young Tobias who, returning to his parents' home after a long journey, finds that his mother Anna and blind father Tobit have sunk into great poverty. Outside, in front of the house, the doorway to which is open, Anna embraces her son, whom she has believed dead but who has in the meantime married and become rich. His travelling companion, the archangel Rafael, dismounts from his ass.[1] The main figure in the composition is the aged, blind father Tobit, who tries to grope his way to the door but blunders into a chair.[2] This chair and the similarly overturned spinning wheel, spool and other equipment with which Anna ekes out a meagre living (cf. cat. no. 28), indicate the place where Anna had been sitting before she ran outside. In the background, to the left of the great open hearth, stands Tobit's chair; beside it lies one of his slippers, which in his haste he had no time to put on. The small white dog that had accompanied the son on his journey has rushed ahead and jumps up to greet his old master.[3]

This impressive painting is remarkably finely worked, and exceptionally close attention has been paid to creating a convincing representation of the many different materials. The brocade and satin of Tobit's worn and patched gown; the aged skin of his face, hands and feet, with their prominent veins; the wood, the earthenware, the bricks and plasterwork; the dog's coat, the cobwebs in the crumbling brickwork of the doorframe; and – above all – the state of decay into which the various materials have declined: all have been rendered with the greatest of care. A high point is the overturned chair, whose wood, cracked and worn smooth through long usage and bearing the traces of the different layers of paint that had once covered it, is reproduced in masterly fashion.

Tobit, Anna and their son Tobias had played a major role in Rembrandt's œuvre since 1626 (see also cat. no. 28).[4] Rembrandt had already depicted the figure of the aged Tobit stumbling to the door in one of his earliest etchings[5] (fig. 67a) in a fashion that – in mirror image – shows striking similarities with the main figure in the painting under discussion here. It is not so surprising, therefore, that there have always been voices calling for attribution of the painting to Rembrandt.

The monogram RL inscribed on the wooden staircase has naturally played an important role in discussions surrounding the attribution of the *Return of Tobias*, all the more so since it was scratched into soft paint. This could have been done immediately after the painting's completion, while the paint was still wet, as is seen, for example, in the case of the Amsterdam *Tobit and Anna* (cat. no. 28). However, the possibility cannot be ruled out that the already-dried paint was re-softened specifically in order for a fake monogram to be scratched into the surface. Indeed, the fact that the paint beneath the monogram has hardly been displaced would seem to imply that the inscription was added at a later date (see for instance cat. no. 34/I). The form of the monogram would seem to corroborate this suggestion. It differs significantly in several

Fig. 67a
Rembrandt, *Tobit Advancing to Welcome his Son*, c. 1629
Etching, plate 79 x 56 mm
Bartsch 153, state II
Rijksmuseum, Amsterdam

respects from Rembrandt's monograms from the Leiden period, the main difference being that the right-hand loop of the R sweeps upwards. The way the stem of the R below curls quite a way up is also unusual. On the basis of the photograph we have seen, a newly-discovered monogram in the lower left corner, wispily applied and with rather transparent paint, would seem to stand even less chance of being an inscription from Rembrandt's own hand.

In 1760 the painting was put up for auction in Amsterdam as a work of ‹Koedyck, no less detailed than by G. Dou›, and again in 1771 as a Dou.[6] In 1882 John Rutter wrote in his *An historical and descriptive sketch of Wardour Castle* (where the painting then was): «Supposed to be by Gerard Douw, but it is probably a Rembrandt, amongst whose etchings is one, in which the subject is treated in a manner strikingly similar to this» (fig. 67b).[7] From then on, the painting always appeared on the market as a Rembrandt, although the authors of œuvre catalogues have continued to exclude it from the canon of Rembrandt's works.

Attempts to explain the painting's singularity in terms of both its execution and format by seeing it as a collaborative product of Rembrandt and Dou, or Rembrandt and Lievens, are unconvincing. The suggestion of the *Rembrandt Research Project* that one might be looking at an imitation from the second half of the seventeenth century fares no better. Their attempt to date the painting to between 1660 and 1680 on the basis of the thread density of the canvas was thwarted by the results of subsequent *RRP* research on seventeenth-century canvases.[8]

If this is an early painting by Rembrandt himself, a position defended in the past by Cevat and Haak – and still maintained by some today – then Rembrandt would have been the first Leiden *Feinmaler*, virtually the immediate precursor of Frans van Mieris.[9] We would then be forced to revise our image of Rembrandt the artist quite radically. Indeed, the painting is only admissible as a work by Rembrandt if one accepts that he could have made just one foray in this artistic direction – in almost every respect different from his own – only to resume his previous course immediately afterwards. The difference from Rembrandt's style, even taking into account the latitude to be found there, is fundamental. In the period in which Rembrandt was profoundly preoccupied with the problem of rendering the surface appearance of different materials – in 1626 – he did this in an essentially different fashion (see cat. no. 22). Afterwards, the representation of light and space, increasingly coupled with a pursuit of a unity of composition, takes precedence. In Rembrandt's paintings, his working of the paint skin primarily serves these ends and does not, as in this painting, have an essentially descriptive purpose. The illusion in Rembrandt is evoked by *the whole* and not by the sum of the constituent parts, as is the case in the painting discussed here, however exceptionally finely the different elements are rendered. The association with Gerard Dou that has occurred to many has to do with this latter quality of the painting.

As outlined in the essay «Delimiting Rembrandt's Autograph Œuvre – an Insoluble Problem?», however, we have no clear picture of Dou's early work. Although he was intensely preoccupied with the ‹description› of the various materials, the Dou we know with reasonable certainty after 1636 also aimed at pictorial unity, as did Rembrandt; he also shared Rembrandt's strong feeling for the logic of illumination, something which is conspicuously lacking in this painting.[10] Given the quantity of often ambitious paintings resembling Dou that make it so difficult to delimit Dou's own œuvre, one could consider this to be a work from Dou's circle. The choice of subject and the conception of the figure of Tobit must have been influenced by Rembrandt's etchings (see figs. 67a and b). In its ambition – but also in the rather clumsy handling of perspective – the painting invites comparison with *The Old Painter at His Easel* in Milwaukee, without wishing necessarily to imply that this is by the same hand.[11] If the painting did originate in Dou's circle, a dating to the first half of the 1630s would seem most likely.

E.v.d.W./M.d.W.

[1] Tob 11:9: «And Anna ran unto him, and fell upon the neck of her son, and said unto him, I have seen thee, my child; from henceforth I will die. And they wept both.»
[2] Tob 11:10: «And Tobit went forth toward the door, and stumbled.»
[3] The dog was referred to as Tobias' travelling companion in Tobit 5:16 and returns in Tob 11:4.
[4] Held 1969, pp. 104–129.
[5] Bartsch 153.
[6] Sale B. Coymans, Amsterdam, 19 March 1760 and Sale Gerrit Braamcamp, Amsterdam, 31 July 1771; see Gelder 1953b, p. 252.
[7] Cevat 1973, p. 84, note 15 and Provenance in Corpus, vol. 1, 1982, no. C 4.
[8] Corpus, vol. 2, 1986, Chapter II «The canvas support», pp. 15–43.
[9] Haak 1969, pp. 52f.; Cevat 1973, pp. 83–88. For a recent attribution to Rembrandt, see research report of Dr. Gregory Wallace (manuscript received Sept. 2000).
[10] See also the reaction of van Regteren Altena in the discussion following Daan Cevat's lecture, see Cevat 1973, p. 90.
[11] Sumowski 1983ff., vol. 1, no. 270. According to Baer and Sluyter, the painting is not by Gerard Dou; see Baer 1990, pp. 29–31 with the reference to a letter from E.J. Sluyter.

## 68

Gerard Dou (Leiden 1613–1675) (?)

# A Leiden Militia Member with an Arms Still-life, c. 1630/35

Panel, 66 x 51 cm
Signed in the centre (on the barrel of the musket): *RHL (?)*
Szépművészeti Múzeum, Budapest, Inv. No. 62.10

Sumowski 1983ff., vol. 1, no. 268; Melbourne/ Canberra 1997/98, no. 38; Baer 1990, no. B1

According to the Leiden burgomaster and historiographer, Jan Jansz. Orlers, Gerard Dou (1613–1675) came to the 21-year-old Rembrandt as a pupil on 24 February 1628.[1] It is assumed that he continued to work in Rembrandt's studio until Rembrandt went to Amsterdam in 1631, after which he established himself as an independent artist in Leiden and – with his widely-admired, extremely precise manner – laid the foundations for the school of the Leiden *Feinmaler*.

A steadily growing number of paintings of wildly varying quality have been identified by art historians as ‹youthful work› of Dou, among them this piece in Budapest.[2] It must, however, be borne in mind that the earliest known signed and dated painting by Dou dates from 1636. We actually know nothing for certain about Dou's œuvre before 1636; it is, as Ernst van de Wetering points out, entirely ‹constructed›.[3] Although Ronni Baer disputes the attribution,[4] the painting is now generally regarded as an early autograph work by Dou. The similarities in the treatment of the light and the detailing between this and Dou's later works would seem to indicate that he is indeed the creator of the painting, but given the above caveats, this can be no more than a supposi-

tion. The situation is further complicated by the Rembrandt monogram «RHL» (?) – not, as far as we know, previously remarked upon – on the musket among the weapons in the foreground. Is this a painting that was created in Rembrandt's Leiden studio by Dou (or another studio assistant)? For the time being, this has to remain a hypothesis. It is in any event very probable that the Budapest painting did originate in Leiden: the banner leaning against the wall on the left bears the gold-embroidered arms of the City of Leiden (with two crossed keys).

In a dim, church-like space, somewhat in the background and surrounded by a veritable armoury of weapons, stands a middle-aged, moustachioed man with his gloved right hand on his hip, wearing a leather jerkin, a gorget and a plumed cap. This dress identifies him as a member of the town militia. He holds a halberd in his left hand and wears a sabre at his side, although only the curved hilt is visible. On the right, in the semi-darkness, we can make out the barrel and carriage of two cannons, while the whole of the foreground is dominated by a martial still life consisting of a cavalry helmet, a leather saddle, a banner bearing the arms of the City of Leiden, a cuirass, a cabasset helmet

337

with a red plume, a fur-trimmed buckler (a round shield with a spike), a curved oriental knife known as a yataghan, a musket with an inlaid stock and a large drum on which lies a bandolier of charges.

The weaponry has been described as contemporary military equipment that would have been in use in Holland in Rembrandt's day.[5] The cavalry helmet, the buckler, the cabasset and the musket appear to be slightly earlier, however, probably dating from around 1600. In any event, this is much more likely to have been the sort of arms and armour that the stadholder's troops would have used in battle than the equipment of the town militia, whose armour, like that of the man in the background, was usually confined to a simple gorget. The yataghan, with the bulbous hilt in the centre

68a
Rembrandt Harmensz. van Rijn, *History Painting (*The *Clemency of Charles V?)* (detail), 1626

foreground, comes from the Middle East and must be regarded as an exotic curio in this context.

Several of the weapons depicted here were favoured props in Rembrandt's studio and were frequently used in paintings by him and by the artists in his circle. We find the yataghan, for instance, hanging on the wall in Rembrandt's *St Paul at his Desk* in Nuremberg of 1629/30 (cat. no. 32), while the buckler with its sunburst ornamentation is prominent in the foreground of the Leiden *History Painting* of 1626 (cat. no. 7). Among the military hardware in the foreground of this latter painting we can also identify the drum, the cuirass and, judging by the decoration, the barrel of the same musket. The sunburst buckler, the drum and the cabasset are also rendered in a very similar way in the foreground of a studio scene by Gerard Dou in Montreal.[6] We also find the buckler and the yataghan in other studio scenes attributed to Dou.[7] In studio scenes, such militaria do not, as has been suggested, represent the *vita activa* of the soldier in contrast to the *vita contemplativa* of the painter;[8] rather they are the attributes by which the painter identified himself as a history painter.[9] It is interesting that in his own studio scene of c. 1628 (cat. no. 61) Rembrandt did not adhere to this convention: in his work these attributes are notable by their absence.

B.v.d.B.

[1] Orlers 1641, p. 380.
[2] Melbourne/Canberra 1997/98, no. 38, where it is dated shortly after 1630.
[3] Cf. the second essay by Ernst van de Wetering.
[4] Baer 1990, no. B1.
[5] P. Sutton in: Melbourne/Canberra 1997/98, p. 228.
[6] Berlin/Amsterdam/London 1991/92, no. 56.
[7] See Amsterdam 1999/2000, fig. 56–57.
[8] C. Brown in: Berlin/Amsterdam/London 1991/92, p. 304.
[9] B. Broos in: Amsterdam 1999/2000, pp. 93ff.

Catalogue III

# Heads in a «Fine» and «Rough Manner»

## 69

Anthony van Dyck (Antwerp 1599–1641 London)

# Study Head, c. 1616

Paper on oak panel,
57 x 41.4 cm
Bayerische Staats-
gemäldesammlungen,
Alte Pinakothek, Munich,
Inv. No. 4809

Glück 1931, fig. p. 30 left,
p. 521; Müller Hofstede
1987/88, pp. 144–156
(148f.), fig. 23; Raatschen
1999, p. 18 with fig., 105
no. 105

Van Dyck's study is the earliest work in the section of the exhibition devoted to «Heads in a Fine and Rough Manner», all of which are grouped around Rembrandt's *Bust of an Old Man with Golden Chain* of 1632 (cat. no. 81). There are close stylistic similarities with the artist's earliest history paintings, which are today dated to 1615/16.[1] The picture belongs to a series of five similar head studies, mostly after the same model, which has been in Munich since the eighteenth century. All were executed as independent works and although some were (re-)used in other paintings, no such use is known for the present study. The works were originally painted as pairs on large sheets of paper. Dendrochonological examinations have shown that they were cut up in the 1650s and pasted on oak panel.[2]

The genre of head studies, to which the Antwerp painter Frans Floris made an important contribution during the sixteenth century, received new impulses in the following century through Peter Paul Rubens.[3] Another important innovator was Anthony van Dyck who, although only sixteen or seventeen years old, did not follow the example of Rubens but instead sought a new direction. Whereas Rubens' facial types were based on his imagination or an idealised view of reality, Van Dyck valued using models and unadorned realism. The choice of model for the present work was clearly influenced by Caravaggism. He is a simple man of the people, whose rough features were reddened by hard physical work. One is struck by the apparent contradiction between the seemingly unintellectual coarseness of his physiognomy and his expression of intensive reflection. His squinting eyes are almost closed, his forehead heavily lined. Both van Dyck's faithful realism and emotional intensity are characteristics leading up to Rembrandt (see cat. nos. 79, 80). Another aspect is its execution in the «rough manner». It is sketchy, quick and spontaneous and thus most suitable to a study, a feature also found in the work of Rubens. But whereas his brushstrokes are broad and curvaceous, van Dyck favours hard forms, sometimes isolated, sometimes abruptly executed. This style had no precedent in the Netherlands but is reminiscent of Venetian works, especially the late paintings of Jacopo Bassano. The execution appears in the first instance shockingly raw,[4] but van Dyck has carefully considered his application of the medium. The hair of the old man is enlivened by a number of colours: in addition to black and white, red and blue-grey. Cast in light, his forehead is encrusted with a thick relief of colour, which the artist mixed on the palette using a yellowish-white and pink. This technique of painting was later used by Rembrandt (cat. nos. 79, 80, 81) and was clearly brought from Antwerp to Leiden by Jan Lievens.[5]                                    B.S.

[1] Cf. the essay by Bernhard Schnackenburg, pp. 120, note 86.
[2] Expertise by Dr. Peter Klein, Hamburg, June 10, 1997: a date after 1652 for the panel support possible, but more likely to date from after 1658. My thanks to Dr. Konrad Renger for permission to consult the files on the painting.
[3] Müller Hofstede 1968 and Müller Hofstede 1987/88, pp. 144–147.
[4] Van Dyck's «plump style» was previously judged only in comparison with Rubens and found wanting, see Glück 1931, p. XXVII.
[5] Cf. the essay by Bernhard Schnackenburg, pp. 92–121.

## 70
## Jacob Jordaens (Antwerp 1593–1678)
# Study of the Head of Abraham Grapheus, c. 1620

Oak panel, 41.4 x 29 cm
Musée de la Chartreuse,
Douai, Inv. Nr. 198

D'Hulst 1982, p. 103, fig.
69, p. 107, 110; Müller
Hofstede 1987/88, p. 147,
151 fig. 21; Antwerp 1993,
no. A 23; Madrid 1995,
vol. 1, p. 624 under no.
1547; Copenhagen 2000,
p. 138, fig. 14

Whereas older generations of artists relied mostly on their imaginations when depicting individual heads (tronies), artists like van Dyck and Jordaens as well as Rembrandt and the painters in his circle preferred to use models. In most cases the identity of these models is unknown, but that of Grapheus is an exception. Abraham Grapheus entered the Antwerp Guild of St Luke as a master in 1572. However, no paintings by his hand are known, and he instead made his living as guild factotum. But it was his expressive face, marked by the ravages of old age, that made him a much sought-after model among painters. Jordaens in particular frequently availed himself of his services.[1]

Jordaen's real interest in head studies started only around 1619/20, when he began to execute them with far greater frequency, a development in which van Dyck demonstrably played an important role.[2] Interestingly, Jordaens employed a variety of techniques for such studies. Like van Dyck, he sometimes painted on paper (which was then pasted onto panel by a later hand), whereby he also depicted two heads on a single sheet.[3] Other works, such as the present tronie, were painted straight onto panel as single figures. As Müller Hofstede has observed, some are more elaborately executed than others. Compared with the study exhibited here, the sketches on paper appear cursory and only half finished. Nevertheless, the manner of painting is essentially similar, with broad, open brushwork and much im-

pasto. This is particularly evident in Grapheus' head, especially in the highlights on the nose, temples, cheeks and neck. The result is a carefully executed work and a brilliant display of virtuosity.

During the early 1620s Jordaens incorporated this study into two large-scale multi-figured scenes.[4] It is, however, improbable that the study was painted solely in preparation for another work. In both history paintings, the head appears only in the background and although practically unchanged, it is reduced in size. Consequently, the nuances of painterly structures that characterise the study have been simplified. Was then the effort put into the study exaggerated and pointless? Certainly not. It is rather the case that such a tronie fulfilled the same function as similar heads of old men by Rembrandt (cat. no. 80, 81): that is, they served to confirm the master's virtuosity to visitors and members of the studio. Such works probably achieved a certain degree of fame, so that it was in Jordaens' interest to cite them in other paintings.                                    B.S.

---

1  On Abraham de Graef, in the Latin form Grapheus, see Antwerp 1993, p. 96.
2  Cf. the essay by Bernhard Schnackenburg, p. 108ff.
3  An example is the *Two Head Studies of Abraham Grapheus*, Museum der Schönen Künste, Ghent. Antwerp 1993, no. A 21.
4  *St Peter Finding the Tribute Money in the Fish's Mouth*, c. 1621, Statens Museum for Kunst, Copenhagen. Copenhagen 2000, pp. 135–140. *Homage to Ceres (Allegory of Fruitfulness)*, c. 1623, Prado, Madrid. Madrid 1995, no. 1547. Illustrations of both paintings also in D'Hulst 1982, figs. 82, 84; Antwerp 1993, p. 102.

## 71
## Jan Lievens (Leiden 1607–1674 Amsterdam)
## Head of a Bearded Man in Profile, c. 1626

Oak panel, 49 x 36. 9 cm
Private Collection, Turin

Sumowski 1983ff., vol. 6,
no. 2358, colour pl. 3967;
Vercelli 1999, no. 28

The famous diary entry written by Constantijn Huygens, the erudite secretary of the stattholder of The Hague, following a visit to the studio of Rembrandt and Lievens in Leiden, records his impressions of that «notable pair of youths» and contains characterisations of their art which are still valid today. Huygens writes that although Lievens does not easily attain the lively inventiveness of Rembrandt when painting «so-called histories», he excells in the rendition of an exhalted and noble form. He achieves wonders in capturing the expression on a face, and Huygens believes Lievens should concentrate on this because in this one part he is able to convey the character of the whole person. He furthermore emphasises that the works of this marvellous youth provide a particularly abundant harvest for one of his age.[1] It is indeed the case that the *tronies*, depictions of individual life-size heads and half-figures, are quite clearly the creative focus of Lievens' early period. Werner Sumowski counted no less than forty-nine such works.[2] Although hardly any are signed, the attributions are convincing and have remained uncontested[3] on account of Lievens' highly original style. Moreover, his figural types unmistakably point to his authorship, and it was their expressive monumentality that so impressed Huygens, even though they frequently appear coarse to present-day viewers. It can without exaggeration be maintained that Jan Lievens provided the impulse for the enormous production of *tronies* by members of Rembrandt's circle. The few *tronies* painted by Rembrandt himself during his early years were conceived to serve a number of different purposes, to which end he developed special types.[4] Such a differentiation was foreign to Lievens, who appears to have painted *tronies* exclusively for the market.

There are, however, variations in his *tronies* which are related to his development and use of different visual sources. In general, Lievens' *tronies* are derived from the half-figure pictures of the Utrecht Caravaggisti, although some were influenced by painters from Haarlem. The present painting points, however, in a different direction, namely to a head study by Anthony van Dyck.[5] Instead of a half-figure depiction in which movement and a narrative are suggested, we find a head in profile. The work has all the characteristics of a study: no notable additions, an unmistakable interest in facial features and in the handling of lighting, and a broad sketchy manner of execution. These particular aspects, also found in other *tronies*,[6] point to these paintings being the precursors of a special Rembrandt type, which is termed here *expressive tronie* (cf. cat. nos. 79, 80, 81).    B.S.

---

[1] English after the German translation of Huygens' Latin text, cf. Braunschweig 1979, p. 33.

[2] Sumowski 1983ff., vol. 3, nos. 1249–1285, vol. 5, nos. 2124–2127, vol. 6, nos. 2358–2364.

[3] See the review by Josua Bruyn (Bruyn 1988b, pp. 327f.).

[4] Cf. the essay by Bernhard Schnackenburg, p. 112ff.

[5] Cf. the essay by Bernhard Schnackenburg, p. 111, fig. 23.

[6] Sumowski mentions the *Old Man in Profile*, previously in the H. J. Hyams Collection, London. Sumowski 1983ff., vol. 3, no. 1249 as c. 1625/26. A date of 1626 is most probable. Kurt Bauch considers the broad open brushwork as reminiscent of Rubens, see Bauch 1960, pp. 217f., fig. 178, p. 266, note 185.

72–73
Jan Lievens (Leiden 1607–1674 Amsterdam)

# Allegory of Fire and the Age of Childhood, c. 1626
# Allegory of Water and Old Age, c. 1626

72
Oak panel, 83 x 58.2 cm
Staatliche Museen Kassel,
Gemäldegalerie Alte
Meister, No. GK 1205

73
Oak panel, 83.7 x 59.7 cm
Staatliche Museen Kassel,
Gemäldegalerie Alte
Meister, No. GK 1208

Braunschweig 1979, no. 2,
5; Sumowski 1983ff., vol.
3, no. 1216, 1217; Tümpel
1993, p. 26; Kassel 1996,
p. 171, pl. 115; Wetering
1997, p. 175f., fig. 229

With single-figure paintings Lievens worked «without constrains. There was no need to follow the requirements of narratively and psychologically-motivated compositions. The single figure is like a still life, and the artist has time for those problems of form and colour which occupy his mind».[1] Werner Sumowski quite rightly pointed out that the search for form and desire for experimentation characterise Lievens' early period. Of particular importance within the first years of his development are two related series of single-figure paintings, both of which are also contextually more discriminating that the numerous single figures «without meaning». Probably in 1627 Lievens executed a series showing the Evangelists, today in the Residenzgalerie Bamberg.[2] It is likely that the allegorical series of the Four Elements and the Four Ages of Man was painted the year before. Of these four, which were acquired by the Kassel Gemäldegalerie in 1993/94, the first and last are exhibited. That Lievens rejected the traditional forms for depicting allegories – Olympian gods or female personifications – in favour of figures taken from everyday life and shown performing typical activities and professions is in keeping with developments in Dutch art. A notable degree of ambition is evident in the combination of at least two levels of meaning; according to Klessmann, the series might even contain a reference to a third level: the Four Seasons.[3]

The *Four Elements and the Ages of Man* were traditionally aligned with the twelve constellations of the Zodiac. Both the year and the beginning of life started in Spring under the constellation of fire, Aries, and ended in Winter with the constellation of water, Pisces. The combination of the elements and the ages of man in the cycle by Jan Lievens thus follows the astrological understanding of the time.

The element of fire and the age of childhood

Fig. 72/73a
Jan Lievens, *Allegory of Air and Youth*, c. 1626
Oak panel, 83.5 x 59.5 cm
Staatliche Museen Kassel,
Gemäldegalerie Alte
Meister, No. GK 1206

are represented by a chubby-faced boy blowing into a glowing piece of coal which he has removed with a set of tongs from the dish so as to light a torch. The motif is not Lievens' invention but was known in antique times: in his *Natural History* Pliny praises the Greek painter Antiphilos for his rendering of a boy blowing into a fire and for the light which the flames threw on the boy's face.[4] In the sixteenth and seventeenth centuries this description was tantamount to a syllabus for depicting light, and many painters used it as a (literary) model. Lievens had already painted two similar depictions.[5] The rendition of the effect of light and the confident brushwork are more advanced in the painting in Kassel, the most mature picture of the series. The areas of light and dark on the boy's face are painted in a loose and fluid impasto; his white shirt is clearly indicated with a few broad sketchy brushstrokes. The impression that Lievens has adopted characteristics of Rubens' style here is reinforced by the stripy

painting of the background, which is typical of sketches by the Flemish master.[6]

The final painting in the series shows an old man throwing water from a copper bucket into a wooden barrel filled with fish. Lievens clearly adapted his use of the «rough manner» to suit each individual head. Whereas for *Childhood* he paints in a flowing and curvy manner, for *Youth* (fig. 72/73a) it is smoother and quieter, for *Adulthood* (fig. 72/73b) he employs a more energetic use of light and shade, and for *Old Age* the style has become brittle. The massive application of impasto to the face of the old fish dealer – clearly visible in a photograph taken under raking light (cf. p. 102, fig. 9) – is stylistically derived from renderings of the heads of old men by Jacob Jordaens (cat. no. 70), and provided impulses for Rembrandt, who developed them to an even higher level (cat. no. 80). In the *Allegory of Water and Old Age* Lievens, once again inspired by Rubens' technique, covered the light brown background with a stripy-translucent layer of grey.

B.S.

---

[1] «[...] arbeitet Lievens unbeschränkt. Der Zwang zur handlungsbedingten und psychologisch motivierten Komposition entfällt. Die Einzelfigur bietet sich wie zum Stilleben an, und der Künstler hat Muße für die Form- und Farbprobleme, die ihn bewegen.» Sumowski 1983ff., vol. 3, p. 1766.

[2] Braunschweig 1979, nos. 10–13; Sumowski 1983ff., vol. 3, nos. 1230–1233.

[3] Cf. Braunschweig 1978, pp. 55–59, 77–83.

[4] Pliny, p. 105, § 138.

[5] *Young Man Blowing on a Glowing Coal* and *Young Man Blowing on a Torch,* both in the Nationalmuseum Warsaw. Braunschweig 1979, nos. 6–7; Sumowski 1983ff., vol. 3, nos. 1225–1226.

[6] For a chronology and on the influence of Rubens, cf. the essay by Bernhard Schnackenburg, pp. 106ff.

Fig. 72/73b
Jan Lievens, *Allegory of the Earth and of Adulthood*, c. 1626
Oak panel, 83 x 60 cm
Staatliche Museen Kassel, Gemäldegalerie Alte Meister, No. GK 1207

## 74

Rembrandt Harmensz. van Rijn
# Bust of a Man in a Gorget and Cap, c. 1626/27

Oak panel, 40 x 29,4 cm
On the right traces of a
dubious identification:
*RH v Rin*
Private Collection, USA

Corpus, vol. 1, 1982, No.
A 8; Schwartz 1984/85/87,
p. 62; Tümpel 1986,
no. 126; Basle 1987,
no. 79; Gutbrod 1996,
pp. 139ff.; Melbourne/
Canberra 1997/98, no. 1;
Ploeg 2000, p. 13

In front of an irregularly plastered wall marked by the unmistakable edge of an oblique shadow, a man turns his head to fix the viewer. Seen from the side, his grey-blue ribboned beret is decorated with two plumes, one bluish-green, the other white tinged with yellow. The combination of this beret, worn at a jaunty angle, his yellow-brown leather jacket, the gorget, which reflects a great variety of colours, and the red-brown cloak is very impressive indeed. A sash lies across his breast and the hilt of his sword is tucked under his right arm. Such a relaxed pose serves to heighten his imposing appearance. His unusual costume is comparable with the type worn by sixteenth-century soldiers and recorded in prints. It is thus unlikely that Rembrandt portrayed a real soldier, but rather executed a study of a man in fancy dress, a *costume tronie*.[1]

This is the first instance of this pictorial type appearing in Rembrandt's œuvre. Formal inspiration seems to have come from the works of the Utrecht Caravaggisti; the clear-cut line of the shadow on the back wall in particular is reminiscent of Caravaggio and his followers.[2] Kurt Bauch thought the model to have been Rembrandt's brother Adriaen.[3] The assumption that the artist used members of his family as models is typical of older literature. Today we know that he also used studio assistants and others. It is thus improbable that the present work is a depiction of a specific soldier. Instead Rembrandt appears to have used the costume to evoke a particular type of person, one that appears regularly in his œuvre, namely the soldier (cf. e. g. cat. no. 79). De Vries noted that the sitter would have made an excellent *Capitano* for a *Commedia dell'arte* troup.[4] Indeed there are a number of similarities with Jacques Callot's *Capitano* of 1618/19[5] (fig. 74a): the self-confident pose and unwavering gaze, the size of the hat with its large feathers. Considering

Fig. 74a
Jacques Callot, *Capitano*,
1618/19
Etching, 220 x 150 mm
Rijksmuseum, Amsterdam

that Rembrandt owned prints by the French artist, such a connection is indeed possible.

As in other *tronies* of the Leiden period, Rembrandt used the depiction as a means of experimenting with his painting technique. The seemingly carelessly applied impasto highlights on the gorget are in marked contrast to the rather flat, rubbed paint of the cloth. The conspicuous use of colour relates this work to his many-figured history paintings of the same period (cf. cat. no. ##), so that a date of 1626/27 for the *tronie* seems plausible. But here Rembrandt attempts to place related tones together. Whereas in the lower half warm, earthy colours dominate – with the exception of the blue seam of the garment – in the upper half the combination of colours is cooler and harder. The metal gorget with its numerous coloured reflexes allows for a clever transition between the two. Finally, the treatment of the light is particularly noteworthy, especially the diagonal shadows which cross the man's forehead.

X-rays of the painting have shown that Rembrandt overpainted an earlier picture, which presumably was also by him.[6] Apparently unhappy with the results, he used the panel for the new painting, and thus once again confirmed the experimental nature of a number of *tronies* in his œuvre.                    J.L.

[1]   Cf. the essay by Bernhard Schnackenburg, p. 112ff.
[2]   Blankert 1986/87.
[3]   Bauch 1966, no. 109.
[4]   He does not, however, mention definite examples. See Vries 1989, pp. 191f.
[5]   Dresden 1992, no. 166.
[6]   Corpus, vol. 1, 1982, p. 125. The overpainted picture showed an old man looking down to the left, and is comparable to a painting by Jacques de Rousseaux in the Bredius Museum, The Hague. Sumowski 1983ff., vol. 4, no. 1675.

## 75

Rembrandt Harmensz. van Rijn

# Bust of an Old Man with Turban, c. 1627/28

Oak panel, 26.5 x 20 cm
Signed right: *RHL*
Collection Fondation
Aetas Aurea

Bauch 1933, p. 220;
Bredius 1935, no. 72;
Sumowski 1983ff., vol. 4,
p. 2506, no. 1675a
(Jacques des Rousseaux);
Wetering 1998

The fascination for oriental culture is already evident in Rembrandt's early work. When in 1626 a Persian delegation arrived in the Netherlands accompanied by a magnificent retinue, it was not simply the exotic goods that generated great interest; so, too, did the oriental costumes and fabulous head-dresses.[1]

Recent stylistic and technical studies have shown that one of the earliest *tronies* in oriental costume can be attributed to Rembrandt.[2] Other names put forward by earlier scholars as author of this work include Jacques des Rousseaux, a pupil of Rembrandt's, and his friend and fellow artist Jan Lievens.[3] A comparable depiction of the monumentally conceived half-figure of an oriental wearing magnificent garments, the so-called Sultan Soliman, would seem to support the attribution to Lievens (fig. 75a).[4] Moreover, the Caravaggesque lighting in both paintings seemed to further strengthen the case for his authorship. Besides, the 1630 autobiography of the Dutch statesman and scholar Contantijn Huygens refers explicitly to the model for the oriental, who may be identical with the present character head. Today we know that this model was very much in demand among artists in Leiden, and appears not just in works by Rembrandt but also in the *Bust of an Old Man with a Feathered Cap* (cat. no. 76) by his pupil Gerard Dou.

In addition to the detailed technical examinations carried out by the *Rembrandt Research Project* on the age of the support and the structure and composition of the paint, it is above all the monogram «RHL» and the stylistic similarities with early works by Rembrandt that promote his authorship. The painting *The Rich Man* (cat. no. 29), attributed to him, was painted around the same time, and is signed with the same initials. The emphasis on light and dark, despite the different sources of light, is comparable, as is the position and form of the head of both protagonists, even though their gazes vary on account of the different thematic contexts. If in the Berlin painting, Rembrandt is especially interested in drawing attention to the various at-

357

Fig. 75a
Jan Lievens, *Old Man in
Oriental Costume*, c. 1629
Canvas, 135 x 100.5 cm
Stiftung Preußische
Schlösser und Gärten
Berlin-Brandenburg

tributes personifying riches, in the present work he seeks to evoke the spirit of the Orient through the headdress and focus on the expressive features of the man's physiognomy. Subtle gradations characterise the transition from the smooth, illuminated side of the face to the darker other side, where forceful brush strokes emphasise the plasticity of the wrinkles and folds of skin.

The handling of light is supported by highlights and the gold tones in the turban. Minute brushstrokes give the headdress a tactile quality. A special feature is the tip of the plume which, although in shadow, appears to catch and reflect the light. The red and golden colour of the plume underpins this effect, and within the composition the tip and jewellery of the feather serve to balance the light which dominates the left of the painting.

Compared with the very elaborate rendition of the headdress, the actual garment is very roughly modelled using only slightly differentiated patches of impasto paint. The details of the cloak-like garment are almost unrecognisable. Only the drapery of what seems to be a scarf tied around his neck forms a transition between the finely modelled area of the head and the very abbreviated painting of the monochrome garment, the simplicity of which is in stark contrast to the rest of his costume.

The oriental as a type appears frequently in Rembrandt's œuvre, especially during the 1630s. The large-scale paintings with half-figures conjure up the image of a far-flung, foreign and mysterious world through their (almost) authentic depiction of oriental costumes and attributes. The basis for Rembrandt's study of this fashion were illustrated travel books such as that by Pieter Coecke van Aelst, who in 1533 undertook a journey to Istanbul and recorded his experience in a series of detailed prints on the *Customs and Habits of the Turks*.[4] These observations on the country and its people as well as other thematically similar graphic works by Melchior Lorch and Nicolas de Nocolay formed the point of departure for Rembrandt's study of the Orient.               B.C.M.

[1]  On the reception of the Orient, cf. Berlin 1989, chapter 8, pp. 739ff.
[2]  Wetering 1998 with additional literature.
[3]  Bauch 1960, p. 283; Bauch 1939, p. 257.
[4]  Cf. Berlin 1989, pp. 240ff.

76–77
Gerard Dou (Leiden 1613–1675)

# Bust of an Old Man with a Feathered Cap, c. 1630
# Bust of an Old Woman with a Fur Collar, c. 1630

76
Oak panel, 24.3 x 19 cm
(oval)
Inscribed right: *G D*
Staatliche Museen Kassel,
Gemäldegalerie Alte
Meister, No. GK 257

77
Oak panel, 24.3 x 19 cm
(oval)
Staatliche Museen Kassel,
Gemäldegalerie Alte
Meister, No. GK 258

Martin 1913, pp. 22, 38;
Sumowski 1983ff., vol. 1,
no. 254; Baer 1990, no. 11;
Kassel 1996, p. 104

Both the identical dimensions and the positioning of the figures point to these paintings having been conceived as pendants.[1] This prompted earlier authors to suggest that the couple were Rembrandt's parents. Kurt Bauch was the first to contradict this proposal when he convincingly showed that the same models appear in different paintings wearing a variety of costumes.[2] Ernst van de Wetering pointed out that the same man also sat for Rembrandt's *Bust of an Old Man with Turban* (cat. no. 75).[3] This in particular is informative, since it not only helps establish a date for Dou's pendants, but also permits a comparative study of the similarities and differences between the two artists.

Dou was first apprenticed to the printmaker Bartholomäus Dolendo and then to the glass painter Pieter Couwenhorn. There he almost certainly learned the techniques of making a fine and exact reproduction of individual forms. From 1625 to 1627 he worked in his father's studio as a glass painter. In 1628 he became an assistant in the studio of Rembrandt, then just twenty-one years old. It was only there that Dou turned to oil painting and created works whose motifs are closely related to those found in Rembrandt's paintings but executed in a style which unmistakably reveals his different artistic training.

The two exhibited pictures are among Dou's earliest signed works. They demonstrate the extent of Dou's debt to Rembrandt but also the life-long differences between teacher and pupil. Joachim von Sandrart (1675) gives a very clear picture of these differences by drawing on an analogy from nature: «Gerhard Dau of Leyden was sown in our artistic garden by Rembrandt, but turned out to be a completely different flower as the gardener thought. I mean to say, he [Dou] adopted a completely different and hitherto unseen manner, by applying his immense diligence and a similarly admirable patience to painting in oil everything that otherwise occurs in a life-size painting, be it drawing, colour, bright light, shade and lustre, most marvellous and complete in small and finger-long pictures, so wonderful, lively, strong, powerful, full of grandeur and harmony that no one before him ever made such comparable small pieces.»[4]

Quite different from Rembrandt, Dou specialised in painting in a consistently fine manner, one in which brushwork is negated as much as possible, so as to create a porcelain-like surface. This characteristic is especially prevalent in Dou's late work, and made him the real founder of the Leiden school of fine painting.[5]

For these pendants Dou took as his pictorial source Rembrandt's work of the 1620s. However, he remains, so to speak, purely on the pictorial surface, so that despite his detailed depiction of physiognomy, he never reaches into the depths to capture the personality of the sitter. It is this psychological penetration of his model that is characteristic of Rembrandt's work. Dou, on the other hand, depicts every detail with the same dedication. The clothing of the sitters does not suggest a particularly pictorial meaning; thus the man with the gorget is not imbued with the specific qualities of a soldier. Moreover, light seems to be employed solely to give the figures a better contour rather than to heighten the pictorial message. The result is a series of masterpieces of fine painting, bust pictures that have an almost still-life quality. While Rembrandt employed the same models for his experiments using colour, and so gave each work its own individual characterisation, they represented for Dou a means of displaying his artistic virtuosity. Dou also sought to achieve colouristic harmony. The greenish-blue of the feather reappears in the man's sash, while the colour of the woman's headdress is found in the reddish glow of her fur collar. Rembrandt's very different treatment of colour can be seen in such works as his *Bust of a Man in a Gorget and Cap* (cat. no. 74).

The appearance of Dou's models in works by Rembrandt and his as yet not quite perfected style of fine painting make a date of around 1630 for the pendants most likely.[6]      J.L.

[1]  On pendants in seventeenth-century Dutch painting showing an old couple, see Moiso-Diekamp 1987, pp. 90ff.
[2]  Bauch 1933, pp. 197f.
[3]  Wetering 1998, p. 17.
[4]  «Gerhard Dau von Leyden wurde zwar von Rembrand in unserm Kunstgarten gesäet, aber es wurde eine ganz andere Blume, als der Gärtner sich eingebildet, ich will sagen, er habe ganz eine andere und zuvor niemalen gesehene Manier angenommen, indeme er vermittelst seines großen Fleißes und demselben zugeselleten verwunderlichen Gedult alles, was sonst in ein Lebens-großes Bild an Zeichnung, Colorit, hohen Liecht, Schatten und Glanz gehörig, ganz verwunderlich und vollkommen in sehr kleine und Fingers lange Bildlein mit Ölfarben gemahlt, so wunderbar, lebhaft, stark, gewaltig, mit guter Erhebung und Harmonie, daß niemals vor ihme einiger dergleichen kleine Stucke verfärtiget.» Sandrart (1675) 1925, p. 195.
[5]  On fine painting in Leiden, see Dresden 2000 (with further literature).
[6]  The dendrochronological examination carried out by Dr. Peter Klein (University of Hamburg) determined the earliest possible dates for the paintings as ‹from 1610 onwards› (GK 285) and ‹from 1616 onwards › (GK 257).

## 78
## Rembrandt Harmensz. van Rijn
# Self-portrait Bareheaded, 1629

Etching, 174 x 155 mm
Signed and dated above
left: *RHL 1629* (reversed)
Bartsch 338, only state
Rijksmuseum,
Amsterdam, Inv. No. RP-
P-OB-273

Chapman 1990, pp. 22ff.;
White 1969, pp. 107f.;
London/The Hague
1999/2000, no. 11;
Amsterdam/London
2000/01, no. 4;
Boston 2000/2001, no. 1

Self-portraits play a special role in Rembrandt's œuvre. On the one hand they convey the physiognomy of the artist, on the other they can offer the viewer an understanding of his manner of working, since Rembrandt used himself as a model for depicting different states of emotion but also different costumes. His pupil Samuel van Hoogstraten expressly recommended such study of oneself when in 1678 he wrote: «One can also achieve the same advantage by depicting one's own emotions, at best by being before a mirror, so that one is both performer and viewer.»[1] Thus Rembrandt shows himself in his paintings as laughing, contemplative, but also in melancholic reflection.

Within the series of self-portraits, the present etching is both technical and artistically an exception. The unusually large format of the sheet gives the work a representative character. It is possible that the artist intended to print a large edition, but obviously rejected this idea later, as only two prints are known (Amsterdam and London).[2]

The upper half of the body of the twenty-three-year-old artist is turned slightly to the right while his head is directed somewhat to the left. As a result he looks directly out of the picture, without, however, catching the viewer's eye. This divergence of movement evokes a sense of momentary tension. The light comes from the right above his head, so that a slight shadow falls on the left half of his face. Strong cross-hatching indicates that his body throws a shadow on the left edge of the picture. The broad white collar of his jacket, which is decorated with stripes on the front, gives the portrait an official character. This is strengthened by the long hair, which on the right falls in a so-called «lovelock» (*Cadenette*).[3] While this aristocratic hair style, which is singular to this self-portrait, points to the intention of the depiction, the extremely sketchy execution of the etching is in strong contrast to its official character.

The technique is unique: in addition to the fine etching needle, Rembrandt employed a type of bird or cane pen, which produced a characteristic double-line when pressure was exerted. This enlivens the contours and creates the impression of spontaneity. It is almost as if Rembrandt attempted here an etching in the «rough manner». The experimental nature of the print is obvious. Just how spontaneous Rembrandt was is evident in the rendering in reverse of his signature, which is related to that in paintings of the same time. The artist apparently forgot for a moment that he was working on a copper plate. This is further supported by the position of the *Cadenette* over his left shoulder in the etching rather than over the right shoulder where it should be – and as it was on the copper plate.

Filippo Baldinucci emphasised in 1686 the uniqueness of Rembrandt's etchings, «a most bizzare manner, [...] singular to him and never used by others [...], which with certain strokes, touches and irregular lines, without contours, lends the whole a profound *chiaroscuro* effect with a strength and painterly taste (*gusto pittoresco*) of the highest degree.»[4] Even if it is improbable that the Tuscan was referring directly to the present sheet, he nevertheless accurately characterises Rembrandt's attempt to translate the specific qualities of his painting, in this case the «rough manner», into the medium of the graphic arts.

J.L.

[1] «Dezelve baet zalmen ook in't uitbeelden van diens hartstochten, die gy voorhebt, bevinden, voornaemilijk voor een spiegel om tegelijk vertooner en aenschouwer te zijn.» Hoogstraten 1678, p. 110.
[2] The presence in the upper left (clearer in the London print) of another scene (Supper at Emmaus?) shows that for his self-portrait Rembrandt apparently re-used a copper plate. See White 1969, pp. 107f.
[3] Meyer 1986, p. 87; Winkel 1999/2000, p. 62.
[4] «una bizzarrissima maniera [...], ancor questa tutta sua propria, nè più usata da altri [...], cioè con certi freghi, e freghetti, e tratti irregolari, e senza dintorno, facendo però risultare dal tutto un chiaro scuro profondo e di gran forza, ed un gusto pittoresco fino all' ultimo segno.» Baldinucci (1686) 1808, vol. 1, p. 197.

## 79

Rembrandt Harmensz. van Rijn

# Laughing Soldier, c. 1629/30

Copper with gold-leaf
ground, 15.4 x 12.2 cm
Signed top left: *Rt*
Royal Cabinet of Paintings
Mauritshuis, The Hague,
Cat. No. 598

The Hague 1978, pp.
48–55; Corpus, vol. 1,
1982, no. B 6; Schwartz
1984/85/87, p. 62; Tümpel
1986, no. 127; Stockholm
1992/93, no. 50;
Phoenix/The Hague
1998/99, no. 46

Situated against a plain background, this youthful man appears to have spontaneously turned to the viewer and, with his mouth slightly open, laughs in an almost coarse manner. The right side of his face is illuminated by the light falling from the upper left, the left half is cast in shadow. Strong brushstrokes, apparently applied in such quick succession that one could almost talk of lashes, give the painting a spontaneity that is unique in Rembrandt's early work, an impression underlined by the sudden turn of the man's head, his unrestrained laughter and the dramatic lighting. In 1920 Wilhelm Fraenger emphasised the incomparably free manner of the painting, noting the coarse and fleshy face modelled in wide brushstrokes and the play of yellowish-red lights and bluish shadows on his flesh. «The broad ray of light has only one purpose in the painting: to add lewdness to the abruptness of his spontaneous expression of coarse merriment.»[1]

Together with the *Old Woman at Prayer* and a *Self-portrait*, the *Laughing Soldier* forms a group of small paintings, all of which have identical dimensions and are painted on copper with a gold-leaf ground.[2] Rembrandt did not, however, use the smooth support to paint in a fine manner and thus create a polished paint surface, but rather to exemplify the power of his brushstrokes. This type of painting can be termed *expressive tronie*, and differs from *costume tronie* both in the concentration on the face and its expression and in the manner of painting (e.g. cat. no. 74). The iron gorget is to be understood not only as a decorative accessory, but also serves to underscore the mimicry – in this case, the uncontrollably wild profession of the soldier. Theodor Hetzer has already emphasised the uniqueness of Rembrandt's brushwork: every stroke has the power to create form and is full of life.[3] The three copper panels probably served as exemplary works in Rembrandt's studio, designed to convey to his pupils three different character types – soldier, young man, old woman – and three different graduations of painting, from the «fine manner» to the «rough manner».[4]

The influence of Adriaen Brouwer has been fre-

79a
Jan van Vliet after
Rembrandt Harmensz.
van Rijn, *Laughing Soldier*
Etching, 226 x 190 mm
Bartsch 21
Rijksmuseum,
Amsterdam

quently mentioned. His paintings, *The Bitter Drink* in Frankfurt and especially the *Peasant with Cocked Hat and Mug* in Basle, show a comparably free use of the brush.[5] Remarkable parallels can also be found in the work of Frans Hals.[6] The Kassel *Peeckelhaering* in particular offers a good comparison,[7] especially in the expressively patchy application of paint. There are, however, differences which underline Rembrandt's individuality. He differs from Hals, for example, in placing patches of unconnected colour next to one another. One thinks of Filippo Baldinucci, who wrote of Rembrandt: «Extremely unusual in the way of painting, he invented a manner of which one can say that it was his alone, without contours, without inner or outer outlines, just with coarse strokes of the brush.»[8]

This quality can only be partly conveyed in Jan van Vliet's reproductive print after Rembrandt's painting (fig. 79a).[9] He himself, however, undertook an attempt to transfer the manner of his expressive painting to the medium of print. Kurt Bauch recognised the relationship with his *Self-portrait Bareheaded* (cat. no. 78) «in the somewhat affected turn of the head, the treatment of the small, slightly crooked eyes and their surroundings, the eyebrows consisting of a few upright hairs, the unkempt beard, and the overall rough modelling of cheek and chin.»[10]                J. L.

---

[1]  «Breithingefleckte Pinselzüge modellieren das grobe und fleischige Gesicht, in dessen Inkarnat mannigfach gelbrote Lichter und bläuliche Schatten spielen. Das breit hereinströmende Licht hat auf dem Bilde nur den Zweck, die Plötzlichkeit des spontanen Ausdrucks derber Fröhlichkeit zu versinnlichen». Fraenger 1920, p. 39

[2]  The *Old Woman at Prayer,* signed *R,* Salzburger Landessammlungen-Residenzgalerie. Corpus, vol. 1, 1982, no. A 27. *Self-portrait,* signed *R ... 1630,* Nationalmuseum, Stockholm. Corpus, vol. 1, 1982, no. B 5, see Stockholm 1992/93, nos. 49–51

[3]  «Jeder Strich hat formbildende Kraft und Lebensausdruck.» Hetzer 1984, pp. 229f. (University lecture, Winter term 1925/26).

[4]  Schatborn 1986b, p. 61; London/The Hague 1999/2000, no. 18.

[5]  *The Bitter Drink*, panel, 47.5 x 35.5 cm. Städelsches Kunstitut, Frankfurt. *Peasant with Cocked Hat and Mug,* 1630s, panel, 15 x 12 cm. Kunstmuseum Basle (Max Geldner Collection). Basle 2000, no. 8

[6]  Sumowski 1973, pp. 94f.

[7]  Cf. the essay by Bernhard Schnackenburg, p. 105, fig. 13.

[8]  «stravagantissimo nel modo del dipingere, e fecesi una maniera, che si può dire che fosse intieramente sua, senza dintorno sì bene, o circonscrizione di linee interiori ne' esteriori, tutta fatta di colpi strapazzati.» Baldinucci (1686) 1808, vol. 1, p. 195.

[9]  Amsterdam 1996, no. 8.

[10]  «... in der etwas gezierten Drehung des Kopfes, der Behandlung der dunklen, kleinen, etwas schiefen Augen und ihrer Umgebung, der aus wenigen gesträubten Haaren bestehenden Brauen, des wüsten Kinnbartes und der gesamten struppig modellierten Wangen- und Kinnpartie.» Bauch 1933, p. 199.

## 80
## Rembrandt Harmensz. van Rijn
# Bust of an Old Man in a Cap, c. 1630

Oak panel, 24.3 x 20.3 cm
Signed top right: *RHL*
Dr. & Mrs. Alfred Bader

Corpus, vol. 1, 1982, no.
C 22; Tümpel 1993, fig.
p. 57, pp. 405f., no. 128;
Amsterdam 1996, no. 10b;
Melbourne/Canberra
1997/98, no. 4; Boston
2000/01, no. 16

States of emotion, be they contemplative, reflective or introspective, repeatedly occur as themes in Rembrandt's early character heads, the so-called *tronies*, whereby the figures can appear on their own or as part of a scene. An example is the *Bust of an Old Man in a Cap*. Its brushwork shows a clear relationship to the Kassel *Bust of an Old Man with a Necklace* of 1632 (cat. no. 81) and the same head appears in other works by Rembrandt.

Particularly notable is the man's high forehead, which spirited brushstrokes have modelled to achieve great plasticity. Up close it appears like a moon landscape, but within the context of the entire picture it conveys strength and energy.

According to the latest research, this *expressive tronie* is unquestionably the work of Rembrandt.[1] It is one of the first paintings in which the artist partly abandons fine painting and begins to experiment with a coarse, rough manner. It was probably executed in the same year as the *Laughing Soldier* (cat. no. 79). Rembrandt reinforces painterly autonomy through the dynamics of his brush. Seemingly unrelated areas of the face are framed by hair and gorget and defined through eyes, nose and mouth. The expressive quality of the brushwork intensifies the mimicry, so that with character heads it is the forehead in particular that conveys the emotional state. An etching of 1634 by J. G.

Fig. 80a
Jan van Vliet after
Rembrandt Harmensz.
van Rijn, *Head of an Old
Man in a Cap*, c. 1634
Etching, 213 x 178 mm
Museum het
Rembrandthuis,
Amsterdam

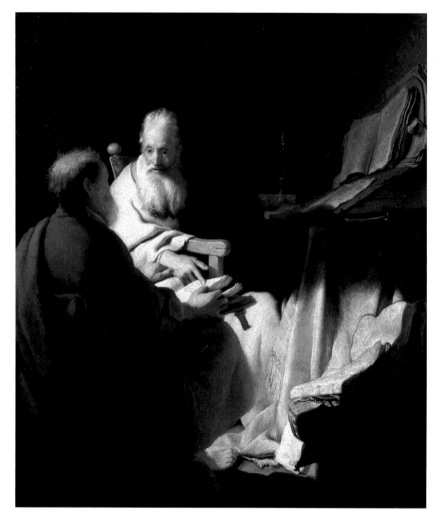

van Vliet probably reproduces in reverse the present *expressive tronie* (fig. 80a).[3] The inscription «RH jnventor» points to Rembrandt as the author of this work, although for a time it was thought that the etching reproduces another original by an unknown artist from Rembrandt's circle.[3] However, recent studies of water marks refute this supposition and support the attribution to Rembrandt; it has been shown that van Vliet used the same paper for his prints as Rembrandt for his drawings, making it probably that the two artists shared a studio.[4]

The *expressive tronie* on exhibit is of a particular character type used by Rembrandt in a number of paintings and etchings from around 1630,[5] such as in his *Peter and Paul in Disputation*[6] of around 1628 (fig. 80b). Instead of two single figures, a pair of erudite men is portrayed together, bathed in light, attentive and deep in concentration as they engage in an intense discourse. In Rembrandt's lost painting *The Baptism of the Eunuch*, which is known through a copy, the head of Philippus shows a close relationship, despite the very different subjects, to the present head, especially in the facial expres-

Fig. 80c
Copy after Rembrandt
Harmensz. van Rijn,
*The Baptism of the Eunuch*
(detail)
Oak panel, 115 x 89 cm
Private Collection

sion, the direction of gaze and the modelling of hair and beard (fig. 80c).[7] Also comparable is the handling of light. In both cases, the left side of the face is illuminated by light coming from the left, while the right half is cast in shadow and the physiognomic details appear as diffuse monochrome areas of colour.

A basic figural type does of course require different characterisations depending on the pictorial context, but the shape of the head, the beard and facial expression do point to the same model. The caravaggesque lighting is similar in the two pictures. It is only in the present character head that the expressive accentuation through painterly structure, such as here in the case of the forehead, becomes the overriding theme of the depiction.                    B.C.M.

[1]  Amsterdam 1996, no. 10b.
[2]  Amsterdam 1996, no. 10a.
[3]  Cf. Bauch 1960, p. 261, note 130; Tümpel 1986, pp. 405f., no. 128.
[4]  Cf. Amsterdam 1996, pp. 27ff.
[5]  Corpus, vol. 1, 1982, no. C 22.
[6]  Corpus, vol. 1, 1982, no. A 13.
[7]  Cf. Tümpel 1993, pp. 51, 424; Sumowski 1983ff., vol. 6, no. 1913, p. 2940.

Rembrandt Harmensz van Rijn

# Bust of an Old Man with Golden Chain, 1632

Oak panel, 59.3 x 49.3 cm
Inscribed on right edge at
eye level: *RHL* (mono-
gram) *van Ryn / 1632*
Staatliche Museen Kassel,
Gemäldegalerie Alte
Meister, No. GK 233

Schwartz 1984/85/87,
p. 197, no. 211 (Rem-
brandt); Corpus, vol. 2,
1986, no. C 53 (Rem-
brandt imitation, seven-
teenth century); Tümpel
1986, p. 424, no. A 36
(Rembrandt pupil);
Sumowski 1983ff., vol. 5,
pp. 3059, 3100, no. 2084,
p. 3216 (Govert Flinck,
c. 1642); Grimm 1991,
p. 91, fig. 49, pp. 96f.
(Rembrandt Studio);
Tümpel 1993, p. 427,
no. A 36 (Rembrandt
pupil); Kassel 1996,
p. 229, colour pl.
p. 236 (Rembrandt)

Of the paintings that left Rembrandt's studio during his early period, the percentage of single-figure pictures without portrait character was notably high. Of the thirty-one paintings mentioned in inventories and other sources for the years from 1628 to 1640, fifteen were *tronies*. In the subsequent period they continued to account for a third of the total output.[1] Their value was only a few guilders, and the addition of qualifying attributions in the inventories («after» Rembrandt or «in his manner») indicate that the majority of these works were not autograph. Instead they were by assistants and pupils, since it was part of their artistic education to execute small-scale, affordable works in the style of the master. Interest in such pieces continued to be high until the eighteenth century; the collection in Kassel possesses four examples from the early 1630s.[2] For the studio, such *tronies* played an important role in ensuring economic prosperity, but an essential precondition for the production of the different types, be it the emphasis on facial expression (*expressive tronies*) or on accessories (*costume tronies*), was the existence of autograph models.

The painting on exhibit is an extremely rare example of an *expressive tronie* by Rembrandt.[3] It probably remained in the studio until 1656, when Rembrandt was force to auction his possessions to stave off bankruptcy. The *tronie* may be one of three listed in the inventory of his estate drawn up in that year as being «naer 't leven» (after life).[4] Such an identification is in accord with the close-up view of the model and the overall study character of the piece, a feature also found in the *Bearded Old Man in a Cap* (cat. no. 80). It is not known if the first documented owner, Valerius Röver the Elder, who died in 1693, acquired the work at the auction in September 1656 or at a later date from someone else.

The Kassel painting has always been highly esteemed but for a brief interruption following the publication of the findings of the *Rembrandt Research Project* and subsequent scholarly works. In 1724 the then-owner Valerius Röver the Younger, who considered the painting to be «extra konstig» (particularly artful), received an offer of 200 guilders for it from the prominent painter Philip van Dijk.[5] The first exact description was by Wilhelm Bode in 1883: «The head of an old man with full, dishevelled hair and beard [...] is as if kneaded in colour; with broad confident strokes of the brush which place, almost unconnected, wrinkle next to wrinkle. »[6]

As in only a few other single-figure paintings by Rembrandt, the attention of the viewer is drawn to the old man's face. Everything else serves to support this effect. The costume is only suggested and remains unidentifiable; the golden chain, a common accessory in *tronies* and self-portraits, has no specific meaning. It has been interpreted as an addition by the artist to indicate that the painting is more than a depiction of everyday life.[7] Rembrandt has for the most part concentrated on painting the face. While the brown of the man's shirt is nothing more than the thin layer of underpaint, the brushstrokes in the face are unusually rich in form and colour. Various tones of yellow, red, grey and brown have been mixed with lead white. An old yellowed varnish has, however, considerably reduced the rich interplay between the cool and warm tones of the strong flesh colours, and the effect probably more closely resembled the flesh colouring in the portrait of *Aechje Claesdr. Pesser* (cat. no. 83), which Rembrandt produced two years later and which shows certain stylistic similarities with the Kassel painting.                                    B.S.

[1]  For this and further information, see Veen 1997/98, pp. 71f.
[2]  Kassel 1996, pp. 245f., nos. GK 229–232.
[3]  On the style and function of the painting, cf. the excursus in the essay by Bernhard Schnackenburg, pp. 114–118.
[4]  Strauss/Meulen 1979, pp. 355, 357; Amsterdam 1999/2000, p. 148, no. 66: «Een tronie naer 't leven van Rembrandt», p. 357, no. 90; «Twee tronien, nae 't leven van Rembrandt». See also Veen 1997/98, p. 71.
[5]  Moes 1913, p. 17, no. 39.
[6]  «Der Kopf eines Greises mit vollem, struffem Haar und Bart [...] ist wie in Farbe geknetet; in sicheren, großen Pinselstrichen ist, fast unvermittelt, Falte neben Falte gesetzt.» Bode 1883, p. 413.
[7]  London/The Hague 1999/2000, p. 104 under no. 10.

## 82
### Rembrandt Harmensz. van Rijn
# Portrait of a Man Trimming his Quill, 1632

Canvas, 105 x 83 cm
Signed: *RHL* (mono-
grammed) and *van Rijn
1632*
Staatliche Museen Kassel,
Gemäldegalerie Alte
Meister, No. GK 234

Corpus, vol. 2, 1986,
pp. 3f., 10, 26, 31, 38, 100,
206ff., no. A 54; Tümpel
1993, p. 415, no. 197;
Grimm 1991, p. 34,
fig. 17, p. 46, fig. 62, p. 54,
fig. 92, p. 75, fig. 133, p.
80; Kassel 1996, pp. 229f.;
Wetering 1997, pp. 94,
110, 113, 310, fig. 141

Only in Kassel

This commissioned portrait was executed in the same year as the *Bust of an Old Man with Golden Chain* (cat. no. 81) and was acquired by the Landgrave of Hesse, Wilhelm VIII, in 1750. It has always been attributed to Rembrandt. The comparison with the Kassel *Old Man with a Golden Chain* demonstrates in an exemplary manner Rembrandt's ability to use very different stylistic means and manners of painting contemporaneously. Whereas for the old man in Kassel Rembrandt powerfully wields his brush on certain sections of the head to heighten his expression, in the case of the portrait the modelling is so fine that hardly any movement of the brush is detectable. Particularly notable in this respect are the face, hands and clothing of the man; but it is only following its recent restoration that the portrait's extreme painterly and colouristic differentiation has come to light.[1]

The man's clothes represent the height of Netherlandish fashion in the 1630s. The long sleeves of his garment are visible beneath the outer so-called hanging sleeves of his doublet, which is decorated by a trim. This trim runs along the edge of the outer sleeve, serves to define the contours of the sitter's shoulder and continues down the side of the breeches. The dot-like holes on the inside of the large sleeves and around the waist connect the doublet with both his inner garment and breeches.[2]

The sitter rests his right elbow on the arm of the chair. There is, however, almost no contrast between it and the deep brown tones of the man's costume. Only his hands in the centre of the painting stand out (fig. 82a). The painterly virtuosity with which Rembrandt conveys their vitality through soft flesh tones is also found in his characterisation of the forehead, cheeks, nose and ears of the man's reddish face. Equally, the red thread on his pleated collar sets an important accent.

The light coming from the left is reflected above all by the white collar. But beyond its brightness, the airy appearance of the various layers of material, the ends of which are ruffled,

gives a sense of lightness to what is basically a static composition. Other sources of contrast with the dark brown tones are the quill, which directs attention to the right half of the painting, and the white sheet of paper bearing Rembrandt's signature and the date.

The portrait is among the first commissions Rembrandt received following his move to Amsterdam. The central motif of cutting a quill was a popular one among other artists such as Gerard Dou, Adriaen Brouwer and Jan Steen. It was seen as a symbol of industry and continual practice. The presence of other writing utensils prompted eighteenth-century scholars to see in the portrait a depiction of a calligrapher, and in particular of Lieven Willemz. Coppenol, who lived and worked in Amsterdam during Rembrandt's lifetime. This identification has, however, been refuted, since it could be shown that no likeness exists between Coppenol and the sitter.[3] Stylistic, compositional and technical parallels instead suggest that it is one of a pair, having as its pendant the portrait of a seated young woman now in the Gemäldegalerie of the Akademie der Bildenden Künste in Vienna.[4]                                    B.C.M.

[1]  The restoration was undertaken between 1999 and 2001 in the Gemälderestaurierungswerkstatt of the Staatliche Museen Kassel. Hans Brammer was responsible for the extensive preliminary scientific examinations; then, together with Jutta Michels, he developed the concept for the restoration. This was carried out by Jutta Michels and Pia Maria Hilsenbeck and comprised the following: restoration of the painting's original dimensions (previously 101.5 x 81.5 cm); making the date completely visible by flattening the turned-over edges of the canvas; removal of the unusually thick layers – eight altogether – of varnish; filling in missing areas at the edges; other small retouches. Cf. also Brammer 1999, p. 177f.
[2]  Cf. Köhler, part 6, p. 55.
[3]  Corpus, vol. 2, 1986, p. 211.
[4]  Rembrandt, *Portrait of a Young Woman in a Chair*, 1632, canvas, 92 x 17 cm, Akademie der Bildende Künste, Vienna, Gemäldegalerie. Corpus, vol. 2, 1986, p. 210; Berlin/Amsterdam/London 1991/92, no. 10, p. 150.

## 83
### Rembrandt Harmensz. van Rijn
# Portrait of Aechje Claesdr. Pesser, 1634

Oak panel, 68 x 53.8 cm
(oval)
Inscribed in the middle
right: *Rembrandt. f/ 1634,*
on the left side: *AE.SVE.83*
The National Gallery,
London, Inv. No. 775

Schwartz 1984/85/87,
No. 139; Corpus, vol. 2,
1986, no. A 104; London
1988/89, no. 3; London
1991, pp. 341–343, inv.
no. 775; Grimm 1991,
p. 64, fig. 122, p. 70,
fig. 34, p. 125, note 88
(Rembrandt Studio);
Berlin/Amsterdam/
London 1991/92, no. 19;
Tümpel 1993, pp. 91 (ill.),
418, no. 234; Dudok
van Heel 1992

This portrait of an old woman has long enjoyed special status because of the penetrating characterisation and the virtuosity of its execution. A few years ago, Dudok van Heel, an Amsterdam expert on archival material, was able to establish the identity of the sitter and the circumstances surrounding the commission. Following his marriage to Saskia van Uylenburgh in Frieseland in June 1634, Rembrandt, then very much in demand as a portraitist, spent a month in Rotterdam in order to accommodate a patron who, unlike others, was unable to undertake the journey to Amsterdam. The person in question was Aechje Claesdochter Pesser, a widow, whose ripe old age of eighty-three has been specially recorded on the painting. It is probable that at the same time two further portraits of family members were at least begun: one of her son, Dirck Jansz. Pesser, a brewery owner in Rotterdam; the other of his wife, Haesje Jacobsdr. van Cleyburg. All three portraits testify to the current fashion for oval supports and all have the same dimensions.[1] It has also been possible to determine how Rembrandt came to receive the commission. In 1633 the artist painted the portrait of the famous preacher Johannes Uyttenbogaert, an advocate of the liberal Calvinist Remonstrant Church, who at that time was living in Rotterdam.[2] Among his followers was the Pesser family, so that Uyttenbogaert was probably responsible for establishing contact between them and Rembrandt.

Rembrandt appears to have been fascinated by the sitter; indeed, so much so that the portrait evolved from a depiction of an individual into a general statement about old age. It is a study of human expression. This may in part be the result of the fact that the old lady apparently was reluctant to sit for Rembrandt, and only agreed because it was the express wish of her children. She remains withdrawn into herself, her face conveys the hardship of old age, and her eyes, with their diverging gaze, are slightly lowered and avoid all contact with the viewer. Rembrandt's expansion of the task of simply recording the reality of the «conterfeis» into one documenting a generalised state of being clearly had an effect on the manner of execution. This was already noted by the authors of the *Corpus,* who in addition to citing other portraits mostly drew comparisons with *tronies* executed by Rembrandt during the 1630s. They failed, however, to mention the closest example: the *Bust of an Old Man with Golden Chain,* painted two years previously and now in Kassel (cat. no. 81).

This portrait of a woman is singular for the period in question because Rembrandt took the liberty of executing it in a sketchy open manner. Moreover, his use of impasto is much in evidence. Individual strokes of the brush cross one another on the sitter's forehead and each appears as if the yellowish and rose-coloured paint, which was mixed on the palette, has been applied with a trowel. The hollows of her wrinkles are executed in red. The demands of portraiture and the soft, padded features of the sitter necessitated a more temperate application of the paint in favour of a finer diffusion of form. Nevertheless, details such as the unconnected black shadows in the corner of the eye are exactly the same as those found in the Kassel painting. In the present portrait these shadows extend to the eyelid, the bridge of the nose and the opening of the mouth. Rembrandt painted no female pendant to the Kassel old man. The portrait of Aechje Claesdr. Pesser creates the impression that here Rembrandt made up for that omission.                    B.S.

1   *Dirck Jansz. Pesser,* oak panel, 67 x 52 cm, later enlarged to a rectangle, inscribed *Rembrandt ft. 1634,* County Museum of Art, Los Angeles. Corpus, vol. 2, 1986, no. A 102. *Haesje Jacobsdr. van Cleyburgh,* oak panel, 68.8 x 53.4, inscribed *Rembran..f. 163(4).* Rijksmuseum, Amsterdam. Corpus, vol. 2, 1986, no. A 103.
2   *The Preacher Johannes Uyttenbogaert,* canvas, 123 x 105 cm, inscribed Rembrandt ft: 1633, Rijksmuseum, Amsterdam. Corpus, vol. 2, 1986, no. A 80.

381

## 84
Jacob Adriaensz. Backer (Harlingen 1608–1651 Amsterdam)
# Old Man with a Mirror Fragment (Sight), c. 1633

Oak panel, 71.5 x 60.5 cm
Inscribed right: *J B*
Staatliche Museen zu
Berlin, Preußischer
Kulturbesitz, Gemälde-
galerie, Cat. No. 935B

Bauch 1926, p. 29f.,
no. 71; Czobor 1969,
p. 22; Berlin 1976, p. 12;
Sumowski 1983ff., vol. 1,
no. 22; Berlin 1996, p. 14,
fig. no. 1138

Against a dark, unidentified background, an old man with a beard is turned slightly to the left and stares at the fragment of a mirror which he holds in his right hand. He thus reveals himself to be a rather original personification of the allegory of sight. The light falling from above left illuminates his head and the left half of his face while leaving the right cast in shadow. The light emphasises the modelling of his wrinkled face. The painting belongs to a series of depictions of the Five Senses scattered among different European collections.[1]

In the sixteenth century, five scantily clad women personified the Five Senses, each holding an attribute (mirror, fruit, etc.) which would enable the viewer to identify the sense she represented. Usually artists depicted the five seated or lying figures grouped together in a landscape. The subject was a particularly popular one in the graphic arts, and inscriptions made the identification even easier. During the turn of the sixteenth to the seventeenth century, the manner of depicting the Senses changed considerably. Artists working in the wider circle of Caravaggio favoured allegorical renderings of the Senses using male half-length figures.[2] An important, perhaps even decisive series for the new interpretation of the subject is that executed by Jusepe de Ribera for a Spanish nobleman during his sojourn in Rome around 1613–15.[3] There we find for the first time male half-length figures, each of whom depicts a Sense. By using everyday objects Ribera abandons the allegorical tradition in favour of a genre-like conception of the subject. Artists from Utrecht – in particular Hendrick ter Brugghen and Gerard van Honthorst, who were in Rome at the beginning of the Seicento – adopted this pictorial type and popularised it in their homeland upon their return.[4] Backer builds on this tradition by moving the figure of the old man to the very edge of his painting so that he directly relates to the viewer. The alteration in the iconographic understanding of the subject goes hand-in-hand with a change in the technique of painting. Backer clearly orientates his style to that of Rembrandt. Especially his use of impasto and the warm reddish flesh tones are reminiscent of the master. Backer also uses the end of the brush to scratch individual hairs in the man's beard. A comparison with Rembrandt's *Bust of an Old Man with Golden Chain* of 1632 (cat. no. 81) reveals moreover that Backer clearly used the same model, so that his painting seems to have been created in close proximity to Rembrandt. Backer does not, however, go as far as to imitate the master. Instead his painting shows in an exemplary manner how Rembrandt inspired the work of other painters. Born in Friesland, Backer was apprenticed to Lambert Jacobsz. in Leeuwarden, where he met Govaert Flinck. Around 1633 both painters moved to Amsterdam, Flinck to work as an assistant in Rembrandt's studio and Backer to establish himself as an independent artist. Nevertheless, Rembrandt's influence on his early Amsterdam production is clearly evident, and one of the paintings executed during this period was the Sense of Sight.

J.L.

[1] *Taste,* Staatliche Museen zu Berlin, Preußischer Kulturbesitz, Gemäldegalerie; *Hearing,* Szépmüvészeti Múseum, Budapest; *Touch,* Museu Nacional de Arte Antiga, Lisbon (Sumowski 1983ff., vol. 1, pp. 225–228) and Smell, Harry J. Moore, Lincolnshire (Sumowski 1983ff., vol. 5, p. 3078).
[2] See Madrid 1997 for an overview of the subject and the literature to date.
[3] New York 1992, pp. 60–65. The man in question is probably Juan de Tassis y Peralta, Conde de Villamediana (1582–1622), who in the 17th. century owned a legendary collection of paintings. On this, see my forthcoming Ph.D. thesis (Justus Lange, *Zum Frühwerk des Jusepe de Ribera,* Dissertation, Würzburg 2000).
[4] Blankert 1986/87.

Rembrandt Harmensz. van Rijn
# The Apostle Paul, c. 1629

85
Red chalk, black pen,
wash, heightened with
white, 236 x 201 mm
Benesch 15
Musée du Louvre,
Départements des Arts
Graphiques, Paris,
Inv. No. 22985

86
Etching, 238 x 200 mm
Bartsch 149, II State (2)
Teylers Museum,
Haarlem, Inv. No. KG
3719

White/Boon 1969,
no. 149; Schatborn 1986a,
pp. 4–5; Paris 1988/89,
no. 3; Gutbrot 1996,
p. 226f.

Only in Kassel

Both sheets, which are exhibited together, belong to the same project, as the design and etching of the same subject.

The Apostle Paul sits in front of a table on which a thick folio volume lies open. His body is turned towards the viewer, whom he fixes with his gaze. The turn of his body is repeated by his arms: while one arm rests on the table, the other supports his energetic twisting movement by gripping the armrest of the chair. At the same time, this pose also suggests that he has momentarily paused in the act of turning. The composition is repeated in reverse in the etching (cat. no. 86). However, a more detailed study shows that it is actually the composition of the preparatory drawing (cat. no. 85) that is reversed. That the Apostle should hold the pen in his left hand is most unusual. It is only in the etching that Paul is shown as right-handed. This indicates that from the beginning Rembrandt conceived the drawing as a preparatory work for the etching.

It is nonetheless not simply the case that the drawn image was replicated as a print. Instead the master changed some details. He eliminated the sword, an attribute of the Apostle,[1] which is placed against the back wall in the drawing, and accentuated the wall of the etching by using darker hatching. Finally, in the second state, known only in the one impression on exhibit, he covered up the Apostle's hand on the armrest. Although seemingly small alter-

ations, they change the character of the depiction. Whereas in the drawing Paul appears to have just interrupted his studies and, as if disturbed by something, still holds onto the armrest, in the etching the impression of movement has been eliminated. The absence of the sword makes the iconographic identification more difficult. One could almost suspect that in the etching Rembrandt was intent on creating a generalised example of a scholar sitting at a writing desk.[2]

The two sheets differ moreover in the placement of light and shadow. In the drawing in Paris the two zones are clearly differentiated. The table with the open book is so enveloped in shadow that it is practically impossible to identify individual details. The etching attempts to lessen this effect. The first state weakens slightly the contrast between light and dark. But Rembrandt apparently wished to unify the composition even more. To this end, in a second step, he applied ink of varying intensities, but did not completely wipe the surface of the plate clean so as obtain less harsh contrasts by staining the paper with different shades of grey. The rare etching is known only in four impressions whereby three reproduce the first state, with the fourth, the exhibited sheet, being the only known example of the second state. Rembrandt does not appear to have been happy with the altered composition, which is why he printed no additional impressions. This situa-

385

tion points once again to the experimental nature of a number of sheets in Rembrandt's œuvre.

Van Rijckevorsel drew attention to an etching by Willem van Swanenburg after a design by Abraham Bloemaert (fig. 85/86a), which could have inspired Rembrandt's depiction of the Apostle.[3] Compositional similarities are evident, although Bloemaert places the Apostle into a scenic context by depicting in the background the conversion of Paul.

Both the drawing and the etching are closely related to a number of works by Rembrandt and members of his studio. The master himself transformed the depiction into a full-length composition for a painting, now in Nürnberg, in which he emphasised the meditative character (cat. no. 32). The drawing and/or etching

provided a studio assistant with one source of inspiration for the painting *St Paul at his Desk* painting in Vienna (cat. no. 87). Another painting of the Apostle by Jan Lievens (Bremen) also contains some comparable elements.[4] These examples attest to the actuality of this particular subject in Leiden.

The issue of the date of the drawing and etching is more difficult to answer. Frits Lugt dated both sheets to around 1627,[5] as did Peter Schatborn.[6] White and Boon on the other hand proposed a date around 1629. A number of compositional similarities are found in Rembrandt's *Rich Man* of 1627 (cat. no. 29), especially in the heavy folio volumes, which for the most are not illuminated and thus form a dark barrier at the bottom of the painting above which the brightly lit Apostle towers. Yet despite these affinities, the more frequently cited date of circa 1629 for the drawing and etching seems more accurate,[7] especially as the draughtsmanship is much freer and differs from the artist's earliest graphic works (e.g. cat. no. 13).

Irrespective of the exact date of execution, both the drawing and the related etching as well as the studio painting from Vienna (cat. no. 87) offer an unique opportunity to study the development and influence of Rembrandt's pictorial invention. J.L.

Fig. 85/86a
Willem van Swanenburg
after Abraham Bloemaert
*St Paul*
Etching, 244 x 273 mm
Rijksmuseum, Amsterdam

---

[1] What appears to be a weak indication of a cross shape behind Paul on the left could be a reminder of the weapon. It is more noticeable in the exhibited second state.

[2] Bauch 1933, pp. 101f. identified both images as «an old man with books».

[3] Rijckevorsel 1932, pp. 73–75.

[4] Canvas, 110.5 x 101.5 cm. Kunsthalle Bremen. Hamburg 2000, no. 4.

[5] He recognised a close relationship with Rembrandt's dated *St Paul in Prison* of 1627 in Stuttgart. Paris 1933, no. 1145.

[6] Schatborn 1986a, p. 3.

[7] Most recently Amsterdam/London 2000/01, p. 69.

# St Paul at His Desk, c. 1636

Canvas, 137 x 112.5 cm
Inscribed below left:
*Rembrandt 163.*
Kunsthistorisches
Museum Vienna,
Gemäldegalerie, Inv.
No. 297

Sumowski 1983ff., vol. 2
no. 643 (Flicnck); Corpus,
vol. 3, 1989, pp. 27–29
(Rembrandt-Studio,
1635/36); Vienna 1991,
p. 99, pl. 509 (Rembrandt)

The exhibition closes with *St Paul at His Desk* from Vienna. Although it lies beyond the period under review, it shows in an exemplary manner the enduring effects of Rembrandt's early work.

The white-haired, bearded Apostle sits in an armchair at a writing desk covered with books. He has for a moment stopped his work to turn to the viewer. He holds a pen in his right hand while his left rests on an open folio volume upon which a half-written sheet of paper has been placed. The depiction of the contemplative Apostle who pauses while writing is a classic reference to Paul's activity as the author of letters to the young Christian community. The large sword leaning against the back wall refers to his martyrdom by decapitation.

The painting is generally dated to the middle of the 1630s. The no longer fully-extant date was deciphered as 1636 in the eighteenth century.[1] But even then doubts about Rembrandt's authorship were raised, and attributions to Govert Flinck, Jacob Adriaensz. Backer and Jan Lievens were suggested.[2] However, the painting still bears the attribution to Rembrandt in the museum. The *Rembrandt Research Project* provided new arguments for the date and for a close connection with Rembrandt's studio production. The canvas came from the same bale of cloth as that was used for a number of Rembrandt paintings: the *Cupid Blowing Bubbles* of 1634, the contemporaneous *Holy Family* in Munich as well as the Berlin *Samson* of 1635.[3] The exaggerated red of the Apostle's head and the undifferentiated brushwork, which lacks rhythm and depth, have been criticised. But the painting's style does not fit any of the identified artists in Rembrandt's circle. For this reason, the frequently-made attribution to Govert Flinck is untenable. Flinck arrived in Rembrandt's studio in 1633 as a fully-fledged painter and remained there for a year as an assistant, during which time he completely assimilated the master's style. He set up his own studio at the time the *Apostle Paul* was being painted. Despite close stylistic similarities with Rembrandt, his signed paintings, such as the 1636 *Shepherdess* in Braunschweig,[4] are marked by a specific looseness of brushwork and an autonomy of pictorial invention.

The latter quality in particular does not apply to the *Apostle Paul*. Instead it is a typical anonymous product of Rembrandt's studio, whereby the goal was to achieve a convincingly authentic effect. To this end a number of different older works by Rembrandt served as models, which could be adapted and combined at will. Von Moltke was the first to point to the etching

389

87a
Rembrandt Studio,
*St Paul at His Desk*
(detail), c. 1636

of 1629 (cat. no. 86). In the *Corpus*, Josua Bruyn correctly drew attention to the preparatory design for this etching, a sanguine drawing in the Louvre (cat. no. 85) which also contains the long sword, the handle of which almost touches the upper edge of the drawing. The Viennese painting also takes account of the change that Rembrandt's style underwent in the 1630s, when his figures became more monumental and displayed greater pathos. This was achieved in a number of ways: by emphasising the twist of the body, with the head turned in one direction, the upper body in the other; by placing greater importance on the heavy mass of the beard, the lively contour of the fluffy hair on the head; and by the gaze, which is no longer directed inward but energetically seeks to fix the viewer.

But one other, equally important pictorial source has gone unnoticed: Rembrandt's *Bust of an Old Man with Golden Chain* of 1632 in Kassel (cat. no. 81). The comparison reveals not just surprising similarities in pose, gaze, the illumination of the forehead and the structure of the wrinkles, but also provides an explanation for the unusual colouring of the Viennese head. The studio assistant was clearly incapable of imitating the warm variegated flesh-tones of his model so that his work contains a disproportionate amount of red. The adaptations which occurred when a study after a model was transformed into a figure in a history painting can be studied in the detailed illustrations of the two figures in Bernhard Schnackenburg's analysis.[5]

B.S.

1   Vienna 1783, p. 88, no. 17 (Rembrandt, «Auf dem Gemälde steht Rembrandt f. 1636»).
2   Vienna 1796, p. 21, no. 15 (doubts about authenticity, by a certain «Heinrich [Ulrich?]»); Vienna 1884, pp. 364f., no. 1145 (manner of painting points to Govert Flinck); Benesch 1935, p. 5 (studio copy after a lost original by Rembrandt); Moltke 1965, pp. 18f., 24, 80, no. 71, pls. 6, 7 (Flinck); Bauch 1966, no. A 9 (perhaps Backer, reworked by Rembrandt); Bredius/ Gerson 1969, p. 612, no. 603 (Flinck or Lievens).
3   Corpus, vol. 2, 1986, nos. A 91 and A 88, vol. 3, 1989, p. 28, fig. 15 and no. A 109.
4   Sumowski 1983ff., vol. 2, p. 1031, no. 656, colour ill. p. 1088.
5   See above, pp. 114–118 (p. 117, fig. 32, 33).

# Appendix

Biographical Data of Rembrandt's
Beginnings

Constantijn Huygens
on Rembrandt and Lievens

Bibliography

List of Photos

# Rembrandt Harmensz. van Rijn (Leiden 1606–1669 Amsterdam)
# Biographical Data of his Beginnings

## 1606

Rembrandt was born on July 15th in Leiden. Unlike many painters of his time, he did not come from a family of artists or craftsmen; his father was a miller.

## 1613

He began attending the Latin school, the only formal education he was to receive. Biblical studies and classics were the main subjects taught. It is not clear whether he finished school. His first biographer, the Leiden burgomaster Jan Jansz. Orlers, suggests that at his own request he was taken from school prematurely and sent to be trained as a painter.

## 1620

On May 20th Rembrandt was enrolled at Leiden University, possibly merely for tax reasons.

## c. 1620–25

He trained as an artist. The exact dates of the training periods are not known. Not uncommonly for the time, he had two masters in succession. The first was the Leiden painter Jacob van Swanenburgh (see cat. no. 1), with whom, according to Orlers, he stayed for about three years, and who must have trained him in the basic skills and knowledge necessary for the profession. His second teacher, Pieter Lastman, who lived in Amsterdam, was well known at the time as a history painter (cat. nos. 2, 4–6); he also helped to develop Rembrandt's abilities and knowledge in the field of history painting.

## c. 1625

Rembrandt settled in Leiden as an independent master. During this period, Rembrandt collaborated closely and may even have shared a studio with the painter Jan Lievens (cat. nos. 8, 14, 15, 18, 20, 21, 23, 24, 71–73), who had also received his final training with Pieter Lastman. A child prodigy, Lievens was one year younger than Rembrandt but had already embarked upon his own career; indeed, it may well be that Lievens had a stronger impact on Rembrandt in these early years than vice versa. Rembrandt's earliest works testify to this collaboration (cat. nos. 9–11), providing a commentary, as it were, on Pieter Lastman's work (see cat. s. 3, 7). His production as a painter in the Leiden period was mainly devoted to small-scale history paintings and *tronies*, single half-figures that – although individuals must have posed for them (cat. no. 74, 75), including Rembrandt himself (cat. no. 78) – were not intended as portraits.

## c. 1626

Rembrandt produced his first etchings. Whereas drawing is the natural pendant to painting, Rembrandt's decision to begin etching meant taking a separate, very important direction in his career. Much of his international fame must have been based on the widely circulated prints he made from these approximately 300 etchings (see cat. nos. 13, 19, 40–45, 49, 50, 52–55). Some 78 of his etching plates have been preserved.

## c. 1628

From 1628 on, Rembrandt had pupils, among them Gerard Dou (see cat. nos. 66, 67, 76, 77). We usually know of the existence of Rembrandt's pupils by chance, no official register of painters' trainees in either Leiden or Amsterdam having survived. We can make only a rough estimate of the number of Rembrandt's pupils; however, over his entire career he must have had at least fifty and quite possibly many more. Joachim Sandrart wrote of «countless pupils» in his studio. Each pupil's parent had to pay 100 guilders annually in tuition expenses, a substantial sum in those days. Rembrandt also profited financially from his pupils through the sale of their works. Rembrandt's early fame attracted many young men – from abroad, as well – who were eager to become his pupil once they had completed their basic training elsewhere. It seems that a number of them, including Isack Jouderville, for some time stayed on as studio assistants.

## c. 1628–1669

Rembrandt collected ethnographic and other objects, which he probably depicted in his works from 1628 onwards (see cat. no. 32). This encyclopedic collection of *naturalia* and *artificialia* also included numerous prints and paintings, goods in which Rembrandt also dealt. The inventory of Rembrandt's goods, drawn up on the occasion of his insolvency in 1656, serves as a catalogue of this enormous collection.

## 1628–29

Rembrandt worked on the *Judas Repentant* (cat. no. 33). This painting was seen in his studio and highly admired for its narrative quality by Constantijn Huygens, the secretary of Prince Frederik Hendrik. This may well have led to the first known purchase by the Prince of a painting by Rembrandt (*The Rape of Proserpine*, c. 1630, today Staatliche Museen zu Berlin, Preußischer Kulturbesitz, Gemäldegalerie). These purchases would continue until 1646.

## 1629

He finished the *Judas Repentant* (cat. no. 33), and among other works painted the *Artist in his Studio* (cat. no. 61). The year 1629 marked a period in which – after an amazingly rapid and consistent evolution from 1625 onwards – Rembrandt reached the first peak in his artistic development. The pictorial problems he set himself in that period (concerning the handling of light and differentiation of the paint substance) would later occupy him again intensively, especially in his later years.

## 1630

Beginning of a collaboration with the etcher Jan Gillisz. van Vliet, who made prints of a number of Rembrandt's early works (cat. nos. 57, 79, 80). This was an accepted way of bringing one's artistic inventions into a wider circulation. The collaboration lasted until 1635/36.

## 1631

Rembrandt became acquainted with Hendrick Uylenburgh, an Amsterdam art entrepreneur with a large workshop in which portraits were painted, restorations carried out and copies produced. Rembrandt apparently decided to leave Leiden, then in decline, for Amsterdam, which at that time was enjoying an economic boom. However, resettling to another town and becoming a master in the painters' guild were neither straightforward nor simple processes. In several towns it was customary to demand that a younger painter first serve an obligatory apprenticeship of about two years in the workshop of a local master before being admitted to the guild. This may be the reason why Rembrandt moved into Uylenburgh's workshop (cat. no. 81). We know that Rembrandt only became a member of the St Luke's Guild in Amsterdam in 1634. In that same year, he married Uylenburgh's niece, Saskia.

## 1631–34

In Uylenburgh's workshop, he produced – with the occasional help of assistants – a substantial number of portraits and group portraits (cat. nos. 82, 83).

# Constantijn Huygens on Rembrandt and Lievens (from his autobiography, c. 1630)

I have deliberately refrained from mentioning a pair of young and noble painters from Leiden in this parade. Were I to say that they were the only ones who can vie with the absolute geniuses among the aforesaid prodigies, I would still be underestimating the merits of these two. And were I to say that they will soon surpass those geniuses, I would merely be expressing what their astonishing beginnings have led connoisseurs to expect. Considering their parentage, there is no stronger evidence against the belief that nobility is in the blood. Some people swear by such nobility, but I recall how cleverly they were confuted by the biting satire of Traiano Boccalini, a modern author who writes in a most painstaking and pure style. In a tale about the anatomical dissection of a nobleman's corpse, he relates how all the doctors, after carefully inspecting the veins, declared unanimously that nobility did not dwell in the blood, for there was no difference between this man's blood and that of a commoner or peasant.

One of our two youths was the son of a commoner, an embroiderer; the other a miller's son, but assuredly not of the same grain. Who could help but marvel that two such prodigies of talent and skill should ripen from such humble seeds?

Enquiring as to their childhood teachers, I discover men whose reputation was scarcely known outside the common classes. Due to their parents' straitened circumstances, the youths were compelled to take teachers whose fees were modest. Were these teachers to be confronted with their pupils today, they would feel just as abashed as those teachers who gave Virgil his first lessons in poetry, Cicero in rhetoric and Archimedes in mathematics. Let it however be said, with due respect for everyone's capacities and without detracting from anyone (for what is it to me?): these two owe nothing to their teachers but everything to their aptitude. Had they never received any tuition but been left to their own devices and suddenly been seized by the urge to paint, I am convinced that they would have risen to the same heights as they indeed have. It would be wrong to think that others have led them to this point.

The first, whom I described as an embroiderer's son, is called Jan Lievens; the other, whose cradle stood in a mill, Rembrandt. Both are still beardless and, going by their faces, more boys than men. I am neither able nor willing to judge each according to his works and application. As in the case of the aforementioned Rubens, I wish these two would draw up an inventory of their works and describe their paintings. Each could supply a modest explanation of his method, going on to indicate how and why (for the admiration and education of all future generations) they had designed, composed and worked out each painting.

I venture to suggest offhand that Rembrandt is superior to Lievens in his sure touch and liveliness of emotions. Conversely, Lievens is the greater in inventiveness and audacious themes and forms. Everything his young spirit endeavours to capture must be magnificent and lofty. Rather than depicting his subject in its true size, he chooses a larger scale.

Rembrandt, by contrast, devotes all his loving concentration to a small painting, achieving on that modest scale a result which one would seek in vain in the largest pieces of others. I cite as an example his painting of the repentant Judas returning to the high priest the silver coins which were the price for our innocent Lord. Compare this with all Italy, indeed, with all the wondrous beauties that have survived from the most ancient of days. The gesture of that one despairing Judas (not to mention all the other impressive figures in the painting), that one maddened Judas, screaming, begging for forgiveness, but devoid of hope, all traces of hope erased from his face; his gaze wild, his hair torn out by the roots, his garments rent, his arms contorted, his hands clenched until they bleed; a blind impulse has brought him to his knees, his whole body writhing in pitiful hideousness. All this I compare with all the beauty that has been produced throughout the ages. This is what I would have those naive beings know, who claim (and I have rebuked them for it before) that nothing created or expressed in words today has not been expressed or created in the past. I maintain that it did not occur to Protogenes, Apelles or Parrhasius, nor could it occur to them, were they to return to earth, that a youth, a Dutchman, a beardless miller, could put so much into one human figure and depict it all. Even as I write these words I am struck with amazement. All honour to thee, Rembrandt! To transport Troy, indeed all Asia, to Italy

is a lesser achievement than to heap the laurels of Greece and Italy on the Dutch, the achievement of a Dutchman who has never ventured outside the walls of his native city.

I believe I have already mentioned Lievens' character in passing. He is a young man of great spirit, and great things may be expected of him if he is granted a long enough life. He has an acute and profound insight into all manner of things, riper than a mature man, as I have often had occasion to note in conversations. My only objection is his stubbornness, which derives from an excess of self-confidence. He either roundly rejects all criticism or, if he acknowledges its validity, takes it in bad spirit. This bad habit, harmful at any age, is absolutely pernicious in youth. After all, a little leaven leaveneth the whole lump. And those ridden with the vice which closely resembles this bad habit, ‹deceive themselves›, according to the Holy Scripture. It is a sign of great sagacity to realize that God has given to each man ‹with a chary hand what is sufficient›, in the words of the poet but that no man has ever received everything; consequently all men, whoever they be, should be approached with a well-disposed heart and an inquisitive mind, in the belief that there is always something to be learned from everyone.

Compared with his age, the production of the illustrious youth is immense. Seeing the maker beside his paintings, it is scarcely credible that such a meagre sapling can put forth so much fruit. In painting the human countenance he wreaks miracles. One

would be rendering him good service by endeavouring to curb this vigorous, untameable spirit whose bold ambition is to embrace all nature, and by persuading the brilliant painter to concentrate on that physical part which miraculously combines the essence of the human spirit and body. In what we are accustomed to calling history pieces, the artist, his astonishing talent notwithstanding, is unlikely to match Rembrandt's vivid invention.

In the collection of our Prince there is a painting of a man purported to be a Turkish potentate with a Dutchman's head [tronie]; Brouart has a portrait [tronie] whose face is sere and wrinkled like that of a philosopher. De Gheyn, I believe, has some portraits [tronies] of youths, and Sohier diverse portraits which the artist painted some time ago, while still a pupil. They are works of inestimable value and unrivalled artistry. May their maker be preserved for us in the length of days.

Allow me to relate in passing that once, in the company of my brother, I called on him; he had no prior acquaintance with me at this time. He was seized with the desire to paint my portrait. I assured him that I should be only too pleased to grant him the opportunity if he would come to The Hague and put up at my house for a while. So ardent was his desire that he arrived within a few days, explaining that since seeing me his nights had been restless and his days so troubled that he had been unable to work. My countenance had lodged so firmly in his mind that his eagerness brooked no further delay. This effect on his imaginative powers was all the

more remarkable in view of his customary aversion to being persuaded to portray a person. It being winter and the days drawing in, and my own affairs leaving me scant time to pose, he was content to paint my clothes and my bare hands (a task of which he acquitted himself most tastefully) and to postpone the portrayal of my face until the advent of spring. Again, he made his appearance long before the appointed date. So evident in the finished work was his enthusiasm that I paid tribute to its excellent maker by allotting it a permanent place amongst my most treasured possessions. Not a day goes by but it is regarded by van Mierevelt and countless others with the utmost admiration. There are however those who opine that the contemplative rendering of the face detracts from the vivacity of my mind, to which I can but respond that the fault is mine. During this period I was involved in a serious family affair of some importance and, as is only to be expected, the cares which I endeavoured to keep to myself were clearly reflected in the expression of my face and eyes.

I do however censure one fault of these celebrated young men, from whom I can scarcely tear myself away in this account. I have already criticized Lievens for his self-confidence, which Rembrandt shares; hitherto, neither has found it necessary to spend a few months travelling through Italy. This is naturally a touch of folly in figures otherwise so brilliant. If only someone could drive it out of their young heads, he would truly contribute the sole element still needed to perfect their artistic powers. How I would welcome their acquaintance with Raphael and Michelangelo, the feasting of their eyes on the creations of such gigantic spirits! How quickly they would surpass them all, giving the Italians due cause to come to Holland. If only these men, born to raise art to the highest pinnacle, knew themselves better!

Let me describe the pretext with which they justify their lack of mobility. They claim to be in the bloom of youth and wish to profit from it; they have no time to waste on foreign travel. Moreover, the best Italian paintings of the genre most appreci-ated and collected these days by kings and princes north of the Alps are to be found outside Italy. What is scattered around in that country and only to be traced by dint of considerable effort, can be found in abundance and even in surfeit here.

The validity of this excuse is a moot point. I feel it incumbent upon myself to state that I have never observed such dedication and persistence in other men, whatever their pursuits or ages. Truly, these youths are redeem-ing the time. That is their sole con-sideration. Most amazingly, they regard even the most innocent diver-sions of youth as a waste of time, as if they were already old men burdened with age and long past such follies. Such indefatigable application to diligent labour may well yield great results quickly, but I have often wished that these excellent young men would practise moderation and consider their constitutions, which a sedentary occupation has already rendered less vigorous and robust.

(Based on C. L. Heesakkers translation from the Latin of Constantijn Huygens' text, pub-lished as *Mijn Jeugd*, Amsterdam 1987.)

# Bibliography

Alpers 1988
Svetlana Alpers, *Rembrandt's Enterprise. The Studio and the Market*, London 1988

Amsterdam 1976a
*All the Paintings of the Rijksmuseum in Amsterdam. A Completely Illustrated Catalogue*, P. J. J. van Thiel et al., Amsterdam/Haarlem 1976

Amsterdam 1976b
*Tot Lering en Vermaak, Betekenissen van Hollandse genrevoorstellingen uit de zeventiende eeuw*, edited by Eddy de Jongh, Rijksmuseum, Amsterdam, 1976

Amsterdam 1983
*The Impact of a Genius. Rembrandt, His Pupils and Followers in the Seventeenth Century,* edited by Albert Blankert et al., Waterman Gallery, Amsterdam, 1983

Amsterdam 1985
*Tekeningen van Rembrandt, zijn onbekende leerlingen en navolgers* (Catalogus van de Nederlandse tekeningen in het Rijksprentenkabinet, Rijksmuseum Amsterdam IV)/*Drawings by Rembrandt, his anonymous pupils and followers* (Catalogue of the Dutch and Flemish Drawings in the Rijksprentenkabinet, Rijksmuseum, Amsterdam, IV), Peter Schatborn, The Hague 1985

Amsterdam 1988/89
*Jan Lievens, 1607–1674. Prenten & Tekeningen/Prints & Drawings*, edited by Peter Schatborn and Eva Ornstein-van Slooten, Museum het Rembrandthuis, Amsterdam, 1988

Amsterdam 1991
*Pieter Lastman, leermeester van Rembrandt/Pieter Lastman, the Man Who*

Taught Rembrandt, edited by Ed de Heer, Museum het Rembrandthuis, Amsterdam, 1991

Amsterdam 1992
*All the Paintings of the Rijksmuseum in Amsterdam. A Completely Illustrated Catalogue. First supplement: 1976–91*, P. J. J. van Thiel et al., Amsterdam/ The Hague 1992

Amsterdam 1993/94
*Dawn of the Golden Age, Northern Netherlandish Art 1580–1620*, edited by B. Bakker, Rijksmuseum, Amsterdam, 1993

Amsterdam 1996
*Rembrandt and van Vliet. A Collaboration on Copper*, edited by Chr. Schuckman, Museum het Rembrandthuis, Amsterdam, 1996

Amsterdam 1997
*Spiegel van alledag. Nederlandse genreprenten 1550–1700*, edited by Eddy de Jongh and Ger Luijten, Rijksmuseum, Amsterdam, 1997

Amsterdam 1999/2000
*Rembrandts schatkamer/Rembrandt's Treasures*, edited by B. van den Boogert, Museum het Rembrandthuis, Amsterdam, 1999

Amsterdam/London 2000/01
*Rembrandt the Printmaker*, edited by Erik Hinterding et al., Rijksmuseum, Amsterdam; British Museum, London, 2000

Amsterdam/Vienna/New York/ Cambridge 1991/92
*Seventeenth-century Dutch drawings. A Selection from the Maida and George*

*Abrams Collection*, edited by William W. Robinson, Rijksmuseum, Amsterdam; Graphische Sammlung Albertina, Vienna; The Pierpont Morgan Gallery, New York; The Fogg Art Museum, Harvard University, Cambridge, New York 1991

Andrews 1985
Keith Andrews, *Adam Elsheimer. Werkverzeichnis der Gemälde, Zeichnungen und Radierungen,* Munich 1985

Angel 1642
Philips Angel, *Lof der Schilderkonst*, Leiden 1642

Antwerp 1993
*Jacob Jordaens (1593–1678). Volume I, Paintings and Tapestries*, edited by R.-A. d'Hulst et al., Koninklijk Museum voor Schone Kunsten, Antwerp, 1993

Antwerp/London 1999
*Van Dyck 1599–1641*, edited by Christopher Brown and Hans Vlieghe, Koninklijk Museum voor Schone Kunsten, Antwerp; Royal Academy of Arts, London, 1999

Antwerpse Kunstinventarissen
*Antwerpse Kunstinventarissen uit de zeventiende eeuw*, edited by Erik Duverger (Fontes historiae artis neerlandicae. Bronnen voor de Kunstgeschiedenis van de Nederlanden, vol. 1), 10 vols., Brussels 1984–1999

Baar/Moerman 1991
P. J. M. de Baar and I. W. L. Moerman, *Rembrandt van Rijn en Jan Lievens, inwoners van Leiden*, in: Leiden 1991/92, pp. 24–38

Baer 1990
Ronni Baer, *The Paintings of Gerrit Dou (1613–1675)*, Ph.D. diss. New York 1990

Baer 2000/2001
Ronni Baer, *The Life and Art of Gerrit Dou*, in: Washington/London/The Hague 2000/01, pp. 26–52

Baldinucci (1686) 1808
Filippo Baldinucci, *Cominciamento e progresso dell' arte dell' intagliare in rame, colle vite di molti de' più eccellenti maestri della stessa professione*, Florence (1686) 1808

Barasch 1978
Moshe Barasch, *Light and Color in the Italian Renaissance Theory of Art,* New York 1978

Baraude 1933
H. Baraude, *Lopez: agent financier et confident de Richelieu*, Paris 1933

Bartsch 1797
A. Bartsch, *Catalogue raisonné de toutes les estampes qui forment l'œuvre de Rembrandt, et ceux de ses principaux imitateurs*, 2 vols., Vienna 1797

Bartsch
Adam Bartsch, *Le Peintre Graveur*, 21 vols., Vienna 1803–1821

Basle 1987
*Im Lichte Hollands. Holländische Malerei des 17. Jahrhunderts aus den Sammlungen des Fürsten von Liechtenstein und aus Schweizer Besitz*, edited by Petra ten-Doesschate Chu, Kunstmuseum Basle, 1987

Basle 2000
*Die Sammlung Max Geldner im Kunstmuseum Basel. Vermächtnis und Ankäufe der Stiftung*, edited by Gian Carlo Bott, Kunstmuseum Basle, 2000

Bassano/Fort Worth 1992/93
*Jacopo Bassano ca. 1510–1592*, edited by Beverly Louise Brown and Paola Marini, Museo Civico, Bassano; Kimbell Art Museum, Fort Worth, 1992

Bauch 1926
Kurt Bauch, *Jakob Adriaensz. Backer. Ein Rembrandtschüler aus Friesland*, Berlin 1926

Bauch 1933
Kurt Bauch, *Die Kunst des jungen Rembrandt*, Heidelberg 1933

Bauch 1939
Kurt Bauch, *Rembrandt und Lievens*, in: *Wallraf-Richartz-Jahrbuch* 11, 1939, pp. 239–268

Bauch 1960
Kurt Bauch, *Der frühe Rembrandt und seine Zeit. Studien zur geschichtlichen Bedeutung seines Frühstils*, Berlin 1960

Bauch 1966
Kurt Bauch, *Rembrandt. Gemälde*, Berlin 1966

Bauch 1967a
Kurt Bauch, *Zum Werk des Jan Lievens (I)*, in: *Pantheon* 25, 1967, pp. 160–170

Bauch 1967b
Kurt Bauch, *Ikonographischer Stil. Zur Frage der Inhalt in Rembrandt's Kunst*, in: *Studien zur Kunstgeschichte*, pp. 123–151

Beck 1624
David Beck and S. E. Veldhuyzen (Eds.), *Spiegel van mijn leven. Een Haags dagboek uit 1624*, Hilversum 1993

Benesch 1935
Otto Benesch, *Rembrandt. Werk und Forschung*, Vienna 1935

Benesch 1940
Otto Benesch, *An Early Group Portrait Drawing by Rembrandt*, in: *Art Quarterly* 3, 1940, pp. 2–14

Benesch 1954
Otto Benesch, *An Unknown Rembrandt Painting of the Leiden Period*, in: *The Burlington Magazine* 96, 1954, pp. 134f.

Benesch
Otto Benesch, *The Drawings of Rembrandt. A Critical and Chronological Catalogue*, 6 vols., London 1954–1957

Benjamin 1963
Walter Benjamin, *Das Kunstwerk im Zeitalter seiner technischen Reproduzierbarkeit: Drei Studien zur Kunstsoziologie*, Frankfurt 1963

Berenson 1902
Bernard Berenson, *Rudiments of Connoisseurship*, in: *The Study and Criticism of Italian Art*, 2 vols., London 1902

Berlin 1975
*Gemäldegalerie SMPK Berlin. Katalog der ausgestellten Gemälde des 13. –18. Jahrhunderts*, Henning Bock et al., Berlin 1975

Berlin 1976
*Holländische und Flämische Gemälde des 17. Jahrhunderts*, Irene Geismeier, Staatliche Museen zu Berlin, Gemäldegalerie, 1976

Berlin 1989
*Europa und der Orient. 800–1900*, edited by Gereon Sievernich and Hendrik Budde, Martin-Gropius Bau, Berlin, 1989

Berlin 1996
*Gemäldegalerie Berlin. Gesamtverzeichnis. Staatliche Museen zu Berlin, Preußischer Kulturbesitz*, Henning Bock et al., Berlin 1996

Berlin/Amsterdam/London 1991/92
*Rembrandt, de meester en zijn werkplaats – schilderijen*, edited by Chr. Brown, Staatliche Museen zu Berlin, Preußischer Kulturbesitz, Gemäldegalerie; Rijksmuseum, Amsterdam; The National Gallery, London, Berlin 1991

Białostocki 1979
Jan Białostocki, *Lievens und Rembrandt*, in: *Braunschweig 1979*, pp. 13–20

Białostocki 1981
Jan Białostocki, *Stil und Ikonographie. Studien zur Kunstwissenschaft*, Cologne 1981 (first edition Dresden 1966)

Blankert 1982
Albert Blankert, *Ferdinand Bol (1616–1680). Rembrandt's Pupil* (Ph.D. diss. Utrecht 1976), Doornspijk 1982

Blankert 1986/87
Albert Blankert, *Caravaggio und die nördlichen Niederlande*, in: Utrecht/ Braunschweig 1986/87, pp. 17–41

Blankert 1997/98
Albert Blankert, *Looking at Rembrandt. Past and Present*, in: Melbourne/Canberra 1997/98, pp. 32–57

Bloch 1937
Vitale Bloch, *Musik im Hause Rembrandt*, in: *Oud Holland* 54, 1937, pp. 49–53

Blok 1916
P. J. Blok, *Geschiedenis eener Hollandsche Stad. Eene Hollandsche stad onder de Republiek*, S-Gravenhage 1916

Bode 1881
Wilhelm Bode, *Rembrandts früheste Thätigkeit*, in: *Die graphischen Künste* 3, 1881, pp. 49–72

Bode 1883
Wilhelm Bode, *Studien zur Geschichte der Holländischen Malerei*, Braunschweig 1883

Bok 1994
Marten Jan Bok, *Vraag en aanbod op de Nederlandse kunstmarkt 1580–1700*, Ph.D. diss. Utrecht 1994

Bol 1977
L. J. Bol, *Rembrandts Musicerend gezelschap: een Vanitas-allegorie*, in: *Bulletin van het Rijksmuseum* 25, 1977, pp. 95f.

Boston 1980
*Printmaking in the Age of Rembrandt*, edited by C. S. Ackley, Museum of Fine Arts, Boston, 1980

Boston 2000/01
*Rembrandt Creates Rembrandt. Art and Ambition in Leiden 1629–1631*, edited by Alan Chong, Isabella Stewart Gardner Museum, Boston, 2000

Both/Vogel 1964
Wolf von Both and Hans Vogel, *Landgraf Wilhelm VIII. von Hessen-Kassel. Ein Fürst der Rokokozeit,* Munich 1964

Brammer 1999
*Firnisschichten. Beobachtungen an Farbfirnisquerschnitten von vier Gemälden der Kasseler Gemäldegalerie Alte Meister*, in:

*Firnis. Material-Ästhetik-Geschichte.* Internationales Kolloquium Braunschweig, Braunschweig 1999

Braunschweig 1978
*Die Sprache der Bilder. Realität und Bedeutung in der niederländischen Malerei des 17. Jahrhunderts*, edited by Konrad Renger et al., Herzog Anton Ulrich-Museum, Braunschweig, 1978

Braunschweig 1979
*Jan Lievens, ein Maler im Schatten Rembrandts*, edited by Rüdiger Klessmann, Herzog Anton Ulrich-Museum, Braunschweig, 1979

Braunschweig 1993/94
*Bilder vom alten Menschen in der niederländischen und deutschen Kunst 1550–1750*, edited by Jutta Desel and Thomas Döring, Herzog Anton Ulrich-Museum, Braunschweig, 1993

Bredius 1881
A. Bredius, *Drie vroege werken van Rembrandt*, in: *Nederlandse Kunstbode* 1881, pp. 182f.

Bredius 1915
A. Bredius, *Rembrandtiana*, in: *Oud Holland* 33, 1915, pp. 126–128

Bredius 1935
Abraham Bredius, *Rembrandt. Gemälde*, Innsbruck 1935

Bredius
Abraham Bredius, *Künstlerinventare. Urkunden zur Geschichte der holländischen Kunst des 17., 18. und 19. Jahrhunderts*, 8 vols., The Hague 1915–1922

Bredius/Gerson 1969
Abraham Bredius, revised by Horst Gerson, *Rembrandt. The Complete Edition of the Paintings*, London 1969

Broos 1975
B. S. J. Broos, *Rembrandt and Lastman's*

*Coriolanus. The History Piece in 17th-century Theory and Practice*, in: *Simiolus* 8, 1975/76, pp. 199–228

Broos 1977
Ben Broos, *Rembrandt Studies*, Ph.D. diss. Utrecht 1977

Broos 1985
B. P. J. Broos, *Rembrandt en zijn voorbeelden*, Amsterdam 1985

Broos 2000
Ben Broos, *Rembrandts eerste Amsterdamse periode*, in: *Oud Holland* 114, 2000, pp. 1–6

Brown 1981
Christopher Brown, *Carel Fabritius. Complete Edition with a Catalogue Raisonné*, Oxford 1981

Brown 1983
Christopher Brown, *Jan Lievens in Leiden en London*, in: *The Burlington Magazine* 1983, pp. 663–671

Brown 1984
Christopher Brown, *Scenes of Everyday Life. Dutch Genre Paintings of the Seventeenth Century*, London/Boston 1984

Bruyn 1974
Josua Bruyn, *Problems of Attributions*, in: *Rembrandt after Three Hundred Years*, Symposium (1969), The Art Institute of Chicago, Chicago 1974

Bruyn 1979a
E. B. de Bruyn, *Sex en Eros bij Martialis. 300 epigrammen*, Amsterdam 1979

Bruyn 1979b
Josua Bruyn, *Een onderzoek naar 17de-eeuwse schilderijformaten, voornamelijk in Noord-Nederland*, in: *Oud Holland* 93, 1979, pp. 96–115

Bruyn 1982
Josua Bruyn, *The Documentary Value of Early Graphic Reproductions*, in: *Corpus*, vol. 1, 1982, pp. 35–51

Bruyn 1987
Josua Bruyn, *Nog een suggestie voor het onderwerp van Rembrandts historiestuk te Leiden. De grootmoedigheid van Alexander*, in: *Oud Holland* 101, 1987, pp. 89–94

Bruyn 1988a
Josua Bruyn, *Jung und alt – ikonographische Bemerkungen zur «tronje»*, in: *Symposium Braunschweig*, pp. 67–76

Bruyn 1988b
Josua Bruyn, Review of W. Sumowski, *Gemälde der Rembrandt-Schüler vol. III*, in: *Oud Holland* 102, 1988, pp. 322–333

Bruyn 1989
Josua Bruyn, *Studio Practice and Studio Production*, in: *Corpus*, vol. 3, 1989, pp. 12–50

Bruyn/Wetering 1982
Josua Bruyn and Ernst van de Wetering, *The Stylistic Development*, in: *Corpus*, vol. 1, 1982, pp. 3–9

Buscaroli 1935
R. Buscaroli, *La Pittura di paesaggio in Italia*, Bologna 1935

Castiglione 1528
Baldassare Castiglione, *Il libro del cortegiano*, Venice 1528

Cevat 1973
Daan Cevat, *The Braamcamp Tobit*, in: *Neue Beiträge zur Rembrandt-Forschung*, Berlin 1973, pp. 83–88

Chapman 1990
H. Perry Chapman, *Rembrandt's Self-portraits. A Study in Seventeenth-century Identity*, Princeton, N. J. 1990

Clark 1966
Kenneth Clark, *Rembrandt and the Italian Renaissance*, London 1966

Clark 1969
Kenneth Clark, *Opening Speech for the Exhibition Rembrandt 1669–1969*, in: *Bulletin van het Rijksmuseum* 17, 1969

Cooney/Malafarina 1976
Patrick J. Cooney and Gianfranco Malafarina, *L'opera completa di Annibale Carracci* (Classici dell'Arte Rizzoli), Milan 1976

Copenhagen 2000
*Flemish Paintings 1600–1800. Statens Museum for Kunst*, Olaf Koester, Copenhagen 2000

Corpus
Josua Bruyn, B. Haak, S. H. Levie, P. J. J. van Thiel, E. van de Wetering (Eds.), A *Corpus of Rembrandt Paintings*, vols. 1ff., The Hague/Boston/London 1982ff.

Couprie 1992
L. D. Couprie, *Rembrandts zelfbeeld in de jaren 1628–1629. De schilder in zijn atelier*, in: *Spieghel Historiael* 27, 1992, pp. 50–56

Czobor 1969
Agnes Czobor, *Rembrandt und sein Kreis*, Museum der Bildenden Künste Budapest, Christliches Museum Esztergom, Privatsammlungen, Budapest 1969

D'Hulst 1982
R. -A. d'Hulst, *Jacob Jordaens*, Stuttgart 1982

Defoer 1977
H. L. M. Defoer, *Rembrandt van Rijn. De Doop van de Kamerling*, in: *Oud Holland* 91, 1977, pp. 2–26

Denucé
Jan Denucé, *Quellen zur Geschichte der flämischen Kunst*, vol. 1, *Kunstausfuhr Antwerpens im 17. Jahrhundert. Die Firma Forchoudt*, vol. 2, *Inventare von Kunstsammlungen zu Antwerpen im 16. und 17. Jahrhundert*, The Hague 1931/32

Douglas Stewart 1990
J. Douglas Stewart, *Before Rembrandt's ‹Shadow› Fell. Lievens, van Dyck and Rubens. Some Reconsiderations*, in: *Hoogsteder Naumann Mercury* 11, 1990, pp. 42–47

Dresden 1992
*Jacques Callot (1592–1635). Das druckgraphische Werk im Kupferstich-Kabinett zu Dresden*, edited by Christian Dittrich, Staatliche Kunstsammlungen Dresden, 1992

Dresden 2000
*Von der lustvollen Betrachtung der Bilder. Leidener Feinmalerei in der Dresdener Gemäldegalerie Alte Meister*, edited by Annegrat Laabs, Staatliche Kunstsammlungen Dresden, 2000

Dublin 1986
*Dutch Seventeenth and Eighteenth Century Paintings in The National Gallery of Ireland. A complete catalogue*, Homan Potterton, Dublin 1986

Dudok van Heel 1991/92
S. A. C. Dudok van Heel, *Rembrandt van Rijn (1606–1669). Een veranderend schildersportret*, in: Berlin/Amsterdam/London 1991/92, pp. 50–67

Dudok van Heel 1992
S. A. C. Dudok van Heel, *Enkele Observaties bij het Portret van een 83-jarige Dame uit 1634 door Rembrandt*, in: *Maandblad Amstelodamum* 79, 1992, pp.6-15

Edinburgh 2001
*Rembrandt's Women*, edited by J. Lloyd

Williams, National Gallery of Scotland, Edinburgh, 2001

Egmond/Mason 1995
F. Egmond and P. Mason, *Een portret van Coenraet van Schilperoort (1577–1636)*, in: *Bulletin van het Rijksmuseum* 43, no. 1, 1995, pp. 36–58

Ekkart 1991/92
Rudolf E. O. Ekkart, *Rembrandt, Lievens and Constantijn Huygens*, in: Leiden 1991/92, pp. 48–59

Ekkart 1998
Rudolf E. O. Ekkart, *Isaac Claesz. van Swanenburg 1537–1614*, Zwolle 1998

Emmens 1968
Jan Emmens, *Rembrandt en de Regels van de Kunst*, Utrecht 1968

Filedt Kok 1972
J. P. Filedt Kok, *Rembrandt. Etchings & Drawings in the Rembrandt House*, Maarssen 1972

Fock 1969
C. W. Fock, *Nieuws over de tapijten, bekend als de Nassause Genealogie*, in: *Oud Holland* 84, 1969, pp. 1–28

Fock 1990
C. W. Fock, *Kunstbezit in Leiden in de 17de eeuw*, in: *Het Rapenburg. Geschiedenis van een Leidse gracht*, vol. Va, Leiden 1990, pp. 3–36

Fraenger 1920
Wilhelm Fraenger, *Der junge Rembrandt*, Heidelberg 1920

Franken 1997
Michiel Franken, *«Aen stoelen en bancken leren gaen». Leerzame vormen van navolging in Rembrandts werkplaats*, in: *Album discipulorum J. R. J. van Asperen de Boer*, 1997

Franken
Michiel Franken, *Varianten binnen de schilderijenproductie in Rembrandts werkplaats*, in: *Corpus*, vol. V (forthcoming)

Frankfurt 1991
*Städels Sammlung im Städel. Zeichnungen*, edited by K. Gallwitz, Städelsches Kunstinstitut und Städtische Galerie, Frankfurt, 1991

Frankfurt 2000
*«Nach dem Leben und aus der Phantasie». Niederländische Zeichnungen vom 15. bis 18. Jahrhundert aus dem Städelschen Kunstinstitut*, edited by A. Strech, Städelsches Kunstinstitut und Städtische Galerie, Frankfurt, 2000

Freise 1911
K. Freise, *Pieter Lastman. Sein Leben und seine Kunst. Ein Beitrag zur Geschichte der hollaendischen Malerei im XVII. Jahrhundert*, Leipzig 1911

Friedländer 1942
Max Friedländer, *On Art and Connoisseurship*, Oxford 1942

Füessli 1803
J. H. Füessli, *Vorlesungen über die Malerei*, transl. by Joachim Eschenberg, Braunschweig 1803

Gelder 1953a
J. G. van Gelder, *Rembrandt and his Circle*, in: *The Burlington Magazine* 95, 1953, pp. 34–39

Gelder 1953b
J. G. van Gelder, *Rembrandts vroegste ontwikkeling*, in: *Mededelingen van de Koninklijke Nederlandse Akademie van Wetenschappen*, Afdeling Letterkunde, Nieuwe Reeks, Teil 16, no. 5, Amsterdam 1953

Gelder/Veen 1999
R. van Gelder and J. van der Veen, *Een kunstcaemer aan de Breestraat. Rembrandt*

*als liefhebber van kunst en rariteiten*, in: Amsterdam 1999/2000, pp. 33–90

Gersaint 1751
Edmonde François Gersaint, *Catalogue raisonné de toutes les pièces qui forment l'œuvre de Rembrandt*, Paris 1751

Gerson 1962
Horst Gerson, *La lapidation de Saint Étienne peinte par Rembrandt en 1625*, in: *Bulletin des Musées et Monuments Lyonnais* 3, 1962, pp. 57–62

Gerson 1963
Horst Gerson, *A Rembrandt discovery*, in: *Apollo* 77, 1963, pp. 371–372

Gerson 1968/69
Horst Gerson, *Rembrandt, Gemälde, Gesamtwerk*, Gütersloh 1969 (first edition *Rembrandt Paintings*, Amsterdam 1968)

Glück 1931
Gustav Glück, *Van Dyck. Des Meisters Gemälde* (Klassiker der Kunst), Stuttgart/Berlin 1931

Godefroy 1982
Frédéric Godefroy, *Dictionnaire de l'ancienne langue française et de tous ses dialectes du 9e au 15e siècle*, 10 vols., Ghent/Paris 1982

Goeree 1670
Willem Goeree, *Inleydinge tot de algemeene teycken-konst*, Middelburg 1670

Goeree 1682
Willem van Goeree, *Natuurlyk en Schilderkonstig Ontwerp der Menschkunde ...*, Amsterdam 1682 (facsimile Soest 1974)

Goeree 1697
Willem Goeree, *Inleydinge tot de algemeene teycken-konst*, Amsterdam[3] 1697

Gombrich 1971
Ernst Gombrich, *The Renaissance Theory of Art and the Rise of Landscape*, in: *Norm and Form. Studies in the Art of the Renaissance*, London/New York 1971 (1966)

GPI 2000
*The Getty Provenance Index Online Databases*, edited by the Getty Research Institute for the History of Art and the Humanities, Los Angeles August 2000 [http://piedi.getty.edu/]

Grimm 1991
Claus Grimm, *Rembrandt selbst. Eine Neubewertung seiner Porträtkunst*, Stuttgart 1991

Groen 1997
Karin Groen, *Investigation of the Use of the Binding Medium by Rembrandt*, in: *Zeitschrift für Kunsttechnologie und Konservierung* 11, 1997, pp. 207–225

Guratsch 1975
H. Guratsch, *Die Untersicht als ein Gestaltungsmittel in Rembrandts Frühwerk: Beobachtungen zum Kompositionsstil des holländischen Meisters*, in: *Oud Holland* 89, 1975, pp. 243–265

Gutbrod 1996
Helga Gutbrod, *Lievens und Rembrandt. Studien zum Verhältnis ihrer Kunst*, Frankfurt/Berlin/Bern/New York/Paris/Vienna 1996

Haak 1968
Bob Haak, *Rembrandt, zijn leven, zijn werk, zijn tijd*, Amsterdam 1968

Haak 1969
Bob Haak, *Rembrandt, his Life, his Work, his Time*, New York 1969

Hamburg 2000
*Rembrandt, oder nicht? Die Gemälde*, edited by Thomas Ketelsen, Hamburger Kunsthalle, 2000

Haverkamp-Begemann 1961
E. Haverkamp-Begemann, Review of Otto Benesch, *The Drawings of Rembrandt*, London 1954–57, in: *Kunstchronik* 14, 1961, pp. 10–14, 19–28, 50–57, 85–91

Heer 1991
Ed de Heer, *Pieter Lastman, ‹den Apelles onzer eeuwe›*, in: *Nieuwsbrief van de Vereniging van vrienden van Museum het Rembrandthuis* 3, no. 2, Nov. 1991, p. 1

Heer 1992
E. de Heer, *Kruisigingsscènes door Pieter Lastman*, in: *Kroniek van het Rembrandthuis* 1992, no. 1, pp. 20–25

Heiland/Lüdicke 1960
Susanne Heiland and Heinz Lüdecke (Eds.), *Rembrandt und die Nachwelt*, Leipzig 1960

Held 1969
Julius Held, *Rembrandt's Aristotle and other Rembrandt Studies*, Princeton 1969

Held 1970
Julius Held, *Einige Bemerkungen zum Problem der Kopfstudie in der Flämischen Malerei. Mit einem Nachsatz von Justus Müller Hofstede*, in: *Wallraf-Richartz-Jahrbuch* 32, 1970, pp. 285–295

Held 1980
Julius Held, *The Oil Sketches of Peter Paul Rubens. A Critical Catalogue* (National Gallery of Art. Kress Foundation Studies in the History of European Art, vol. 7), 2 vols., Princeton 1980

Held 1990/91
Julius Held, *Van Dyck's Oil Sketches*, in: *Washington 1990/91*, pp. 327–329

Henkel/Schöne 1967
Arthur Henkel and Albrecht Schöne (Eds.), *Emblemata. Handbuch zur Sinnbildkunst des XVI. und XVII. Jahrhunderts*, Stuttgart 1967

Herzog 1969
Erich Herzog, *Die Gemäldegalerie der Staatlichen Kunstsammlungen Kassel*, Hanau 1969

Hetzer 1984
Theodor Hetzer, *Rubens und Rembrandt*, in: *Schriften Theodor Hetzers*, edited by Gertrude Berthold, vol. 5, Mittenwald/Stuttgart 1984

Hind 1923
Arthur M. Hind, *A History of Engraving & Etching – from the 15th Century to the Year 1914*, London ³1923

Hinterding 1995
Erik Hinterding, *The History of Rembrandt's Copperplates with a Catalogue of those that survived*, Zwolle 1995

Hinterding 1996
Erik Hinterding, *Appendix: Catalogue of Watermarks in Prints by Jan van Vliet*, in: Amsterdam 1996, pp. 27–37

Hinterding 2001
E. B. M. Hinterding, *Rembrandt als etser. Twee studies naar de praktijk van productie en verspreiding*, Ph.D. diss. Utrecht 2001

Hirschfelder/Raupp 2001
Dagmar Hirschfelder and Hans-Joachim Raupp, ‹Tronies› in de Italiaanse, Vlaamse en Nederlandse schilderkunst van de 16de en 17de eeuw, Tagungsbericht, Symposium, Den Haag, Königliche Bibliothek, 19. –20. Oktober 2000, in: *Kunstchronik* 54, no. 5, 2001, pp. 197–202

Hofstede de Groot 1899
C. Hofstede de Groot, *Die Rembrandt-Ausstellungen zu Amsterdam (September-October 1898) und zu London (Januar-März 1899)*, in: *Repertorium für Kunstwissenschaft* 22, 1899, pp. 159–164

Hofstede de Groot 1922
C. Hofstede de Groot, *Die holländische Kritik der jetzigen Rembrandt-Forschung und neuest wiedergefundene Rembrandt-bilder*, Stuttgart/Berlin 1922

Hollstein
*Hollstein's Dutch and Flemish Etchings, Engravings and Woodcuts. 1400–1700*, vols. 1ff., Amsterdam 1949ff.

Hoogewerff 1947
G. J. Hoogewerff, *De geschiedenis van de St. Lucas gilden in Nederland*, Amsterdam 1947

Hoogewerff/Regteren Altena 1928
G. J. Hoogewerff and J. Q. van Regteren Altena, *Arnoldus Buchelius ‹Res Pictoriae›. Aanteekeningen over kunstenaars en kunstwerken voorkomende in zijn Diarium. Res Pictoriae. Notae Quotidianae en Descriptio Urbis Ultrajectinae (1583–1639)*, The Hague 1928

Hoogstraten 1657
Samuel van Hoogstraeten, *Den Eerlyken Jongeling, of de edele Kunst, Van zich by Groote en Kleyne te doen Eeren en Beminnen*, Dordrecht 1657

Hoogstraten 1678
Samuel van Hoogstraten, *De Inleyding tot de Hooge Schoole der Schilderkonst anders de Zichtbaere Werelt*, Rotterdam 1678

Houbraken
Arnold Houbraken, *De groote schouburgh der Nederlantsche konstschilders en schilderessen. Waar van 'er vele met hunne Beeltenissen ten Tooneel verschynen, en hun levensgedrag en Konstwerken beschreven worden: zynde een vervolg op het Schilderboek van K. v. Mander*, 3 vols., Amsterdam 1718–1721

Huygens/Heesakkers 1987
C. L. Heesakkers (Ed.), *Constantijn Huygens. Mijn jeugd*, Amsterdam 1987

Jaffé 1989
Michael Jaffé, *Rubens. Catalogo completo*, Milan 1989

Jager 1990
Ronald de Jager, *Meester, leerjongen, leertijd*, in: *Oud Holland* 104, 1990, pp. 69–111

Jongh 1986
Eddy de Jongh, *Portretten van echt en trouw. Inleiding*, in: *Haarlem 1986*, pp. 13–64

Judson/Ekkart 1999
Richard Judson and Rudolf E. O. Ekkart, *Gerrit van Honthorst 1592–1656*, Doornspijk 1999

Kahr 1973
Madlyn Kahr, *Rembrandt and Delilah*, in: *The Art Bulletin* 55, 1973, pp. 240–259

Kassel 1996
*Staatliche Museen Kassel. Gemäldegalerie Alte Meister. Gesamtkatalog*, Bernhard Schnackenburg, 2 vols., Mainz 1996

Kingston 1984
*Pictures from the Age of Rembrandt*, edited by David McTavish, Agnes Etherington Art Centre, Queen's University, Kingston (Ontario) 1984

Kingston 1997
*Wisdom, Knowledge & Magic. The Image of the Scholar in Seventeenth-Century Dutch Art*, edited by Volker Manuth et al., Agnes Etherington Art Centre, Queen's University, Kingston (Ontario) 1997

Klooster 1990
L. J. van der Klooster, *Opnieuw de Nassause tapijten*, in: *Oud Holland* 104, 1990, pp. 140–148

Knuttel 1955
G. Knuttel, *Rembrandt's Earliest Works*, in: *Burlington Magazine* 97, 1955, pp. 44–49

Kobayashi-Sato 1994
Yoriko Kobayashi-Sato, *The Portrait and the Tronie in the Art of Rembrandt*, in: *Faces of the Golden Age. Seventeenth Century Dutch Portraits*, edited by Eddy de Jongh et al., The Yamaguchi Prefectural Museum of Art, Yamaguchi; Kumamoto Prefectural Museum of Art, Kumamoto; Tokyo Station Gallery, Tokyo 1994, pp. 11–17

Köhler
Bruno Köhler, *Allgemeine Trachtenkunde in 7 Teilen*, Leipzig n. d.

Lairesse 1707
Gerard de Lairesse, *Het groot Schilder-boek*, Amsterdam 1707

Lankheit 1952
Klaus Lankheit, *Das Freundschaftsbild der Romantik*, Heidelberg 1952

Leiden 1949
*Stedelijk Museum De Lakenhal, Leiden. Beschrijvende catalogus van de schilderijen en tekeningen*. E. Pelinck, Leiden 1949

Leiden 1976
*Geschildert tot Leyden Anno 1626*, edited by M. L. Wurfbain et al., Stedelijk Museum De Lakenhal, Leiden, 1976

Leiden 1983
*Stedelijk Museum De Lakenhal, Leiden. Catalogus van de schilderijen en tekeningen*, M. L. Wurfbain et al., Leiden 1983

Leiden 1991/92
*Rembrandt en Lievens in Leiden, ‹een jong en edel schildersduo›/Rembrandt and Lievens in Leiden, ‹a pair of young and noble painters›*, edited by M. L. Wurfbain, Stedelijk Museum De Lakenhal, Leiden, 1991

Liedtke 1989
Walter Liedtke, *Reconstructing Rembrandt*, in: *Apollo* 129, Mai 1989

London 1988/89
*Art in the Making. Rembrandt*, edited by David Bomford et al., The National Gallery, London, 1988

London 1991
*National Gallery Catalogues. The Dutch School 1600–1900*, edited by Neil MacLaren, revised and extended by Christopher Brown, 2 vols., London 1991

London/The Hague 1999/2000
*Rembrandt by Himself*, edited by Ernst van de Wetering et al., The National Gallery, London; Royal Cabinets of Paintings Mauritshuis, The Hague, Stuttgart 1999

Longhi 1957
R. Longhi, *Una traccia per Filippo Napoletano*, in: *Paragone* 95, 1957, pp. 33–62

Lugano 1998
*Rabisch. Il grottesco nell'arte del Cinquecento. L'Accademia della Val di Blenio, Lomazzo e l'ambiente milanese*, edited by Giulio Bora et al., Museo Cantonale d'Arte, Lugano, 1998

Madrid 1995
*El Siglo de Rubens en el Museo del Prado. Catalogo razonado de Pintura Flamenca del Siglo XVII*, Matías Díaz Padron, 3 vols., Barcelona 1995

Madrid 1997
*Los cinco sentidos y el arte*, edited by Sylvia Ferino-Pagden, Museo del Prado, Madrid, 1997

Mander 1604
Karel van Mander, *Het schilder-boeck, waer in voor eerst de leerlustighe jueght den grondt der edel vry schilderconst in verscheyden deelen wort voorghedraghen*, Haarlem 1604

Mander 1617 (1991)
Karel van Mander, *Das Leben der niederländischen und deutschen Maler (von 1400 bis ca. 1615)*, transl. and annotated from the edition of 1617 by Hanns Floerke, Worms 1991 (Reprint of the first edition Munich/Leipzig 1906)

Mander/Hoecker 1916
Rudolf Hoecker, *Das Lehrgedicht des Karel van Mander. Text, Übersetzung und Kommentar nebst Anhang über Manders Geschichtskonstruktion und Kunsttheorie*, The Hague 1916

Mander/Miedema 1973
Karel van Mander, *Den grondt der edel vry schilder-const*, edited, transl. and annotated by Hessel Miedema, 2 vols., Utrecht 1973

Martin 1901
W. Martin, *Een ‹kunsthandel› in een Klappermanswachthuis*, in: *Oud Holland* 19, 1901, pp. 86–87

Martin 1913
W(illem) Martin, *Gerard Dou. Des Meisters Gemälde in 247 Abbildungen* (Klassiker der Kunst, vol. XXIV), Stuttgart/Berlin 1913

Mason Rinaldi 1984
Stefania Mason Rinaldi, *Palma il Giovane. L'opera completa*, Milan 1984

Meijer 2000
Bert W. Meijer, *Italian Paintings in 17th Century Holland. Art Market, Art Works and Art Collections*, in: Max Seidel (Ed.), *L'Europa e L'Arte Italiana*, Venice 2000, pp. 377–417

Melbourne/Canberra 1997/98
*Rembrandt. A Genius and His Impact*,
Albert Blankert et al., National Gallery
of Victoria, Melbourne; National
Gallery of Australia, Canberra,
Melbourne/Sydney/Zwolle 1997

Merrifield 1849
M. P. Merrifield, *Original treatises on the
arts of painting*, London 1849 (Reprint
New York 1967)

Meyer 1986
Maria Meyer, *Das Kostüm auf niederländischen Bildern. Zum Modewandel im
17. Jahrhundert*, Münster 1986

Miedema 1989
Hessel Miedema, *Kunst historisch*,
Maarssen/The Hague 1989

Miedema
*Karel van Mander, The Lives of the Illus-
trious Netherlandish and German Painters,
from the first edition of the Schilder-boeck
(1603–1604). Preceded by the Lineage,
Circumstances and Place of Birth, Life and
Works of Karel van Mander, Painter and
Poet and likewise his Death and Burial,
from the second edition of the Schilder-
boeck (1616–1618)*, edited, transl. and
annotated by Hessel Miedema, 5 vols.,
Doornspijk 1994–1998

Moes 1894
E. W. Moes, *Een brief van kunsthistorische
beteekenis*, in: Oud Holland 12, 1894,
pp. 238–240

Moes 1913
E. W. Moes, *Het Kunstkabinet van
Valerius Röver te Delft*, in: Oud Holland
30, 1913, pp. 4–24

Moiso-Diekamp 1987
Cornelia Moiso-Diekamp, *Das Pendant
in der holländischen Malerei des 17. Jahrhunderts*, Frankfurt/Bern/New York
1987

Moltke 1965
J. W. von Moltke, *Govaert Flinck 1615-
1660*, Amsterdam 1965

Montias 1982
J. M. Montias, *Artists and Artisans in
Delft*, New Jersey 1982

Montias 1991
John Michael Montias, *Works of Art in
Seventeeth-century Amsterdam. An Analy-
sis of Subjects and Attributions*, in: Art in
History, History in Art. Studies in Seven-
teeth-century Culture, edited by David
Freedberg and Jan de Vries, Santa
Monica 1991, pp. 331–372

Müller Hofstede 1968
Justus Müller Hofstede, *Zur Kopfstudie
im Werk von Rubens*, in: Wallraf-Richartz-
Jahrbuch 3, 1968, pp. 223–252

Müller Hofstede 1987/88
Justus Müller Hofstede, *Neue Beiträge
zum Œuvre Anton Van Dycks. Teil VI: Zur
Kopfstudie bei Rubens, Jordaens und Van
Dyck. Die Münchner Ausdrucksstudien
und ihr Umfeld im Werk des frühen Van
Dyck*, in: Wallraf-Richartz-Jahrbuch
48/49, 1987/88, pp. 144–163

Munich 1986
*Bayerische Staatsgemäldesammlungen.
Alte Pinakothek München. Erläuterungen
zu den ausgestellten Gemälden*, edited by
Erich Steingräber, Munich ²1986

Münz 1952
Ludwig Münz, *Rembrandt's Etchings. A
Critical Catalogue*, 2 vols., London
1952

Münz 1953
Ludwig Münz, *Rembrandts Bild von Mutter und Vater*, in: Jahrbuch der kunsthistorischen Sammlungen in Wien 50, 1953,
pp. 141–190

Muylle 1994
Jan Muylle, *Groteske koppen van Quinten
metsijs, Hieronymus Cock en Hans
Liefrinck naar Leonardo da Vinci*, in: De
zeventiende eeuw. Cultur in de Nederlanden in interdisciplinair perspectief 10,
no. 2, 1994, pp. 252–265

MW
*Middelnederlandsch Woordenboek*, edited
by E. Verwijs and J. Verdam, 11 vols.,
The Hague 1885–1952

Nederlands kunsthistorisch jaarboek
1999/2000
*Kunst voor de markt 1500–1700 (= Neder-
lands kunsthistorisch jaarboek 50,
1999/2000)*

Neumann 1905
Carl Neumann, *Rembrandt*, Munich
1905

New York 1992
*Jusepe de Ribera 1591–1652*, edited by
Alfonso E. Pérez Sánchez and Nicola
Spinosa, The Metropolitan Museum of
Art, New York, 1992

New York 1995/96
*Rembrandt/Not Rembrandt in the Metro-
politan Museum of Art. Aspects of Connoisseurship*, edited by Hubert von Sonnenburg et al., 2 vols., The Metropolitan
Museum of Art, New York, 1995

Nicolson/Vertova 1990
Benedict Nicolson, edited by Luisa
Vertova, *Caravaggism in Europe*, 3 vols.,
Turin ²1990

Obreen
F. D. O. Obreen, *Archief voor de Nederlandse Kunstgeschiedenis*, 7 vols., Rotterdam 1877–1890

Orlers 1641
Jan Jansz. Orlers, *Beschrijvinge der Stadt
Leyden*, Leiden ²1641

Ottawa 1968/69
*Jacob Jordaens 1593–1678*, edited by

Michael Jaffé, The National Gallery of Canada, Ottawa, 1968

Ottawa 1987
*Catalogue of the National Gallery of Canada. European and American Painting, Sculpture, and Decorative Arts,* Ottawa 1987

Padua/Rome/Milan 1990
*Pietro Paolo Rubens (1577–1640),* edited by Didier Bodart, Palazzo della Ragione, Padua; Palazzo delle Esposizioni, Rome; Società per le belle Arti ed Esposizione permanente, Milan, 1990

Paris 1933
*Musée du Louvre. Inventaire géneral des dessins des école du nord. École Hollandaise, Tome III Rembrandt ses élèves, ses imitateurs, ses copistes,* Frits Lugt, Paris 1933

Paris 1986
*Rembrandt, eaux-fortes. Collectiion Dutuit,* edited by S. de Bussière, Musée du Petit Palais, Paris, 1986

Paris 1988/89
*Rembrandt et son école, dessins du Musée du Louvre,* edited by Emmanuel Starcky and Menehould de Bazelaire, Musée du Louvre, Paris, 1988

Paris 1999
*Le Cabinet des Dessins. Rembrandt – Les Figures,* E. Starcky, Paris 1999

Pauw-de Veen 1969
Lydia de Pauw-de Veen, *De begrippen ‹Schilder›, ‹Schilderij› en ‹Schilderen› in de zeventiende eeuw* (Verhandelingen van den Koninklijke Vlaamse Academie voor Wetenschappen, Letteren en Schone Kunsten van Belgie. Klasse der Schone Kunsten, vol. 22), Brussels 1969

Pelletier 1998
S. William Pelletier, *From Rembrandt and His Studio: Two Paintings from the*

*Bader Collection,* Broschüre Georgia Museum of Art 1998

Perth/Adelaide/Brisbane 1998
*The Golden Age of Dutch Art. Seventeenth Century Paintings from the Rijksmuseum and Australian Collections,* edited by Norbert Middelkoop, Art Gallery of Western Australia, Perth; Art Gallery of South Australia, Adelaide; Queensland Art Gallery, Brisbane, 1998

Phoenix/The Hague 1998/99
*Copper as Canvas. Two Centuries of Masterpiece Paintings on Copper 1575–1775,* edited by Isabel Horovitz et al., Art Museum, Nelson-Atkins Museum of Art, Phoenix; Royal Cabinets of Paintings Mauritshuis, The Hague, 1998

Pigler 1954
Arnold Pigler, *Neid und Unwissenheit als Widersacher der Kunst,* in: *Acta Historiae Artium I,* Budapest 1954, pp. 215–235

Pliny
C. Plinius Secundus the Elder, *Naturkunde, Lateinisch-deutsch, Buch XXXV,* edited and transl. by Roderich König and Gerhard Winkler, Düsseldorf/Zürich ²1997

Ploeg 2000
Peter van der Ploeg, *Ontmoetingen in het Mauritshuis. Face to Face at the Mauritshuis,* in: *Mauritshuis in focus* 13, no. 2, 2000, pp. 10–21

Pochat 1986
Götz Pochat, *Geschichte der Ästhetik und Kunsttheorie. Von der Antike bis zum 19. Jahrhundert,* Cologne 1986

Pommier 1998
Edouard Pommier, *Théories du Portrait. De la Renaissance aux Lumières,* Paris 1998

Posner 1971
D. Posner, *Annibale Carracci,* 2 vols., London/New York 1971

Potterton 1982
Homan Potterton, *Recently-cleaned Dutch pictures in the National Gallery of Ireland,* in: *Apollo* 115, 1982, pp. 104–107

Prins/Smit 1997
Y. Prins and J. Smit, *De naaste verwanten van Jan Steen,* in: *Jaarboek Centraal Bureau voor Genealogie* 51, 1997, pp. 153–235

Raatschen 1999
Gudrun Raatschen, *Van Dyck in der Alten Pinakothek, Bayerische Staatsgemäldesammlungen,* Munich, 1999

Rammelman Elsevier 1848
W. C. J. Rammelman Elsevier, *Iets over Leidse schilders van 1610, in verband met het geslacht der Elsevieren,* in: *Berigten van het historisch gezelschap te Utrecht* 2, 1848, pp. 35–45

Raupp 1984
Hans-Joachim Raupp, *Untersuchungen zu Künstlerbildnis und Künstlerdarstellung in den Niederlanden im 17. Jahrhundert,* Hildesheim/Zürich/New York 1984

Raupp 1986
Hans-Joachim Raupp, *Bauernsatiren. Entstehung und Entwicklung des bäuerlichen Genres in der deutschen und niederländischen Kunst ca. 1470–1570,* Niederzier 1986

Raupp 1995
Hans-Joachim Raupp, *Einführung,* in: *Niederländische Malerei des 17. Jahrhunderts der SØR Rusche-Sammlung,* vol. 1, *Porträts,* edited by Hans-Joachim Raupp, Münster/Hamburg/London 1995, pp. 1–14

Regteren Altena 1936
J. Q. van Regteren Altena, *The Drawings of Jacques de Gheyn*, Amsterdam 1936

Regteren Altena 1983
J. Q. van Regteren Altena, *Jacques de Gheyn*, The Hague/Boston/London 1983

Reznicek 1961
E. K. J. Reznicek, *Die Zeichnungen von Hendrick Goltzius*, Utrecht 1961

Rijckevorsel 1932
J. L. A. Rijckevorsel, *Rembrandt en de traditie*, Rotterdam 1932

Roeber 1998
Urs Roeber, *Zur Stellung und Funktion alter Figuren im Werk Caravaggios*, Ph.D. diss. Kiel 1998

Roethlisberger 1993
Marcel G. Roethlisberger, *Abraham Bloemaert and his Sons, Paintings and Prints*, 2 vols., Doornspijk 1993

Rosier 1990
Bart Rosier, *The Victories of Charles V. A Series of Prints by Maarten van Heemskerck, 1555–56*, in: *Simiolus* 20, 1990/91, pp. 24–38

Rotterdam 1956
*Rembrandt Tentoonstelling: ter herdenking van de geboorte van Rembrandt op 15. juli 1606*, Museum Boymans-Van Beuningen, Rotterdam; Rijksmuseum, Amsterdam, 1956

Rotterdam 1976
*Kabinet van tekeningen. 16ᵉ en 17ᵉ-eeuwse Hollandse en Vlaamse tekeningen uit een Amsterdamse verzameling*, edited by J. C. Ebbinge Wubbe, Museum Boymans-van Beuningen, Rotterdam, 1976

Rotterdam 2000/01
*Jezus in de Gouden Eeuw*, edited by

Albert Blankert et al., Kunsthal Rotterdam, Zwolle 2000

Rotterdam/Braunschweig 1984
*Malerei aus erster Hand. Ölskizzen von Tintoretto bis Goya*, edited by Jeroen Giltay, Museum Boymans-van Beuningen, Rotterdam; Herzog Anton Ulrich-Museum, Braunschweig, 1984

Royalton Kisch 1984
Martin Royalton Kisch, *Over Rembrandt en Van Vliet*, in: *Kroniek van het Rembrandthuis* 1984, pp. 3–23

Royalton Kisch 1994
M. Royalton Kisch, *Some further Thoughts on Rembrandt's «Christ before Pilate»*, in: *Kroniek van het Rembrandthuis* 1994, no. 2, pp. 2–13

Sacramento 1974
*The Pre-Rembrandtists*, edited by Astrid Tümpel, E. B. Crocker Art Gallery, Sacramento, 1974

Sandrart 1675
Joachim von Sandrart, *Teutsche Academie des Bau-, Bild- und Mahlerey-Künste*, Nuremberg 1675

Sandrart/Peltzer 1925
A. R. Peltzer (Ed.), *Joachim von Sandrarts Academie der Bau-, Bild, und Mahlerey-Künste*, Munich 1925

Schama 1987
Simon Schama, *The Embarrassment of Riches. An Interpretation of Dutch Culture in the Golden Age*, New York 1987

Schatborn 1986a
Peter Schatborn, *Tekeningen van Rembrandt verband met zijn etsen*, in: *Kroniek van het Rembrandthuis* 1986, no. 1/2, pp. 1–38

Schatborn 1986b
Peter Schatborn, Review of *Josua Bruyn et al., A Corpus of Rembrandt Paintings,*

vol. I, *The Hague/Boston/London 1982*, in: *Oud Holland* 100, 1986, pp. 55–63

Schatborn 1989
Peter Schatborn, *Notes on Early Rembrandt Drawings*, in: *Master Drawings* 27, 1989, no. 2, pp. 118–127

Scheller 1969
R. W. Scheller, *Rembrandt en de encyclopedische kunstkamer*, in: *Oud Holland* 84, 1969, pp. 81–147

Schillemans 1987
R. Schillemans, *Gabriel Bucelinus and ‹the Names of the Most Distinguished European Painters›*, in: *Hoogsteder-Naumann Mercury* 6, 1987, pp. 25–37

Schillemans 1989
Robert Schillemans, *Bijbelschilderkunst rond Rembrandt*, Utrecht 1989

Schipper 2000
Claudia Schipper, *Mit Lust unter den Händen. Darstellungen der fünf Sinne in der bildenden Kunst des 17. Jahrhunderts*, 2 vols., Ph.D. diss. Utrecht 2000

Schnackenburg 1987
Bernhard Schnackenburg, Exhibition review *Holländische Malerei in neuem Licht. Hendrick ter Brugghen und seine Zeitgenossen*, in: *Kunstchronik* 1987, pp. 169–177

Schneider 1932
Hans Schneider, *Jan Lievens. Sein Leben und seine Werke*, Haarlem 1932

Schneider 1990
C. P. Schneider, *Rembrandt's landscapes*, New Haven, Conn. 1990

Schneider/Ekkart 1973
Hans Schneider with a Suppl. by R. E. O. Ekkart, *Jan Lievens. Sein Leben und seine Werke*, Amsterdam 1973 (Reprint of the edition Haarlem 1932)

Schwartz 1984/85/87
Gary Schwartz, *Rembrandt, zijn leven, zijne schilderijen*, Maarssen 1984 (English edition: *Rembrandt. His Life, His Paintings*, Harmondsworth 1985, German edition: *Rembrandt, Sämtliche Gemälde in Farbe*, Stuttgart/Zürich 1987)

Schwartz 1989
Frederic Schwartz, *The Motions of the Countenance. Rembrandt's Early Portraits and the Tronie*, in: *Res. Anthropology and Aesthetics* 17/18, 1989, pp. 89–116

Seelig 1997
Gero Seelig, *Abraham Bloemaert (1566–1651). Studien zur Utrechter Malerei um 1620*, Berlin 1997

Segal 1991
*Jan Davidsz. de Heem en zijn kring*, edited by S. Segal, Centraal Museum, Utrecht; Herzog Anton Ulrich-Museum, Braunschweig, 1991

Slatkes 1981/82
Leonard. J. Slatkes, Review of *Benedict Nicolson, The International Caravaggesque Movement*, Oxford 1979, in: *Simiolus* 12, 1981/82, pp. 167–183

Slatkes 1992
Leonard J. Slatkes, *Rembrandt. Catalogo completo* (I Gigli dell' Arte, 23), Florence 1992

Slive 1953
Seymour Slive, *Rembrandt and his Critics, 1630–1730*, The Hague 1953

Slive
Seymour Slive, *Frans Hals*, 3 vols., New York/London 1970–1974

Sluijter 1988
E. J. Sluijter, *Schilders van cleyne, subtile ende curieuse dingen. Leidse ‹fijnschilders› in contemporaine bronnen*, in: *Leidse fijnschilders: van Gerrit Dou tot Frans van*

*Mieris de Jonge 1630–1760*, Stedelijk Museum De Lakenhal, Leiden, 1988, pp. 29–34

Sohm 1991
Philip Sohm, *Pittoresco, Marco Boschini, his Critics, and their Critiques of Painterly Brushwork in Seventeenth- and Eighteenth-century Italy*, New York/Port Chester/Melbourne/Sydney 1991

Sonnenburg 1979
Hubert von Sonnenburg, *Rubens' Bildaufbau und Technik*, in: Hubert von Sonnenburg, Frank Preusser (Eds.), *Rubens. Gesammelte Aufsätze zur Technik*, Bayerische Staatsgemäldesammlungen, Munich, 1979 (off-print from Maltechnik-Restauro 2 and 3, 1979)

Sonnenburg 1995/96
Hubert von Sonnenburg, *Rubens and Rembrandt. A Comparison of Their Techniques*, in: *New York 1995/96*, pp. 71–79

Stechow 1969
Wolfgang Stechow, *Some Observations on Rembrandt and Lastman*, in: *Oud Holland* 84, 1969, pp. 184–262

Stockholm 1992/93
*Rembrandt och hans Tid-Rembrandt and his Age, Människan i Centrum-Focus on Man*, edited by Görel Cavalli-Björkman et al., Nationalmuseum Stockholm, 1992

Straten 1991
Roelof van Straten, *Rembrandts Leidse ‹Historiestuk›. Een iconografisch standpunt*, in: *Leids Jaarboekje* 83, 1991, pp. 89–107

Straten 1992
Roelof van Straten, *Een nieuwe interpretatie van Rembrandts Musicerend gezelschap*, in: *Bulletin van het Rijksmuseum* 40, 1992, pp. 158–160

Strauss/Meulen 1979
W. L. Strauss and M. van der Meulen, *The Rembrandt Documents*, New York 1979

Strengholt 1987
L. Strengholt, *Constanter. Het leven van Constantijn Huygens*, Amsterdam 1987

Stukenbrock 1993
Christiane Stukenbrock, *Frans Hals – Fröhliche Kinder, Musikanten und Zecher. Eine Studie zu ausgewählten Motivgruppen und deren Rezeptionsgeschichte* (Europäische Hochschulschriften, Reihe 28, Kunstgeschichte, vol. 167), Frankfurt/Berlin/Bern/New York/-Paris/Vienna 1993

Stumpel 2000
Jeroen Stumpel, *A Twelfth Attempt. The Subject of Rembrandt's History Piece in Leiden*, in: *Simiolus* 28, 2000–2001, pp. 44–50

Sumowski 1970
Werner Sumowski, *Rötelzeichnungen von Pieter Lastman*, in: *Jahrbuch der Hamburger Kunstsammlungen* 14/15, 1970, pp. 129–132

Sumowski 1973
Werner Sumowski, *Kritische Bemerkungen zur neuesten Gemäldekritik*, in: *Neue Beiträge zur Rembrandt-Forschung*, edited by Otto von Simson and Jan Kelch, Berlin 1973, pp. 91–110

Sumowski 1983ff.
Werner Sumowski, *Gemälde der Rembrandt-Schüler*, 6 vols., Landau 1983–1994

Sumowski
Werner Sumowski, *Drawings of the Rembrandt School*, 10 vols., New York 1979–1992

Symposium Braunschweig
R. Klessmann (Ed.), *Hendrick ter Brugghen und die Nachfolger Caravaggios in Holland. Beiträge eines Symposiums im Herzog Anton Ulrich-Museum Braunschweig, 1987*, Braunschweig 1988

Taverne 1978
E. Taverne, *In 't land van belofte: in de nieue stadt. Ideaal en werkelijkheid van de stadsuitleg in de Republiek 1580–1680*, Maarssen 1978

Taylor 1992
Paul Taylor, *The Concept of Houding in Dutch Art Theory*, in: *Journal of the Warburg and Courtauld Institutes 55*, 1992, pp. 210–232

The Hague 1977
*Mauritshuis. The Royal Cabinet of Paintings. Illustrated General Catalogue*, F. Duparc et al., The Hague 1977

The Hague 1978
*Rembrandt in the Mauritshuis. An interdisciplinary study*, A. B. de Vries et al., The Hague 1978

The Hague 1997
*Vorstelijk Verzameld. De kunstcollectie van Frederik Hendrik en Amalia*, P. van der Ploeg et al., Royal Cabinets of Paintings Mauritshuis, The Hague, 1997

Thiel 1989a
Pieter J. J. van Thiel, *Rembrandt. Musicerend gezelschap*, 1626, in: *Bulletin van het Rijksmuseum 37*, 1989, pp. 207–210

Thiel 1989b
Pieter J. J. van Thiel, *Rembrandt. Tobias en Anna met het bokje*, 1626, in: *Bulletin van het Rijksmuseum 37*, 1989, pp. 211–213

Thiel 1999
Pieter J. J. van Thiel, *Cornelis Cornelisz van Haarlem 1562–1638. A Monograph and Catalogue Raisonné*, Doornspijk 1999

Timmers 1947
J. J. M. Timmers, *Symboliek en Iconographie der Christelijke Kunst*, Roermond/Maaseik 1947

Tokyo 1989
*In Darkness and Light. A Rembrandt in Tokyo Reconsidered*, edited by The Bridgestone Painting Research Group, Bridgestone Museum of Art, Ishibashi Foundation, Tokyo, 1989

Tours 1998
*Musée des Beaux-Arts à Tours. Guide des Collections*, Philippe Leyzour et al., Paris 1998

Trésor de la langue française
*Trésor de la langue française. Dictionnaire de la langue du 19ᵉ et 20ᵉ siècle (1789–1960)*, 16 vols., Paris 1971–1994

Tümpel 1967
Christian Tümpel, *Katalog zur Geschichte der Rembrandtforschung*, Ph.D. diss. Hamburg 1967

Tümpel 1969
Christian Tümpel, *Studien zur Ikonographie der Historien Rembrandts. Deutung und Interpretation der Bildinhalte*, in: *Nederlands Kunsthistorisch Jaarboek 20*, 1969, pp. 107–198

Tümpel 1974
Christian Tümpel, *Claes Cornelisz. Moeyaert*, in: *Oud Holland 88*, 1974, pp. 1–163

Tümpel 1986
Christian Tümpel, *Rembrandt. Mythos und Methode*, mit Beiträgen von Astrid Tümpel, Antwerp/Königstein im Taunus 1986 (second revised edition Antwerp 1993)

Tümpel 1991
Christian Tümpel, *Pieter Lastman en Rembrandt/Pieter Lastman and Rembrandt*, in: Amsterdam 1991, pp. 54–84

Tümpel 1992
Christian Tümpel, *Rembrandt*, Nijmegen 1992

Tümpel 1993
Christian Tümpel, *Rembrandt. All Paintings in Colour*, Antwerp 1993

Tuynman 1999
P. Tuynman, *Een oud Rembrandt-raadsel opgelost. De drie Horatiërs voor koning Tullus op het Leidse historiestuk uit 1626*, in: *Kroniek van het Rembrandthuis 1999*, pp. 2–7

Urbach 1983
Susan Urbach, *Preliminary Remarks on the Sources of the Apostle Series of Rubens and Van Dyck*, in: *Essays on van Dyck*, edited by A. McNairn (= *Racar. Canadian Art Review 10*, no. 1, 1983), pp. 5–22

Utrecht/Braunschweig 1986/87
*Holländische Malerei in neuem Licht. Hendrick ter Brugghen und seine Zeitgenossen*, edited by Albert Blankert and Leonhard J. Slatkes, Centraal Museum, Utrecht; Herzog Anton Ulrich-Museum, Braunschweig, 1986

Valentiner
Wilhelm Valentiner, *Rembrandt in Wort und Bild*, edited by Wilhelm Bode, Berlin n. d.

Vasari 1550/1568
*Lives of the Painters, Sculptors and Architects*, transl. by Gaston du C. de Vere, with an introduction and annotations by David Ekserdjian, 2 vols., New York 1927 (Reprint 1996)

Veen 1997/98
Jaap van der Veen, *Faces from Life. Tronies and Portraits in Rembrandt's Painted Œuvre*, in: Melbourne/Canberra 1997/98, pp. 69–80

Velde 1975
Carl van de Velde, *Frans Floris (1519–1570). Leven en Werken*, 2 vols. (Verhandelingen van de Koninklijke Academie voor Wetenschappen, Letteren en schone Kunsten van Belgie. Klasse der schone Kunsten 37, no. 30), Brussels 1975

Venice 1990
*Palma il Giovane 1548–1628. Disegni e Dipinti*, edited by Stefania Mason Rinaldi, Museo Correr, Venice, 1990

Venice 1999
*Renaissance Venice and the North. Crosscurrents in the Time of Bellini, Dürer and Titian*, edited by Bernard Aikema and Beverly Louise Brown, Palazzo Grassi, Venice, 1999

Vercelli 1999
*Ut Pictura Ita Visio. Dipinti Olandesi del Secolo d'Oro da Collezzioni Private Italiane*, edited by Gianni Carlo Sciolla, Fondazione Museo Borgogna Vercelli, 1999

Verhoef 1994
Margriet Verhoef, ‹Brantjes› en ‹Maneschijntjes›: over lichteffecten in de nacht, in: *Rotterdamse Meesters uit de Gouden Eeuw*, Rotterdams Historisch Museum, Zwolle 1994, pp. 125–131

Vey 1962
Horst Vey, *Die Zeichnungen Anton van Dycks*, 2 vols., Brussels 1962

Vienna 1783
*Verzeichniß der Gemälde der Kaiserlich Königlichen Bilder Gallerie in Wien*, verfaßt von Christian von Mechel ..., Vienna 1783

Vienna 1796
Joseph Rosa, *Gemälde der k. k. Gallerie, Zweite Abtheilung. Niederländische Schulen*, Vienna 1796

Vienna 1884
*Kunsthistorische Sammlungen des Allerhöchsten Kaiserhauses. Gemälde. Beschreibendes Verzeichniss. II. Band. Niederländische Schulen*, Eduard R. v. Engerth, Vienna 1884

Vienna 1991
*Die Gemäldegalerie des Kunsthistorischen Museums in Wien. Verzeichnis der Gemälde, mit 2341 Abbildungen*, Sylvia Ferino-Pagden et al., Vienna 1991

Vinne
Vincent Laurensz. van de Vinne, *Dagelijckse aentekeninge; Reisjournaal van een Haarlems schilder, 1652–1655*, edited by Bert Sliggers jr., Haarlem 1979

Vlieghe 1998
Hans Vlieghe, *Flemish Art and Architecture 1585–1700* (Pelican History of Art), New Haven/London 1998

Vries 1989
Lyckle de Vries, *Tronies and Other Single Figured Netherlandish Paintings*, in: *Nederlandse Portretten. Bijdragen over de portretkunst in de Nederlanden uit de 16de, 17de en 18de eeuw*, in: *Leids Kunsthistorisch Jaarboek* 8, 1989, pp. 185–202

Vries 1991
B. de Vries, *De Leidse textielnijverheid in de 17ᵉ en 18ᵉ eeuw*, in: *Leidse Historische reeks*, edited by J. K. S. Moes et al., 1991, pp. 77–90

Vries 1995
Huub de Vries, *Van lachende man tot Democritus. Gedaanteverwisselingen en andere transformaties in prenten naar inventies van Rembrandt*, in: *Kroniek van het Rembrandthuis* 1995, 2, pp. 24–39

Warners 1956/57
J. D. P. Warners, *Translatio-Imitatio-Aemulatio*, in: *De Nieuwe Taalgids* 49, 1956 and 50, 1957

Warnke 1986
Martin Warnke, *Zur Herkunft und zur Deutung der ‹Lobpreisung Simeons› von Rembrandt in der Kunsthalle*, in: *Idea. Jahrbuch der Hamburger Kunsthalle* 5, 1986, pp. 35–45

Warnke 1996
Martin Warnke, *Hofkünstler: zur Vorgeschichte des modernen Künstlers*, Cologne² 1996

Wartburg
Walther von Wartburg, *Französisches etymologisches Wörterbuch. Eine Darstellung des galloromanischen Sprachschatzes*, vols. 1ff., Tübingen 1948ff.

Washington 1990/91
*Van Dyck Paintings*, edited by Arthur K. Wheelock Jr., National Gallery of Art Washington, 1990

Washington/Amsterdam 1980
*Gods, Saints & Heroes. Dutch Painting in the Age of Rembrandt*, edited by Albert Blankert et al., The National Gallery of Art, Washington; Institute of the Arts, Detroit; Rijksmuseum, Amsterdam, 1980

Washington/London/Haarlem 1989/90
*Frans Hals*, edited by Seymour Slive, The National Gallery of Art, Washington; Royal Academy of Arts, London; Frans Hals-Museum, Haarlem, 1989

Washington/London/The Hague 2000/01
*Gerrit Dou 1613–1675*, edited by Ronni Baer, The National Gallery of Art, Washington; Dulwich Picture Gallery, London; Royal Cabinets of Paintings Mauritshuis, The Hague, 2000

Wellesley 1969
*The Collection of Dutch Drawings of Maida & George Abrams. A Loan Exhibition,* edited by Franklin W. Robinson, Wellesley College Museum, Wellesley, Mass. 1969

Wetering 1976
Ernst van de Wetering, *Leidse schilders achter de ezels,* in: *Leiden 1976*

Wetering 1977a
Ernst van de Wetering, *Rembrandt doorgelicht,* in: *Kunstschrift* 21, 1977, pp. 173–181

Wetering 1977b
Ernst van de Wetering, *De jonge Rembrandt aan het werk,* in: *Oud Holland* 91, 1977, pp. 27–65

Wetering 1983
Ernst van de Wetering, *Isaac Jouderville, a Pupil of Rembrandt,* in: *Amsterdam 1983,* pp. 59–69

Wetering 1986
Ernst van de Wetering, *Studies in the Workshop Practice of the Early Rembrandt,* Amsterdam 1986

Wetering 1988
Ernst van de Wetering, *Some Remarks on Light, Colour, and Form with the Dutch Carravaggists,* in: Symposium Braunschweig, pp. 45–50

Wetering 1991/92a
Ernst van de Wetering, *Rembrandts Malweise. Technik im Dienst der Illusion,* in: Berlin/Amsterdam/London 1991/92, pp. 12–39

Wetering 1991/92b
Ernst van de Wetering, *De symbiose van Lievens en Rembrandt,* in: Leiden 1991/92, pp. 39–47

Wetering 1995
Ernst van de Wetering, *Rembrandt's*

‹Satire on Art Criticism› Reconsidered, in: *Shop Talk. Studies in Honor of Seymour Slive,* edited by Cynthia P. Schneider et al., Cambridge, Mass. 1995, pp. 264–270

Wetering 1997
Ernst van de Wetering, *Rembrandt. The Painter at Work,* Amsterdam 1997

Wetering 1997/98
Ernst van de Wetering, *The Miracle of Our Age. Rembrandt through the Eyes of His Contemporaries,* in: *Melbourne/Canberra 1997/98,* pp. 58–68

Wetering 1998
Ernst van de Wetering, ‹Old Man with Turban›, *an Early Rembrandt Rediscovered,* in: Katalog PAN Amsterdam, De Kunst- en Antiekbeurs van de Lage Landen, 11–18. Oktober 1998, pp. 17–20 (Dutch pp. 11–17)

Wetering 1999/2000
Ernst van de Wetering, *Die mehrfache Funktion von Rembrandts Selbstporträts,* in: London/The Hague 1999/2000, pp. 8–37

Wetering 1999/2001
Ernst van de Wetering, *The Aged Painting and the Necessities and Possibilities to Know its Original Appearancee,* in: *Conservare necesse est, Festskrift til Leif Einar Plahter,* International Institute of Conservation (IIC) Nordic Group, Oslo 1999, pp. 259–264; also in: H. Cantz (Ed.) *Horizons. Essays on art and art research. 50 Years Swiss Institute for Art Research,* Zürich, 2001, pp. 399–406

Wetering 2000/01
Ernst van de Wetering, *Remarks on Rembrandt's Oil-sketches for Etchings,* in: Amsterdam/London 2000/01, pp. 36–63

White 1969
Christopher White, *Rembrandt as an Etcher. A Study of the Artist at Work,* 2 vols., London 1969

White 1982
Christopher White, *The Dutch Pictures in the Collection of her Majesty the Queen,* Cambridge et al. 1982

White 2000
Christopher White, *Rembrandt as an Etcher. A Study of the Artist at Work,* New Haven/London ²2000

White/Boon 1969
Chr. White and K. G. Boon, *Rembrandt's Etchings. An Illustrated Critical Catalogue,* 2 vols., Amsterdam/London/New York 1969

Winkel 1999/2000
Marieke de Winkel, *Costume in Rembrandt's Self-portraits,* in: London/The Hague 1999/2000, pp. 58–74

WNT
*Woordenboek der Nederlandsche Taal,* founded by M. de Vries and L. A. te Winkel, vols. 1ff., Leiden/The Hague 1882ff.

Worp 1891
J. A. Worp, *Constantijn Huygens over de schilders van zijn tijd,* in: *Oud Holland* 9, 1891, pp. 106–136

Zanker 1995
Paul Zanker, *Die Maske des Sokrates. Das Bild des Intellektuellen in der antiken Kunst,* Munich 1995

# List of Photos

We thank the following people and institutions for allowing us to reprint photos from their collections:

Archives of the Rembrandt Research Project, Amsterdam: Fig. 24a; Essay Wetering I, fig. 1–31; Essay Wetering II, fig. 1-5, 7–32

Museum het Rembrandthuis, Amsterdam: Cat. no. 14, 39, 40, 51, 52, 53, 54, 57, fig. 33b, 64a, 64c, 66c, 67b, 79a, 80a; Essay Hirschfelder fig. 4

Rijksmuseum, Amsterdam: Cat. no. 13, 19, 22, 25, 27, 28, 34, 41, 43, 44, 45, 47, 49, 55, 56, 78; fig. 4a, 7a, 7b, 13a, 19a, 22a, 23a, 27b, 28a, fig. 41a–b, 46a, 47a, 48a, 51a, 53a–b, 58a, 64b, 67a; Essay Schnackenburg fig. 24

Rubenshuis, Antwerp: Essay Schnackenburg fig. 16

Dr. & Mrs. Alfred Bader: Cat. no. 59, 80

Kunstmuseum, Basle: fig. 15a; Essay Schnackenburg fig. 12

Staatliche Museen zu Berlin, Preußischer Kulturbesitz, Gemäldegalerie (Photos: Jörg P. Anders): Cat. no. 29, 84; fig. 27a, 34/Ib; Essay Hirschfelder fig. 3; Essay Schnackenburg fig. 18

Museum of Fine Arts, Boston (Reproduced with permission © Museum of Fine Arts Boston. All Rights reserved): Cat. no. 61

Maida & George Abrams, Boston: Cat. no. 21

Herzog Anton Ulrich-Museum, Braunschweig: Essay Schnackenburg fig. 19

Szépmüvészeti Múzeum, Budapest: Cat. no. 68, fig. 62a

Fitzwilliam Museum, Cambridge (© The Syndics of the Fitzwilliam Museum, Cambridge): Cat. no. 36

The Cleveland Museum of Art: Essay Schnackenburg fig. 11

Musée de la Chartreuse, Douai (Photo: Béatrice Hatala): Cat. no. 70

Kupferstich-Kabinett, Staatliche Kunstsammlungen Dresden: Cat. no. 23; fig. 44a

The National Gallery of Ireland, Dublin: Cat. no. 62; Fig. 6b

Trinity College, Dublin: Cat. no. 6

Gabinetto Disegni e Stampe degli Uffizi, Florence: Fig. 26a

Städelsches Kunstinstitut, Frankfurt am Main (Photo: © Ursula Edelmann, Frankfurt am Main): Cat. no. 38

Royal Cabinet of Paintings Mauritshuis, The Hague: Cat. no. 65, 79; fig. 52a; Essay Korevaar fig. 6

Teylers Museum, Haarlem: Cat. no. 48, 86

Hamburger Kunsthalle (Photo: Elke Walford): Cat. no. 30; fig. 6a

Tiroler Landesmuseum Ferdinandeum, Innsbruck: Essay Hirschfelder fig. 1

Staatliche Kunsthalle Karlsruhe: fig. 2a

Staatliche Museen Kassel, Gemäldegalerie Alte Meister (Photos: Ute Brunzel): Cat. no. 72, 73, 76, 77, 81, 82; fig. 24b, 72/73a–b, 74a, 82a, 85/86a; Essay Schnackenburg fig. 1, 2, 4, 5, 9, 10, 13; Essay Wetering II, fig. 6

Stedelijk Museum De Lakenhal, Leiden: Cat. no. 1, 7, 24; Essay Korevaar fig. 1, 2, 3

Prentenkabinet van de Universiteit Leiden: Cat. no. 15

British Museum, Department of Prints and Drawings, London: Cat. no. 37; fig. 6d, 39a

The National Gallery, London (© National Gallery Picture Library): Cat. no. 63, 83

London (© Prudence Cuming Associates Ltd.): Cat. no. 9, 75

Spier Collection: Cat. no. 8

The J. Paul Getty Museum, Los Angeles (© The J. Paul Getty Museum): Cat. no. 66; fig. 66a–b

Musée des Beaux-Arts, Lyon: Essay Schnackenburg fig. 6

The National Gallery of Victoria, Melbourne: fig. 80b

Bayerische Staatsgemäldesammlungen, Munich: Cat. no. 69; Essay Hirschfelder fig. 2; Essay Schnackenburg fig. 17, 20

Staatliche Graphische Sammlung, Munich: fig.7c

The State Pushkin Museum of Fine Arts, Moscow: Cat. no. 12

The Metropolitan Museum of Art, New York: Essay Schnackenburg fig. 8, 15, 25

Germanisches Nationalmuseum, Nuremberg: Cat. no. 32

Christ Church Picture Gallery, Oxford: Essay Schnackenburg fig. 21

Fondation Custodia, Institut Néerlandais, Paris: Cat. no. 2, 4

Musée du Louvre, Départements des Arts Graphiques, Paris: Cat. no. 16, 35, 42, 85; fig. 57a

Stiftung Preußische Schlösser und Gärten Berlin-Brandenburg, Potsdam (photographer): fig. 75a

Nationalmuseum, Stockholm: Cat. no. 17; Essay Schnackenburg fig. 26

Bridgestone Museum of Art, Ishibashi Foundation, Tokyo: Cat. no. 58

Musée des Beaux-Arts de Tours (Photo: Arsicaud): Cat. no. 60

Galleria Sabauda, Turin: Cat. no. 31

Museum Catharijneconvent, Utrecht (Photo: Ruben de Heer): Cat. no. 3

The National Gallery of Art, Washington: Essay Schnackenburg fig. 29

Graphische Sammlung Albertina, Vienna: Fig. 6c

Kunsthistorisches Museum, Vienna: Cat. no. 87

The Royal Collection, Her Majesty Queen Elisabeth II, Windsor Castle (© 2001): Essay Hirschfelder fig. 5; Essay Schnackenburg fig. 27

and the following photos lent by private individuals: Cat. no. 5, 10, 11, 18, 20, 26, 33, 46, 50, 64, 67, 71; fig. 29a, 33a, 80c; Essay Schnackenburg fig. 3, 14, 22, 23, 30